THE LEGACY

THE LEGACY

The Vietnam War
in the
American Imagination

Edited by D. Michael Shafer

BEACON PRESS
BOSTON

Beacon Press
25 Beacon Street
Boston, Massachusetts 02108-2800

Beacon Press books
are published under the auspices of
the Unitarian Universalist Association of Congregations.

97 96 95 94 93 92 91 90   8 7 6 5 4 3 2 1

Text design by Michael Fender

Library of Congress Cataloging-in-Publication Data

The Legacy : The Vietnam War in the American imagination / edited by
  D. Michael Shafer.
      p.   cm.
  Includes bibliographical references.
  ISBN 0-8070-5400-3 : $22.95
    1. Vietnamese Conflict, 1961–1975—United States.   2. United
States—Civilization—1970–   .   3. Vietnamese Conflict, 1961–1975—
Influence.   I. Shafer, D. Michael, 1953–
DS558.L4   1990
959.704′3373—dc20   89-46138
                                                              CIP

CONTENTS

PREFACE

The Tet offensive which broke Americans' political will to win in Vietnam happened more than twenty years ago, yet the war's legacies still enter our daily lives in myriad subtle and not so subtle ways. In 1980, Ronald Reagan ran on the slogan "America Is Back"—by implication from Vietnam and the associated time of tumult, self-doubt, and self-laceration. During his presidency, Congress debated whether or not Central America was "another Vietnam," and the leaders of student protests against everything from aid to the Contras to CIA recruiting on campus and apartheid in South Africa congratulated their followers that their rallies were "just like the sixties." The idioms of Vietnam combat and antiwar protest infuse our day-to-day language, and riveting images of the war and the fall of Saigon, of Woodstock, Kent State, and Chicago '68 are part of our shared culture. Vietnam has become not only a major subject in literature, film and television, but also a powerful symbol of an America out of balance. And, most painfully, the war lives on among us in the memories of the three million men and women who served in Vietnam, in the thoughts of the mothers, fathers, brothers, sisters, wives, and children of the 59,000 Americans killed there and of the 2,500 still missing in action, and in the yearnings of the millions of Indochinese Americans whose presence enriches us with the culture of the countries they have lost forever.

While for these Americans the Vietnam War still has claws that cut to the quick, for most it has been fenced off as a time apart, its disturbing memory safely domesticated. For high school and college students too young to remember the fall of Saigon, the war is ancient history. For them, the turbulent age of Aquarius holds a special fascination, but they often need help understanding the lyrics of "Hair." For their parents, the once radical protest songs of Country Joe and the Fish now evoke a certain nostalgia, and the once innovative riffs of Jimi Hendrix must now be sought out on "Golden Oldies" shows. TV and Hollywood have begun to do to Vietnam what "Hogan's Heroes" and *The Dirty Dozen* did to World War II, while slightly paunchy Vietnam veterans have now largely replaced aging World War II vets in the ranks of American Legion and Veterans of Foreign Wars contingents marching in Memorial Day and Fourth of July parades. Even Jane Fonda, whose wartime visit to

Hanoi enraged so many, has given up political protest to profit from exercise videos intended to tighten the sagging tummies of the now visibly middle-aged Vietnam generation. At long last, it would appear, the wounds are scabbing over, and Americans can finally put "all that" behind them. Or can they?

We, the writers of these essays, don't think so, and this book is about why not. We don't believe that Vietnam was an aberration, nor do we believe that the issues it raised can be set aside. We see the war both as a powerful magnifying glass, enlarging critical themes in American life, and as a burning glass, searing our consciousness and leaving scars that are now themselves part of who and what we are. *The Legacy* is not a book about the Vietnam War; rather, it probes how and how much Vietnam shapes America and Americans today. In doing so, this book examines issues that have been with us since the Revolution: questions of what it means to be an American and what rights and obligations citizenship entails; questions of race, gender and ideology in American life; questions of the role of the press and of the limits of both government action and popular protest.

The Legacy explores topics as diverse as military manpower policy, Hollywood depictions of Vietnam, the transformation of American popular culture, democratic education, the rise of the women's movement, and the Vietnam War novel. It is meant to be a *tour d'horizon,* not an exhaustive treatment of the subject; it is intended to provoke further thought and dialogue, not to close them off, for the thing we fear most in the domestication of the memory of Vietnam is the silencing of discussion. Not at issue for us are specific answers to the perennial questions raised by the war; for two hundred years, these have changed as America has changed. Rather, we seek to highlight the dilemmas these questions pose, and so to force our readers to confront the fundamental contentiousness of the issues they raise. All of us hold strong personal beliefs about what the right answers are. We believe equally strongly that what matters is not our conclusions per se, but open and honest confrontation among citizens over the questions themselves. Such debate is an essential ingredient in a strong democracy. With this book we hope to make much more of this debate a positive element in the enduring legacy of Vietnam.

The Legacy is arranged in four parts. The first, "The Importance of Remembering," sets the stage, sketching the history of the 1960s and of American involvement in Vietnam and laying the philosophical groundwork for the arguments that follow. Thereafter, the book moves to the present and future, and from immediacy to abstraction. "Part Two, Going to War: The Human Legacy," addresses the experiences of those who literally embody the Vietnam legacy—Vietnam veterans—through examination of the Vietnam combat experience and veterans' accounts of it. Most Americans, however, experienced the war only vicariously; thus, the chapters of "Part Three, The Recreation of Vietnam—and America," examine how the war has been mediated to us via the press, literature and the movies, and how both the war and who we are have been given new meanings in the process. Finally, our survey of the Vietnam legacy looks forward. "Part Four, Facing the Future," analyzes the war's impact on the black community, the women's movement, ideology, and domestic politics, and considers the experience of Vietnamese Americans and how changes wrought or exaggerated by the war shape the nation we are—and will be.

Books are not conjured from thin air, and *The Legacy* is no exception. Without generous institutional support and the encouragement of many friends and colleagues, it would never have been written. Funding from Rutgers University, Rutgers College, Douglass College, the New Jersey Department of Higher Education, and the New Jersey Committee for the Humanities made the Vietnam Project possible; help from Phyllis Cohen, John Glascock, Mary Hartman, and Michael Moffatt made it happen. Friends and colleagues Elsa Auerbach, David Berman, Nguyen Ngoc Bich, John Chambers, James Creedle, Richard Dunn, Dee Garrison, Todd Gitlin, Dao Thi Hoi, Art Huddleston, Greg Hung, Chris Jespersen, Jim Livingston, Michael Musuraca, Martin Novelli, Elliott Shore, Steven Tischler and Ron Ward; poets Jan Berry, Bill Ehrhart, Wendy Larson, Lamont Steptoe and Trâm Ti Nga; authors Fred Downs, John Del Veccio, Ky Lam, Myra MacPherson, Robert Mason, Nuoy Sok and Thang Nham; and Vietnam veterans, Vietnamese Americans, ex-antiwar protesters and other "just plain folks" too numerous to name all contributed time, ideas and criticism to the effort. Deborah Chasman at Beacon Press smoothed our rough prose with a deft editorial touch, applied the whip where necessary and, amazingly, managed to do both without ruffling too many feathers. Finally, special thanks are due to the many students who helped frame the Vietnam Project and whose research laid its foundations: Judy Bieber, Lynn DeLean, Jennifer DuFault, Maureen Hall, Jeffrey Lipkin, Valery Mann, Trâm Dieu Nguyen, Annette Saddek, Dawn Shea, Elisabeth Spector, and Philippe Zimmerman.

PART ONE

THE IMPORTANCE OF REMEMBERING

1

THE IMPORTANCE OF REMEMBERING:
The Vietnam Legacy's Challenge to American Democracy

BENJAMIN R. BARBER

Alexis de Tocqueville reminds us that "as the past has ceased to throw light upon the future, the mind of man wanders in obscurity." We need our past to illuminate our present, yet what we need most to remember is what pains us most and is thus hardest to hold onto. There is no event in America's recent history more painful—more memorable yet less remembered—than our long and futile military engagement in Southeast Asia. Single events like Kennedy's assassination or Watergate are deep traumas of loss, but they invite memory and reflection, and may even seem instructive. But Vietnam is an invitation only to amnesia—a hard and numb scar we prefer not to notice.

In certain ways, the war in Vietnam has become America's Dreyfus case; an entire generation of resisters and antiwar youths on trial, rather than one man, the honor of the American military put to an impossible test. As the arrest of a French captain of Jewish ancestry on charges of espionage at the end of the last century became a cause celebre through which all of France's passions about its nationhood, its military honor, and the character of French citizenship were ignited, so our engagement in Vietnam became a litmus test of attitudes towards America, the cold war, the Third World, and the place of the military in our democracy. Just as his case continued to trouble the French spirit long after Alfred Dreyfus was tried and retried and finally acquitted and restored to rank and honor, so the war in Vietnam has continued to trouble Americans long after the last chopper took off from the American Embassy in Saigon in 1975, leaving behind a broken world only midway on its voyage of suffering.

It was like no other war America had experienced, this peculiar, horrific, escalating war into which America seemed to have entered almost by default, first trying to fill the vacuum left by the defeat of the French in the early fifties, then in the early sixties trying to prop up a faltering military regime supposedly bent on democracy with a few thousand advisors. By 1965, America was protecting its own investment, concerned less with Vietnam's democracy than its own honor, with 185,000 men in the field. Finally, by 1969, 543,000 frustrated soldiers engaged in a war against an enemy that, as the Tet offensive made clear, even in defeat would not succumb to firepower—a war no longer just in Vietnam, but a war in the United States, the country split in two, casualties falling not only on the sulphured desolation of Da Nang, but also on the green quads of Kent State and Jackson State Universities.

Not until 1985, a full decade after America's ignoble withdrawal, did the nation begin to consider the war's many somber meanings. The building of a memorial in Washington had intimated a certain calm, but the special issues of the *New York Times Sunday Magazine,* the *New Republic,* and other journals in 1988 did not so much explore as refight the war in Vietnam—now on the new turf of Central America, where, once again, the promise and peril of American military intervention were under scrutiny. Evaluation and analysis strayed quickly into recrimination. Rather than examine their views, the protagonists often continued to defend old positions. As the horrors of Vietnam and Cambodia unfolded, as the new proxy battles of Chinese and Russians played themselves out, those who originally opposed the war saw in the ongoing horrors further confirmation of their initial opposition. And those who had supported the war were again reassured that had they been permitted to fight the war full out the cruel fate of the boat people and the retraining centers could have been avoided. If, said the war's opponents, the army had lost the war through ignorance and pigheadedness, it also was responsible for the tragic aftermath. If, rejoined the proponents, the antiwar movement sold the army down the river and made it impossible to fight in the early years, it also sold the Vietnamese down the river later, its naiveté opening the way for the horrors that followed in Vietnam as well as in Pol Pot's Cambodia.

We are now in the aftermath of the aftermath, and there is a new generation in American high schools and colleges for whom the war in Vietnam has no more resonance than Korea or World War II. These young men and women were in nursery school when President Nixon and Henry Kissinger negotiated a peace treaty rationalizing America's defeat, were not yet born when the Tet offensive broke Americans' political will to prevail militarily in Southeast Asia. What are they to learn from recrimination or amnesia? Little more than cynicism, one suspects.

Is there something else to be learned from America's collective Dreyfus case? Has time enough elapsed for deeper lessons to be taught? Can we now explore Vietnam without refighting questions of honor—whether it is the honor of the men who fought, the young people who resisted, or the politicians who watched and waffled? Is it possible to take the measure of the war without refighting it by analogy? Or does the lesson lie precisely in the analogies? With the victims still among us—300,000 wounded, nearly a million veterans—and Vietnam still a tortured nation at war with itself, are we ready to learn? A somber memorial has finally risen in Washington to commemorate our war dead, but it is also a monument to discreet political neutrality. There is no heroism, no glory, only an endless roll of the dead. The stark and beautiful wall commemorates individuals but shoves aside the cause for which they died. We dare not remember too vividly.

T. S. Eliot wrote:

> Neither fear nor courage saves us. Unnatural vices
> Are fathered by our heroism. Virtues
> Are forced upon us by our impudent crimes.

Where are the virtues lurking in the tragic history of the war in Vietnam? Do we retain the strength to use the first great defeat of a country founded on optimism and reared in self-confidence to better our nation?

For a democracy to flourish, there must be connections between present and past and between past and future. One of America's troubles now is its inability to read and remember its own past, and so to converse with its future. Memory is how we confront ourselves and legitimize our citizenship. Thus the story of the American founding remains a vital source not just of civic pride but of actual citizenship; Lincoln's rededication at Gettysburg bespeaks the moral force of the nation as a collective entity, reasserting its unity over 600,000 victims of fratricide; Memorial Day is a remembering no less poignant to veterans than the ancient Greek Olympic festival was to those relatives and friends of fallen soldiers who were commemorated as part of the festival's civic ceremonies. To remember is finally to accept, to possess, and to acquire—to make of memories a force for living.

This collection is a study in memory—which may help Americans not simply to remember, which is painful, but also to learn, which is even more painful. The lessons it tries to teach are not only the short-term lessons of what we did wrong and what we did right and what conclusions are to be drawn for foreign policy today, but also the longer-term lessons that, as citizens of a democracy, Americans must learn if they are to preserve their liberties. The larger lessons are about democracy itself. They vary from observer to observer. For me they have these common themes: that war and democracy make uneasy, perhaps dangerous partners; that citizen and conscript armies are the least unsafe form the military can take in a democracy; that war is often a futile instrument of national policy, a self-contradictory instrument of the defense of democracy. I will say a word about each of these themes and then permit this eloquent book to speak for itself.

War always compromises democracy, even where it is fought in the democracy's name. Ancient Athens' participatory democracy was wrecked by the Peloponnesian War, Lincoln felt compelled to suspend habeus corpus during the Civil War, and both world wars were followed in America by assaults on the freedom of expression, those infamous Red scares which, almost immediately after the nation had proved its mettle to the world, left it trembling and self-doubting from within. The imperatives of national security in wartime play havoc with tolerance, dissent and the imperatives of an open society. Vietnam reaped a harvest of recrimination, polarization, and bitterness that came, in time, to endanger not only the foreign policy consensus but the consensus on which the successful operation of the political system *tout court* depended.

"Resist illegitimate authority!"—a popular slogan in the anti-war movement—was directed against governmental legitimacy itself, not just government policy in Vietnam. The government responded with a distrust of the citizenry no less outraged than the citizenry's distrust of government, a response that resulted eventually in enemies lists and the extra-constitutional shenanigans of Watergate, and brought down two presidents (Lyndon Johnson opting out of the race for a second term, Richard Nixon forced out by the threat of impeachment). Even a popular war can imperil a democracy; a controversial or an unpopular war may undo it.

Yet wars *are* fought, and even for peaceable democracies separated by vast oceans from their enemies there are wars that cannot be avoided if democracy is to be defended. The question then is "by whom?" The answer that emerges again from the evidence of the Vietnam War is that in a democracy citizen soldiers must do the fighting. This ensures that the war is legitimate, and offers a litmus test for illegitimacy. The ideal of the citizen soldier is an ancient one—citizens of the Greek *poleis* fought their own battles and, as Machiavelli rediscovered on the threshold of the modern age, citizen armies often make war more effectively (if also more bloodily) than professional or mercenary armies, while guaranteeing that the war has a certain currency at home.

It was because the American army in Vietnam was a cross section of America, with conscripts from every class (though still not class-balanced because of college deferments) serving and dying side by side, that America experienced the war as *its* war, and was moved to doubt, to criticism, to resistance, and ultimately to the formation of a political will to withdraw. Would the voices of professionals have ever been raised? Would the blood of volunteers from America's poorer ranks have troubled the nation's conscience? Would body bags containing the remains of mercenaries excite the public to outrage or, for that matter, to support? Invisible casualties make war seem costless, and democracies must always understand what their wars cost them.

The "Ballad of the Green Berets" sings of "silver wings upon their chest, these are men, America's best." It is not the best a democratic army must field, however, it is the ordinary and everyday, Everyman's son and brother. If the Vietnam years were the years of the imperial presidency (in part the consequence of war), they were also the years of the conscript army and it was the conscript army as much as anything else that held the imperial presidency in check and, in time, helped to bring it under control. Draft cards were symbols—of honor for those who fought, of resistance for those who burned them, of citizenship for everyone. The draft card embodied the relationship between duties and rights, between popular will and policy action, that is the special virtue of democracy.

Today, when armed forces volunteers are sought with the marketing techniques of corporations and market inducements are the only effective come-on for privatized youngsters who must be talked into a military "job" or "career," the very idea of citizen military service is in disrepute, ironically, principally because of the very war that a conscript army helped bring to an end. It will not be the first time in the life of a democracy that the erosion of citizenship began with the erosion of the citizen-soldier ideal, or that democracy withered because the relationship between citizenship and rights could no longer be discerned.

In fact, the most profound lesson that can be drawn from our Vietnam experience is the fragility of democracy under the pressure of war. War is never a very useful instrument of national affirmation, although it is an apt empire-builder. Wars of defense have to be fought, particularly by democracies, though little more than national and institutional survival can be hoped for from so blunt and undiscriminating an instrument. But wars in the name of extending or enlarging or creating democracy rarely realize their objectives. President Wilson went down to Mexico to make the world safe for democracy and managed only to make it unsafe for Mexico. The Great War we know now as World War I was "the war to end war," but its fruits were a far more destructive Second World War, which in its turn has spawned cold war and hot war and a divided world safe for no nation. The spirit with which I would urge readers to come to this book about war and its somber lessons is the spirit of Wilfred Owen, the young British poet who lost his life in a war he understood all too well. Before he died in the trenches of France in World War I, he wrote these prophetic lines, which resonate still, above all for soldiers:

> Oh, Death was never enemy of ours!
> We laughed at him, we leagued with him, old chum.
> No soldier's paid to kick against his powers.
> We laughed, knowing that better men would come,
> And greater wars; when each proud fighter brags
> He wars on Death—for life; not men—for flags.

2

AMERICA'S WAR IN VIETNAM: The End of Exceptionalism?

LLOYD GARDNER

For most Americans the Vietnam War did not begin until the summer of 1963, when they first saw the horrifying spectacle of saffron-robed Buddhist monks setting fire to themselves on the streets of Saigon. Then they heard national leaders warning the country that the main battlefront of the Cold War had shifted to Southeast Asia, and soon they began to read of Americans serving and dying in Vietnam. But no one—least of all the decision makers in Washington—anticipated a war that would eventually cost more than $100 billion and see half a million men fighting a maddeningly elusive enemy in the steaming jungles of Vietnam. No one would have predicted that the war would drive two presidents from office—and nearly tear the country apart.

Yet it all happened. In the bitter aftermath of "America's longest war," everyone wanted to know how the nation got trapped in the "quagmire." Miscalculation, said some, miscalculation and the cold war background. Whatever mistakes were made—and the very term quagmire implied a false or ill-advised turning off main policy roads—could be attributed to the all-pervading cold war atmosphere. After all, it was pointed out, the Cuban missile crisis of 1962, perhaps the high point of cold war tension, had only just occurred when the American military buildup began in Vietnam. If U.S. policymakers mistook Ho Chi Minh's nationalist revolution for another Kremlin probe, there was ample reason to do so.

Antiwar critics insisted, on the other hand, that while specific policy miscalculations might explain some things about Vietnam, they could not begin to account for *why* America had plunged into the struggle; citing errors in military or political judgment too easily assumed the war was "winnable." Understanding American involvement required a longer perspective, and a degree of self-awareness that was still absent. In their view, persistent questions of racial and cultural conflict that went back to the years of the westward movement had yet to be addressed, as had the roles of ideology and political economy. "American imperialism," they said, should no longer be put in quotation marks; it was imperialism, like any other expansionist thrust in history.

Deeply troubled by either set of explanations, Americans feared that the war had drawn a line across the nation's history and the way one looked at that history. Did the relative decline in America's world economic position stem from military overspending during the war and from a neglect of basic research? Was that decline reversible? Novelists like Robert Stone used their fiction to illustrate the tragic consequences of what they saw as a Vietnam-inspired drug epidemic in America. Could that moral decay be reversed?

Presidential candidates from both parties and both ends of the political spectrum promised they would restore America's faith in itself. Talking about the national mood (*moodiness*) he faced at the outset of the Nixon years, Henry Kissinger wrote: "A new isolationism was growing. Whereas in the 1920s we had withdrawn from the world because we thought we were too good for it, the insidious theme of the late 1960s was that we should withdraw from the world because we were too evil for it."[1]

It is often remarked that Americans are predisposed by the circumstances of their national development to think in these *exceptionalist* terms, by which historians mean that Americans see themselves as removed by much more than an ocean barrier from a common history with their ancestors. As Kissinger (and others) have frequently complained, this deeply ingrained belief causes problems for the policymaker, as the public becomes impatient with the outside world, and/or its supposedly corrupting influences.

Americans lurch between two extremes; at the internationalist end, they seek to spread the American dream to the most remote places on earth, while at the isolationist end, they draw back horrified at what they have seen in those places. But while decrying one manifestation of exceptionalism, Kissinger himself has not been immune to other tenets of the credo: "I believed in the moral significance of my adopted country. America, alone of the free countries, was strong enough to assure global security against the forces of tyranny. Only America had both the power and the decency to inspire other peoples who struggled for identity, for progress and dignity."[2]

Reading back from such a perspective, American expansionism is seen not as a European-style annexation of lands and minerals and a reduction of natives to the status of colonial subjects, but as a unique experiment in human history, a confirmation of the nation's special Manifest Destiny. Historian Patricia Nelson Limerick, author of a biting study of westward expansion entitled *The Legacy of Conquest,* notes that presidents throughout the nation's history, ignoring complex reality, have always seen the frontier, however misleadingly, as "a simple and attractive metaphor for challenge, struggle, and mastery."[3]

The history of the settling of the West—with all of its universal human complications and struggles, its extravagances matched against an often numbing isolation, its greed set against nobility of spirit, and its pitiless racial wars—has never stood a chance, she argues, against the inventions of contemporary and later celebrants of American exceptionalism. And when America went abroad, these myths provided a comfortable rationale for deeds of empire-building.

By the end of the nineteenth century the frontier, or at least the continental frontier, had run out. "The census takers of 1890 informed us," future president Woodrow Wilson wrote in 1902,

> that they could no longer find any frontier upon this continent . . . We had not pondered their report a single decade before we made new frontiers for ourselves beyond the seas, accounting the 7,000 miles of ocean that lie between us and the Philippine Islands no more than the 3,000 which once lay between us and the coasts of the Pacific.[4]

From the time of the Philippine annexation and their initial appearance on the stages of world diplomacy in a major role, American policymakers always believed they were specially endowed by their heritage of revolution against George III's England to undertake a similar mission to *give* Asians self-determination. As Dean Acheson once put it (without ever realizing the irony), "We are willing to help people who believe the way we do, to continue to live the way they want to live."[5]

What might appear to foreign observers to be a typical imperial pattern unfolding was always, in American eyes, a justified assault on European colonialism. There were dissenters, of course, and the presidential election of 1900 was called a referendum of sorts on imperialism. But the ruling party, the Republicans, had little difficulty dispelling the notion that they sought to plant the flag in every "vacant" space around the world. In the Philippine case, plans were made and laws passed promising eventual independence as early as 1916.

Side by side with that zeal to demonstrate American understanding of Asian aspirations, however, there was always an assumption that Americans knew what was best; to be worthy of this gift of independence from the American republic, Filipinos must transform their society so as to conform with "progressive" ideas about sanitation and business contracts.

Typical of the turn-of-the-century conception of the American mission in Asia was an editorial in the *Army and Navy Journal* which justified the surprisingly difficult and bloody campaign against the Philippine guerrillas, who had a different vision of the future, with these words: "While it is true that a people have a certain right to say what shall be done in a political way on their own soil, it is equally true that a narrow-minded race have not the right to shut out from use by other peoples vast natural resources . . ."[6]

Certain patterns were thus established that would hold throughout the century, through World Wars I and II, and through the Vietnam War as well. Declining always to become too closely involved with European colonialism, the United States declared itself a logical spokesman for, and defender of, Asian nationalism. An unacknowledged ambiguity dwelt beneath this self-proclaimed role. While U.S. presidents and secretaries of state claimed to speak, for example, for China's interests at international conferences, the specter of a truly awakened Chinese nationalism sweeping out of Asia disturbed the sleep of White House occupants from Woodrow Wilson to Lyndon Johnson.

All these feelings, many of them obviously contradictory, were in place well before World War II and the Cold War. All nations, it should be noted, have exceptionalist visions of themselves, and all have to deal with such contradictions. What can be said about the dominant American self-perception is that its assumption of uniqueness had not really been challenged until Vietnam. Until then its Fourth-of-July optimism had conformed closely enough to reality to dispel doubts.

Serious American interest in the fate of French Indochina did not manifest itself until the months immediately preceding the Japanese attack on Pearl Harbor in December, 1941. At that time, of course, Tokyo was also proclaiming for itself a special place in world affairs and, like the United States, justifying its actions against the dominant European colonial system as support for nationalist aspirations. Japan said its goal was a "greater East Asian co-prosperity sphere." What it really wanted, behind that phrase, was to make itself independent of European colonies for supplies of raw materials. What most concerned American policymakers in pre–Pearl Harbor days was the threat Japan posed to the economic lifelines of the British Empire in Asia.

Already defeated and humiliated by Nazi Germany in Europe, the rump French government at Vichy had no ability to resist Japanese demands that Japan be allowed to occupy Indochina to insure an uninterrupted supply of foodstuffs and rubber. President Franklin Delano Roosevelt took it upon himself to offer Japan a carrot-and-stick deal. He would participate in a scheme to "neutralize" Indochina so as to guarantee all nations access to the French colony's rich supplies of rice and other products. At the same time, however, State Department officials announced that Japanese assets in the United States were being frozen.

Roosevelt already had in mind, vaguely, a postwar order based on the elimination of colonialism and on the universal rule of liberal political and economic ideas. This Wilsonian vision cropped up twenty-five years later in another proposal to avoid war over Southeast Asia; when President Lyndon Johnson offered Ho Chi Minh and North Vietnam (the Democratic Republic of Vietnam) a chance to participate in a Mekong River development plan which would improve the economy of all Vietnam—if Hanoi would cease and desist from its attempt to conquer South Vietnam (the Republic of Vietnam) by military force.

Interestingly, especially for later developments in American thinking about Vietnam, it was not the Japanese that Roosevelt blamed for the situation so much as the French. Throughout World War II, FDR spoke contemptuously of the French regime in Indochina. Sometimes his pronouncements on the postwar fate of the colony were put in the general context of the rising forces arrayed against European colonialism and the need to promote a peaceful transition to independence; often, however, they were directed towards the specific failings of French rule.

Whoever happened to be present in the Oval Office of the White House when Indochina came up was likely to hear Roosevelt inveigh against French shortcomings. "France has had the country," FDR told Secretary of State Cordell Hull on one occasion, "—thirty million inhabitants—for nearly one hundred years, and the people were worse off than they were at the beginning."[7]

Roosevelt's ambassador to Vichy France, Admiral William D. Leahy, delivered a fateful new message from Washington. If Japan won the war, "the Japanese would take over French Indo-China; and if the Allies won, *we* would take it."[8]

Too much can be made of such statements. Roosevelt and his aides had too overloaded an agenda of "big" issues to worry about during the war, including problems about the conduct of the war and proposed designs for the post-victory world, to be constantly concerned about one French colony. Even so, it is noteworthy that the president himself boasted that he had raised Indochina with Churchill and Stalin on several occasions, always with the firm intention of denying the French any chance to return.

France no longer had any right to expect anyone to respect its claims to sovereignty, Roosevelt insisted, much less to aid its return to that colony. He seemed not to be bothered about assurances given the Free French authorities at the time of the 1942 Anglo-American invasion of North Africa that the French Empire would be restored intact after the war. Such promises were made to save the lives of American soldiers and could not be expected to govern postwar questions, the president would say.[9]

By the end of the war, consequently, there was no settled policy on Indochina, only FDR's vows to drive the French out. These would be recalled in future years when someone asked what happened, as, for example, when John Foster Dulles actually blamed the 1954 Dienbienphu crisis on a failure to follow through on Roosevelt's plans. As Americans watched the final agony of the French effort to recapture Indochina from its people, Secretary of State Dulles said,

> The fundamental blunder . . . was made after 1945. . . . The question then was whether or not the United States . . . would use its power to put the French back into Indochina. Originally, President Roosevelt was against this on the ground that France did not have a good record as a colonial power and its return would not be accepted by the people. Nevertheless, our Government allowed itself to be persuaded in this matter by the French and the British and we acted to restore France's colonial position in Indochina.[10]

That was easy to say in 1954. The legend of Roosevelt's determination to save Indochina from the French colonialists added a peculiar twist to subsequent self-justifications, but it was a very superficial reading of what happened at the end of World War II. Roosevelt himself had wavered on the issue in early 1945, withdrawing into an obscurantist nonpolicy of postponement. Had Dulles then been serving as secretary of state, he very likely would have urged President Harry S. Truman to do exactly what was done—not stand in the way of a French return—and for the same reasons, the need for French support in Europe and fears of Asian communism, especially after 1947.

The Vietminh leader, Ho Chi Minh, appealed to Truman on several occasions in 1945 and early 1946, asking for his moral support against the French. Truman and his policy aides were embarrassed by any appearance of American support for colonialism, but they felt trapped. By 1947 Washington confessed its inability to do anything to halt the developing tragedy. No one could escape the fact that colonial empires were a thing of the past, as new Secretary of State George C. Marshall explained to the American ambassador in Paris, but no one in Washington wanted to see those regimes replaced by "organizations emanating from and controlled by Kremlin . . . Frankly we have no solution of problem to suggest."[11]

The contention that the Kremlin controlled Ho Chi Minh was challenged both then and later, but the official mood in 1947 was dictated by the need to simplify the world to fit the black and white colors of the Truman Doctrine. On March 12, 1947, the president appeared before a joint session of Congress to request $500 million to aid Greece and Turkey. Did that include Indochina? And, if it did, which party was attempting the subjugation? Ho Chi Minh claimed he was the legitimate ruler of Vietnam and that the French were the ones seeking to use outside pressure to impose a disenfranchised emperor, Bao Dai, on the majority of the nation. In part, the question turned on Ho's nationalist credentials. Was he a nationalist, or was he a Kremlin agent posing as a nationalist? In May 1949, Secretary of State Dean Acheson dismissed the "question [of] whether Ho [was] as much nationalist as Commie [as] irrelevant. All Stalinists in colonial areas are nationalists." [12]

Actually, the question had been dismissed even earlier; the atmosphere of the Truman Doctrine had already made it irrelevant. During secret testimony on the Greek-Turkish aid plan, Senator Walter George was among those who worried about the possibility of a holy war developing. George pondered the implications of leaving the United Nations on the sidelines in favor of unilateral action:

> I do not see how we are going to escape going into Manchuria, North China, and Korea and doing things in that area of the world . . . [W]e have got the right to exercise common sense. But I know that when we make a policy of this kind we are irrevocably committing ourselves to a course of action, and there is no way to get out of it next week or next year. You go down to the end of the road. [13]

During those secret hearings, Secretary of State Acheson assured the senators that the administration knew the limits of the Truman Doctrine geographically. There were places where you could not go, he stressed. Indeed, the Truman administration came under fierce criticism for its reluctance to send more aid to Chiang Kai-shek's nationalist government as it tried to turn back Mao's communist armies. Given Chiang's limitations and the nature of the Kuomintang regime, reeking of corruption, it is doubtful that anything Washington could have done would have saved the nationalists.

But the lesson of China's "loss" was not lost on politicians of both parties over the next twenty-five years. Having put the struggle in universal terms, policymakers became accountable for every square mile of territory "lost" to communists anywhere. The political risks of not doing anything crowded out any concern that Asia offered few parallels to Europe, where the containment policy had proven to be a stunning success. By mid-1950, in what General Omar Bradley would call the wrong war, in the wrong place, at the wrong time, the United States was engaged in protecting the territorial integrity of the Republic of South Korea against an invasion from the north, even though the Joint Chiefs of Staff had frequently recommended against fighting on that peninsula for any reason.

Divided at the end of World War II into two occupation zones, Korea had become, de facto, two countries. Defending South Korea was considered a nightmare assignment by the American military, with the exception of General Douglas MacArthur, who was more than ready to try to turn back the communist tide at the 38th parallel. Republican party leaders insisted that it was illogical to aid Greece and Turkey (or the NATO countries one and all) while turning one's back to the threat of Asian communism, but the best that could be made out of the Korean War was a stalemate. Eisenhower came into office in 1953 determined to extricate American forces from that imbroglio as soon as possible. But, while the American military vowed "never again" to become involved on the Asian continent in that kind of war, the unsatisfactory outcome in Korea made it virtually impossible not to accept the "challenge" elsewhere in Asia for fear that the Kremlin's piecemeal tactics would eat away at the frontiers of the "free world."

The French, moreover, now definitely wanted America involved in Indochina—if on their own terms. By the end of the Truman administration, Washington was putting up 80 percent of the costs of the war, and there was growing impatience in the American capital about the way it was being fought. American policymakers firmly believed that what was missing in Vietnam was not men or ordnance, but morale, and that the Vietnamese were never going to fight well until Paris made unequivocal promises of independence. (The French had even refused to create a Vietnamese army, for fear that it would turn on its creators.)

Little wonder, charged American officials, that by the spring of 1954 the French were themselves surrounded in the besieged remote fortress of Dienbienphu. When Paris appealed for direct and immediate American military intervention, Eisenhower played a cagey game. Some of his military advisers recommended using an atomic bomb or bombs to lift the siege. Looking back on the crisis, Air Force General Nathan Twining regretted that such a decision had not been made: "You could take all day to drop a bomb, make sure you put it in the right place. No opposition. And clean those Commies out of there and the band could play the Marseillaise and the French would come marching out of Dien Bien Phu in fine shape." [14]

Ike, however, did not have it in mind to provide an easy way out for the French. His goal, and that of Secretary Dulles, was to save the area for the "free world." To do that, the French would have to stop making themselves an obstacle to efforts to mount anticommunist nationalist campaigns in what would soon be called the Third World. Hence Eisenhower set certain conditions. If Congress approved, he said, and if the British and French agreed to stay the course, and finally, if Paris came through with the promises for complete independence, then, and only then, would the United States intervene. It would not act alone, he ruled.

The president would do his part, meanwhile, to educate public opinion about what was at stake. On April 7, 1954, the president introduced the domino theory—if Indochina fell, it would knock over a line of neighboring states in Southeast Asia, reaching even across water to Indonesia. "Now you are talking really about millions and millions and millions of people," Eisenhower said, and that besides the loss of so many souls to communism, and so many natural resources the free world would be deprived of, there was the Japanese connection. Japan was the biggest domino of all. "It [the loss of Indochina] takes away, in its economic aspects, that region that Japan must have as a trading area or Japan, in turn, will have only one place in the world to go—that is, toward the Communist areas in order to live." [15]

The conditions were not met and the United States did not intervene to save the French at Dienbienphu. One can argue that Ike set unobtainable conditions in order not to have to face the question squarely; even if that is so, his legacy was the fateful domino theory, cited again and again by his successors to justify American policy and applied even after the end of American involvement in Vietnam to developing situations in Central America.

Moreover, while Washington did not like to see communists win any military victories anywhere, the long-term effect of American policy was to turn the situation from a colonial war to a cold war confrontation. After Dienbienphu fell, France made its peace with Ho Chi Minh at the 1954 Geneva Conference. Few expected the solution would stick, however, because it called for all-Vietnam elections within two years. According to the Geneva agreements, Vietnam was to be temporarily divided at the 18th parallel. The elections were never held. The United States did not sign the final agreements at Geneva, but issued a statement promising not to undo them. Within months of the conference, on the other hand, Secretary of State Dulles had obtained the signatures of the British, the French, the Thais, the Filipinos, the Australians and the New Zealanders on a Southeast Asian Treaty Organization (SEATO) protocol, that pledged them all to extend protection to Laos, Cambodia, and the "free territory" of Vietnam.

This was the first step in a carefully plotted campaign to redefine the Vietnamese situation from an internal civil war to a case that could come under the "rules" laid down in the Truman Doctrine: "to support free peoples who are resisting attempted subjugation by armed minorities or by outside pressures." Almost at once, Dulles was talking about South Vietnam as a full-fledged nation, not as part of a country temporarily divided at the 18th parallel. It was little short of amazing how fast the notion took hold that the 1954 Geneva Conference had created two countries.

Dulles, meanwhile, started recalling for reporters the Philippine example (and legend) as a model for the salvation of a non-communist Republic of South Vietnam: "We granted independence to the Philippines and now after they get their independence they in turn are helping another country, Vietnam, to become independent. There is a certain drama about it which appeals to me, at least, and it is having an excellent effect in Vietnam."[16]

The time for the 1956 elections came and went, and Dulles became increasingly confident that the drama he had put on stage was going to end happily. The American protégé picked to lead the Republic of South Vietnam was Ngo Dinh Diem. Diem did in fact have nationalist credentials, but it soon became evident that he had severe deficiencies as a political leader. He was a Catholic in a Buddhist country. Instead of building a solid base of support, he depended for advice upon an inner circle, mostly family members, who were little help in addressing the pressing problems in the countryside. Land reform, probably the only way to counter the growing insurgency, was simply ruled out by Diem.

For the time being, nevertheless, and with the help of large-scale American aid, he appeared to represent in person the elusive "Third Force" Washington hoped would emerge to stand between communism and colonialism. The French were unhappy at being shoved aside, but there was little they could do, and their warnings sounded like sour grapes.

John Kennedy came into office even more determined, if anything, than Eisenhower had been to man all the stations on the watchtowers of freedom and not to fail in Southeast Asia. After the Bay of Pigs debacle at the outset of his administration in 1961, notes former presidential adviser Walt Whitman Rostow, JFK told him:

> The British could have a nervous breakdown in the wake of Suez, the French over Algeria. They each represent six to seven percent of the free world's power—and we could cover for them. But we can't afford a nervous breakdown. We're forty percent, and there's no one to cover for us. We'd better get on with the job.[17]

And, says Rostow, "so we did."

At the Vienna summit conference later that summer, Soviet leader Khrushchev wanted to talk about Berlin and what he said was the abnormal situation of a divided Germany. Kennedy, however, kept coming back to the Third World and Khrushchev's announced support for so-called wars of national liberation. Kennedy had campaigned on the issue of Republican paralysis in foreign policy, which, he claimed, had been caused by Eisenhower's neglect of conventional forces in developing the doctrine of massive retaliation. That doctrine left a president no choices between appeasement and nuclear war. When one looked around the world, and when one listened to Soviet leader Nikita Khrushchev's speeches trumpeting Russian support for wars of national liberation, could there be any doubts that nuclear war was the least likely of the challenges that the United States would face in the future?

It was true, of course, that such wars could escalate into superpower confrontations, hence it was necessary to have the ability to outdo the Russians at every rung of that ladder. So Kennedy and his aides asserted, at any rate, as they went about building up the special forces, the Green Berets, an elite corps trained in counterinsurgency techniques. Vietnam seemed tailor-made for something like the Green Berets. As it turned out, the Green Berets would do very little of the fighting; most of it fell to regulars.

When Kennedy entered office there were about 1,500 American advisors in Vietnam. At his death there were over 15,000. Vice President Lyndon Johnson, who had earlier provided Kennedy with a strong recommendation for staying the course, vowed on the day of Kennedy's assassination in November 1963, that he would not be the president to lose Vietnam. Furthermore, surrounding Johnson were New Frontier advisors who had convinced themselves that Vietnam was to be the ultimate test of an experiment in nation-building. As one former member of the National Security Council wrote after resigning his position in despair about what endowed policymakers with such confidence:

> As they see it, that endowment is composed of, first, our unsurpassed military might; second, our clear technological supremacy; and third, our allegedly invincible benevolence (our "altruism," our affluence, our lack of territorial aspirations). Together, it is argued, this threefold endowment provides us with the opportunity and the obligation to ease the nations of the earth toward modernization and stability: toward a full-fledged *Pax Americana Technocratica*. In reaching toward this goal, Vietnam is viewed as the last and crucial test. Once we have succeeded there, the road ahead is clear.[18]

It is very doubtful, on the other hand, whether LBJ ever subscribed to all these beliefs. A passionate man, Johnson was convinced that the keys to success in politics were personality and, above all, personal contact. That was the way he had run the Senate as majority leader and that was the way he would push through the Great Society programs, but Vietnam stymied him. "If only I could get Ho in a room with me," he remarked on occasion, "I'm sure we could work things out."[19]

But no one knew better than Johnson that, as things stood, Ho had no need to go into any room to negotiate. A few weeks before Kennedy's death Ngo Dinh Diem's regime had been overturned in a military coup. Diem was killed along with his brother-in-law, his chief political adviser. American involvement in the coup remains one of the debated questions about Vietnam. Certain officials in Washington had come to feel that the war could not be won with Diem, but many were also reluctant to "give a green light" to the Vietnamese military. Bad as Diem was, what was there to replace him?

In the confusion, the generals who carried out the coup came to believe, probably correctly, that there was a strong possibility that the Buddhist immolations, combined with all the other "bad press" Diem was receiving in the United States, could very well mean a cutoff in military aid. In that case, there would be no chance for a victory. Diem's principal concern, furthermore, had become to exploit the military to bolster his political position against dissident forces. He was also determined to prevent a military phalanx from arising against his rule. Under those conditions, it was clear that the war against the Vietcong guerrillas was unlikely to have any chance of success. Military men do not like to lose, especially for what they perceive as political reasons.

In Washington, meanwhile, there was a growing fear that President Diem might, as a last resort, attempt to secure his position by opening negotiations with Ho's government. While this might seem farfetched to casual observers, it set off warning bells in Washington. Immediately after he took the oath of office, President Johnson sent high-ranking emissaries to Saigon to tell Diem's successors that there was to be no more talk of neutralism or negotiations. America was in for the duration. Nevertheless, during the 1964 presidential campaign the Democrats cast LBJ as the peace candidate, as opposed to Republican Barry Goldwater, whose itchy trigger finger (Goldwater was a reservist Air Force General) supposedly insured a wider war. Johnson promised not to send American boys to Vietnam to undertake the burden of the fight. Early in the campaign, however, Johnson suddenly appeared on television to report that he had ordered retaliatory strikes against North Vietnamese PT boat bases. American naval forces in the Gulf of Tonkin, he told the nation, had been attacked twice, and it was his job to protect those forces. Within days Congress had passed the Gulf of Tonkin Resolution, empowering the president to use American military forces to repulse future attacks.

Much controversy developed about the motive and nature of the North Vietnamese attacks. Were they as unprovoked as administration witnesses were to claim? Did the second attack even take place? Johnson was in a very good position at this time, able to rely upon all his old friends in the Senate and House to advance the argument, as many did, that such a resolution was in safe hands with LBJ—especially if it stole what little thunder Goldwater had generated thus far in the presidential race.

The Gulf of Tonkin Resolution would later be cited as the authority—and all the authority needed—for the administration to send half a million men to Vietnam. At one point, Under Secretary of State Nicholas Katzenbach told the Senate Foreign Relations Committee that the Gulf of

Tonkin Resolution was "the functional equivalent" of a declaration of war. Truth was, of course, that the United States had engaged in war in Korea under the rubric of a police action, but by the time Katzenbach caused an uproar with this assertion in 1967, Johnson was under assault for the so-called credibility gap.

The longer the war went on—without any prospect of a victory despite Secretary of Defense Robert McNamara's optimistic predictions of light at the end of the tunnel—the more skeptical the nation became about administration statements. The daily press briefings in Saigon became known as the five o'clock follies because of the dubious "body count" figures supplied to reporters. In a war without front lines, a war fought with booby traps on one side and napalm on the other, how was one to tell who was winning?

General Maxwell Taylor, a key policy planner in the Kennedy and Johnson years, admitted to mystification:

> The ability of the Viet Cong continuously to rebuild their units and to make good their losses is one of the mysteries of this guerrilla war. We are aware of the recruiting methods by which local boys are induced or compelled to join the Viet Cong ranks and have some general appreciation of the amount of infiltration of personnel from the outside. Yet taking both of these sources into account, we still find no plausible explanation of the continued strength of the Viet Cong if our data on Viet Cong losses are even approximately correct. Not only do the Viet Cong units have the recuperative powers of the phoenix, but they have an amazing ability to maintain morale.[20]

No hint of this mystification reached the public from official channels. Instead there were constant reiterations that the measured steps the administration was taking would produce results. Antiwar "teach-ins" had already begun on college campuses in the spring of 1965, stimulated in part by the decision to begin bombing North Vietnam. The raids began on a tit-for-tat basis after a particularly damaging mortar attack on American forces stationed at Pleiku, but soon gave way to a regular military operation. Over the next decade more bombs would be dropped on Vietnam than in all the previous wars the nation had fought!

Johnson's response to the nascent antiwar movement came on 7 April 1965, the eleventh anniversary of Eisenhower's description of the domino theory. There were three compelling reasons why America was in Vietnam, the president told an audience at Johns Hopkins University. First, there was the nation's pledged word from the time of 1954; second, American credibility as the main supporter of world order was on the line; third, the central lesson of our time was that appeasement always failed. "We must say in southeast Asia—as we did in Europe—in the words of the Bible: 'Hitherto shalt thou come, but no further.'"[21]

If North Vietnam would agree to beat its swords into plowshares, Johnson promised, he would ask Congress to join in a billion-dollar investment in regional development. All the nations of the area could participate, as could the Soviet Union. He would sponsor a Mekong River plan for dams and reservoirs "on a scale to dwarf even our own TVA." A variety of negotiating formulas were advanced by Washington over the remaining three and a half years of the Johnson administration. The sticking point was always the role the Saigon government would have, with the North insisting that internal affairs of Vietnam were up to the Vietnamese "in accordance with the program of the NFLSV [the vietcong] without any foreign interference."

On 22 July 1965, Johnson took the decision to send 100,000 troops to Vietnam. His advisors had warned that things had gotten so bad that the VC was about to abandon guerrilla war in favor of large unit battles. Secretary McNamara and Pentagon generals then advanced the remarkable thesis that it was precisely because things had gotten so bad that if the United States responded properly, and the VC and its North Vietnamese ally attempted to stand toe-to-toe, this would allow us, as General Earl Wheeler said, "to cream them."

Johnson still tried to probe what would happen if Ho sent his own hundred thousand or more troops into the fray, but seemed to accept the logic of the situation, even when warned that the 100,000 might be only half enough—or less. Only a few days earlier he had told his staff "There's one thing you ought to know. Vietnam is like being in a plane without a parachute when all the engines go out. If you jump, you'll probably be killed, and if you stay in you'll crash and probably burn. That's what it is." [22]

So American ground forces went in, first 100,000, then 200,000, and finally more than half a million. By the end of 1967 Johnson had drawn the administration wagon train into a tight circle against antiwar critics. But there were defections, including a very shaken Secretary of Defense McNamara. At a November 1967 meeting of the senior foreign policy advisory group (prominent citizens who had served at one time or another), dubbed "the wise men," Johnson got the reassurance he now so desperately wanted. The meeting ended with almost unanimous agreement against getting out. "Absolutely not," said Dean Acheson. "As impossible as it is undesirable," said McGeorge Bundy. "Definitely not," repeated C. Douglas Dillon. "Unthinkable," said Henry Cabot Lodge, "we are trying to divert a change in the balance of power." "The public would be outraged if we got out," said Abe Fortas. [23]

Across the street from the executive mansion, crowds chanted, "Hey, hey, LBJ! How many kids did you kill today?" Public opinion polls continued to show support for the war, but increasing numbers of people were saying that the original decision to intervene had been a mistake. Few wanted to concede defeat in Vietnam, but the wisdom of American foreign policy was now being openly disputed for the first time, really, since the Truman Doctrine was first announced twenty years earlier. Young men were fleeing to Canada to escape the draft, and draft boards in small towns were pleading with Washington that the system was punishing those areas who loyally sent in their quotas each month. The fabric of American society had come under a terrific strain.

The final blow for Johnson was the Tet offensive in February, 1968. This all-out offensive by the VC failed to win the war, but it left in shattered ruins the credibility of the Johnson administration. At a meeting with the Democratic Congressional leadership on 6 February 1968, Johnson faced for the first time the defection of a key figure, Senator Robert Byrd, hitherto absolutely loyal. Byrd charged that Tet demonstrated a whole series of flaws in government thinking about the war. "I am concerned," he said, offering his list: "(1) That we had *poor intelligence*. (2) That we were not prepared for these attacks. (3) We underestimated the morale and vitality of the Viet Cong. (4) We overestimated the support of the South Vietnamese government and its people." Johnson shot back that he did not agree with anything Byrd said: "It seems to be an American trait to ask why. I just hope that we don't divert our energies and our talents by criticizing unnecessarily. We've got all we can take of this 'What's wrong with our country?'" Byrd was not dissuaded. "I do not want to argue with the President. But I am going to stick by my convictions."[24]

It was now clear that even if one agreed with the commander in Vietnam, General William Westmoreland, that Tet had been a defeat for the Vietcong, to win the war would require many more troops and perhaps a decade. And after that, what? Was it reasonable to believe that South Vietnam could be held like South Korea with a small occupying force?

The Vietnamese terrain, so completely unlike the rocky hills of Korea, did not offer much encouragement to that view. When General Westmoreland asked for 100,000 more troops to pursue the "defeated" VC, internal debates began in the administration that ended with Johnson's decision to announce that he would not stand for reelection.

The president had already summoned "the wise men" to the White House again to solicit anew their pledges of support. They were supposed to recommend hanging tough, but Acheson and Clark Clifford, the new secretary of defense, were now skeptics about Vietnam. The latter had been unable to get an answer from the Joint Chiefs when he asked how many men and how long it would take to defeat the VC. Acheson was blunter: The Joint Chiefs had been leading Johnson down the primrose path. The wisemen went over all the issues, not just military questions. They surveyed the economic consequences of the war. The gold drain caused by the president's reluctance to raise taxes to pay for the war could not go on. There was the question of whether the Democratic party could hold together much longer. And so forth.

There had to be another way to end the war, concluded "the wisemen." Declaring a moratorium on the bombing of North Vietnam above a certain line, the president said that he intended to devote the remainder of his term in office to the search for peace. His efforts brought the opening of formal discussions in Paris, but no progress had been made on any key issue by the time he left office. Still, the very fact discussions had begun was important.

Johnson had been challenged within the Democratic party in the presidential primaries by Senators Eugene McCarthy and Robert Kennedy. Kennedy's assassination, after a triumph in the California primary, left McCarthy to battle it out with Vice President Hubert Humphrey for the nomination. The turmoil of the Democratic Convention in Chicago that summer was unprecedented in American political history. While a startled nation watched, Chicago police chased demonstrators through the streets, waving billy clubs and hurling teargas at yippies and whoever else got in the way.

The staid CBS commentator, Walter Cronkite, looked at the scene outside the convention hall on his monitor, and declared it to be a police riot. Humphrey won the nomination and was opposed by Richard M. Nixon. The most remarkable thing about the campaign was that Vietnam was not debated at all! Humphrey said that discussions would hinder the peace efforts. This allowed Nixon to claim that he had a plan to end the war, without having to answer questions. The 1968 election was a mirror image of the one Nixon lost to Kennedy eight years earlier, only this time the razor-thin margin went to the Republican.

Nixon's plan, it turned out, was to offer the Russians promises of trade and technology if they would put pressure on Hanoi to negotiate on American terms. Combined with this, Nixon would seek to inject the Paris negotiations with a sense of urgency. He wanted his negotiators to let it slip that the president was irrational in his determination to end the war quickly. This madman theory was supposed to bring rapid concessions from the other side.

One trouble with the madman theory was that Nixon had determined to begin reducing the American force in Vietnam. He was perfectly capable of letting loose massive bombing raids, as the world would soon know, but the Vietnamization program of turning over more and more of the fighting to the South Vietnamese was a rational way of dealing with domestic opposition to the war. All Hanoi had to do was wait him out.

Henry Kissinger, Nixon's national security advisor, was confronted by his North Vietnamese counterpart with precisely that challenge. How, asked Le Duc Tho, did the United States expect to win with puppet troops, if it could not win with America forces? Kissinger had no answer. In the spring of 1970, on 30 April, United States and Vietnamese forces invaded Cambodia in an effort to destroy North Vietnamese camps and demonstrate South Vietnamese capabilities to carry the burden on their own.

For more than a year, the United States had been secretly bombing suspected bases in Cambodia as part of the Vietnamization of the war. The Cambodian "incursion" was disastrous from every point of view. It was touted as a masterstroke against the principal North Vietnamese military headquarters in Cambodia, the main source of infiltration from North to South. The base was never found, but that was the least of President Nixon's troubles.

The war instantly became "Nixon's War." Up until the invasion, the administration could claim that it was simply cleaning up the mess left by Johnson. No more. The incursion demonstrated that Vietnamization, instead of narrowing the war, threatened to spread it across Indochina. Perhaps worst of all was the domestic reaction. Tragic shootings occurred at Kent State University in Ohio and at Jackson State in Mississippi, where nervous military and police forces resorted to bullets to stop protests. Nixon had promised to bring the nation together again, but his policy now depended upon divide and rule. From the infamous list of enemies kept by the White House, to the egging-on of the "hard hats" against students and antiwar demonstrators, to Vice President Spiro Agnew's intemperate attacks on the "media manipulators," the administration behaved like a prizefighter blinded with rage, swinging wildly in the hopes of landing a knockout blow.

All the more remarkable, then, that the administration was scoring diplomatic successes elsewhere. No Democratic president since Harry Truman had considered an opening to Communist China. Nixon not only did consider breaking the old taboo, he went to China to initiate American relations with the Communist leadership. He went to Russia to sign SALT-1, a strategic arms limitation pact, and to present to the Soviets the opportunity to join in what he and Kissinger called the structure of peace.

But there was always Vietnam. The president could not find a way out of the war that would not betray his own commitment to the exceptionalist view, now supported by his own creation, the so-called Silent Majority. The president had summoned forth the image of Woodrow Wilson in a television address to the nation, declaring that the Vietcong and North Vietnamese could never defeat the United States, only Americans could do that. He meant the war protestors, of course, but having called upon the Silent Majority to support the noble American cause, he could not suddenly turn around and pursue his détente policies toward the Soviet Union on the bodies of dead Americans in Vietnam. He needed some semblance of a victory to hold things together.

Nixon wanted to get past the war to the business of restructuring Soviet-American relations, with the objective of creating political stability across the lines of the cold war. The Russians made it clear, however, that they had little influence over Hanoi's decisions, no matter how much aid they were providing Ho's armies. (The Soviets have recently admitted that Russian soldiers manned anti-aircraft batteries in North Vietnam. Reminiscences of Russian veterans of the Vietnam War stress their pride in the success of their Vietnamese pupils in downing American bombers. What other Russian forces served in Vietnam has yet to be revealed.)

Time was fast running out for Vietnamization. Nixon had never expected the war to be an issue in the 1972 campaign, but it was. A tentative truce plan was ready for signature just before the election, but Nixon repudiated it at the last moment. He had opened the way to China and to new relations with the Soviet Union, but the specter of rightist attacks on his foreign policy, the great fear Democrats had suffered since 1949, caused him to hesitate.

After winning reelection, Nixon ordered the "Christmas bombings" against Hanoi and environs. Claims would be made later that the bombings had brought the North Vietnamese back to the negotiating table to sign a better truce agreement. Comparisons of the October draft truce agreement with the one finally signed in January 1973 revealed very little change. The essential fact in each instance was that the North Vietnamese were permitted to keep their forces in place in South Vietnam pending the final political settlement of the war, vaguely left to a proposed commission of national reconciliation.

South Vietnam's president, Nguyen Van Thieu, refused to sign the accord, seeing in it only an escape route for Washington, while his regime was sacrificed. Thieu's resistance infuriated Nixon. "If the current course continues," the American president wrote Thieu, "and you fail to join us in concluding a satisfactory agreement with Hanoi, you must understand that I will proceed at whatever the cost." [25]

On the other hand, Nixon did promise that if the North Vietnamese violated the terms of the truce, America would come to Saigon's aid. The issue became moot when Nixon was forced to resign the presidency in the Watergate crisis to avoid impeachment in the summer of 1974. Henry Kissinger and others were to argue that, for this reason, Congress bore the major responsibility for the "loss" of Vietnam—and indeed for American weaknesses in meeting the communist threat in Africa and else-where. It is a most improbable argument. Nixon knew when he began the Vietnamization program that he was entering a one-way street, and once the war in Vietnam became "Mr. Nixon's War" after the Cambo-dian invasion, secret "doves" of the Johnson years could come forward to join in the chorus of protest, released from party loyalty. True, Congress did not repeal the Gulf of Tonkin Resolution until after Watergate had rendered Nixon largely powerless. But to say Watergate caused, via Con-gress, the loss of Vietnam is to reverse cause and effect.

In the spring of 1975 the final act was played out. A North Vietnamese offensive quickly ended the war. Saigon was renamed Ho Chi Minh City. The North Vietnamese victory did not bring the millennium with it. The land began to recover from the wounds left by American bombs, but the communists proved no more able than other leaders in the Third World to alleviate the economic situation that put Vietnam near the bot-tom among nations.

Americans wanted to blame someone or something for what had hap-pened. It did little good to blame everything on the "Vietnam syndrome," when there were so many other limitations on American power. The world had vastly changed in the twenty-five years since the end of World War II, when the United States and Russia were left alone glaring at one another across the ruins of Europe.

Ten years after the war in Vietnam, Ronald Reagan and the Republi-cans boasted that "America is back," but the unique circumstances of the 1960s that had convinced Americans they could "have it all" were not to be repeated. Still, Reagan harked back to the exceptionalist faith in his second inaugural address, reminding Americans of what they had ac-complished in the westward movement:

> The men of the Alamo call out encouragement to each other; a settler pushes west and sings his song, and the song echoes out forever and fills the unknow-ing air. It is the American sound: It is hopeful, big-hearted, idealistic—daring, decent and fair. That's our heritage, that's our song. We sing it still.

For eight years Reagan challenged Congress to live up to that heritage by supporting his determination to oust the Sandinista regime in Nicara-gua. Congress gave him some of what he wanted, but there were to be no more Gulf of Tonkin resolutions. It passed huge new appropriation bills for defense, but incrasingly the major issues confronting American lead-ers in domestic and foreign policy involved finding the way to overcome the budget deficit, yet maintain domestic and foreign commitments.

General Maxwell Taylor, who had played a key role in developing the Vietnam policy, looked back with concern at how lightly the United States had undertaken this mission in nation-building.

We certainly had a feeling after World War II that we could go almost any place and do almost anything. Well, we did many things at enormous cost, but henceforth we're going to have trouble feeding and keeping happy our own growing population just as every other nation is. This is not a time for our government to get out on limbs which are not essential.[26]

The lessons of Vietnam would become the subject of debates as controversial as the war itself. America would take a long time to come to terms with the trauma and to overcome it. The key words were in Taylor's ruminations—"just as every other nation is." Having gone through the Reagan years, the nation had at last seen a president complete two full terms—for the first time since the Eisenhower era. Despite Reagan's initial obsession with the "evil empire," his targeting of Nicaragua, his fumbling in the Iran/Contra affair, and the fancifulness of "Star Wars," there emerged, thanks in part to events over which he had absolutely no control in the "Communist world," a growing sense from the White House down that like no man, no nation could be an island unto itself. The nature of global issues in the next century (again, as Taylor's comments implied) would not yield to the exceptionalist myth of any nation; rather they would present themselves as challenges to humanity in general. Finally Vietnam was a searing flame that cut through such myths to force a recognition that America could not remake the world in its own image. Russia was to find the same reality in Afghanistan. Superpower hegemony had ended. The Vietnam legacy in foreign policy, like all other historical legacies, was a mixed one, but exceptionalism was not part of it.

NOTES

1. Henry Kissinger, *White House Years* (New York: Little, Brown & Co., 1979), pp. 56–57.

2. *Ibid.,* p. 229.

3. Patricia Nelson Limerick, *The Legacy of Conquest* (New York: W. W. Norton & Co., 1987), p. 324.

4. Reprinted in William E. Dodd and Ray Stannard Baker, eds., *The Public Papers of Woodrow Wilson* (New York, 1925), vol. 1, pp. 425–26.

5. Quoted in William Appleman Williams, *The Tragedy of American Diplomacy* (New York: Dell Publishing Co., 1962), p. 10.

6. Quoted in Roy Flint, "The United States Army on the Pacific Frontier, 1899–1939," in Joe C. Dixon, ed., *The American Military and the Far East* (Washington, D.C.: GPO, 1980), p. 151.

7. Cordell Hull, *The Memoirs of Cordell Hull,* 2 vols. (New York: MacMillan, 1948), vol. 2, p. 1597.

8. Lloyd C. Gardner, *Approaching Vietnam: From World War II Through Dienbienphu* (New York: W. W. Norton & Co., 1988), p. 27.

9. For an example of concern about the president's pledges to the French, and a brief list of the occasions on which he offered them, see Hull, *The Memoirs of Cordell Hull* 2, p. 1597.

10. Draft by John Foster Dulles, 9 July 1954, in *Papers of John Foster Dulles*, Seeley Mudd Library, Princeton University, Princeton, New Jersey.

11. Quoted in Gardner, *Approaching Vietnam*, p. 78.

12. Quoted in William Appleman Williams et al., eds., *America in Vietnam: A Documentary History* (New York: Doubleday & Co., 1985), p. 56.

13. Senate Foreign Relations Committee, *Hearings held in Executive Session: Legislative Origins of the Truman Doctrine*, 80th Cong., 1st sess., 1973, p. 198.

14. Quoted in Walter LaFeber, *America, Russia and the Cold War, 1945–1975*, 3rd ed. (New York: John Wiley, 1976), p. 162.

15. United States National Archives, *Public Papers of the Presidents of the United States: Dwight D. Eisenhower, 1954* (Washington: GPO, 1958), pp. 381–90.

16. John Foster Dulles, press conference, Manila, 2 March 1955, *Papers of John Foster Dulles*.

17. W. W. Rostow, "Beware of Historians Bearing False Analogies," *Foreign Affairs* 66 (Spring, 1988), pp. 863–68.

18. James C. Thomson, Jr., "How Could Vietnam Happen? An Autopsy," *The Atlantic Monthly* 22 (April, 1968), pp. 47–53.

19. Quoted in Richard N. Goodwin, "The War Within," *The New York Times Magazine*, 21 August 1988, pp. 34–38, 42, 48.

20. Quoted in *The Senator Gravel Edition. The Pentagon Papers*, 4 vols. (Boston: Beacon Press, 1971), 3, p. 668.

21. The National Archives, *Public Papers of the Presidents of the United States: Lyndon B. Johnson, 1965* (Washington: GPO, 1967), pp. 394–99.

22. Quoted in Goodwin, "The War Within."

23. Larry Berman, *Lyndon Johnson's War* (New York: W. W. Norton & Co., 1989), p. 101.

24. Notes of the President's Meeting with the Democratic Congressional Leadership, 6 February 1968, Tom Johnson's Notes of Meetings, Box 2, *The Lyndon Baines Johnson Library*, Austin, Texas.

25. Quoted in Nguyen Tien Hung and Jerrold L. Schecter, *The Palace File* (New York: Harper and Row, 1986), p. 135.

26. Taylor interview in Michael Charlton and Anthony Moncrieff, *Many Reasons Why: The American Involvement in Vietnam* (New York: Hill and Wang, 1978), pp. 239–40.

3

PROMISE AND PARADOX: The 1960s and American Optimism

BARBARA TISCHLER

Nearly twenty years later, the decade of the 1960s has come to signify turmoil and change in American politics and culture. The period was characterized by a genuine reform impulse to use government as an agent for social change and by a "cop on the beat" mentality that placed the United States in the forefront of post–World War II anticommunism. This optimistic, perhaps even naive perspective, with roots in both the New Deal and the Cold War, inspired a significant effort to resolve the social problems of poverty and racial injustice. The same spirit led the country into a deepening quagmire in Southeast Asia from which it has not yet fully recovered. Cold war liberal ideology led American governments in the 1960s to pursue both social reform and anticommunism throughout the world with enthusiasm and optimism. Expectations were high, and when the possibilities of the period were not fulfilled, optimism gave way to a profound cynicism. The legacy of the 1960s comprises not only an optimistic, if slightly out of fashion, faith in reform but also a mistrust of government and politics. The result has been a privitization of political perspective in the "Me" era of the 1970s and 1980s.

Particular reflections on recent history can be as numerous as the historical actors themselves, but two clusters of images of America in the 1960s predominate in the popular mind. The first is a view of the 1960s that stresses the conviction that the social mission of the New Deal could finally be accomplished. For those who look back in the 1960s with nostalgia, a number of phrases and slogans evoke "Big Chill" memories of an ethos that is no longer in fashion as we enter the 1990s. These include Camelot, "Freedom

Now!", student power, the summer of love, and the War on Poverty that could be won. In contrast, other Americans remember the 1960s as a decade when America went wrong. The goal in recent decades for proponents of this view has been to "correct" the aberrations of the period in order to "put America back on track." Those who see the 1960s as a decade out of phase with the orderly progress of American history attach negative meanings to remembered phrases and slogans, including Black Power and "Burn, Baby, Burn," SDS and the Weathermen, yippies, hippies, and other less than desirable non-conformists, and see ignominy, if not actual defeat, in Vietnam, a war lost because of political constraints placed on an otherwise valiant military.

In taking these perspectives into account and avoiding both the nostalgia and the hostility that romanticize the 1960s, scholars are beginning to consider the period as part of the broader spectrum of American history, not simply as an isolated episode of political radicalism, social experimentation, or cultural craziness. The period that we have conceptualized as "the sixties" was characterized by the continuation of many cherished American political and social traditions—what could be more American, for example, than revolutionary political protest and confidence in the ability of the nation to solve its most pressing social problems—but it also included important departures from "the way things had always been," as groups without a voice, black Americans, women, and young people, found that their "place" was in the center of the political and social action.

The issue of the uniqueness of the 1960s raises the question of how to frame the period chronologically. The passing of the 1950s and the emergence of the "Me" decade of the 1970s hardly provide a satisfactory time span for analysis. Many of the issues that we define as products of the 1960s clearly predate the start of the decade, and still more of the issues raised by the events of the 1960s have remained important in our culture beyond the passage of the 1970s. Indeed, several histories of the 1960s can be written, each with a different focus, series of critical events, and historical protagonists. Consider just a few of the ways to conceptualize the period:

1954–73: the years of the United States' most important involvement in Vietnam, from the French defeat at Dienbienphu to the American withdrawal of military forces.

1954–68: the period of civil rights activism which focused on legal changes achieved through the courts and the political process in general, from the *Brown* v. *Board of Education* decision by the Supreme Court to the election of Richard Nixon, in part a white backlash against civil rights activism. An overlapping and related history of black nationalism and Black Power begins in the mid-1960s and continues after the police killings of members of the Black Panther Party in Chicago in 1969.

1960–68:   the period between two elections, characterized by images of Camelot and the Great Society. This was a period of power for the Democratic party which set the political agenda well into the Nixon presidency between 1969 and 1974. The Kennedy-Johnson years saw the United States' deepest Involvement in Viet Nam and most serious attempt since the New Deal to come to grips with social problems through the agency of the federal government.

1957–69:   from the launching of Sputnik by the Soviet Union and the at-tendant scrambling for superiority in space to the Apollo moon landing. This history is of scientific achievement for public use, ranging from the mass marketing of oral contraceptives to intro-duction of the computer and the Xerox copier into American life. It was also a period of growing concern about the social ramifications of scientific discoveries, as illustrated in growing opposition to war research and the emergence of an environmen-tal preservation movement.

1964–84:   from the passage of the Civil Rights Act, whose Title VII man-dated equal protection under the law for women, to the most recent defeat of the Equal Rights Amendment. This was a period of activism and organization for women that serves as a model in many important ways for continuing the quest for equality under the law.

1963–72:   from the early popularity of the Beatles to the emergence of disco music. This was a musically exciting and creative period in American culture, not only because of the so-called British inva-sion, but also because of the rediscovery of African-American musical styles such as blues and soul and the vitality of folk mu-sic as a vehicle for protest and social commentary.

This multi-theme approach provides several ways to study the 1960s, but it is limited in providing a short and simple answer to the question "What were the 1960s about?" The simplicity of the question yields less-than-satisfactory responses for *any* period in American history; however, it is useful to strive for an integrated narrative that will take into account the diversity 1960s of American culture.

One approach to such a narrative of recent American history is to con-sider what difference the 1960s made in the political and cultural life of the nation. Putting the question this way allows for analysis of change without either nostalgia or regret. Whatever our assumptions about the decade and its legacy, the political, military, legal, and cultural events of the 1960s did make a difference in a variety of behaviors and attitudes.

From the perspective of the late 1980s, it is interesting to consider that because of events in the 1960s:

- eighteen-year-olds can vote in the United States.
- there is no draft at present, although there *is* preliminary draft registration for all young men on their eighteenth birthday.
- the Civil Rights and Voting Rights Acts, to the extent that they have been enforced by the federal government, have made participation in the political process and in the economic realm possible for African Americans, women, and members of other minority groups.
- legislation regarding employment, credit, sexual harassment, and divorce, to name only a few areas, has made possible significant changes in the status of America women.
- birth control is legal and somewhat safer than it was prior to the 1960s. As a result of the Supreme court decision in *Roe* v. *Wade,* abortion is legal and is the subject of heated public debate rather than part of a clandestine, illegal, and dangerous medical subculture that costs women their lives.
- children no longer pray in public schools as a matter of public policy.[1]
- persons arrested and accused of criminal activity are informed of their legal rights, and the right to legal counsel under many circumstances has been established by the Supreme Court.
- in spite of the efforts of the powerful tobacco lobby, the federal government has used its authority to warn consumers about the dangers of smoking cigarettes and to ban tobacco advertising from radio and television.
- in many important respects, from eclecticism to the emergence of a recognizable "sixties image," the counterculture has become part of the mainstream popular culture.

The dynamism of the 1960s and the conviction that the nation was ready for rapid and unconventional reform renders the decade almost unique in modern history. Not since the Depression had the nation experienced such dramatic tension and conflict over the legitimacy of individuals and institutions in positions of authority to make policy. It was this tension that inspired many calls for meaningful social reform. As the major reform causes, racial inequality and the Vietnam War, remained unresolved, that tension created important generational, ethnic, and class rents in the American social fabric.

In January of 1960, ten months prior to a closely contested presidential election that would bring an end to the Eisenhower years, historian

Arthur M. Schlesinger, Jr. contributed an article on "The New Mood in American Politics" to *Esquire*. The "upscale" readership of this sophisticated men's magazine was accustomed to reading about the most current political debates, and Schlesinger used his mass-circulation forum to assess the decade coming to an end and to offer some prescriptions for the new era about to unfold. Describing what he called the "politics of fatigue" of the 1950s as a response to the activism of the nation in times of depression, hot war, and cold war, Schlesinger deplored the ideology of the prosperous decade in which consumption seemed to triumph over social conscience. "Materialism—the belief that the needs of life can be fulfilled by material opulence—is not enough," he argued, noting further that "under the spell of materialism, our nation has allocated its abundance to private satisfaction rather than to public need, with the result that the wealthiest nation in the world suddenly seems to be falling behind in education, falling behind in science, falling behind in technology, falling behind in weapons, falling behind in our capacity to stir the minds and hearts of men."

Schlesinger optimistically predicted that the new decade of the 1960s would see a renewed commitment to the public interest and a renewed trust in government as the agent for positive social change. He predicted that the new focus would unleash creative energies that would at first seem chaotic as they were directed to overcoming the nation's pressing problems in unconventional ways. "The Sixties," he predicted, "will probably be spirited, articulate, inventive, incoherent, turbulent, with energy shooting off wildly in all directions. Above all, there will be a sense of motion, of leadership and of hope."[2]

In the 1960 campaign, John Fitzgerald Kennedy attempted to modernize the image of the presidency and of American political leadership in general. As a product of wealth and privilege, he was hardly different from most prior occupants of 1600 Pennsylvania Avenue; but as a young man of only forty-three and an Irish Catholic, he surprised many political pundits by attaining the highest office in the land. He capitalized on the idea that the Eisenhower administration, including Vice President Richard Nixon, stood for the politics of fatigue which Schlesinger had described, and he called for a change, not only in the party affiliation of the president, but also in the focus of political leadership in the United States. Fatigue would be replaced by energy and stagnation would give way to progress on America's "New Frontier' of world leadership.

Kennedy captured the traditionally Democratic votes of city dwellers, blacks, and members of self-defined ethnic groups, while the religion issue cost him votes in the predominantly Protestant South. In the first campaign fought in front of television cameras as well as at rallies and on whistle stop tours, Kennedy appeared more vigorous and attractive than Nixon, whose popularity flagged as he stiffened before the camera's eye. Television was crucial to this and to succeeding campaigns. This relatively new medium brought images of leadership to the American people, as it would soon bring war, urban disruption, and assassinations into living rooms across the land. Indeed, it was the series of television debates, watched by 70 million Americans, that helped Kennedy capture a very narrow victory, with 49.9 percent of the popular vote to Nixon's 49.6 percent. But the very closeness of the election made it immediately clear that many Americans approached the excitement and spirit of change promised by the new decade and the new president uneasily.

The "ask not what your country can do for you, ask what you can do for your country" spirit of John Kennedy's inaugural address emanated from the optimism in the political air that Schlesinger's article had predicted. Given the close ties between the historian and the new president and his policies, this connection is not surprising, but the extent to which this enthusiasm took hold in the public mind as the governing idea during the brief period often described as Camelot helps to locate the spirit of change and dynamism often associated with later, more radical events of the 1960s. It was during John Kennedy's thousand days in office that Americans got themselves into shape on fifty-mile hikes, joined the Peace Corps to bring American technology and ideology to "less-developed" nations, and watched by the millions as Jackie Kennedy took them on a tour of the newly redecorated White House. If, more than twenty years later, the president and the presidency are tainted by public knowledge of private indescretion and the cynical exploitation of altruistic impulses by the Central Intelligence Agency and other government operatives, our skepticism only highlights the optimism, even naiveté, of the early part of the decade.

Rhodes scholars in the Cabinet, Harvard intellectuals among the presidential advisors, classical music and high style for visiting dignitaries, and a face lift for the White House interior revealed only the surface of the Camelot image. In the realm of government policy, the trappings of liberalism were combined with an adherence to cold war anticommunism. The United States continued to play the role of guardian against world communism. Stressing the irreconcilability of what Kennedy called "freedom under God versus ruthless, godless tyranny," and the sense of mission that the United States was to carry into the new decade, the young president declared at his inauguration; "In the long history of the world, only a few generations have been granted the role of defending freedom in its hour of maximum danger. I do not shrink from this responsibility. I welcome it." With the mission to eradicate communist influence and prevent its spread came the imperative for the nation to "pay any price, bear any burden, meet any hardship, support any friend, oppose any foe, to assure the survival and success of liberty."[3]

Kennedy faced tests of his cold war mettle in Laos, on the shores of Cuba's Bay of Pigs, along the border between East and West Berlin, and in the Caribbean waters surrounding Fidel Castro's revolutionary experiment ninety miles from the Florida coast. In all cases, American foreign policy was focused, directly or indirectly, on the Soviet Union. The administration accepted the domino theory as a first principle and sought to contain the progress of communism wherever it seemed to be gaining a foothold. For Kennedy, the stakes were high, in terms of the political and military reputation of the United States as well as his personal image as a president who would "stand up" to Nikita Krushchev. Finally, the perceived need to extend United States influence throughout the world to counter Soviet "expansion" contributed to America's longest war, the conflict in Southeast Asia.

As Kennedy faced global challenges that placed the United States at the focal point of a bilateral world conflict, events in the domestic realm reflected the excitement and optimism generally associated with the decade of the 1960s. Even before Kennedy came to power, two groups that were to play a critical role in the unfolding of domestic politics and culture in the 1960s, black Americans and students, asserted their willingness to "put themselves on the line" for social change.

February 1, 1960 saw the first of a long series of lunch counter sit-ins that drew attention and public outrage to the stubborn phenomenon of segregation in the South. Starting in the "nice-nasty" city of Greensboro, North Carolina, where a degree of civility and pride in good manners had long diverted the possible disapprobation of outside observers, the lunch counter sit-ins eventually drew attention to the high moral ground on which the protesters stood in their quest for equal treatment in establishments that allowed them to spend money on clothing or school supplies but denied them the privilege of sitting down to order a cup of coffee or a meal. Students from North Carolina Agricultural and Technical College, dressed in jackets and ties, politely asserted their right to equal treatment under the law which the *Brown* v. *Board of Education* case had promised them in the public schools and which the year-long bus boycott in Montgomery, Alabama (1955–1956) had realized with great sacrifice.

In the Greensboro sit-in at Woolworth's, the manager closed the lunch counter rather than serve the students, who returned the next day with more than a thousand supporters. The protests were orderly and received scant attention at first from major newspapers and magazines. When the Greensboro story finally reached the national press, two important images emerged of the protesters and their goals. The first was that these young people were bypassing the traditional strategy of working through organizations like the NAACP in order to tackle head-on the system of segregation that many Americans from both the North and the South had long considered abhorrent. The second was that they did so with dignity and pride. As long as young black Americans *asked* for their rights in the South and as long as they dressed in a respectable manner and maintained a nonviolent posture, even in the face of police force and public violence, they were heroes who deserved and received public support.

The Kennedy administration was less committed than many Northern liberals to the right to protest peacefully in support of civil rights, as illustrated by the experience of the Freedom Riders, black and white Americans who challenged the prevailing codes of segregation in public transportation facilities. These men and women were exposed to extreme danger with no guarantee of federal government protection as they traveled the interstate bus routes. Attorney General Robert Kennedy at first accepted assurances from Southern governors and public safety officials that the buses would get to their destinations safely, but the absence of any state force to realize this promise and the savage beating in Montgomery of John Siegenthaler, the attorney general's representative on the scene, finally convinced the Kennedy administration that the deployment of federal marshalls was the only course of action that would prevent further beatings, harassment, and the fire-bombing of buses.

What captured the Northern imagination about the Freedom Rides was not the debate over who was responsible for protecting the bus riders as they traversed state borders, nor the extent of Democratic commitment to the broader cause of civil rights; it was the dedication to nonviolence of the riders themselves. Trained by members of the Southern Christian Leadership Conference in the techniques of Gandhian nonresistance, these silent protesters took their dignity from the cause itself as they transmitted their high moral purpose to the broader public. Martin Luther King wrote of the importance of nonviolent protests in the early 1960s:

> Nonviolence had a tremendous psychological importance to the Negro. He had to win and to vindicate his dignity in order to merit and enjoy his self-esteem. He had to let white men know that the picture of him as a clown—irresponsible, resigned and believing in his own inferiority—was a stereotype with no validity. This method was grasped by the Negro masses because it embodied the dignity of struggle, of moral conviction and self-sacrifice. The Negro was able to face his adversary, to concede to him physical advantage and defeat him because the superior force of the oppressor had become powerless.[4]

The tenets of nonviolence remained with the civil rights movement throughout the early and mid-1960s. The nonviolent response to taunts, arrests, and the use of fire hoses and police dogs in Selma, Montgomery, in Birmingham, Alabama and in Albany, Georgia, among many other Southern cities, prompted public outcry, not only at the evils of a segregated culture, but also at the obvious disregard of First Amendment rights by local police authorities. Within a few years, the nation would witness a similar disregard for the basic right to express political dissent, as protests against the war in Vietnam were often met with similar violence in the name of law and order.

While the civil rights movement was infused with outrage and high moral purpose coupled with a strong emphasis on the teachings of Jesus and Gandhi and practical lessons learned in the nonviolent struggle, the Kennedy administration was slow to take up the cause, arguing that "the time was not yet ripe" for an all-out struggle for civil rights. After convincing black leaders that it was more "prudent" to focus on voter registration than to continue the freedom rides or lunch counter sit-ins, Robert Kennedy's Justice Department failed to provide protection for Southern Christian Leadership Conference and Student Non-Violent Coordinating Committee workers who labored in the black belt to make the right to vote a reality for citizens who had long been intimidated from exercising their rights as citizens. The image of FBI agents collecting information while civil rights workers were beaten, ambushed, and terrorized contributed to a profound disillusionment on the part of civil rights leaders with the Kennedy administration and to the conviction that the president and his attorney general would act only when the authority of the federal government was clearly in question, as in the eventual deployment of federal marshalls to protect freedom riders in Montgomery and the use of federal troops to facilitate the enrollment of James Meredith at the University of Mississippi in 1962. For blacks who had voted for Kennedy in large numbers in 1960, the clear message from the White House that civil rights was a low-priority political issue was distressing. The conviction that moral outrage and concerted action for the right cause could change the hearts and minds of both segregationists and the United States government was giving way to a mistrust of the promises of liberals.

For a time, the moral principle of nonviolence, the media images of racist attacks on peaceful protesters, and the conviction that such protests would bring victory kept together civil rights groups and individuals who would otherwise have been pulled apart by fundamental disagreements over strategy and tactics. In the face of increased official Southern intransigence and the painfully slow process of legislative and social change, groups within the civil rights coalition began to question the viability of the reform approach, arguing instead for a change in power relationships and economic reality in America.

By 1966 the Student Non-Violent Coordinating Committee posed a clear challenge to the leadership of Martin Luther King and the Southern

Christian Leadership Conference. Prior to that time, SNCC had recognized the utility of muting the differences between its own grass-roots, anti-authoritarian, black-led movement and the more institutionalized and orderly SCLC. For a time, even Stokely Carmichael, who later would lead SNCC on a path that diverged from that of the older civil rights organizations, accepted the principle that an association with Dr. King would help his organizing efforts in black belt areas such as Lowndes County, Alabama: "People loved King . . . They even saw him like a God. These were the people we were working with and I had to follow in his footsteps when I went in there. These people didn't know what was SNCC. They just said, 'You one of Dr. King's men?' "Yes, Ma'am, I am." [5]

As early as 1963, the partnership between the SCLC and SNCC was beginning to dissolve under the weight of political and tactical realities. Questions of how to respond to the murder of Medgar Evers in Mississippi, the failure of the movement to achieve successful integration in Albany, Georgia, and the continued protests and arrests of school children in Birmingham raised the specter of a nonviolent movement, provoked beyond all rational limits, that might respond in kind to the treatment it was receiving at the hands of Southern law enforcement.

Many Americans remember the August 1963 march on Washington as a triumph for the civil rights movement and the occasion which inspired Martin Luther King's famous "I have a dream" speech. The event did inspire increased white liberal support for legislative reforms, just as it was an important catalyst to congressional consideration (but not passage) of a comprehensive civil rights act; but the day was also one in which the divisions within the movement became all the more apparent. One of the scheduled speakers was John Lewis, SNCC chairman, who planned to deliver a scathing attack on the Kennedy administration and on Congress for their failure to address the plight of the masses of poor black American citizens. Lewis's speech was consciously provocative, to the displeasure of march organizers who hoped to stress unity in the movement. An advance draft revealed the intensity of Lewis's attack, including this challenge:

> Listen, Mr. Kennedy, listen, Mr. Congressman, listen, fellow citizens—the black masses are on the march for jobs and freedom, and we must say to the politicians that there won't be a 'cooling-off period.' We won't stop now. All of the forces of Eastland, Barnett, and Wallace won't stop this revolution. The next time we march, we won't march on Washington, but we will march through the South, through the Heart of Dixie, the way Sherman did. We will make the action of the past few months look petty. And I say to you WAKE UP AMERICA! [6]

Many groups participating in the march declared that if Lewis delivered his speech as written, they would withdraw their support, insisting on the omission of references to Sherman's march through Georgia and the intimation of a scorched earth policy, and of references to the black "masses" and "revolution." Lewis complied reluctantly and, with the help of James Forman, recast the speech, but not without a clear sense that SNCC was headed in a different direction from the SCLC-led mainstream of the civil rights movement.

The liberal perspective may have held the day at the triumphant March on Washington, but events would soon overtake the reformers who counted on government and individuals to follow a moral course toward true equality and integration. The bombing of Birmingham's Sixteenth Street Church in September of 1963, which killed four young girls, and the continued harassment of civil rights workers engaged in voter registration drives throughout the South led to continued frustration with the absence of a clear government commitment to black equality.

Many black Americans, like their white counterparts, expressed shock and horror at the assassination in Dallas of President John F. Kennedy on November 22, 1963. But the remark by Muslim leader Malcolm X that "now the chickens have come home to roost" signified increased militance in the movement. Even though Malcolm was temporarily silenced by Elijah Muhammed in a split that was eventually to lead to his expulsion from the Nation of Islam and Malcolm's murder in the spring of 1965, it was becoming clear that many black activists, followers of Malcolm or members of SNCC, had no faith in the promises of white liberals. Nevertheless, it was just such a liberal consensus in the Congress that passed, with the support and leadership of the new Johnson administration, a comprehensive civil rights act in 1964 that placed the federal government in the civil rights arena as a defender of equal opportunity. The Voting Rights Act of the following year brought the promise of the Fifteenth Amendment (1870) closer to reality for blacks in the South, but the disappearance of civil rights workers James Chaney, Andrew Goodman, and Michael Schwerner in Philadelphia, Mississippi in June of 1964 and the discovery of their bodies in August dampened some of the optimism regarding the efficacy of legislative action. As the Mississippi murders dominated the news throughout the summer, thousands of American military advisors were coming perilously close to a combat role in Vietnam, a nation few Americans knew existed. Once a series of covert actions, the fighting in Vietnam was becoming a major theme of the mid-1960s.

The presidential election of 1964 seemed to mark a triumph of progressive American politics. The outcome was never seriously in doubt, as Lyndon Baines Johnson had successfully wrapped himself in the mantle of the martyred president while continuing to push through the Congress legislation which his predecessor had been unable to move. Johnson was also able to cut taxes and inaugurate programs that became part of the War on Poverty. Johnson faced challenges from conservative Republican Barry Goldwater and from insurgent states' rights candidate George Wallace, who scored surprising early primary victories but eventually dropped his third party bid for the White House at Goldwater's urging. Johnson clearly held the center, and his landslide victory with 61.1 percent of the popular vote came as no surprise. With a popular mandate, Johnson felt secure in engaging the nation in a two-front war against poverty at home and the communist enemy in Vietnam.

The vote count of Johnson's resounding victory over Goldwater masked dissension within the Democratic party over civil rights. At issue was the right of black voters to organize themselves into independent state Democratic parties when the regular party organization discriminated against them in county conventions and primary votes. In political terms, Johnson had to weigh the importance of votes gained as a result of the Mississippi Freedom Democratic Party's organizing efforts against the regular white delegations of the other Southern Democratic state organizations. Johnson was willing to recognize the efforts of the SNCC organizers and others who had elected a MFDP slate, but he was not willing to seat the entire delegation at the Atlantic City nominating convention and risk a walkout by all of the Southern white delegations.

The 1964 Democratic nominating convention also marked a turning point for the civil rights movement. The split between white liberal supporters in the Democratic party and the insurgent members of the Mississippi Freedom Democratic Party who had spent a brutal summer organizing and registering black voters in preparation for a showdown in Atlantic City brought about a dramatic change in the complexion of the movement. Unwilling to accept Johnson's proposal that they yield to the political interests of the national Democratic party and accept token representation in the Mississippi delegation, the black activists left the convention convinced that it was no longer possible to work within the political system or with white liberals.

By mid-1966, John Lewis had been forced to resign as chairman of SNCC. The firebrand who had frightened liberals with his sharp attacks on American racism and the slow pace of change was now criticized for leaning too close to the liberal reform position. Lewis's continued membership on the SCLC board was now a liability in an organization that sought a revolutionary rather than a reform path. Lewis's militant rhetoric of 1963 was now far surpassed by Stokely Carmichael's position of "Black Power for Black People." Carmichael, SNCC's new chairman, was willing to lead the organization in a militant direction, in spite of Dr. King's plea that the "Black Power" slogan would "confuse our allies, isolate the Negro community and give many prejudiced whites, who might otherwise be ashamed of their anti-Negro feeling, a ready excuse for self-justification."[7] The ousting of whites from leadership positions in the Congress of Racial Equality, the expulsion of whites from SNCC, the success of Malcolm X in organizing poor, potentially militant blacks in urban ghettos, and the founding of the Black Panther Party all pointed to new ideas of separatism, radicalism, and potential violence. The message of black nationalism and independence was one that could no longer be ignored, and when Dr. King abandoned his coat and tie (and, for many militants, his "Uncle Tom" image) for the overalls and work shirt of SNCC activists, media analysts and the American public at large were quick to note the contrast.

In the face of the new black militancy, many white Americans abandoned the "center" of the civil rights movement that had taken the form of legal and legislative battles. The language of revolution and the sensationalist reporting of very real frustration in black communities and of violence in ghetto streets in New York City's Harlem and Rochester, New York in 1964, in the Watts ghetto of Los Angeles in 1965, and throughout the country in a series of "long, hot summers" became part of the day-to-day reality of the United States. At the same time, self-consciously black and angry voices began to be heard in more strident and demanding tones. Faced with militant demands rather than polite requests for civil and economic rights, it was possible for many Americans to lose their moral commitment to the cause.

Images of protesters as victims who turned the other cheek to their oppressors could move the average American television news viewer, if not to action, then at least to sympathy. But cries of "Black Power," "Burn, Baby, Burn," "Get Whitey," and H. Rap Brown's declaration that "violence is as American as apple pie" inspired no confidence on the part of those white Americans who came to feel that the movement had gone too far. By the end of the decade, presidential candidate Richard Nixon would be able to appeal to these voters of the "Silent Majority" with a law and order platform clearly aimed at halting black militance as well as violence. The concept of a white backlash in politics and the formation of groups like SPONGE, the Society for the Prevention of Negroes Getting Everything, could not be far behind.

The political orientation of Lyndon Johnson's War on Poverty toward helping the poor contributed to the loss of vigor and enthusiasm in white support for civil rights. From the outset in 1964, Johnson was faced with the problem of ending poverty without alienating the affluent. This was to be a war with no casualties, but even as Americans recognized the validity of Michael Harrington's analysis of the "Other America," they adhered to notions of the traditional work ethic and the American Dream of individualism. As a result, many antipoverty programs were examples of piecemeal legislation that attacked a specific problem while leaving basic issues of income distribution untouched. Further, the focus on aid to "the disadvantaged" often alienated middle-class taxpayers. Loopholes and political problems plagued the implementation of the Economic Opportunity Act of 1964 (which included the much-maligned Job Corps), the Elementary and Secondary Education Act (1965), Medicare (1965), and various Community Action Programs, including legal services, health care centers, Upward Bound, and Head Start, a program that worked well in preparing children for school but ultimately could not fulfill its far too ambitious goal of solving the problem of poverty through education. By 1967, when Johnson had to choose between fighting his War on Poverty at home and continuing the non-war in Vietnam, he chose the latter, as the politics of anticommunism and military strength were more powerful than the ambitious goal of ending poverty.

Throughout the Kennedy-Johnson years, numerous challenges to traditional authority emerged, some from the civil rights movement and the black community and others from the ranks of young people. Americans in college or of college age comprised a large cohort within the population, as they represented the post–World War II baby boom now nearly grown up. Because of the size of this segment of the population, the activities of students and young people received considerable notice in the press and on television. This was a generation that had grown up with the new visual medium and had learned to use it effectively to promote an antiauthoritarian and countercultural message.

Student and faculty radicalism posed many challenges to the prevailing cold war consensus on the wisdom of containing communism abroad and encouraging conformity and consent at home. Perceiving themselves to be at odds with the sectarian approach of what came to be known as the old Left, student activists often organized around particular issues rather than a broad political platform, at least at first. Harvard's TOCSIN pressed the case for nuclear disarmament publicly in the late 1950s, and organizers of the University of California at Berkeley's SLATE party, a broadly based coalition in which no one in a leadership position could identify with any political party, ran on a platform in 1958 that called for "taking college politics out of the sand box." The SLATE candidates won and focused on civil rights in the community, picketing San Francisco hotels that discriminated in employment and boycotting local merchants who refused to hire black workers. In May of 1960, SLATE made headlines when Berkeley students protested at local hearings held by the House Committee on Un-American Activities. Many were dragged down the steps of San Francisco's City Hall and taken to jail for voicing their opposition to the Committee's anticommunist witch hunts.

Local protest and even civil rights activism did not, however, create a

New Left student movement, although the students did borrow the tactics of mass picketing, singing, and asserting moral superiority from the older movement. In the spring of 1960, sociologist and activist C. Wright Mills published a "Letter to the New Left," in which he issued a call to young intellectuals to become the vanguard of revolutionary social change. In a response, "Letter to the New (Young) Left," activist Tom Hayden argued that any movement of young people needed philosophical ideas with which to transcend a simple rejection of the old politics and provide a sense of purpose and a basis for the new politics. In 1962, Hayden and others in the new Students for a Democratic Society (SDS), which had emerged earlier out of the League for Industrial Democracy, composed the Port Huron Statement, a document Jeffersonian in tone and broadly radical in content, which was to form the basis for the growth of SDS. A rejection of "Victorian Marxism," the Port Huron Statement articulated a commitment to social change that transcended liberalism but did not have a specific radical platform. The absence of a precise platform allowed SDS to appeal to students in a broad coalition which, like the civil rights movement, held high moral goals and had within it the seeds of dissension over specific policy issues.

Prior to 1965, student activism, often including mass demonstrations, did not focus on specifically radical issues. Two early catalysts for demonstrations on the campus of the University of California at Berkeley, for example, were the theme of cultural alienation and the issue of free speech. The question of the extent to which the university resembled a factory, turning out educated "products" in the form of graduates who had little or no perceived connection with their teachers or the subjects they went to class to study, was debated at Berkeley as students recognized that the so-called modern multiversity served interests far-removed from their lives. Students continued to press for civil rights in the San Francisco area through pickets and "shop-ins"; they also sought to bring the issue of the right to free speech to the campus in a dispute over a small parcel of city street known as the Bancroft Strip, long identified as Berkeley's "Speakers' Corner." The closing down of all public activities on the Strip by University authorities in September of 1964, led to mass protests, sit-ins, and the eventual occupation of Sproul Hall and the arrest of eight hundred students. The compromise that restored order to the Berkeley campus held, as the Free Speech Movement slate was victorious in campus elections. Mario Savio, leader of the Free Speech Movement, was instrumental in mobilizing students and in negotiating concessions from the university. By December of 1964, the Free Speech Movement voted to disband, as it had achieved its immediate goals. A later incarnation, the Filthy Speech Movement, which sought to test university tolerance for exercise of the right of free speech with language that was generally deemed unacceptable (at least by college administrators), emerged briefly in the spring of 1965. Free speech, the use of obscenities, even the flying of National Liberation Front banners and the defacing of the American flag, all became, by 1965, aspects of student opposition to the fighting in Vietnam.

Ironically, the event that historians now see as a major turning point in United States military involvement in Southeast Asia inspired little protest, as the passage of the Gulf of Tonkin Resolution was seen as an appropriate defensive response to hostile fire against American ships by North Vietnamese torpedo boats. The president withheld from Congress and the public the fact that the destroyer Maddox was in North Vietnamese waters on August 1, 1964 for the purpose of conducting electronic surveillance authorized as part of a larger program of covert activities against the North. Nor did the president reveal that weather conditions and instrument readings on August 4 made it likely that the attack on a second destroyer, the Turner Joy, never took place. Nevertheless, with only minimal objection, the Congress authorized Johnson to "take all necessary measures to repel any armed attack against the forces of the United States." Johnson's victory as a peace candidate who had taken strong action against aggression was now assured. Shortly after his election, Johnson ordered the systematic and regular bombing of targets in North Vietnam which would become the focus of serious protests at home.

In response to the attack on American soldiers at Pleiku on February 6, 1965, the United States escalated the bombing of North Vietnam in what came to be known as Operation Rolling Thunder. American citizens who opposed continued American involvement in Southeast Asia soon realized that writing letters to legislators and speaking privately among themselves were not effective forms of protest, especially after the decision early in March to send ground troops to protect American bases in South Vietnam. Opponents of the fighting, especially in the academic community, sought a way to express their outrage at Johnson's Vietnam policies, and March 24 and 25 saw the first major teach-in at the University of Michigan, at which the issues surrounding American involvement in this undeclared war were discussed and debated seriously, even in the face of a bomb scare. University rules on curfews for women students were suspended so that participation was open to all. Teach-ins on other campuses followed immediately (Columbia on March 25, Wisconsin on April 1, New York University on April 14, Rutgers and the University of Oregon on April 23, and Berkeley on May 21 and 22), as many students and faculty members responded to the import of the sudden escalation in hostilities that the bombing represented.

The Johnson administration resented such public challenges to its prerogatives and took the teach-ins seriously, even though most student participants were not yet old enough to vote. The President issued a white paper designed to justify the bombing and also sent so-called truth teams to debate students and antiwar faculty members. This practice stopped, however, when many of the truth team members were either heckled off the stage or simply out-argued by opponents of the bombing and the use of ground troops, who numbered 50,000 by mid-April.

As they received coverage by the press and television, the teach-ins caught the public imagination. These early expressions of opposition to American foreign policy were not always received sympathetically, especially by veterans' groups and by parents who felt that their children should be spending time and energy on more traditional learning than all-night discussions of a distant war. Clearly, the activities of students and faculty members did not change any minds in the Johnson administration and, coming as they did in reaction to the bombing that was already in progress, they were unable to inspire a policy shift. Indeed, the situation seemed to worsen when, on April 1, Johnson authorized the troops to become involved in active combat in the face of a threat. The perception of an enemy threat led to pre-emptive actions in the air and on the ground. Campus protests could not change the fact that, even without formal declaration, the United States was at war.

Reactive as they were, the teach-ins served a valuable educational purpose. They raised the issue of the legitimacy of American involvement in Vietnam in a very public way for students as they encouraged serious debate. By bringing students and faculty members together against American military policy and the draft that threatened the lives of young men, the teach-ins helped to bridge some traditional barriers between young people and their mentors. Further, the teach-ins began the process of making opposition to the conflict in Vietnam a public matter. Very soon, they were superceded by larger, less academic, and often more emotional and violent demonstrations of antiwar feeling.

On April 17, 1965, SDS sponsored its first major march on Washington in opposition to the war in Vietnam. Contrary to right-wing notions that SDS represented a Soviet attempt to undermine America, march organizers welcomed participants who were "not committed to any form of totalitarianism nor drawing inspiration or direction from the foreign policy of any government." Indeed, the antiwar coalition transcended New Left politics to include not only radicals who wanted to end the fighting in Vietnam and revolutionize American society at the same time, but also many who held the more mainstream position that it was more prudent simply to bring American soldiers home and let the Vietnamese solve their own problems, as well as individuals who opposed the war and the draft for strictly personal reasons.

In addition to taking part in marches, antiwar rallies, and Moratorium Days in the mid-1960s, American opponents of the war burned their draft cards, sought conscientious objector status or left the United States; in a few cases, they followed the example of Buddhist monks in 1963 who had set themselves aflame in protest over their treatment at the hands of the Diem regime. Individual and group actions that were labeled "extreme" or "radical" caught the public imagination, as they received enthusiastic press coverage. Protests at induction centers, defacing of draft records (especially by dousing them with animal blood), the public consumption of illegal drugs as the hippie and political currents in America's youth culture came together, and a Yippie-inspired demonstration in 1967 that was intended to levitate the Pentagon, all brought attention to the movement to end the war.

By 1967, participants in the antiwar movement were weary of what they saw as the "liberal bullshit" of the Johnson administration, but it was also clear that mass demonstrations were not bringing about an end to the fighting. As an increasing number of patriotic Americans who had been disposed to support "Lyndon's War" began to learn about how the war was actually being fought, with napalm, defoliation agents, and "pacification" policies, and as a significant number of strongly pro-military citizens began to ask why we weren't winning, public support for the administration waned. The press, at first a faithful medium for the administration's military message, broke stories of American atrocities, fragging in the military, and inflated body counts, and labeled the daily Saigon briefings the "Five O'Clock Follies."

As public support declined, the antiwar coalition showed signs of schism over strategy and tactics. Women who had labored for years in the civil rights and antiwar movements grew increasingly dissatisfied with their male-imposed marginality. No longer content to gain access to power in the movement through their boyfriends and not willing be assigned roles as cooks or typists while men made policy decisions, women began to consider their role as women in protest movements, as they searched for a voice with which to speak of their dissatisfaction *as women* with their status in American society.

As early as 1964, when Mary King and Casey Hayden had articulated the grievances of the women in the Student Non-Violent Coordinating Committee, activists had come to see the futility of simple complaint. The "women question" was not treated seriously by SNCC men, just as it was largely ignored or considered insignificant to many male leaders of the New Left. Women had to learn to develop their own political networks, from grass-roots campus and community groups that organized the unorganized and used street protest to voice their outrage, to the larger, more institutional and middle-class National Organization for

Women and similar groups that labored carefully within the political system to change laws that restricted women's access to equal participation in the political and economic life of the nation. Many feminists of the 1960s and after began their careers as activists in the civil rights and antiwar movements.[8]

Although large and successful antiwar demonstrations continued through November of 1969 and again after the murders at Kent State and Jackson State Universities in May of 1970, the broadly based coalition politics of the streets that the antiwar movement represented began to suffer the exhaustion of government indifference. In this context, the emergence of groups like the Weathermen, who sought to "bring the war home" through militant action that sometimes led to violence, was not a surprise. As SDS split in 1969, the Weathermen took the task of revolution in the United States seriously and were willing to risk their own lives commiting acts of political violence to bring the message of the war's horror and the repressive nature of American politics home to a public that was tired of the war, tired of the protests, and tired of America's tarnished imperialist image in the world.

The Dump Johnson Movement of 1967, spearheaded by Long Island Congressman Allard Lowenstein, was fortuitous, as political forces were preparing for an assault on the Johnson administration and its war. In contrast to SDS and the Weathermen, who proposed the revolution and a complete class realignment of American society, Lowenstein's Conference of Concerned Democrats and ACT-68, the student arm of the Dump Johnson Movement, worked in a traditional political context, challenging the party leader in his own domain rather than in the streets. Lowenstein was among the first Democrats to support the presidential candidacy of Eugene McCarthy, who publicly supported American withdrawal from Vietnam.

As McCarthy campaigned among working-class and middle-class voters, his student supporters presented an image of hard-working and serious young people who were willing to operate within "legitimate" political parameters of the electoral process to bring about significant military policy changes. McCarthy's candidacy represented a fresh voice in the Democratic party, although his intellectual posture was often regarded as a liability. His primary campaign was helped by the American psychological defeat in the Tet offensive. The lunar New Year had brought with it coordinated attacks on American bases on January 30, 1968, and, although technically the United States did not lose any territory, the fact that our embassy in Saigon was held under seige for more than six hours by a force of only nineteen guerrilla fighters presented a challenge to American claims of superiority and invulnerability in Vietnam.

With less than one percent of the New Hampshire primary vote separating the incumbent president from his liberal challenger in February of 1968, it was clear that McCarthy had "won" the primary and scored a victory for the Dump Johnson Movement. Having demonstrated that Americans of varying political perspectives were ready for a change, McCarthy paved the way for the late entry into the presidential race of Robert Kennedy, then a Senator from New York. Kennedy was criticized for letting McCarthy take the major political risk while assessing his own political options (banners appeared with slogans like "Bobby Kennedy: Hawk, Dove, or Chicken?"). Nevertheless, the charismatic Senator attracted the support of young campaign workers away from McCarthy, whose political political aspirations faded after Kennedy's entry into the race. For those who wanted to rid the country of its unpopular president, the Kennedy candidacy came as a boost. On March 31, 1968, Lyndon Johnson announced to the nation that he would neither seek nor accept the nomination of the Democratic party for the office of president of the United States.

With the assassination of Martin Luther King, Jr. in Memphis on April 4, the jubilation of a broad spectrum of Americans at LBJ's withdrawal gave way to profound sadness and fear for the future of the nation. King, who had been moving toward a wider critique of American racism and militarism and who had been developing his own program of economic as well as political civil rights for blacks, was in the Southern city to support a strike of city sanitation workers, most of whom were black. In the wake of John Kennedy's assassination, the murder of Malcolm X in 1965, violent disturbances in ghetto streets, and the extreme violence of the war in Vietnam that was taking American and Vietnamese lives at an appalling rate with no end in sight, King's murder seemed to stand as testimony to the racism and violence of America. Around the country, black ghettos exploded in violence that took days and troops to quell. In Chicago, Mayor Richard Daley ordered police officers to shoot to kill those who were caught looting or committing arson in black neighborhoods. Robert Kennedy, who became the victim of an assassin's bullet only two months later, told a black audience in Cleveland the day after King's murder that "violence breeds violence, repression brings retaliation, and only a cleansing of our whole society can remove this sickness from our soul."[9]

Observers in 1968 saw few signs of such a cleansing. Robert Kennedy's murder in Los Angeles on June 4, as he was on his way to greet supporters after his victory in the important California primary, signaled an end to optimism for those who had trusted the system and the political process. Even many militant blacks had seen Kennedy as the last politician with whom it was possible to talk. With its frontrunner gone, McCarthy in retreat to his own introspection, and antiwar Senator George Mc-

Govern unable to get a campaign started, the Democratic party was in disarray. Hubert Humphrey, a Senator with a liberal record on civil rights early in his political career but the albatross of Vietnam weighing him down as Johnson's vice president, won the nomination in a convention that was characterized by discontent with the old political ways. Even though Humphrey's forces were able to defeat a platform plank calling for "an unconditional end to all bombing in North Vietnam," the very presence of the minority plank on a test vote was an indication of the Democrats' serious political trouble. In addition to the battles over the party's position on Vietnam, the refusal to seat the segregationist Mississippi delegation and the allotment of half of the seats on the Georgia delegation to a black insurgent group led by legislator Julian Bond assured George Wallace Southern Democratic support in his third party crusade against "pointy-headed intellectuals" of the "Eastern Establishment."

Outside of the convention, thousands of people gathered in Chicago to show their dissatisfaction with the political show inside. Many were Yippies who joined with Abby Hoffman and Jerry Rubin in taunting Mayor Daley's police force of more than twelve thousand and capturing television attention from the more staid proceedings inside by nominating a pig for president, while others were peace activists who had come to the convention to bear witness. As the convention wore on and demonstrators were denied permission to march or sleep in city parks, tempers rose. The jeers were met with outbursts of police violence of an intensity that shocked television viewers. The indiscriminate beating and gassing of protesters and bystanders, with or without provocation, spoke volumes about the violence of American society of which Richard Daley's Chicago was only a microcosm. The police lawlessness in the streets stood in sharp contrast to Humphrey's acceptance speech on law and order, the theme that eventually secured victory for the Republican candidate, Richard Nixon.

The 1968 Republican National Convention presented calm and confidence rather than chaos and indecision. Like the more populist George Wallace, Nixon was hostile to the Eastern liberal wing of his party. He effectively eliminated Nelson Rockefeller from serious contention for the nomination and was equally adept at turning back a challenge from the Republican right, represented by Ronald Reagan. Nixon's law and order campaign was aimed at what he called the Silent Majority of Americans who wanted a change from Democratic policies and a return to stability at home and strength in the larger world political arena. Nixon chose as his running mate Maryland Governor Spiro Agnew, who shared with Chicago's Mayor Daley a willingness to unleash the police on black "troublemakers," even advocating the shooting of looters in Baltimore.

Agnew blasted the press for not being more supportive of government policy, calling reporters "nattering nabobs of negativism," and he had no patience with antiwar protesters, deriding them as "naughty children."

It was on a platform of "peace with honor" in Vietnam, and a return to a respectful America in which men and women, blacks and whites, knew and kept to their places that the Nixon-Agnew ticket garnered 43.4 percent of the popular vote, with 42.7 percent for Humphrey and 13.5 percent for Wallace. The optimistic 1960s, in which civil rights could be won through dedication to justice and the war in Vietnam could be brought to an end simply because it was "right" to stop the slaughter of our soldiers, had come to an end.

The decade was far from over, as Black Nationalism and Black Power influenced the call for justice, as seen in increased militance on college campuses, the raising of the Black Power salute by victorious American athletes at the 1968 Olympics in Mexico City, and the murder of Black Panthers Fred Hampton and Mark Clark in Chicago. The antiwar movement continued, with a massive Washington demonstration in November of 1969 and with protests after the invasion of Cambodia in May of 1970 that led to the killing of four students on the campus of Kent State University in Ohio. The Weather Underground continued its attempts to "bring the war home" with destruction of government property and other protests.

The GI antiwar movement that emerged after 1967 presented a strong and credible voice against the continuation of the war. Soldiers printed their own newspapers, engaged in "Armed Farces Day" demonstrations, ran coffee houses, held rap sessions and gave counseling on First Amendment rights and military harassment, drug abuse, desertion, and other issues. The movement reflected a growing mistrust of military authority, an effort to combat institutionalized racism and sexism in the military, and a commitment to ending the war.

With the Nixon administration's policy of Vietnamization, which relied increasingly on bombing, it had become clear that the United States could no longer mount an effective fighting force on the ground in Vietnam. Instances of fragging, increased drug use among soldiers, and, occasionally, the refusal of orders to fight, were prevalent enough to cause genuine concern that the war might not be winnable after all. At home, members of Vietnam Veterans Against the War threw back their combat medals in the Dewey Canyon demonstration in Washington in 1971. In the Winter Soldier Investigation of 1972, more than eight hundred former soldiers testified publicly about atrocities they had witnessed in the war. No longer an undercurrent, Vietnam dominated American life. As the soldiers told of the horrors of the war, the Congress passed the first version of the War Powers Act, a law that, in a limited way, was intended to actualize the antiwar slogan "No More Vietnams."

Richard Nixon's campaign for a second term seemed to bring an end to the 1960s. The break-in at Democratic National Committee headquarters in the Watergate office complex on June 17, 1972 was only the first of many events that convinced many Americans of the lesson they had begun to learn earlier: government was run cynically and could not be trusted. The majority of Americans agreed that the "dirty tricks" that characterized the Watergate scandal constituted unethical behavior on the part of presidential staff members, even though Americans could not agree on the wisdom of pursuing the investigation to the point of impeachment hearings or on the necessity for Richard Nixon's resignation on August 9, 1974. But the response of Americans to the outrage of Watergate is significant; instead of taking to the streets, most retreated to the private domain of their living rooms to watch the impeachment hearings on television.

In spite of the cynicism and the retreat to privatism of the 1970s "Me" generation, the organizational efforts of the early part of the 1960s continued and even expanded to encompass rights for homosexuals, disabled people, and many others who had been considered marginal to American political and economic life. In the midst of the era of the fifties revival and disco music in the 1970s, the spirit of Camelot was being transformed into a less naive and more sophisticated effort to achieve equality and justice through the use of political and economic power. As the decade of the 1980s neared its end, young people, some describing themselves as activists and others simply curious, flocked to courses about the 1960s. Their presence and the commitment on the part of some to social change reflects the strength of a sixties legacy that is still finding its way, challenging accepted norms and searching for the bonds of community.

NOTES

1. The status of school prayer changed in 1961. It is difficult to credit sixties activism with bringing this change about; nevertheless, it marks an important watershed in the interpretation of civil rights and civil liberties in the United States.

2. Arthur M. Schlesinger, Jr., "The New Mood in American Politics, *Esquire,* January 1960.

3. John F. Kennedy, Inaugural Address, 20 January 1961.

4. Martin Luther King, Jr., *Why We Can't Wait* (New York: New American Library, 1963), p. 40.

5. Stokely Carmichael, quoted in Clayborne Carson, *In Struggle, SNCC and the Black Awakening of the 1960s* (Cambridge: Harvard University Press, 1981), p. 164.

6. John Lewis, speech written for the march on Washington, 23 August 1963, in Joanne Grant, ed., *Black Protest: History, Documents, and Analysis 1619 to the Present* (Greenwich, Connecticut: Fawcett Publications, Inc., 1968), pp. 376–77.

7. Martin Luther King, Jr., quoted in Carson, *In Struggle,* p. 210.

8. See Sara Evans, *Personal Politics* (New York: Vintage, 1978).

9. Robert Kennedy, quoted in William H. Chafe, *The Unfinished Journey, America Since World War II* (New York: Oxford University Press, 1986), p. 368.

PART TWO

GOING TO WAR: THE HUMAN LEGACY

4

THE VIETNAM-ERA DRAFT:
Who Went, Who Didn't, and Why It Matters

D. MICHAEL SHAFER

The issue of the proper relationship between citizen and state is one of the oldest questions in the history of the West. It grows out of the tension between the state's need to survive and the freedom that Western civilization believes makes life worth living, the freedom that is one of the fundamental reasons for the state's existence in the first place.

—CASPER WEINBERGER

In recent years, the defense debate has focused on the size of the Pentagon budget, the numbers and esoteric technology of the weapons bought, and the competing grand strategies for their use. But it has largely ignored questions that have exercised the passions of Americans since the Revolution: Who shall serve those weapons and how shall they be chosen? These are not questions of interest to just a handful of generals and defense buffs. Answers to them not only determine who will die for the rest of us in time of war, they also touch the core questions of our political life: What does it mean to be an American? What rights and obligations does citizenship confer? How do we balance the demands of individual conscience against obligations to our fellow citizens and the dictates of the majority? What is our country's role in the world and what requirements does that role impose?[1]

Answers to these larger questions are not set in stone; they have been fought over by Americans since colonial times. Still, there is a disturbing pattern to them. From the Revolution to the present, the seemingly prosaic issue of military manpower policy has offered a mirror to America—and the image it reflects is not a pretty one. It contrasts our idealized visions of who we are with how we act, and the high rhetoric of civic virtue and equal obligation with the reality of gross inequalities in the distribution of the putatively common rights we enjoy and of the putatively common obligations we bear. For the history of military manpower policy in America is marked by a deep divide between those who make decisions and those who suffer their consequences, a schism resulting from the systematic and successful efforts of the former to shirk the obligations of both citizenship and conscience. While this problem is as old as the Republic, it was highlighted as never before in the workings of the Vietnam-era draft and is today institutionalized in the All Volunteer Force (AVF), created in response to protests against the draft.

Most Americans hold sharp images of that antidraft protest. Depending on political bent, they may conjure nasty visions of long-haired protesters defiling the flag, burning draft cards and shouting obscenities at the police, or heroic ones of mobilized citizens taking on the state to stop an immoral war. Few realize, however, that the Vietnam-era draft was not the first to arouse the ire of Americans, nor has its elimination removed the underlying questions of who shall serve and how they shall be chosen. In 1814 Daniel Webster declared conscription "incompatible with any notion of personal liberty," hundreds died protesting the Civil War draft, and congressional opponents of the World War I draft warned that it would "Prussianize America" and "destroy democracy at home while fighting for it abroad."[2] Such concerns are not a thing of the past. Today those who fought to end the draft and defenders of the AVF must address both the AVF's waning ability to raise the manpower needed to defend this country and the disturbing political implications of a form of military organization which exempts the better-off and depends on the poor, uneducated and politically weak to protect the benefits of being American which we all hold so dear.

Every country's military institutions respond to a unique blend of internal and external imperatives, and the United States is no exception. On the one hand, American armed forces reflect our geopolitical position, threats to our national security, the military requirements of meeting them, and our ideological conception of our international role. On the other, they reflect our national values, our unique blend of liberal and republican political ideals, and the pluralism of our politics. The basic pattern was set early and although this pattern has evolved as American society and our position in the world have changed, it is important to explore these enduring themes and highlight enduring value conflicts before examining the history of the draft.

American opinion on military service and the draft is torn between liberalism and republicanism, the two competing conceptions of the state and the citizens' relationship to it that underpin most American thinking about politics.[3] The keys to the former are a citizenship defined by rights (not obligations) and minimal government, the chief aim of which is the protection of life, limb, and property. Despite big benefits at home, from a national security standpoint liberalism confronts the state with a dilemma: If its primary aim is each citizen's survival, how can it ask, let alone require, citizens to risk their lives in the military? From the beginning, of course, Americans have recognized the need for national defense, but have never very successfully reconciled its requirements with individual rights. Over time, however, we have developed a widely accepted, if imperfect, three-part rationale, each element of which posed problems during the Vietnam war. First, limited government limits the ends for which citizens can be made to serve—they can be asked to defend the country against a clear and present danger, but not, for example, to enlarge it. Second, since all citizens share in the benefits of the commonwealth, all are equally obligated to defend it when threatened. Third, we have faith in voluntarism, believing that in crisis citizens will step forward to defend the nation, thus obviating the need to oblige them to serve.

Equality of obligation and the importance of voluntarism also lie at the heart of republicanism. In contrast to liberalism, however, republicanism demands citizens' active participation in the affairs of state and celebrates the notion of *civic virtue,* particularly the belief that citizenship and military service are inextricably linked. Republican ideas came to America with the first British settlers and remain with us in our belief in the value of citizen service. As early as 1663, Plymouth Colony required all settlers to serve in the militia, and in 1792 the Militia Act required that "each and every free able bodied white male citizen . . . be enrolled in the militia." This was more than a matter of providing for the national defense. As General Henry Knox put it in 1786, with military service:

> A glorious national spirit will be introduced with its extensive train of political consequences. The youth will imbibe a love of their country; reverence and obedience to its laws; courage and elevation of mind; openness and liberality of character; accompanied by a just spirit of honor; in addition to which their bodies will acquire a robustness, greatly conducive to their personal happiness, as well as the defense of their country; while habit, with its silent but efficacious operations will durably cement the system.[4]

By republican lights, in short, military service is evidence of civic virtue, an essential obligation of citizenship, and a school teaching both.

With these deep and opposing roots, Americans' conceptions of the state and of citizens' obligations to it have changed as the country has developed. Indeed, it is because of this fluidity that the question of military obligation is so contentious and revelatory. As John Whiteclay Chambers observes, "the nexus between a nation's needs and an individual's obligations is the concept of national citizenship";[5] but in the United

States this concept evolved very slowly. The Founding Fathers had to fashion a federal government that recognized the continued vitality of local, state, and regional interests and loyalties. Thus, "to the extent that they dealt with citizenship, the fundamental charters of the American national government—the Declaration of Independence, Articles of Confederation, U.S. Constitution, and the Bill of Rights—emphasized rights and privileges, not obligations, as they sought to build popular support for a new national government."[6] This, however, left unresolved two critical questions: To what community are citizens loyal? What obligations to the state do citizens' rights entail? Absent answers to these, the concept of national citizenship remained contested ground. Republican sentiments, expressed in a continued attachment to the militia system, held sway at the local level; liberal ideals, evidenced by the lack of effective national armed forces, predominated at the federal level.

By the mid-nineteenth century two new forces were at play. On the one hand, the creation of a national market, communications system, and transportation infrastructure gave Americans a stronger national, as opposed to local or regional, identity, and set the stage for a more active federal government. On the other, wave after wave of immigrants forced Americans to ask, what can we do to integrate these new citizens into American life? Military service in a national army seemed to offer an answer. Indeed, the ranks of the armed forces have long been disproportionately foreign-born or the sons of recent immigrants, while black Americans have also long viewed the right to perform military service as a key to the achievement of full citizenship rights. Here, too, lie the roots of one of the most contentious issues raised by Vietnam-era manpower policies—the tension between a conception of military service as an avenue for social and political upward mobility for the poor, disenfranchised, and foreign-born, and the belief that military service is an obligation of all citizens, privileged and underprivileged.

Finally, military organizations are not solely the product of domestic forces. States exist in an anarchic world in which there is no overarching authority to make and enforce rules or protect the weak from the strong; if a state is to survive and flourish, it must be able to defend itself. The security threats a state faces, however, vary by its geopolitical position, change over time, and are as much a reflection of citizens' views of their state's international role as they are externally imposed. Thus, Americans' definition of the requirements of national security, and so of the military forces needed, were shaped initially by the absence of threatening neighbors, by the comforting presence of the great natural defensive barrier of the Atlantic, and by a fear that our experiment with democracy would be sullied by contact with decadent Europe or destroyed in one of its silly dynastic wars. This definition has changed as technology has eliminated geographical isolation, as development has given us global interests, and as we have adopted an increasingly expansive notion of American security as comprising not only the security of the United States, but also the security of our European allies and eventually that of the new nations of Africa and Asia. But broadening the definition of national security had critical consequences. While most Americans believe that the security of Europe is unambiguously tied to our own, many doubt the broader claim that Third World security is as well. Thus, the deployment of American forces and the aims of American military policy in the Third World are naturally contentious issues, as is the related issue of how to raise the needed manpower. These questions dominated the political debate during the Vietnam War, while the supposed lessons of Vietnam figure prominently in the foreign policy debate today.

Military Manpower Policy from the Revolution to Vietnam

Americans are raised on the heroic myth of a ragtag army of minutemen standing up for their beliefs and defeating the greatest power of the day. It is a potent myth, one which embodies many of our core values—localism, pluralism, devotion to liberty, voluntarism, egalitarianism—but it is a myth just the same. Indeed, one of the striking things about the Revolution is how General Washington's manpower problems prefigured ours in Vietnam—in particular, the unwillingness of most citizens to serve in the Continental Army (and so its dependence on the poor and disenfranchised) and the post-independence decision to depend on local militias, made possible by the United States' isolated geopolitical position and Americans' deep-seated isolationism (and so the embedding of the myth and institutions of voluntarism in the military manpower system).

Middle-class unwillingness to serve in the militia was not a new problem even in 1776. Colonial governors had always had difficulty raising forces to repel Indian attacks, even though, in principle, all able-bodied citizens were obligated to serve. To find the needed manpower, they offered bonuses to the poor and ne'er-do-wells or "drafted" the rich, who then paid poor substitutes to take their places. Commented a Boston orator in 1773, "It is highly absurd, though not uncommon, that those who have the most to lose by the destruction of a state, should be the least capable of bearing a part in its defense."[7] His observation—and its political barb—remain as apt today as two centuries ago.

During the Revolution, Washington faced the same problems as the colonial governors before him. His letters to the Continental Congress complain constantly about the inadequacy of his forces because of a general unwillingness to serve after the enthusiasm of the war's first year had faded. Congress refused to consider a draft, however, and so the Continental Army, too, was "composed overwhelmingly of the young and the poor whites and blacks—the sons of marginal farmers, laborers, drifters, indentured servants—and recent immigrants without roots in America,"[8] some lured into military service by enlistment bonuses and others hired as substitutes by affluent citizens unwilling to risk their lives for their beliefs.

With the victory at Yorktown, Americans put military matters aside. On January 2, 1784 Congress discharged the entire Continental Army except for eighty-three veterans kept on to guard the West Point arsenal. At the Constitutional Convention, the framers gave Congress the power "to raise and support Armies," but Congress hesitated to establish a national army or raise taxes to support it. In the ensuing years, Federalists such as Washington and Alexander Hamilton, who wanted a strong central state, did battle with the states'-rights, locally oriented Jeffersonian Democratic-Republicans over what sort of military the United States needed. The former called for a standing army to deter European attacks and to make the United States a "respected" member of the community of nations. The latter clung to the militia ideal of citizen participation and local control. The result was a compromise—a small regular army supported by local militias. The compromise was possible because of the United States' natural security from attack, but it left unresolved the tension between the federal and state governments over control of the military, and kept citizens' primary attachment to their local communities, not the nation. Some state militias even refused to fight outside their own states, denying the very idea of a "common defense."

The Civil War offered the world a first glimpse of a new kind of warfare, combat between huge armies equipped with sophisticated weapons which tripled the size of the battlefield "killing zone" and resulted in 10–20 percent casualty rates. (Battles commonly killed 20,000 to 40,000 Union and Confederate soldiers and the total death toll topped 600,000 in four years.)[9] The size of the armies and the casualties they suffered made recruitment critical in the North and South. Both preferred volunteers, but too few came forward, even with huge enlistment bonuses. Thus, first the Confederacy and then the Union turned to conscription, and although ultimately only 50,000 of the two million men who served in the Union Army were draftees, the Civil War draft set the main themes of the continuing debate over conscription in America.

The draft provoked intense debate and required all Lincoln's political finesse to implement. To appease states' rights forces, he avoided any confusion of the draft with the militias, referring instead in the Enrollment Act of 1863 to "national forces" (a novel concept at the time), and giving control of the draft to local "enrollment boards." To appease liberals, he stressed not citizens' obligations to the nation, but the state's right to defend itself. Further, to give the semblance of voluntarism and make conscription acceptable to the middle class and industrialists (who feared losing skilled labor), Lincoln allowed draftees the option of paying a "commutation fee" or hiring a substitute to go in their place. When implemented in July 1863, the draft sparked violent resistance among those who were its target, the poor. In New York, Boston, and many other cities, thousands of workers and new immigrants took to the streets. Scores were killed and hundreds injured when troops fired on the protesters.

The Civil War draft produced few draftees, but did have important political consequences. Of the 300,000 men called in 1863, 9 percent sent substitutes, 18 percent paid the commutation fee, and 70 percent found medical or other exemptions—in the end only 3 percent of the original total saw service.[10] Ultimately more than 80 percent of all those called to service did not perform it. (Hence the bitter cry: "A rich man's war but a poor man's fight!") Still, the draft symbolized the federal government's power and determination to oppose challenges to its supremacy. Moreover, although it fostered a return to a professional army, the Civil War draft offered later military manpower planners an example of how the draft could be used to encourage voluntarism. (In Vietnam, draft-induced volunteers far outnumbered draftees.)

The inequity of the Civil War draft was not accidental, and the reasons for it continue to provoke controversy in American politics and discussions of military manpower policy. On the one hand, Lincoln's decision to permit commutation and substitution reflected the need to appease the politically powerful middle class by shifting the common burden of defending the Union to the disenfranchised (the new immigrants) and the politically impotent poor, that is, to those who already enjoy a disproportionately small share of the putatively common benefits of American life. On the other hand, modern mass warfare requires manpower policies that channel individuals into those jobs where they can contribute the most to the total war effort. Thus, industrialists who pressured Lincoln to exempt skilled workers argued that mass enlistments would damage the industrial capacity to sustain the war effort. This argument provided the rationale for the selective service system constructed during World War I and used through the Vietnam War. The issue then and now is clear, however: How shall the cost of freedom be distributed? How shall we choose who goes to war and who stays home?

This question obsessed President Wilson and his advisers during World War I and their answers are still with us. Unlike Lincoln, who dared only to nibble at conscription, Wilson committed himself to it; of the 3.5 million men he called to arms, 72 percent were draftees. To understand how Wilson and his advisers answered the question of who shall serve, we must understand the changes underway in the United States at the time.[11]

In the decades after 1865 the United States grew from an agricultural nation divided by strong regional ties to one of the most advanced industrial countries in the world with a national economy and strong international ties. These changes brought a new elite to the fore whose interests were industrial, not agricultural; national, not regional; and internationalist, not isolationist. One of the critical issues they championed from 1915 to 1920 in their campaign to reshape America was the necessity for universal military training (UMT). In part to this end they formed the National Security League and the Military Training Camps Association (the Plattsburg Movement).

For men such as Teddy Roosevelt, Elihu Root and Henry Stimson, a strong, conscripted military was a necessity in itself and a vehicle for achieving other ends. Confident in America, they were not content to hide behind the Atlantic, merely reacting to foreign events; they wanted the power to shape them. UMT's advocates also believed UMT would undercut regional parochialism, reduce class conflict, "Americanize" new immigrants, improve the quality of the military, and ensure efficient allocation of manpower in wartime.[12] Some black leaders, like James Weldon Johnson, also supported UMT for this reason, arguing that from military service would come full citizenship rights.

An equally active movement of immigrants, agrarians, industrial workers, and pacifists counter-organized against UMT. Like those they opposed, groups such as the Grange, the AFL, Jane Addams' Women's Peace Party, and the American Union Against Militarism (AUAM) focused on both conscription itself and on what it represented. At issue was not only the draft, but what sort of country this was to be. Thus, while UMT's champions argued that conscription would make the U.S. a great power, educate Americans in their democratic duties, break class barriers and Americanize new immigrants, anti-conscription forces argued the opposite. They feared a bigger military would invite an interventionist foreign policy and believed that conscription was (in William Jennings Bryan's phrase) a "munitions-military conspiracy against democracy." Labor organizations feared, too, that industrialists would use UMT to break strikes and create a docile work force. For their part, AUAM-allied immigrant groups asserted that conscription and the implied precedence of the state over the individual was what they had come to America to get away from.

Against the backdrop of these profound changes, Wilson took up the question of conscription. Although he had opposed permanent UMT and peacetime conscription, once he decided (in March 1917) to take the United States into the war, Wilson quickly determined to raise the wartime army by temporary selective national conscription. From the beginning he faced serious opposition. As during the Civil War, many resisted the very idea of conscription for what it did or might do to the relationship between citizens and the state. Others objected to the implied end of isolation-ism and the idea that American boys should die, as one Senator put it, in "European squabbles . . . to decide who shall have Alsace or Lorraine or Bosnia or Herzegovina, or some other outlandish country over there."[13]

Responding to criticisms and yet sensitive to the requirements of the United States' changing position in the world, Wilson offered a tempo-rary wartime draft built on three principles: equality of obligation, fed-eral direction, and local administration. He argued that the draft was "in no sense a conscription of the unwilling [but] rather selection from a na-tion which has volunteered in mass,"[14] and went on to assert—as Lincoln had not dared—that citizenship entailed not only rights, but obligations. Wilson often noted the symbolic import of using voter registration rolls to register men for the draft, while flatly refusing to consider commuta-tion or substitution. In the name of efficient manpower planning, how-ever, he insisted on federal control over who served and how, eventually forbidding voluntary enlistment altogether. To soften the shock of this unprecedented assertion of federal authority, final implementation of the draft was left to local draft boards composed of civilian volunteers. The resulting system was imperfect, but as John Whiteclay Chambers notes, "What most impressed . . . contemporaries and subsequent policymak-ers and scholars was the compatibility of the wartime Selective Service System with American ideals—localism, individualism, civilian control of the military—and with the economic and military needs of the nation in modern mass warfare."[15]

As World War II loomed, President Roosevelt and his advisers framed the Selective Service Act of 1940 around the system which had served so well in World War I. And again it worked, easing the 45-fold expansion of the military and bringing 10 million draftees to arms. The system also made possible the efficient allocation of manpower between military and civilian needs which allowed the U.S. to fight on two fronts simultane-ously and meet the allies' combined production requirements as well. The centrality of efficient manpower allocation, as embedded in the Se-lective Service machinery, was to have important and divisive conse-quences during the Vietnam War. To understand how and why, it is nec-essary to understand the dramatic shift in Americans' perception of our world role born of World War II.

World War II and its aftermath fundamentally altered Americans' worldview and this, in turn, altered our ideas about citizens' rights and obligations. When the Senate rejected the Versailles Treaty and League of Nations, it rejected Wilson's vision of the United States as a world leader with concerns beyond its borders. Thus, when reinstated in 1940, the draft was seen as a temporary measure responding to a clear and present danger from abroad. With victory, the U.S. demobilized rapidly in 1945 and allowed the Selective Service Act to lapse in early 1947. Within months, however, a new selective service bill was under debate which, in 1948, gave the United States its first peacetime draft.[16]

This new departure reflected a profound change in how the great majority of Americans perceived their world role. From isolationism, the U.S. shifted to world leadership as voters and politicians alike came to believe that past failure to lead had contributed to World War II and that American involvement in world affairs was needed to avoid future wars. This shift and its consequences are clear in the words of New Jersey Senator Alexander Smith speaking for the draft in 1946:

> We are . . . not a militaristic nation. We seek no conquest, and as a people we are wedded to the paths of peace and good will toward our neighbors. Why, then, should we even consider continuation of the Selective Service Act? . . . We have found . . . after the experiences of World Wars I and II, that we as a people cannot live alone. Time and space have been annihilated, and the conquest of the air, coupled with the discovery and dreadful possibilities of the atomic bomb, make us realize that, whether we desire it or not, we have . . . responsibilities to cooperate in preserving the peace of the world . . . I look upon this measure as an indication of our cooperation with the world to preserve the peace, not to strengthen ourselves for war with other countries. It is difficult for me to endorse a national policy which calls upon our young men . . . to accept responsibility to be on call to help our country meet its international obligations. But I have come to the conclusion that our country and our international responsibilities are the primary consideration.[17]

As the Cold War got colder such statements became more common until, in the midst of the debate over the Selective Service Act of 1950, the North Korean invasion of South Korea convinced the last holdouts that, as one of them put it, "no longer can we continue to bury our heads like an ostrich in a sand dune . . . and expect peace to come to a shattered and war-torn world."[18] Thereafter the peacetime draft would go largely unchallenged until the late 1960s—as would the fundamental shift in American values from the old belief that the role of government is to protect individual rights to a belief that the national interest takes precedence over individual interests and, thus, that the role of government is (if necessary) to compel individuals to act in the national interest.

This new international role also forced the United States to develop the capacity to meet two entirely different kinds of military threat. On the one hand, the United States required large conventional forces to defend Europe. On the other, having adopted the role of imperial policeman once played by France and Britain, the United States also required the forces to defend the rimlands of the "Free World"—for example, Korea and Indochina. Such wars place very different demands on government and the military, however. Big wars involve a clear and present danger, require national mobilization, and call forth public support and a willingness to accept sacrifices. Small wars in the periphery involve no such clearcut threat, do not require full mobilization, and engender neither public support nor a willingness to sacrifice. They require the services of professional forces, a tiny portion of a country's young men, and the political capacity to sustain a costly, painful and inconclusive commitment for years in the absence of public support. In short, while the Selective Service system inherited from World War II met the requirements for defending Europe, it was inappropriate for meeting the challenge of small wars.

The Vietnam Draft

Between 1964 and 1973, 53 million Americans reached draft age, 26.8 million of them men. Of these, 60 percent escaped military service. Of the remaining 40 percent, only one-quarter, 10 percent of the male age-cohort, served in Vietnam and of these, only approximately 20 percent—or 2.0 percent of the male age-cohort—served in combat. Within these totals, draftees never constituted a majority except among those who served in combat. The draft, however, led many to become "reluctant volunteers" in order to control their service assignments and avoid Vietnam. Reluctant volunteers ultimately outnumbered draftees about two to one. Thus, directly or indirectly, the draft brought far more men into the military than did true voluntarism. Of the nearly 16 million young men who did not serve, 15.4 million were exempted or disqualified, 570,000 evaded the draft illegally (of whom 360,000 were never caught, 198,000 had their cases dismissed, 8,750 were convicted and 3,250 received jail terms), and 30,000 (perhaps as many as 50,000) fled the country.[19]

The selectivness of the Vietnam-era draft reflects supply and demand. On the demand side, the military grew from 2.7 to 3.5 million between 1964 and 1968, American forces in Vietnam jumped from 23,000 to 543,000 in the same period, and draft calls tripled from an average of 100,000 men per year in the five years preceding American intervention to 300,000 per year, from 1966 to 1970, peaking at 340,000 in 1966. By comparison, however, this *yearly* maximum is less than the number of men drafted *monthly* after August 1941, and just one-half the number drafted in 1951 for service in the Korean War.[20] On the supply side, the draft's selectiveness reflects the baby boom's coming of age. In 1955 1.15 million men reached eighteen, by 1960 the figure was 1.33 million, by 1965 1.72 million, and by 1970 1.93 million—a 68 percent increase in fifteen years. Thus, where in 1958, 70 percent of twenty-six-year-olds had served in the military, by 1962 this figure had fallen to 58 percent, by 1966 to 46 percent and by 1973 to 40 percent—despite the war.[21]

Given the selectiveness of the draft, who served and who didn't? The short answer is that white, middle-class, better-educated young men

Table 4.1: Likelihood of Vietnam-Era Service

	MILITARY SERVICE	VIETNAM SERVICE	COMBAT SERVICE
By educational achievement:			
High-school dropouts	42%	18%	14%
High-school graduates	45%	21%	17%
College graduates	23%	12%	9%
By social class background:			
Low-income	40%	19%	15%
Middle-income	30%	12%	7%
High-income	24%	9%	7%

Source: Lawrence Baskir and William Strauss, *Change and Circumstance: The Draft, the War and the Vietnam Generation* (New York: Knopf, 1978), p. 9.

Table 4.2: Distribution of Casualties between Regular Army Volunteers and Draftees in Vietnam

	1968	1969	1970
Draftees:			
Percentage Army in Vietnam	42%	39%	39%
Percentage total casualties	58%	62%	65%
Regular Army volunteers:			
Percentage Army in Vietnam	58%	61%	61%
Percentage total casualties	42%	38%	35%

Source: Paul Savage and Richard Gabriel, "Cohesion and Disintegration in the American Army," *Armed Forces and Society* 2:3 (May 1976), p. 364.

managed to avoid military service or to avoid combat in Vietnam if they did serve, while non-white, working-class, less-well-educated men were far more likely to serve and to see combat (table 4.1). Furthermore, among those who served during the Vietnam era, draftees were far more likely to serve in Vietnam and to see combat. Indeed, the average draftee had a 50 percent to 80 percent chance of being sent to Vietnam. Thus, in mid-1970, draftees filled more than two-thirds of U.S. Army combat roles, although they constituted less than one third of total Army personnel.

The unequal distribution of the burdens of the Vietnam War are revealed most poignantly by casualty statistics. Draftees suffered casualties out of all proportion to their share of both total military manpower and American forces in Vietnam (table 4.2). In 1968, for example, the year of the heaviest fighting in the war,

the Army volunteer had an 8.4 percent chance of becoming a casualty . . . (1.6 percent chance of death and 6.8 percent of injury). For the conscript, the rate was 15.7 percent (3.9 death, 11.8 injury). Thus . . . for every Army volunteer wounded or killed in action, nearly two (1.8) Army draftees were casualties; for the five years of most active fighting, the overall ratio stood at 1:1.5. Combining the chance of being shipped to Vietnam with the probability of suffering serious injury or death, the person drafted during the height of the war stood a 5 to 10 percent chance of becoming a casualty.[22]

Furthermore, since draftees were disproportionately from poor or working-class backgrounds, it was largely poor and working-class families who paid the ultimate cost of American involvement in Vietnam. For example:

- Between 1962 and 1972, Harvard and M.I.T. graduated 21,593—14 died in Vietnam. During the same period, some 2,000 young men came of draft age in the South Boston, a working-class neighborhood not far from Harvard and M.I.T.—25 died in Vietnam. Coming from South Boston meant being 20 times more likely to die in Vietnam than going to Harvard or M.I.T.
- A study of Vietnam War dead from Salt Lake City indicates that 97 percent came from areas where the median family income lay between $4,000 and $8,000, although only 80 percent of Salt Lake's population lived in such neighborhoods.
- A study of Wisconsin's Vietnam War dead found that the poor and working class were overrepresented about two to one relative to their proportion in the population.
- In a personal survey of one hundred inductees from his Wisconsin district, Repulican Congressman Alvin O'Konski found not one from a family with an annual income over $5,000. (Commented O'Konski, "They say the poor are always with you. If the draft goes on as it has, they may not be with us much longer.")
- A study of Chicago's Vietnam War dead found that men from poor neighborhoods were three times as likely to die in Vietnam as those from rich neighborhoods, while those from neighborhoods with low educational levels were four times more likely to die than those from neighborhoods with high educational levels.[23]

Finally, blacks bore a still heavier portion of the burden of Vietnam. Though they made up just 11 percent of the American population and 12.6 percent of American forces in Vietnam, blacks accounted for 20 percent of Army combat deaths from 1961 to 1966. These figures fell over the course of the war, but black casualties in Vietnam ultimately accounted for 15.1 percent of total Army casualties and 13.7 percent of total U.S. casualties—a casualty rate 30 percent higher than should be expected had the draft been color-blind. David Curry notes: "Black Americans, who share least in the benefits brought by the existence of the

American political structure, paid most heavily its costs. As a result of their lower socioeconomic status, they were more likely to serve and more likely to die." [24]

Draft Resistance and Evasion

Images of protesters burning draft cards and pouring blood on draft board files are part of Americans' collective memory of the 1960s. But while such things happened, antidraft protest was more symbolic than effective because of the nature of the Selective Service system. The Selective Service had two functions: to provide manpower to the armed forces and to allocate manpower resources between military and civilian requirements. The latter was accomplished through "channeling" or encouraging young men to pursue either their studies or needed professions by offering them draft deferments or exemptions. As the committee which drafted the deferment scheme in 1952 put it, "men of high ability constitute a national resource that is in short supply. From among them come our leaders and experts in every field. . . ." Thus, it concluded, national security requires use of the draft to give the capable added incentives to develop their talents. [25] In the 1950s, the limited supply of draft-age men left little room for channeling, but with the coming of age of the baby boom in the 1960s the draft became far more selective, channeling 60 percent of draft-age men into civilian occupations. This is precisely how the system was intended to work, but as with the Civil War draft, it raised the equity issue—how shall the cost of the common defense be distributed when only a few must pay?

The key to the equity issue is the selection process itself. Selection took place at three levels; that of the individual (his health, mental ability, and socioeconomic status), of the community (where local draft boards set their own criteria), and of the federal government (where Selective Service officials established a complex system of deferments and exemptions for the purposes of channeling). While fine in principle, this process was open to bias and manipulation at every level. Thus, in the name of the common defense, the Selective Service shifted the burden of Vietnam service to the poor, uneducated, politically impotent and minorities. The draft favored the better-off both because it provided exemptions and deferments only they could use and because the poor and uneducated lacked the knowledge and skills to find and take advantage of the loopholes offered by the tangle of Selective Service regulations. Either way, equity suffered.

The Selective Service served genuine national security interests and strictly political ones. For example, the II-S student deferment did encourage many young men to go to college or graduate school who might otherwise not have done so. Similarly, occupational exemptions channeled many more into education, farming, missile production, and other occupations defined as "necessary to the maintenance of the national health, safety, or interest." But, as General Westmoreland put it, the draft aimed also "to extend the nation's staying power by forestalling premature public pressure to 'bring the boys home'." [26] It did so in several ways. First, because college attendance and access to many draft-exempted occupations were strongly associated with the politically potent middle class, the draft damped protest by channeling the silent poor, uneducated and politically impotent into the military and the vocal, well-educated and potentially troublesome into civilian security. Second, because the draft tapped individuals and offered them individual avenues of escape, it made collective action by draft opponents extremely difficult. Third, because the draft tapped scattered individuals, it was politically preferable to mobilizing the Reserves or the National Guard, which would have touched large numbers of people in concentrated areas. [27] Finally, because it controlled enforcement of draft regulations, the government could simply avoid confrontation with vocal, well-educated draft resisters by selective prosecution. Thus, of nearly 600,000 apparent draft offenders, only 210,000 were accused, 13,000 tried, 8,750 convicted, and 3,250 imprisoned. In fact, many officials bent over backwards to avoid trouble, as did those in Boston who told Harvard and M.I.T. students arriving for their draft physicals, "If you cooperate with us, we'll cooperate with you." [28]

The actions of local draft boards and individuals further exaggerated the draft's inequitable selectivity. The more than four thousand local boards were both powerful and unrepresentative of the communities they served. They operated virtually without supervision and reflected the values and aspirations of the white, middle-class professional segment of the communities from which they were drawn. [29] Thus, note Baskir and Strauss, in the hands of local draft boards "channeling became less a means of allocating manpower to different beneficial national pursuits than a means of enforcing a set of political and social mores." [30] For their part, middle- and upper-class young men exploited the opportunities for evasion offered by the Selective Service regulations and their draft boards. As the chairman of the Los Angeles draft attorney's panel told the press, "any kid with money can absolutely stay out of the Army—with 100 percent certainty." [31] Those with money or connections prolonged their educations, turned to family doctors, dentists, psychiatrists and lawyers for help, or appealed to their draft boards for special treatment. The Beverly Hills draft board, for example, gave actor George Hamilton a hardship exemption since his mother depended on his $200,000 income. [32] All in all, 60 percent of draft-age men who did not see combat took positive steps to avoid military service.

Against this backdrop a small, vocal and committed resistance movement fought the draft.[33] Its members organized public forums and rallies to protest the draft, some risked arrest and prison by confronting the government directly, and perhaps as many as 30,000 (some estimate 50,000) went into exile in Canada, Britain, Sweden, and elsewhere. But while there is no mistaking the sincerity and commitment of the draft resistance movement's core members, there is also no mistaking the movement's shallowness. The problem was that like the early antiwar movement it was comprised of white, middle-class college students. As such, the great majority of draft resistance organization members were draft-exempt. (A survey by the New England Resistance indicated that 80 percent of its members had deferments, while it was later revealed that ten out of ten participants at one highly publicized draft card burning were exempt.)[34] Consequently, protest did not and could not affect the workings of the draft, as they would have if large numbers of draft-eligible men had refused induction.

Most young Americans, including those opposed to the draft, pre-ferred the easy escape mechanisms offered them to the risks of opposing the draft and foregoing the many available deferments and exemptions. For their part, leaders of SDS and other organizations which might have mobilized antidraft protest refused to do so, fearing that if they asked students to give up their deferments they would alienate their key constituency and so fail in their larger political program.[35] Thus, the commonest form of draft protest was draft evasion. It was "morally correct," accord-ing to the evaders—and had the added advantage of not requiring that they make any personal sacrifice or give up their educations and careers. Draft evasion had no effect on the draft, however, given the baby-boom surplus of draft-age young men. It merely shifted the war's burden to those who lacked the means to escape its reach. No less important, draft evasion subverted the very aim of draft resistance as the draft evaders in effect conspired with the Selective Service "to extend the nation's staying power" by exempting the middle and upper classes from the conse-quences of the war.

The All-Volunteer Force

Faced with mounting antiwar protest, President Nixon appointed a Com-mission on an All-Volunteer Force to study the feasibility of ending con-scription and so of removing a highly visible target of protest. The Gates Commission, as it was called, concluded that the draft was unnecessary and an unjustifiable infringement upon citizens' rights. The President thus proposed, and Congress accepted, an All-Volunteer Force (AVF). In 1973 the peacetime draft came to an end, but although ending the draft reduced the president's immediate problems, the larger political and moral questions that have long troubled American manpower policy re-main: Who shall serve? How shall they be chosen?

Table 4.3: Education Background, Male Army Entrants
(No Prior Service)

	% 1964 DRAFTEES	% 1979 ENLISTEES	% 1978 18–19-YEAR–OLD MALES
Some college	17.2	3.2	40.1
High-school graduate	54.1	55.4	39.9
Non-high school graduate	28.7	41.4	20.0

Source: Sam Sarkesian, "Who Serves?" *Society* 18:3 (1981), p. 59.

From the beginning, critics and defenders have battled over whether the AVF is truly voluntary or represents a form of "economic conscription." The Gates Commission addressed the issue directly, asserting that "our research indicates that an all-volunteer force will not differ significantly from the current force of conscripts and volunteers. Maintenance of current medical, physical, and moral standards will ensure that a better paid, volunteer force will not recruit an undue proportion of youth from disadvantaged socioeconomic backgrounds."[36] Experience shows this assertion is incorrect. In adopting the AVF, the nation shifted even more of the burden of military service to the poor, and deprived itself of a way to bring college-educated people into the armed services. Indeed, by comparison to the pre-AVF military and American society at large the AVF is very unrepresentative as shown by the statistics of educational attainment (a proxy for socioeconomic status) and racial composition. Since 1973 the educational qualifications of enlistees have fallen sharply (table 4.3). Of the 100,860 men serving their first tours in the Army's combat arms (infantry, armor and artillery) in 1980, for example, just *twenty-five* held a college degree of any sort, while 1980 nearly 50 percent of new enlistees scored in the lowest acceptable category on the Armed Forces Qualifying Test.[37] In fact, asserts one expert, "had the Army not expanded the opportunities for women soldiers, it is doubtful if the [AVF] could have survived the 1970s" since female enlistees were, on average, far better educated than their male counterparts.[38] Recession in the early 1980s improved matters, but with declining numbers of young people and low unemployment in the mid- and late-1980s the AVF again faces serious problems.

By the same token, in June 1969 the armed forces were 9.5 percent black (although forces in Vietnam were 11 percent black, the same percentage as in the population at large, and Army units were 14.5 percent black). By 1982 the military was 19.9 percent black with Army enlisted ranks 32.9 percent black and 41.1 percent minority. Some units, such as the Second Division in Korea, were 50 percent black.[39] In recent years, the aggregate statistics for first-time enlistees have improved, but problems remain as combat units (as opposed to technical and service units) continue to be composed disproportionately of minorities, and blacks continue to reenlist in much higher numbers than whites because they lack employment possibilities in the civilian economy. Thus, General Westmoreland's assessment still holds—the AVF is "forcing the responsibility for the manning of our military services . . . on the underprivileged segments of our society in totally disproportionate numbers." [40]

These statistics suggest three issues of concern to all Americans. First, the decline in the educational qualifications of those entering today's high-tech military raises concerns about the AVF's combat effectiveness. A 1980 Defense Department study found, for example, that 98 percent of tank turret and artillery repairmen failed the Army's Skill Qualification Test—as did 86 percent of artillerymen, 90 percent of nuclear technicians, 77 percent of computer programmers, 89 percent of tracked-vehicle mechanics, and 82 percent of Hawk surface-to-air-missile crewmen. [41] In 1986, General William DePuy concluded that the all-volunteer Army "cannot meet the training prerequisites established by its schools" and therefore performance in the field "falls substantially below the levels . . . required." [42] Furthermore, removal of even the limited number of better-educated, middle-class men brought into the military by the draft has hurt discipline and reduced positive socialization in the military.

Second, the AVF highlights the contentious equity issue central to the debate over the Civil War and Vietnam War drafts: Should poor and black kids bear arms, while middle-class kids go to college? In keeping with the liberal tradition in American politics, the Gates Commission contended that "when not all our citizens can serve, and when only a small minority are needed, a voluntary decision to serve is the best answer, morally and practically, to the question of who should serve." [43] From a republican perspective, however, this view debases the notion of social obligation, and reduces military service from a sacrifice for the common good to a mercenary occupation. Lt. Colonel Jim Williams worries, "We're setting up a kind of class warfare. I wonder about the morality of a nation that lets the disadvantaged do the fighting." [44] Thus, one congressman attacked the AVF as "a system in which those who have the least in our society are offered the opportunity to be trained to risk all in exchange for the very thing they have been denied by the society they are asked to defend, a job," while an expert on the military noted that the AVF's composition "raises the question of [the] representativeness and political legitimacy of institutions that are at the core of democratic society." [45] Observes Joseph Califano,

> The draft never achieved perfect egalitarianism in distributing the burdens of military service, but at least it made the attempt. The all-volunteer concept . . . legislates into government policy the Civil War practice of having the better-off hire the worse-off to serve their time . . . In effect with the all-volunteer army we write into law the concept of one man's money for another man's blood. [46]

Finally, the AVF raises questions about the control of foreign and military policy. First, limiting military service to the lower classes means that few of our leaders have military experience, and this raises "the risk that they will be buffaloed, either by the services or by equally passionate groups on the left, and virtually eliminates the possibility that they will bring their own, uncoached sense of nuance and perspective to the military reports they hear."[47] Second, the AVF divorces those who make policy from those who suffer its consequences. As Joseph Califano notes, however, what ended the Vietnam War was

> the realization that the vast middle class of America would not permit *their* sons to die in a war which they considered meaningless. It was middle- and upper-class Americans who know how to contact Congressmen, influence their local communities—and most all of whom vote and finance campaigns—who posed the sharp dilemma to Washington: get out of Vietnam or get out of office. An all volunteer force that subjects only the ones at the bottom to military service will effectively reduce the need for future leaders to be concerned about the more affluent majority of America and its judgments about foreign adventures, at least until those adventures are so far along that they will be virtually impossible to stop.[48]

This is not an argument for one foreign policy or another, but for a *democratic* policy, whatever it may be. For foreign policy to be democratic, the United States requires a military manpower system which ensures that the consequences of policy will be borne by the same public that votes for it, rather than one that shifts the consequences to the least influential. Sadly one of the consequences of raising armed forces by strictly voluntary means has been the institutionalization of the divide between the two.

Conscience and Obligation in a Liberal Democracy

Today a new debate is underway about military manpower policy, one which reflects not only the changing requirements of high-tech defense and the hard realities of budgetary constraints, but also, like similar debates that have punctuated American history since independence, changing notions of citizenship and perceptions of the United States' international role. This debate reflects the continuing vitality of both a liberal attachment to individual rights and republican belief in citizens' obligations. It reflects Americans' sense of what is fair and just, and perhaps most immediately, it reflects the political and institutional legacy of the Vietnam draft. How then are we to defend ourselves? Who shall serve when not all must serve?

Answers to these questions will never be fixed; they will change as the United States changes. But if they are to be asked honestly—and if we are to be proud of the answers—there are two unexamined aspects of the Vietnam legacy to be faced. The first is the human legacy of Vietnam-era manpower policy. There is an indictment in the Vietnam casualty figures that the middle-class majority of Americans must acknowledge. They shifted the burden of the common defense to poor, politically impotent, and minority citizens through the workings of the draft and now the AVF. Knowing this, can we—will we—ignore the issue of equity in future discussions of military manpower policy? Or will a future war, too, be "a poor man's fight"?

The second issue raised by Vietnam is the complex question of conscience and obligation. It is the question which faced the thousands of young men who did not believe that the Vietnam War was morally acceptable or in the national interest. Most of them cheated on it, however, serving neither conscience nor obligation, for the mere evasion of military service is not an act of conscience if it shifts the burden to another. Indeed, the deaths of draftees in Vietnam must in part be laid to those who sent them to die in their stead. Nor is the obligation of citizenship merely to serve; it is an obligation to active involvement whether in the pursuit of policy or protest against it. Those who bought in to the system by using its carefully conceived loopholes to avoid the draft did neither. They passively accepted national policy while exempting themselves from its consequences. It is not a legacy to be proud of, but it is a lesson for the future—a lesson to be borne in mind when next we confront the perennial question: Who shall serve when not all must serve?

NOTES

The author wishes, in particular, to thank John Whiteclay Chambers II for his editorial and bibliographic suggestions, and for his meticulous fact checking without which this essay might still suffer many embarrassing lapses.

1. Three recent studies which put these questions in historical perspective are Eliot A. Cohen, *Citizens and Soldiers: The Dilemmas of Military Service* (Ithaca: Cornell University Press, 1985), John Whiteclay Chambers II, *To Raise an Army: The Draft Comes to Modern America* (New York: Free Press, 1987), and David R. Segal, *Recruiting for Uncle Sam: Citizenship and Military Manpower Policy* (Lawrence: University of Kansas Press, 1989).

2. See, for example, the historical documents reprinted in Martin Anderson, ed., *The Military Draft: Selected Readings on Conscription* (Stanford: Hoover Institution Press, 1982), John Whiteclay Chambers II, ed., *Draftees or Volunteers: A Documentary History of the Debate over Military Conscription in the United States, 1787–1973* (New York: Garland Publishing Co., 1975), and John O'Sullivan and Alan M. Meckler, eds., *The Draft and Its Enemies: A Documentary History* (Urbana: University of Illinois Press, 1974).

3. See Michael X. Delli Carpini, "Vietnam, Ideology, and Domestic Politics," in this volume.

4. Cited in Cohen, *Citizens and Soldiers,* p. 129.

5. Cited in Chambers, *To Raise an Army,* p. 268.

6. Ibid., p. 28.

7. Cited in Philip Gold, *Evasions: The American Way of Military Service* (New York: Paragon House, 1985), p. 56.

8. Chambers, *To Raise an Army*, pp. 21–22. More than five thousand black troops served in Washington's forces in both integrated and all-black units.

9. To put these figures in perspective, the contemporaneous Austro-Prussian and Franco-Prussian wars killed thirty-six thousand and seventy thousand respectively.

10. Michael Useem, "Conscription and Class," *Society* 18:3 (1981), p. 30. The best available study of the Civil War draft is Eugene C. Murdoch, *One Million Men: The Civil War Draft in the North* (Madison: Historical Society of Wisconsin, 1971).

11. The following account of the World War I draft draws particularly from Chambers, *To Raise an Army*.

12. Thus Henry Hooker, a Wall Street lawyer, argued the need for UMT "to obliterate the so-called class distinctions," while former Assistant Secretary of War and steel magnate Henry Breckinridge contended that UMT would make the military "a real melting pot, under which the fire is hot enough to fuse the elements into one common mass of Americanism." Cited in Chambers, *To Raise an Army*, pp. 89, 92–93.

13. Sen. Thomas W. Hardwick, *Cong. Rec.* 65:1st, (April 27, 1917), pp. 1319–24.

14. Cited in Chambers, *To Raise an Army*, p. 17.

15. Ibid., pp. 253–54.

16. Although the United States was still technically at peace, the 1940 draft was clearly approved as part of this country's immediate preparations for war. For discussion of the World War II draft, see John Gerry Clifford and Samuel R. Spencer, Jr., *The First Peacetime Draft* (Lawrence: University of Kansas Press, 1986) and John O'Sullivan, *From Voluntarism to Conscription: Congress and the Selective Service, 1940–1945* (New York: Garland Press, 1982).

17. Cited in Richard Gillam, "The Peacetime Draft: Voluntarism to Coercion," in Anderson, *The Military Draft*, p. 106–7

18. Congressman Dewey Short, cited ibid., p. 111.

19. Lawrence Baskir and William Strauss, *Chance and Circumstance: The Draft, the War and the Vietnam Generation* (New York: Knopf, 1978), p. 5; and Cohen, *Citizens and Soldiers*, p. 108.

20. Michael Useem, *Conscription, Protest and Social Conflict: The Life and Death of a Draft Resistance Movement* (New York: John Wiley and Sons, 1973), pp. 77–80.

21. Thomas D. Morris, Assistant Secretary of Defense, Manpower Procurement, "Department of Defense Report on Study of the Draft, 1966," in Anderson, *The Military Draft*, pp. 550–51.

22. Useem, *Conscription, Protest and Social Conflict*, p. 107.

23. Ibid., p. 108; M. Zeitlin, K. G. Lutterman, and J. W. Russell, "Death in Vietnam: Class, Poverty and the Risks of War," *Politics and Society* 3 (Spring 1973); Baskir and Strauss, *Chance and Circumstance*, p. 9; and Gilbert Badillo and David Curry, "The Social Incidence of Vietnam Casualties: Social Class or Race?" *Armed Forces and Society* 2:3 (May 1976).

24. G. David Curry, *Sunshine Patriots: Punishment and the Vietnam Offender* (Notre Dame, Ind: Notre Dame University Press, 1985), p. 61. See also John Helmer, *Bringing the War Home: The American Soldier in Vietnam and After* (New York: Free Press, 1974), p. 17; and Peter B. Levy, "Blacks and the Vietnam War" in this volume.

25. Cited in Useem, *Conscription, Protest and Social Conflict,* p. 91. See also, George Q. Flynn, *Lewis B. Hershey: Mr. Selective Service* (Chapel Hill: University of North Carolina Press, 1985).

26. General William C. Westmoreland, *A Soldier Reports* (New York: Dell, 1980), p. 392.

27. Furthermore, note Baskir and Strauss, "Reservists and guardsmen were better connected, better educated, more affluent, and whiter than their peers in the active forces, and the administration feared that mobilizing them would heighten public opposition to the war." Thus, 71 percent of reserve and 90 percent of National Guard enlistments were draft-motivated and in 1968 the Army National Guard had a waiting list of 100,000. Indeed, between 1967 and 1970, twenty-eight thousand more college-educated men joined the reserves or National Guard than enlisted or were inducted into all of the active duty forces combined (Baskir and Strauss, *Chance and Circumstance,* pp. 49–51). During the 1988 presidential campaign, Republican vice presidential candidate Dan Quayle's draft-evading enlistment in the National Guard provoked a flood of angry protest from Vietnam veterans that is captured in such jokes as: "Q: What's the difference between Dan Quayle and Jane Fonda? A: Jane Fonda's been to Vietnam"; and "Q: What's the name of Dan Quayle's Vietnam movie? A: *Full Dinner Jacket.*"

28. Gold, *Evasions,* p. 96; and Baskir and Strauss, *Chance and Circumstance,* pp. 5, 47.

29. A 1966 survey of draft board members found 1.3 percent to be black; 7 percent blue collar workers; and 70 percent professionals, officials, managers, technical workers and proprietors, although these groups constitute 11, 35 and 40 percent of the American population. Useem, *Conscription, Protest and Social Conflict,* pp. 89–90.

30. Baskir and Strauss, *Chance and Circumstance,* p. 24.

31. Cited in ibid., p. 39.

32. Ibid., p. 33.

33. See chapters by Michael X. Delli Carpini and Barbara Tischler in this volume. For studies of opposition to the Vietnam War draft, see Stephen M. Kohn, *Jailed for Peace: The History of American Draft Law Violators, 1685–1985* (New York: Praeger, 1986), and Charles DeBenedetti with Charles Chatfield, *An American Ordeal: The Antiwar Movement, 1955–1975* (Syracuse: Syracuse University Press, forthcoming).

34. Baskir and Strauss, *Chance and Circumstance,* pp. 64–66.

35. See chapters by Michael X. Delli Carpini and Barbara Tischler in this volume.

36. *Report of the President's Commission on an All-Volunteer Armed Force* (New York: Collier Books, 1970), p. 16.

37. James Fallows, *The National Defense* (New York: Random House, 1981), pp. 126–28.

38. Martin Binkin, *America's Volunteer Military: Progress and Prospects* (Washington, D.C.: The Brookings Institution, 1984) p. 8.

39. Sam Sarkesian, "Who Serves?" *Society* 18:3 (1981), p. 59.; Robert Fullinwider, "The AVF and Racial Balance," in *Conscripts and Volunteers: Military Requirements, Social Justice and the All-Volunteer Force,* ed. Robert Fullinwider (New York: Rowman and Allen, 1983), p. 176; and Peter B. Levy, "Blacks and the Vietnam War," in this volume.

40. General Westmoreland interviewed in *U.S. News and World Report,* 17 May 1980.

41. David H. Marlowe, "The Manning of the Force and the Structure of Battle," in Fullinwider, *Conscripts and Volunteers,* pp. 51–52.

42. General William DePuy, "Technology and Manpower: Army Perspective," in *The All-Volunteer Force after a Decade,* ed. William Bowman, Roger Little and G. Thomas Sicilia (New York: Pergamon-Brassey's, 1986), p. 134.

43. *Report of the President's Commission,* pp. 13–14.

44. Cited in Fallows, *The National Defense,* p. 133.

45. Congressman John Cavanaugh, *Presidential Commission on National Service and the National Commission on Voluntarism,* Hearings before the Subcommittee on Child and Human Development, Committee on Labor and Human Resources, U.S. Senate, 96th Cong., 2nd Sess., 13 March 1980, p. 432; and Morris Janowitz, "Focus on Blacks and the Military," *Focus,* June 1975, p. 3.

46. Joseph A. Califano, Jr., "Doubts About an All-Volunteer Army," in Anderson, *The Military Draft,* p. 533.

47. Fallows, *The National Defense,* p. 137.

48. Califano, "Doubts About an All-Volunteer Army," p. 554.

5

THE VIETNAM COMBAT EXPERIENCE:
The Human Legacy

D. MICHAEL SHAFER

Fifty-nine thousand Americans were killed in Vietnam, 270,000 wounded, 21,000 disabled, and untold others carry the hidden wounds of Agent Orange and post-traumatic stress. But the human legacy of Vietnam afflicts not only these men and women; it affects all three million who served in Vietnam—and the rest of us too.

Powerful and pervasive stereotypes dominate most Americans' understanding of the Vietnam War and Vietnam veterans. In the minds of many, Vietnam was just a police action, a limited war, nothing like "the big one" which was fought by "real soldiers." Many still think the Vietnam War was fought by drug-smoking incompetents and baby-killers incapable of defeating a ragtag collection of black-pajama-wearing peasants. Since the war, we have ignored Vietnam veterans or treated them with a hostility reflecting the common view that they are a "bunch of whining vets," or losers, druggies and, possibly, psychopaths. Recently, some politicians have lionized Vietnam veterans for their own purposes, but have paid little attention to veterans' real interests or concerns. President Reagan, for example, made "America Is Back" his rallying cry and elevated the Veterans Administration to cabinet-level status, but cut or froze programs for Vietnam veterans and refused to attend the dedication of the Vietnam Memorial in Washington. Similarly, beribboned Vietnam veterans in camouflage were required stage decorations for both candidates during the 1988 presidential campaign, though candidate George Bush simply brushed off Vietnam veterans' outrage over vice presidential candidate Dan Quayle's use of family connections to evade the draft by joining the National Guard.

Powerful and pervasive as these stereotypes may be, they are the product of ignorance, misunderstanding, and false or ill-informed comparisons with America's past wars and warriors. They obscure our understanding of both the Vietnam War and its human legacy. No less important, they blind us to how badly we as a nation have dealt with the war and, in particular, with those who bear the Vietnam legacy most directly, the Vietnam veterans. Nor is this all, for in this blindness Americans also ignore the deep divisions left by the war and the erosion of our national community revealed by our treatment of Vietnam veterans. If not addressed, it is a legacy that does not bode well for our future.

The Vietnam Combat Experience

What does the Vietnam combat experience share with that of other wars? What about it is unique? How do these differences explain the special legacy of hurt which veterans brought from home from Vietnam? To answer these questions, it is first necessary to choose the proper frame of reference for studying combat. The traditional one—from which most history is written—embodies Clausewitz's dictum that "war is but the extension of politics by different means,"[1] and treats battles merely as the pieces of wars. What matters is not the battles themselves, but the final score: who won, who lost, and the implications of winning and losing in terms of the strategic or political goals of the nations involved. Similarly, most military historians take a general's-eye view of battles. They begin by asking "What were the opposing generals' objectives?" and go on to discuss the strategy and tactics each employed to achieve his ends.

At one level, these approaches are essential and informative. War is the *ultima ratio* in international politics, the final test of any nation. Strategy, tactics, weaponry, logistics, economic capacity, and national will are essential to understanding the course of battles and wars and the sense of purpose of combatants. They cannot answer the questions posed here, however, because they say nothing about the actual experience of combat. The world looks very different to infantrymen than it does to politicians or generals. For Henry V's swordsmen at Agincourt, Napoleon's guardsmen at Waterloo, Pickets' ragged scavengers, Patton's tankers, and the Marine "grunts" who retook the Citadel at Hue, winning and losing had an entirely personal meaning—surviving or dying.[2] To enter this world requires an understanding of the elements of the combat experience itself.

Perhaps the best place to begin is with the writings of General S. L. A. Marshall.[3] During World War II, Marshall headed a U.S. Army project to evaluate the performance of units in combat and recommend how to improve it. Marshall's observations apply more generally, however, and provide the basis for comparing combat in different wars. No less important, his analysis also offers the means to understand the lingering consequences of combat on veterans and to compare the different legacies of combat left by different wars.

Marshall observed that "the battlefield is a place of terror" and went on to ask: What are the specific conditions of a combat situation that either mitigate this terror, or enhance it? These can be divided into conditions affecting the environment in which soldiers must fight and those affecting their ability to cope with battlefield terror. Of the first type of conditions, we will focus on the nature of the war being fought and on the degree and kind of exposure soldiers experience in combat. As for the second, we will focus on who the soldiers are as individuals, the quality of battlefield leadership, and the strength of the small groups in which soldiers live and from which they draw moral support.

Analysis of the Vietnam combat experience in Marshallian terms reveals conditions likely to leave especially deep and lasting scars on veterans. The combined effects of the nature of the war, the kind of exposure to combat the soldiers suffered, who they were, poor battlefield leadership, and the disintegration of the small groups that traditionally provided support for the individual soldier in combat add up to a combat experience that maximized the terror soldiers faced and minimized the effectiveness of the means by which soldiers in past wars have coped with combat.

Having said as much, it is important to remember two things. First, although there was no one Vietnam combat experience (experiences of individuals varied dramatically according to assignment, theater of operations, and the period of the war during which they served), there are critical elements of combat in Vietnam that form a common denominator and allow us to compare Vietnam and other wars. Second, because our subject is the Vietnam legacy, this chapter treats the "Vietnam experience" as a combat experience, although only 20 percent of those sent to Vietnam served in combat units. The reason is simple—the "grunt" carried the weight of the war, and he carries the war's most painful legacy today.

Perhaps the easiest way to understand the nature of the Vietnam War is to begin with what it was not. Soldiers and historians traditionally assume that battles possess the classic Aristotelian dramatic unities of time, place and action: they have a beginning, middle and end; they take place in a clearly defined locale; and the action proceeds in a logical and continuous fashion from beginning to end. They assume, for example, that it is possible to distinguish battles from the far longer periods of relative calm between them. This temporal distinctness of battle is captured in the expressions D-day and H-hour, designating the planned day and hour on which a battle begins. Similarly, it has traditionally been easy to distinguish a battle's end by the defeat of one side or the disengagement of forces and the return to a period of recovery and preparation.

The traditional geographical organization of battles also imposed a clear unity and structure of place. Armies faced one another from defined positions, easily labeled our lines and their lines with no-man's-land in between. Moreover, there was a clear hierarchy to each side. At the front were the fighting lines, but the further back one went into the rear areas, the safer one got, and units regularly rotated to the rear for periods of rest in complete safety. (Paul Fussell reports a sign behind the British trenches in World War I that had two arrows, one pointing to the front labeled "To the War" and the other pointing to the rear labeled "To Heaven.")[4]

Finally, this traditional neat ordering of the battlefield structured and unified action, which began from our trenches and moved forward toward theirs. Battles had defined objectives. Attacks aimed to take a physical target and the action could be understood as a logical series of sub-actions directed toward a single goal. Subsequently, the success of actions could be measured in terms of how much of the initial object was achieved. Furthermore, just as clear objectives defined the purposes of action, they also defined *who* the players were in the drama. The aims of action were military—the destruction of the enemy's fighting forces and the capture of the territory they held. This enemy could be easily identified by the very uniform he wore. There was, in short, a clear distinction between "us" and "them" and between soldiers and civilians.

Combat in Vietnam possessed none of these unities of time, place, or action. In many places, it was a guerrilla war against an elusive enemy indistinguishable from the civilian population and unwilling to commit itself to open battle. Combat ranged across an undefined territory without clear beginning or end, front or rear, objective or enemy. For "grunts," the battlefield became a psychological region corresponding to the concept of being "in the bush," a mentality combat soldiers carried with them always and from which they could never really be relieved, even at a firebase, a base camp, or while on R-and-R in Thailand.[5] Even where American troops faced North Vietnamese Army regulars, as they did in the Central Highlands and along the DMZ, the war was not fought in the style of set-piece battles, and major actions took place in the midst of a more fluid, murkier battlefield than the battles of earlier, conventional wars. Throughout the war, American military commanders attempted to set up classic encounters—in the Ia Drang valley, at Dak To, in the A Shau, at Khe Sanh and "Hamburger Hill"—only to prove repeatedly the inappropriateness of classic conceptions in Vietnam.

For individual soldiers, the Vietnam War's lack of structure had serious implications beginning with the psychological consequences of the lack of clear objectives and of distinctions about who the players were. The objectives of the Vietnam War were doubly obscure to American soldiers in the field. First, like soldiers in many conflicts before Vietnam, they often lacked a clear grasp of the abstract principles for which the war was being fought and their lives risked. But those serving in Vietnam had particular reason to wonder, for Washington never offered them a credible, widely accepted justification for American involvement. Indeed, the Johnson and Nixon administrations both went to great lengths to preserve the semblance of normalcy at home and to avoid admitting the seriousness of the Vietnam conflict. Thus, those fighting faced the bitter irony that back in "The World" life went on as normal while they risked their lives in a war their government did not acknowledge and many fellow citizens considered unnecessary or even immoral.

Second, soldiers in Vietnam seldom perceived the objectives of the specific actions in which they were engaged. As the testimony of the veterans of other wars makes clear, this was not unique to the Vietnam war, but soldiers in Vietnam were often particularly sensitive to the absurdity of their actions and the loneliness of risking one's life for no obviously valuable end. No clear objectives were set, no territory was captured and held, no milestones marked their advance toward victory as they had for the allied armies in Europe. Units swept the same areas repeatedly, taking casualties each time and never seeming to achieve any lasting effect. No less confusing, the very rules of engagement changed regularly, shifting villages, farm animals and farmers from protected "friendlies" to targets from one day to the next—and maybe then back again. (As Michael Herr reports one chopper pilot commenting bitterly, "Vietnam, man. Bomb 'em and feed 'em, bomb 'em and feed 'em.")[6] Even Khe Sanh, the great set-piece battle of the war, proved inconclusive. The Marines set up, were besieged, took horrendous casualties for months, and then pulled out without having achieved the hoped for "knockout blow," or indeed any conclusion at all.

In the absence of any clear territorial objectives, the war in Vietnam became a war of attrition. In this, it resembled World War I, described by a British captain as "absolutely, certainly a war of attrition . . . and we have got to stick to it longer than the other side and go on producing men, money and material until they cry quits."[7] But unlike World War I, the enemy's identity and location were seldom clear during the Vietnam war. Thus, units were sent out as lures to attract the enemy in order that they could then be subjected to superior American firepower.[8] (According to a Defense Department study in mid-1967, American forces had the initiative in just 14.3 percent of engagements, while the enemy had it 78.6 percent of the time.)[9] Repeated over and over, such actions bred a sense of hopelessness. Unable to seize the initiative, American soldiers were powerless to do anything but react in situations defined by the enemy to his own advantage.[10]

The focus on reactive firepower also had important consequences. In part, it reflected "the American way of war"—the use of bullets, not American lives—learned from the bitter lessons of the slaughter of the Civil War and of World War I, lessons no democracy could ignore. And the firepower employed in Vietnam was fantastic, eclipsing even that used in the two world wars. The problem, however, was that American firepower was meant for use on a conventional battlefield where it is clear *who* and *where* the enemy is. But for much of the war in Vietnam and in most areas except the Central Highlands and DMZ, it proved almost impossible to distinguish the enemy from the rest of the population and attack him directly. As one vet put it,

> No matter how much effort you put into it, you can't find him. You can't lay your hands on him. And the fact that he also might be anywhere, you know . . . as though you were hunting a specific deer and you don't know which one it will be and there's a deer herd all over you.[11]

As a result, this American way of war, with its underlying assumptions about the conventional nature of the battlefield, inevitably had horrendous, if unintended, consequences for the very people the American effort was supposed to be helping.

But the problem went deeper. In a war of attrition, the "body count" became the primary measure of success. The military offered justifications for the body-count-based strategy, but as one soldier put it, "All that's just a *load,* man. We're here to kill gooks. Period."[12] This unique feature of the Vietnam War inflicted a terrible psychic and emotional toll on the nineteen-year-olds ordered to get the body counts. It echoes through one young soldier's questions: "What am I doing here? We don't take any land. We don't give it back. We just mutilate bodies. What the fuck are we doing here?"[13] In the field the rule became "if it's dead, it's VC," from which it was but a short step to a constant, haunting question: Where does combat end and murder begin? In part, this question arose because this was a guerrilla war, but it also raises the final element of the nature of the war in Vietnam—its racial aspect.

Wars always involve a process of stereotyping and dehumanizing the enemy. Soldiers have always thought of those opposing them as having different thoughts, even different corpses. Thus, "we" are individuals, normal, natural, and superior; and "they" are collective, grotesque, bizarre, and inferior.[14] But stereotyping the enemy took on a new racial dimension in Vietnam. In World War II American propaganda, military planning, and soldiers' attitudes also reflected a sharp distinction between Western, white Germans and the "yellow hordes" of Japan; in Vietnam the issue of race was all-pervasive, however, and made little distinction

between our allies and the enemy—they were all "slopes," "dinks,"
"gooks," and so below human consideration. Americans were involved
in a war with *Vietnam*, not with a specific Vietnamese enemy; racial stereotyping of the Vietnamese left soldiers without allies.[15] The entire population was potentially hostile both because it was a guerrilla war and because American attitudes made the entire population alien

The second element of the combat experience for the individual soldier
is *exposure*—that is, his personal exposure to the terror of the battlefield
and the intensity of that terror. It is a function of the length of time he is
in combat and the nature and intensity of the threat he faces.

Few Americans appreciate the issue of exposure because of a common
misperception of the Vietnam War as a low-intensity conflict. But while
for political reasons the war was fought with limited means for limited
ends, there was nothing limited about combat for those involved. Indeed, there is reason to believe that those who served in Vietnam suffered
greater exposure than those who served in World War II. True, total casualty figures for World War II are higher, but they are misleading for three
reasons: total U.S. forces in World War II numbered twelve million, total
U.S. forces in Vietnam numbered three million; a greater percentage of
servicemen saw combat in World War II than in Vietnam; and improvements in battlefield medical services meant that in Vietnam many men
survived wounds which would have killed them in World War II. To
understand what this means for the individual soldier, however, it is necessary to look at the key elements of his personal exposure.

The first of these is time in combat. Edward Luttwak, a military ana-
lyst, notes that though soldiers were "in for the duration of hostilities" in
World War II, most saw little combat. A soldier who enlisted after Pearl
Harbor, was mustered in England, and participated in D-day probably
saw only a few *weeks* of combat during the eleven months between
D-Day and V-E Day.[16] In the Pacific, the Marine "Battle Cry" Division
saw a total of just *six weeks* combat between Pearl Harbor and V-J Day. In
Vietnam, however, those assigned to combat units often spent months in
the field. The Marines, for example, committed units to combat for
eighty days at a time—eleven and a half weeks—and many men served
three or more eighty-day rotations, a total of 240 days in combat. In
short, *each* Marine combat rotation of the Vietnam war was nearly twice
as long as the *total* amount of time a World War II Marine was exposed to
combat. To understand what this meant to the individual soldier, consider the conclusions of the official World War II U.S. Army report,
Combat Exhaustion: "Each moment of combat imposes a strain so great
that men will break down in direct relation to the intensity and duration
of their exposure . . . Most men were ineffective after 180 or even
140 days."[17]

Exposure is also shaped by the objective and subjective danger of the combat situation. Here the Vietnam experience was divided. Vietnam offered few instances of the prolonged, total exposure of the landings at Normandy or Iwo Jima. But while the objective danger may have been lower, the subjective danger was exaggerated by the nature of the war. Combat involved constant patrolling, days and days of suspense waiting for an ambush or a booby trap, and then short, intense firefights followed by more suspense. Moreover, the deliberate helicopter insertion of units into known hostile territory, their deliberate use to lure attacks, and their deliberate stationing in isolated firebases, meant that the war had no front and no rear. Nor was there any temporal distinction between battle and rest. The war was all the time and everywhere. For the individual soldier, terror could be constant because the killing zone was inescapable. As one vet put it, "Complete safety was always relative in Vietnam, and therefore combat paranoia was endemic."[18]

To understand the Vietnam combat experience, it is essential to understand not only the combat environment, but also how and how well soldiers coped with it. This requires a shift of focus to the "human element," for as John Keegan observes:

> What battles have in common is human: the behavior of men struggling to reconcile their instinct for self-preservation, their sense of honor and the achievement of some aim over which other men are ready to kill them. The study of battle is therefore always a study of fear and usually of courage; always of leadership, usually of obedience; always of compulsion, sometimes of insubordination; . . . always of violence, sometimes also of cruelty, self-sacrifice, compassion; above all, it is always a study of solidarity and usually also of disintegration—for it is toward the disintegration of human groups that battle is directed.[19]

How well individuals cope with combat is largely a function of who they are; how mature, how intelligent, and how educated. During and after World War II, sociologist Samuel Stouffer and his collaborators in the *American Soldier* study found that older, smarter, better-educated men made better soldiers. Similarly, the U.S. Army's Human Research and Resources Organization's *Fighter* studies during the Korean War found that more intelligent, more socially mature and emotionally stable men performed better in combat.[20] The military manpower system brought such men into the armed services in World War II and the Korean War. During Vietnam, however, it did not. As one veteran put it, "We were capriciously plucked from our relatively selfish lives and tossed into a world we had neither the wisdom and experience to understand nor the resources to defend against . . . Just a bunch of kids hoping we had a life ahead of us."[21] Vietnam might have been called the Children's Crusade.

The average age of those who saw combat in Vietnam was just nineteen—compared to twenty-seven in World War II and even older in Korea. As adolescents, they lacked the balance and emotional maturity of older men and so were far more vulnerable to the psychological trauma of combat. Moreover, because of their age and the fact that the weight of the Vietnam draft fell most heavily on the disadvantaged, few had the educational background or worldliness to assess their experiences or to integrate them into an already varied personal history. Finally, because of the draft's biases, there were no older or better-educated men in the same units who could serve as role models.[22] Thus, the first combat legacy of the Vietnam-era military manpower system was an army of the emotionally vulnerable, one comprised of those least likely to possess the wisdom and maturity to cope with the terrors of combat.

But men do not face combat alone. To understand the human element of the combat experience fully requires understanding of the dynamics of the small group—the unit, platoon or fire team—in which the individual lives and from which he draws his strength. For in abstact discussions about war aims, strategy and weapons, it is easy to forget that in war *the* essential elements are men and the bonds of trust, respect and loyalty that bind them together on the battlefield, "the lonesomest place which men may share together."[23] The keys to these—and so to combat effectiveness and soldiers' psychological well-being—are leadership and unit cohesion. Unfortunately, here too the effects of the American manpower system eroded the cohesion of fighting units and thus increased the pressure on individuals.

Combat leadership requires that troops respect the professional competence of their officers and believe that their officers will fight and die with them. Both have long been the hallmark of the British and German armies. British Field Marshall William Slim, who personally led the campaign to retake Burma (one of the nastiest of World War II), is famous for admonishing his officers upon taking command, "I tell you, as officers, that you will not eat, sleep, smoke, sit down, or lie down until your soldiers have had a chance to do these things. If you hold to this, they will follow you to the ends of the earth. If you do not, I will *break you in front of your regiments*."[24] His men followed him proudly, confident in the example he set and his obvious professionalism. Similarly, the German Wehrmacht performed well in World War II because German officers *led* their men into combat—as evidenced by the fact that one-third of German generals were killed in combat and casualty rates for the officer corps as a whole exceeded those of enlisted men.[25]

American policy in Vietnam, however, removed senior officers from the field and eroded soldiers' respect for their professional competence. During the entire war just four American generals were killed—three in non-combat-related helicopter crashes and one by sniper fire. Casualty figures for officers as junior as captain were also very low. And because those directing operations "led" from helicopters circling two thousand feet above the battle, there was little experienced leadership on the battlefield for the troops to follow. Indeed, most combat took place under the command of inexperienced, twenty-one-year-old lieutenants just out of ROTC or Officer Candidate School and with less than two years in the service. Moreover, the military placed officers with units for six-month tours—half the enlisted man's tour. This gave a maximum number of officers combat experience, but minimized the professionalism of American combat leadership. Effective command of units in combat often devolved to their noncommissioned officers (NCOs), but as the war went on, high casualty rates among senior NCOs meant the promotion of increasingly inexperienced and often incompetent men from the ranks.[26] In short, combat infantrymen had little leadership, and hence the Marine Corps joke: "What's the difference between the Marine Corps and the Boy Scouts?—The Boy Scouts have adult leadership."[27] The price of absence of leadership in Vietnam is readily apparent in the rapid fall of troop morale after 1968 and the rapid rise in the incidence of drug use, insubordination, and, most seriously, of fragging.

The soldier's second defense against the terror of combat is the small group. Effective fighting forces—and soldiers feel safest in such units—are not composed of militarists or patriotic zealots. In fact, studies of successful units often reveal troops who hate the military, are indifferent to the big issues of the war, and just want to go home. As military sociologist Charles Moskos notes, a unit's members must share "an underlying commitment to the worth of the larger social system for which [they are] fighting,"[28] but what makes them effective are the ties binding the unit together and a shared professional competence born of long experience together. As S. L. A. Marshall observes, "the thing which enables an infantry soldier to keep going with his weapons is the near presence or presumed presence of a comrade," because

> in life and death situations, ordinary soldiers do not think of themselves as subordinate members of whatever formal military organization [they are assigned to], but as equals within a very tiny group—perhaps no more than six or seven men. They are not exact equals, of course, because at least one . . . will be looked to for leadership. But it will not be because of his or anyone else's leadership that the group member will begin to fight and continue to fight. It will be . . . for personal survival, which individuals will recognize to be bound up with group survival, and . . . for fear of incurring the group's contempt by cowardly conduct.[29]

As General Volnay Warner put it more bluntly, "soldiers fight and die for one another, not for country, or even 'Ma' and 'apple pie'."[30] Indeed, the common thread running through virtually all studies of which units stand and which break is the importance of bonds of friendship and trust that unite the members of units and make them willing to sacrifice for one another. No less important, the more cohesive the unit, the better individual soldiers cope with the trauma of combat.

Traditionally, military organizations have gone to extraordinary lengths to foster unit cohesion. The British, for example, cultivate regimental identities by teaching new recruits their regiment's history and lore. During World War II the German General Staff sought to nurture similar unit identities by moving units into and out of the line as units. Initially, American soldiers also trained, shipped out and fought together; in some cases they had years to develop intimate ties with their fellows. As casualties mounted, however, the military found it more efficient administratively to replace losses piecemeal rather than to rotate units out of the line and rebuild them. The resulting system degraded combat performance and "possessed a strong inherent tendency to turn men into nervous wrecks."[31] (As one new replacement put it, "Being a replacement is like being an orphan.")[32] During the Korean War this practice was continued in the form of a system of individual rotations. This dulled public criticisms of the war effort and eased the problems of managing manpower, but it played havoc with unit cohesiveness and combat effectiveness.[33] Despite these well recognized drawbacks, however, individual rotations were continued in Vietnam in the form of the 365-day system.

The 365-day rotation system offered great political and managerial benefits. Politically, limiting an individual's tour in Vietnam to 365 days (thirteen months for a Marine) spread the burden of combat as widely as possible across the American population and served, as General Westmoreland put it, to "extend the nation's staying power by forestalling premature public pressure to 'bring the boys home.'"[34] By the same token, the piecemeal assignment of soldiers to units as needed posed far fewer managerial problems than training, committing and withdrawing units as units. Conversely, however, the 365-day rotation destroyed unit cohesiveness and left each man to look out for himself. As psychiatrist Peter Bourne observed,

> The war becomes a highly individualized and encapsulated event for each man. His war begins the day he arrives in the country and ends the day he leaves. He feels no continuity with those who precede or follow him; he even feels apart from those who are with him but rotating on a different schedule. The universal objective is the personal DEROS—Date Expected to Return from Overseas—a day known exactly to each man from the moment he arrives in Vietnam . . . In this and other ways the system [creates] the combat ethos which distinguishes Vietnam from Korea or World War II—namely, the intensely personalized struggle of each individual to survive emotionally and physically until his own day to return to the United States.[35]

Friendships did develop—they had to—and many units did develop an identity.[36] But of the possible ways of organizing combat forces, the system of 365-day individual rotations minimized the prospects for unit cohesion and maximized the psychological pressures placed on the individual infantryman.

Taken together, these elements of the combat experience—the nature of the war, exposure, the individual, battlefield leadership and small group—also account for veterans' readjustment and so for a war's long-term legacy.

The Human Legacy of Vietnam

Despite the Hollywood stereotype of the emotionally crippled Vietnam veteran, most are now settled middle-class family men with solid jobs and mortgages. According to a study by Josefina Card analyzing data on thousands of young men from the high school class of 1963 who served and did not serve, Vietnam veterans *on average* have not been severely handicapped.[37] By the age of thirty-six, their average educational attainment actually surpassed that of non-veterans in certain areas and black veterans appear to be better-educated than black non-veterans.[38] Similarly, on average veterans show rates of home ownership and levels of savings equal to non-veterans. Substance abuse and criminality, two often discussed problems, are not disporportionately evident. Still, Card discovered, even in 1981 Vietnam veterans continued to pay a high price for their service—and will do so for the rest of their lives. On average, they had lower-prestige jobs than non-veterans, earned $3,000 less per year, suffered higher job instability and rates of unemployment, and "had more problems than their peers in getting on track in their work and in abiding by rules to stay on track." Equally important, they showed higher incidents of problems related to social interaction, anxiety, and depression than their peers.[39]

But aggregate statistics for Vietnam veterans as a whole are misleading, for they lump together the 20 percent who faced combat with the 80 percent who did not. And although we largely ignore the human legacy of Vietnam, it is clear from the evidence that for the combat veteran it is a terrible one.

We are not the first to ignore the ways in which the combat experience haunts veterans long after the guns fall silent. Until recently, how men behaved in combat was assumed to be a simple matter of courage or cowardice, "with no sense that there might be a lasting price to be paid even for bravery."[40] (When asked how long it takes soldiers to get over combat, Audie Murphy, the most decorated soldier in World War II, replied, "I don't think they ever do." Murphy himself had nightmares the rest of his life and could not sleep without a loaded pistol by his bed.) Since

World War I, the military has studied combat psychology, but with the aim of returning men to battle as quickly as possible; little effort has been devoted to healing its lasting psychological trauma. Today, however, there is no mistaking either the continuing price combat veterans pay for their service or the fact that the price exacted by this war is singularly high by comparison to other wars.

Comparisons of Vietnam combat veterans with their non-veteran peers reveal a pattern of continuing psychological problems including nightmares, panic attacks, emotional numbing, withdrawal, hyperalertness, anxiety, and depression which fit the American Psychiatric Association diagnosis of post-traumatic stress disorder (PTSD) almost perfectly.[41] Studies indicate that at any time PTSD afflicts between 12 and 19 percent of the population at large (for example, people who have survived terrible car accidents, muggings, and floods), but afflicts between 27 and 35 percent of Vietnam veterans who saw heavy combat.[42] Indeed, a recently completed study conducted over five years by Steven and Jeanne Mager Stellman indicates that 65 percent of veterans who saw heavy combat suffer from PTSD.[43] Among them, PTSD manifests itself in two basic forms. For some the war continues; mistrust, hyperalertness and aggressiveness—the requirements for survival in combat—continue to dominate. For most, however, it is the mourning that never ends, mourning related to guilt at having survived when friends died, or guilt over actions committed or witnessed in Vietnam. In both cases, veterans are often clinically depressed and, even if they do not behave destructively or demand attention, "their anguish is all the greater from keeping it to themselves." They fear that their Vietnam experience may hurt those they love or estrange them; for, as one put it, "killing both makes you unclean and sets you apart from others."[44]

In its acute forms, PTSD manifests itself in broken families, substance abuse, criminal activity and suicide.[45] Here, too, lies the bitter, sad irony of the stereotype Vietnam veterans suffer under—many feel compelled to hide the source of their anguish lest they be stereotyped and so ostracized or discriminated against. The statistics are sketchy and controversial, but the pattern seems clear. PTSD-afflicted veterans are more likely than their non-veteran peers to be divorced, separated or living alone. Their wives and lovers, too, pay an unrecognized price for their men's service in Vietnam in the form of emotional withdrawal, family disruption, and both emotional and physical abuse. Drug and alcohol abuse is also commonly associated with Vietnam veterans, but often inaccurately. Drug and alcohol abuse among combat veterans is not a continuation of addictions begun in Vietnam, as many believe; in most, it is a *postwar* development tied to PTSD. Similarly, while the great majority of Vietnam veterans returned to law-abiding lives, those who saw heavy combat are disproportionately represented in American prisons. Most of these men had no past criminal record; their criminality is linked to PTSD. Finally, while some PTSD sufferers vent their rage in crime and others dull their pain with drugs and alcohol, many try to protect their loved ones from the former and escape from the latter by suicide. Thus, for example, the Centers for Disease Control reported in 1987 that five years after the war's end Vietnam veterans were dying at a rate 45 percent higher than those who did not serve in Vietnam, had a 72 percent higher suicide rate, and a higher incidence of violent deaths in general (homicides, suicides, motor vehicle accidents, accidental poisonings and drug overdoses).[46]

But if PTSD is the inevitable price of war for combat veterans, it is necessary to look to the Vietnam combat experience itself to explain why the incidence of PTSD is so very high among Vietnam combat veterans.[47] The simplest, but most often overlooked explanation is Vietnam veterans' relatively greater exposure to combat. In her study of Vietnam veterans, for example, Josefina Card found that "it is almost completely the intensity of the combat experience that determines who will come down with [PTSD] after the war is over and how severe the disorder will be."[48] Other authors agree, but suggest that additional elements of the Vietnam combat experience play a role as well.

Two aspects of the nature of the war in Vietnam cause veterans particular anguish. First, a crucial element in a veteran's readjustment is the belief that the war and his experiences have "purpose and significance beyond the immediate horrors he witnessed. He can then connect his own actions with ultimately humane principles, and can come to feel that he had performed a dirty, but necessary, job." The chaotic way this war was fought, however, led many to conclude that it—and the risks they faced— had no purpose; "there was no genuine 'script' . . . of war that could provide meaning or even sequence or progression, a script within which armies clash, battles are fought, won, or lost, and individual suffering, courage, cowardice, or honor can be evaluated." Without a sense of purpose, noted a Veterans Administration psychiatrist, many saw the war as just "an exercise in survival rather than a defense of national values."[49] Indeed, many veterans returned bitter that their "government's commitment was less than wholehearted, and that their lives and those of their friends were being wasted."[50] This sense of purposelessness deepened with the veteran's return to a country which by 1971 believed that veterans were "suckers, having to risk their lives in the wrong war, in the wrong place, at the wrong time."[51] Faced with a largely indifferent or hostile reception, many veterans were unable to reintegrate themselves into the fabric of their communities. They remain alienated and alone in their effort to give meaning to their combat experiences.[52]

Second, the guerrilla nature of the Vietnam War and the military command's decision to pursue a policy of attrition left many combat veterans with a lasting legacy of guilt for their actions. Note Hendin and Haas:

> To a degree unparalleled in our earlier wars, combat in Vietnam involved the killing of women, children, and the elderly; some of who were armed fighters, some of whom were killed inadvertently, and some of whom were killed in retaliation for deaths caused by their countrymen. Regardless of the circumstances, and even in situations where the veteran had to kill to save his life, guilt over such killing is profoundly disturbing to most veterans and plays, in comparison with other wars, a far more significant role in the stress disorders of Vietnam veterans.[53]

This guilt is a particularly heavy burden to bear, since perhaps more than any other aspect of the Vietnam legacy, both it and its origins repel the average American.

The high incidence of PTSD among Vietnam veterans also reflects the legacy of military manpower policy during the war. First, the extreme youth of American soldiers in Vietnam made them particularly susceptible to psychological trauma. At nineteen many simply lacked the maturity, "the inner sense of structure, purposefulness, judgment, and emotional balance," required to cope with combat. Those few combat veterans who have largely escaped PTSD are those who possessed "calmness under pressure, intellectual control, ability to create and impose a sense of structure, [and] acceptance of their own and others' emotions and limitations"—i.e., the mature few.[54] Second, the vulnerability of youth was exaggerated by poor battlefield leadership.[55] Most important, however, is the 365-day system which had the effect of "insuring that more veterans would experience stress symptoms after they returned home" by destroying unit cohesiveness in Vietnam.[56] Veterans with the fewest negative effects from their service in Vietnam are those who report the greatest trust and cohesiveness in their units, while those with the most negative effects report the least.[57]

Bringing the War Home

After World War II American soldiers returned en masse to joyous parades.[58] They came home by troop ship or troop train to be greeted by brass bands and speeches, respect and admiration. Vietnam veterans returned alone. Without fanfare, they were reinserted into civilian life one by one as they completed their tours, just as they had been inserted into combat one by one a year earlier. They came home the orphans of the war, returning to a country busy with other things and too deeply split by the war to face the needs of those who had been sent to fight it. Washington would not defend them, for neither the Johnson nor the Nixon administration wished to call attention to the war's human cost; indeed, both depended on the atomizing effects of the draft and the 365-day system to minimize public opposition and, as General Westmoreland put it, "extend the nation's staying power." To many who supported the American cause in Vietnam, they came home defeated, responsible for having lost a war that could and should have been won. To many who opposed the war, they came home criminals, responsible for the murder of civilians and the rape of Vietnam. Embittered by their reception, many veterans hid their service from friends, employers and coworkers and bottled up their hurt inside. As one veteran blurted out to others complaining about their treatment, "Well, we bring it on ourselves by telling them we're Vietnam veterans. Next time someone asks me where I was I'll say I spent three years in Arkansas."[59]

America finally rediscovered the Vietnam veteran in the late 1970s, but for most veterans the rediscovery was a mixed blessing. On the one hand, a handful of responsible journalists gave their story serious treatment. In 1978, for example, Tracy Kidder introduced the *Atlantic's* readers to the "Soldiers of Misfortune," and in 1979 Marlene Cimons informed readers of the *Los Angeles Times* about PTSD.[60] Far more common, however, were Hollywood and television depictions of veterans as deranged and violent psychopaths. Ironically, both images of the Vietnam veteran served a similar and pernicious end. As Tim O'Brien, himself a Vietnam veteran, observed,

> The nation seems too comfortable with—even dependent on—the image of a suffering and deeply troubled veteran. Rather than face our own culpabilities, we shove them off onto ex-GIs and let them suffer for us. Rather than relive old tragedies, rather than confront our own frustrations and puzzlements about the war, we take comfort in the image of the bleary-eyed veteran carrying all that emotional baggage for us.[61]

Even before allied troops hit the beaches of Normandy, the United States government was planning for veterans' return to civilian life. "If society owes an obligation to these men and women," asked *Marching Home,* a Columbia Teachers College report on the subject, "how is it to be discharged? . . . They do not ask for charity, and no form of dole, 'relief' or 'made work' will satisfy them. They ask only absorption in the economic, governmental, and social life of the nation as rapidly and as painlessly as possible."[62] To this end, the government mounted an extraordinary organizational and publicity campaign to educate and mobilize families, communities, and state and local government agencies. At its heart was the GI Bill of Rights which sent nearly 40 percent of eligible veterans to college in the five years after World War II and laid the educational foundation for postwar American prosperity.[63]

Vietnam veterans received very different treatment; for a decade and a half they have fought an uphill battle for recognition in the White House and Congress. In 1966, President Johnson signed the first Vietnam-era GI

Bill into law. It offered exactly the same benefits World War II veterans received—despite the doubling of state college tuitions and the quadrupling of private college tuitions.[64] Subsequent efforts to raise GI benefits to reflect inflation and the real cost of education fell short. In 1969 the Nixon administration opposed a proposed 46 percent increase, cutting it to 25 percent; in 1972 a proposed 43 percent increase was also cut in half; and in 1974 the administration impounded extra funds set aside by Congress to supplement veterans' educational stipends. Behind in the beginning, the GI Bill served less and less well with each reduction in needed increases. As a result, where the original GI Bill opened new opportunities for working-class families, in the Vietnam era those who needed it the most were the least likely to be able to use it. As early as 1969 a government study commission found that

> nearly 50% of the veterans who already have college training at the time of discharge and therefore have the best prospects for immediate employment seek to upgrade their education under the G.I. Bill. On the other hand, those who have serious education deficiencies show participation rates as low as 10%.[65]

In 1978, a study by the Veterans Administration found that while World War II veterans were 46 percent more likely to have a college diploma than their non-veteran peers, Vietnam veterans were 45 percent less likely.

No less cruel has been Vietnam veterans' often callous treatment by the VA hospital system.[66] Most scandalous, of course, has been the VA's well-documented denial of the long-term consequences of Agent Orange exposure for veterans and their children.[67] Far less well known, but no less painful, has been the VA's poor handling of the lingering trauma of Vietnam veterans' battlefield wounds. In part, the problem reflected breakthroughs in battlefield medicine, especially helicopter medical evacuation, which meant that far more critically wounded men were surviving to burden the VA. In large measure, however, the problem was that the VA was no longer organized to provide acute care for several hundred thousand young, seriously wounded combatants. Since 1945 it had become a chronic care facility for millions of aging World War II veterans. Their numbers and political clout outweigh those of Vietnam veterans to the extent that, until recently, the VA responded to their needs, not to those of Vietnam veterans.

In addition to often mediocre care for their physical complaints, Vietnam veterans received no psychological readjustment assistance from the VA. Indeed, despite pressure from key congressmen and senators since 1971, as late as 1977 "the VA had yet to do a serious, empirical study of the actual adjustment needs of Vietnam veterans."[68] In 1971 a group of senators sought to create a new program to provide readjustment, drug, and alcohol counseling for Vietnam veterans. The bill died in the House, the victim of lobbying by the major veterans' organizations, which viewed it as a threat to the VA health program for their constituents. Again in 1973, 1975, and 1978 they and House Veterans' Affairs Committee leaders blocked passage of the Readjustment Counseling Program. Finally, in 1979, the bill became law, and by late in the year counseling centers were opening. A year later, newly elected President Ronald Reagan's first act in office was to freeze hiring in the Readjustment Counseling Program. He soon moved to eliminate all Vietnam veteran outreach programs, including an employment training program for disabled veterans, though Congress saved some of the funding.[69] References to veterans' sacrifices aside, even the Reagan administration was unwilling to confront the uglier aspects of the human legacy of Vietnam.

Three things explain Vietnam veterans' inability to make their needs heard. The first is the divisiveness of the war itself. Even now, Americans have yet to face its legacy and are still unready to recognize its most painful reminder among us, the veterans. Second, until recently, Vietnam veterans were ignored or opposed by the major veterans organizations, the American Legion and the Veterans of Foreign Wars. On the one hand, members of both organizations strongly supported the American cause in Vietnam and often blame Vietnam veterans for defeat. On the other, Legion and VFW leadership believed that programs to serve Vietnam veterans' needs and interests threatened those serving the needs and interests of their constituents, aging World War II veterans. Thus, until the early 1980s, the Legion and the VFW lobbied aggressively and successfully to block development of outreach, drug rehabilitation, and psychological counseling programs for Vietnam veterans unless they were funded independently of the VA and would have no impact on programs for older veterans. This opposition has now been reversed as Vietnam-ear veterans have come to constitute a substantial portion of total membership of these organizations and have at last risen to leadership positions.

Finally, Vietnam veterans lack the political clout to get their way. In part, this is merely a matter of numbers: three million young, politically innocent Vietnam veterans versus twelve million mature, politically sophisticated World War II veterans—and every other interest group in Washington. More important, Vietnam veterans' political impotence is the final, sad legacy of Vietnam-era military manpower policy. Just two years after World War II, there were ninety-two veterans in Congress, 20 percent of the combined House and Senate. In 1980, seven years after American troops left Vietnam, there were four Vietnam veterans in Congress, just .7 percent of the combined Congress. Nor were Vietnam veterans represented indirectly by congressmen and senators whose sons had served, because virtually none *had* served.[70] Being disproportionately poor, minority and working-class, Vietnam veterans were both underrepresented in Congress and handicapped in their efforts to organize to represent their own interests. It is the final insult; sent to a war the well-heeled could avoid, they are now unable to win either recognition for their service or help in coping with its lingering consequences.

Conclusion

What, then, is the human legacy of the Vietnam War? It is a legacy of pain, a legacy of physical and emotional hurt born of the trauma of veterans' combat experience and their rejection upon returning home. It is a legacy of unfulfilled promises and lingering, unmet needs. It is a legacy of disillusionment, of veterans not proud of their service to their country, but embittered by it, whose most common response to the question "How did military service affect you?" is that it reduced their civic pride and faith in America.[71]

But for Americans, veterans and non-veterans alike, the legacy of Vietnam is also a double challenge. On the one hand, we face the challenge of the past, not to deny it as we did for ten years, or swaddle it in rhetoric and rationalizations as we do today, but to confront it. "We are a people divided," observe Robert Muller and Jan Scruggs, "Antiwar activitists and proud veterans are separated by more than the war itself. They are divided by a contentiousness that threatens to become the only permanent legacy of the Vietnam War. There must be something better to be won from the war years."[72] If there is not, the Vietnam War will go down in history not only as a military defeat, but as a moral, political, and cultural one, as a time when a dispute over national policy poisoned the wellspring of the nation itself. The legacy of Vietnam is also a challenge for the future. "For societies, as for individuals some decisions have to count," note Muller and Scruggs, "We have to honor them despite changes in circumstances . . . War is one of those decisions that should be neither easily undertaken nor quickly pushed aside." The Vietnam legacy marks our past failure to heed this warning—and foreshadows the consequences of future failures to do so. Given the price we have paid for Vietnam, it is an admonition we can ill afford to ignore.

NOTES

1. Karl von Clausewitz, *On War,* trans. Peter Paret and Michael Howard (Princeton: Princeton University Press, 1976), pp. 69, 605.

2. Military historian John Keegan offers a brilliant analysis of the battlefield experience in *The Face of Battle* (New York: Viking Press, 1976).

3. S. L. A. Marshall, *Men Against Fire* (New York: William Morrow, 1947).

4. Paul Fussell, *The Great War in Modern Memory* (New York: Oxford University Press, 1975), p. 83.

5. I am indebted to Richard Sullivan for this point. For a powerful evocation of "being in the bush," see James Webb, *Fields of Fire* (New York: Bantam, 1979), chaps. 4–6.

6. Michael Herr, *Dispatches* (New York: Alfred A. Knopf, 1977), p. 10.

7. Captain G. B. Pollard, cited in Fussell, *The Great War in Modern Memory,* pp. 9–10.

8. One veteran commented on an earlier draft of this chapter: "The most notorious example of this in my experience was General Bersanti's revision of the 101st [Airborne] SOP [standard operating procedure] at the end of my tour. He made the bait idea into a division battle strategy. The idea was to send out platoon- or company-sized units into an NVA AO [North Vietnamese Army Area of Operations] and to have a battalion-sized reaction force standing by . . . The bait would wiggle around until it got hit, then . . . the reaction force [would] encircle the contact area and move in until the 'enemy' was surrounded and destroyed. Problem was, it . . . took hours (sometimes a full day) for the reaction force to arrive . . . Then, when they did arrive, the gooks generally *had* split, or if they hadn't, the 'bait' caught the same shit as the 'enemy'. It got really tight when Blood'n Balls [Bersanti] had us doing it at night. This was the main 'strategy' of the second (August) A Shau sweep, when the 101st got its ass really kicked—60% casualties." Personal communication.

9. Alain Enthoven, Memorandum for the Secretary of Defense, 4 May 1967, in *The Senator Gravel Edition: The Pentagon Papers* (Boston: Beacon Press, 1971), p. 462.

10. Comments a soldier in Charles Durden's fictional *No Bugles, No Drums* (New York: Charter Books, 1978), "grunts" were "the ultimate in throwaway people . . . The ultimate luxury of a throwaway society."

11. Cited in Robert Jay Lifton, *Home from the War: Vietnam Veterans, Neither Victims nor Executioners* (New York: Basic Books, 1985), p. 45.

12. Quoted in Herr, *Dispatches,* p. 20.

13. Cited in Lifton, *Home from the War,* p. 37.

14. Lists culled from various literary works, Paul Fussell, *The Great War in Modern Memory,* chap. 3.

15. GIs' feelings show clearly in the macabre humor of jokes such as this one about how to win the war: "What you do is, you load all the Friendlies [the South Vietnamese] onto ships and take them out into the China Sea. Then you bomb the country flat. Then you sink the ships." Quoted in Herr, *Dispatches,* p. 59.

16. Edward N. Luttwak, "With the Boring Parts Left Out" (review of *Acts of War,* by Richard Holmes, and *Soldiers,* by John Keegan and Richard Holmes), *New York Times Book Review,* 23 March 1986, p. 13.

17. Study by Lt. Col. J. W. Appel and Capt. G. W. Beebe, cited in Richard Holmes, *Acts of War: The Behavior of Men in Battle* (New York: Free Press, 1985), p. 215

18. Cited in Myra MacPherson, *Long Time Passing: Vietnam and the Haunted Generation* (New York: New American Library, 1985), p. 58. Or, as Michael Herr observed: "You could be in the most protected space in Vietnam and still know that your safety was provisional, that early death, blindness, loss of legs, arms or balls, major and lasting disfigurement, the whole rotten deal—could come in on the freaky-funky as easily as in the so-called expected ways." *Dispatches*, p. 14.

19. Keegan, *The Face of Battle*, pp. 297–98.

20. See David Marlowe, "The Manning of the Force and the Structure of Battle," in *Conscripts and Volunteers: Military Requirements, Social Justice and the All-Volunteer Force*, ed. Robert Fullinwider (Rowman and Allen, 1983), p. 50.

21. Personal communication. See D. Michael Shafer, "The Vietnam-Era Draft: Who Went, Who Didn't, and Why It Matters," in this volume.

22. One of the most important findings of S. L. A. Marshall's research during World War II was that units mixed as to education, social class, and age performed much better, and (no less important) that individual soldiers in them both performed and felt better.

23. Marshall, *Men Against Fire*, p. 47.

24. Cited in James Fallows, *The National Defense* (New York: Random House, 1981), p. 110.

25. Paul L. Savage and Richard Gabriel, "Cohesion and Disintegration in the American Army," *Armed Forces and Society* 2:3 (May 1976), pp. 343–44.

26. Even General William Westmoreland, commander of U.S. forces in Vietnam, admitted that "we had to lower our standards to provide the officers and noncommissioned officers to man this Army. . . ." Cited Lawrence Baskir and William Strauss, *Chance and Circumstance: The Draft, the War and the Vietnam Generation* (New York: Knopf, 1978), p. 149. The major study of leadership breakdown in Vietnam is Richard Gabriel and Paul L. Savage, *Crisis in Command* (New York: Hill and Wang, 1978).

27. Quoted in Herr, *Dispatches*, p. 101.

28. Charles Moskos, Jr., *The American Enlisted Man* (New York: Sage, 1970), pp. 145–46.

29. Marshall, *Men Against Fire*, p. 42.

30. Interview in the *Senior Officers Oral History Project*, U.S. Military History Institute, U.S. Army War College, Carlisle Barracks, Carlisle Barracks, Pa., p. 232. The classic study of unit cohesion is Edward Shils and Morris Janowitz, "Cohesion and Disintegration in the Wehrmacht in World War II," *Public Opinion Quarterly* 12 (Summer 1948). See also J. Glenn Gray, *The Warriors: Reflections on Men in Battle* (New York: Harcourt Brace, 1959) and, for Vietnam, James Martin Davis, "Vietnam: What It Was Really Like," *Military Review* 69 (January 1989).

31. Martin van Creveld, *Fighting Power: German and U.S. Army Performance, 1939–1945* (Westport: Greenwood, 1982), p. 79.

32. Quoted in Samuel Stouffer et al., *The American Soldier*, vol. 2, *Combat and Its Aftermath* (Princeton: Princeton University Press, 1949), p. 273.

33. Asked about the rotation system in Korea, S. L. A. Marshall observed that the Chinese "sit there year after year. The longer they stay, the smarter they get. Our youngsters keep moving in and out. They're smart and they've got guts, but they don't stay long enough to learn." Ten years later, Colonel John Paul Vann commented, "We don't have twelve years' experience in Vietnam. We have one year's experience twelve times over." Cited in Eliot Cohen, *Citizens and Soldiers:*

The Dilemmas of Military Service (Ithaca: Cornell University Press, 1985), pp. 104, 107.

34. General William C. Westmoreland, *A Soldier Reports* (New York: Dell, 1980), p. 392.

35. Peter Bourne, *Men, Stress and Vietnam* (Boston: Little, Brown & Co., 1970), pp. 41–42.

36. These identities often had a distinctly subversive quality. A veteran commenting on an earlier draft of this chapter noted that commanding officers often "tried to instill pride in unit history, at base camp formation and funeral services, where the guidons would be unfurled. But the grunts typically made it all into a series of obscene jokes. My unit [the 327th] was called the 'Bastogne Bulldogs' . . . and we had signs about that shit all over base camp at Phu Bai. We had all our fire bases named for World War II battles—Bastogne, Veghle, etc. But we heard through rumor central about how many of our glider-riding predecessors had been greased at Bastogne and Veghle and so on. Among ourselves, we called our platoon the 'Shades of Wierd' . . . You might . . . say a word or two here about the vast numbers of macabre, unauthorized unit patches and names that were cooked up in Vietnam, mostly directly in opposition to official unit histories and names." Personal communication.

37. Josefina Card, *Lives After Vietnam: The Personal Impact of Military Service* (Lexington, Mass.: D.C. Heath, 1983).

38. Ibid., pp. 37–38, 49, 51.

39. Ibid., pp. 70–71, 91–92, 100.

40. Herbert Hendin and Ann Pollinger Haas, *Wounds of War: The Psychological Aftermath of Combat in Vietnam* (New York: Basic Books, 1984), p. 16

41. The American Psychiatric Association, *Diagnostic and Statistical Manual,* 3rd ed. (Washington, D.C: American Psychiatric Association, 1980), lists four indicators of PTSD: (1) "Exposure to recognizable stressor or trauma;" (2) "Re-experiencing of trauma through flashbacks, nightmares, or intrusive memories;" (3) "Emotional numbing to or withdrawal from external environment;" and (4) "The experience of at least two symptoms from a list including hyperalertness, sleep disturbance, survival guilt, memory impairment, and avoidance of situations that may elicit traumatic recollection." See, too, C. B. Scrignar, *Post-Traumatic Stress Disorder: Diagnosis, Treatment, and Legal Issues* (New York: Praeger, 1984) and Ghislaine Boulanger, "Post-Traumatic Stress Disorder: An Old Problem with a New Name," in *The Trauma of War: Stress and Recovery in Viet Nam Veterans,* ed. Stephen M. Sonnenberg (New York: American Psychiatric Press, Inc., 1985).

42. Card, *Lives After Vietnam,* p. 115. Given the disproportionately large number of blacks in combat units, the incidence of PTSD—and it ravages—is also disproportionately high among black veterans. See Peter B. Levy, "Blacks and the Vietnam War," in this volume.

43. The study was based on questionnaire and interview data from 6,810 American Legion members in Colorado, Indiana, Maryland, Minnesota, Ohio and Pennsylvania. See all five articles of the December 1988 Special Issue of *Environmental Research* ("New Light on the Health of Vietnam Veterans") vol. 47:2 (December 1988).

44. Hendin and Haas, *Wounds of War,* pp. 109, 119.

45. Ibid., pp. 133–36, 160–61, 183–88.

46. Cited in Richard Severo and Lewis Milford, *The Wages of War: When America's Soldiers Came Home—From Valley Forge to Vietnam* (New York: Simon and Schuster, 1989), pp. 410.

47. Indeed, note Hendin and Haas, "perhaps the most frequent question raised by the psychological aftermath of Vietnam is why stress responses to combat should be more pervasive after this particular war." *Wounds of War,* p. 15.

48. Card, *Lives After Vietnam,* pp. 107, 108–09.

49. Lifton, *Home from the War,* pp. 38–39, 190, 40–41.

50. Hendin and Haas, *Wounds of War,* pp. 8–9.

51. Louis Harris poll, cited in Baskir and Strauss, *Chance and Circumstance,* p. 6.

52. See Richard Moser, "Talkin' the Vietnam Blues: Vietnam Oral History and Our Popular Memory of War," in this volume.

53. Hendin and Haas, *Wounds of War,* p. 4.

54. Ibid., pp. 233, 214.

55. Indeed, psychiatrist Peter Bourne contends that "foremost in importance" in explaining variance in combat stress in Vietnam "was the quality of leadership and the effect it had upon the morale of the troops." *Men, Stress and Vietnam,* p. 16.

56. Hendin and Haas, *Wounds of War,* p. 7.

57. Card, *Lives After Vietnam,* p. 128.

58. Interestingly, World War II was the exception in this. See Severo and Milford, *The Wages of War.*

59. Cited in Lifton, *Home from the War,* p. 288.

60. Tracy Kidder, "Soldiers of Misfortune," *Atlantic Monthly* 241:3 (March 1978); and Marlene Cimons, "Delayed Stress: Vietnam's Deadly Legacy," "Two Stories of War Veterans as Victims," "Rap Session as Therapy," and "A Mother to the World," *Los Angeles Times,* 29 July 1979, 30 July 1979.

61. Tim O'Brien, "The Violent Vet," *Esquire* 92:6 (December 1979), p. 100. See, too, Severo and Milford, *The Wages of War,* pp. 421–2.

62. Morse Cartwright, *Marching Home: Educational and Social Adjustment After the War* (New York: Teachers College, Columbia University, 1944), pp. 19–20.

63. John Helmer, *Bringing the War Home: The American Soldier in Vietnam and After* (New York: Free Press, 1974), p. 224.

64. David Bonior, Steven Champlin and Timothy Kolly, *The Vietnam Veteran: A History of Neglect* (New York: Praeger, 1984), p. 80.

65. Committee on the Vietnam Veteran, cited in Bonior, Champlin and Kolly, *The Vietnam Veteran,* p. 81.

66. See Robert Klein, *Wounded Men, Broken Promises* (New York: Macmillan, 1981).

67. See John Dux and P. J. Young, *Agent Orange: The Bitter Harvest* (Sydney: Hodder and Stoughton, 1980); Fred Wilcox, *Waiting for an Army to Die: The Tragedy of Agent Orange* (New York: Vintage Books, 1983); Peter H. Schuck, *Agent Orange on Trial: Mass Toxic Disasters in the Courts,* enlarged edition (Cambridge: Harvard University Press, 1987); and Severo and Milford, *The Wages of War.*

68. Bonior, Champlin, and Kolly, *The Vietnam Veteran,* p. 113. See, too, Severo and Milford, *The Wages of War,* chaps. 23–27.

69. Bonior, Champlin and Kolly, *The Vietnam Veteran,* p. 76.

70. See the previous chapter in this volume, "Who Went, Who Didn't, and Why it Matters."

71. Card, *Lives After Vietnam,* p. 138. As one veteran told Hendin and Haas, "In Vietnam I lost my feelings for God, for my family, and for my country. My feelings for my family and for God are returning, but I don't think I'll ever get over my anger toward the United States." *Wounds of War,* p. 242.

72. Robert Muller and Jan Scruggs, Foreword to Bonior, Champlin and Kolly, *The Vietnam Veteran,* pp. vii–viii.

6

TALKIN' THE VIETNAM BLUES:
Vietnam Oral History and Our Popular Memory of War

RICHARD MOSER

I think I've gone through life being able to stand aside, look at myself as someone in the stream of history, wanting to know where I've been . . . where we're going and what's the meaning of it all. I have a need to try and understand Vietnam, its place in our history and to fit it into my life, to fit my own experience into my life, and try to make it more coherent, more meaningful.

–MIKE HEANY

Like Mike Heany, our nation still struggles to understand the Vietnam War and its impact on all of us. Clearly the most divisive event in recent American history, the Vietnam War threatened to dissolve the bonds which held us together. The war pulled us apart, and then reshaped us as individuals and as a nation. But what, exactly, is the story of Vietnam?

Listen closely to Vietnam veterans speak and you will hear the war and its legacy come alive, for the complexities, ambiguities, and contradictions of a nation coming to terms with war are nowhere more richly expressed than by veterans themselves. They are not specialists, like academics, journalists, film makers, or novelists; they are our neghbors. For too long we have ignored them, and so ignored a critical source in our collective effort to understand the war. But listening to their stories, it is easy to hear how Vietnam has crept into our everyday lives, language, and culture—and how jarringly memories of the war resonate with the grander harmonies of our cherished rendition of America's history and future.

Collecting stories, understanding them in terms of theme and story line, and analyzing their larger social meaning is the practice of oral history.[1] Like a well-written book, the tales soldiers spin can be understood and interpreted on a number of different levels if treated as narratives with themes, plots, and subplots. Consider, for example, the following narrative fragments, which exemplify emerging trends in Vietnam storytelling. In the first, a soldier struggles with himself and those around him to begin to remember and talk about the war:

Bob: It wasn't until the New York parade that I came out of the closet . . . I couldn't talk to any person in America my age about Vietnam. There was many of them against the war and I was not going to talk about it with them. And the Vietnam veterans—I couldn't find them . . . It was all coming together all about this time now so it's making sense. I began to talk to people who hadn't been old enough to form opinions about it . . . didn't have political thoughts, didn't march against the war, didn't call us baby killers and spit in our faces . . . Maybe I was better off in the 70's when I didn't mention anything to anybody. I don't know what I was gaining by not mentioning it but right now I begin to think I'm making too much out of it . . . For twenty years I have thought about Vietnam every single day—that makes no sense . . . I feel as though I want to put it behind me.[2]

In the following narrative segment an American advisor remembers his Vietnam experience as part of America's idealistic mission and historic cultural traditions:

Stephen: In my freshman year at Harvard, 1963–64, we raised money for Martin Luther King. And when he came to Boston I helped organize his march and argued with other students on behalf of civil rights. But I drew the line with friends over Vietnam who said Hanoi was right and Johnson was wrong. I couldn't accept such narrow-minded thinking about Southeast Asia, where the stakes for the people were so great . . .

Communism as an ideology is inconsistent with being Vietnamese. Because Vietnameseness depends on two underlying traits: One is individualism . . . As anybody who knows them can see, it's very hard to get them to work together . . . They don't believe in a collective approach or an overbearing government.

The second trait is that the Vietnamese believe in private property. Through the Buddhist notion of karma, to have property, lots of kids, and things going well for you is good fortune. No government or other person can legitimately take that away from you . . . The Communists know this, so they have tried to stomp out traditional culture and religious beliefs.

The American value scheme, based on individualism and private property, is very close to Vietnameseness in some curious ways. There's also remarkable parallels between the Vietnamese belief in fate and virtue and the old American Puritan notions of predestination.[3]

The next remembrance returns to the Vietnam War as a time when honorable expectations were dashed and cherished beliefs challenged in the contradictions and conflicts of that war:

Jan: After you were there for awhile . . . you begin to realize that something strange was going on here. They would claim things out of Washington that had nothing to do with the reality of what was going on in South Vietnam—starting with the fact that it was a dictatorship and they were claiming it was a democracy. You begin to realize at a certain point that we were the palace guard. Protecting those idiots from the people who were fed up with them . . . Some of the special forces people would come back from their missions and say we should be supporting the other side because these people have legitimate grievances, and the other side is the only ones who are really trying to do something for these people . . . This was a rather startling thing to hear because we had been led to believe that communists were behind everything . . . It became clear that this was a homegrown rebellion . . . And when the Buddhist demonstrations took place because the Saigon army started shooting Buddhists on Buddha's birthday, there were non-violent demonstrations in the streets all over South Vietnam. You would look out and see people you knew, people you drank in bars with, people who did our laundry, who shined our boots . . . You had several things going on that were tremendously contradictory for someone who wanted to be a professional soldier.[4]

These narratives introduce the main plots and themes which run through interviews with Vietnam veterans though there is, of course, a practically infinite inventory of stories, tales, jokes, and anecdotes. These may tempt us to consider them as a kind of pure recounting of the reality of the past—as the ultimate, or real story of the war—indeed, published collections of oral narratives often promote them as such. But the memories of Vietnam veterans, like all remembrances, show the telltale traces of social and cultural forces that actively shape both personal and collective memory. And while this evidence of transformation may discredit oral narratives as pure historical "documents," it makes analyzing the way veterans have attempted to make sense of their war experiences a powerful tool for understanding how we as a nation have come to understand Vietnam.

Although culture and memory may combine in many ways, particular ways of remembering become widely elaborated and win adherence from broad segments of our society. These patterns of remembrance—their structure, content, and interaction—comprise popular memory. Veterans' narratives help us understand popular memory, because like formal history, popular memory is expressed in the narrative form that storytelling takes. By allowing access to popular memory, veterans' narratives help us to understand how history, memory, and experience produce our conceptual understanding of the world, our worldview. Worldviews can be explicit and coherent, or absorbed uncritically as just "common sense." A person's worldview is their philosophy of life and is largely articulated through memory of the past. Much as contending political philosophies are related to opposing interpretations of history, different worldviews are related to different versions of popular memory.

Each veteran's story is a cultural construction, a tapestry woven from two threads; one is the more or less direct recall of events, the other is a more subtle meditation on the past animated by the present. Thus, while certain events are minimized, others loom large in the stories that constitute popular memory. Psychological, political, and social needs—in short, all the demands of life—inevitably impress themselves upon and reshape an individual's memory. Culture and memory interact to link the past and present in a comprehensible and meaningful way.

From this perspective, it is the patterns of remembrance, meaning and understanding in which the Vietnam legacy is to be found, not in the events as such. Through the welter of individual narratives it is possible to identify an emerging stock of stories we may consider as the expression of the Vietnam legacy—or rather legacies. For the divisive nature of the Vietnam War is reflected in the many, varied, and opposed readings of both the war and its cultural representations. These reduce to three basic types, or modes of popular memory, however, illustrated by three story lines that emerge from oral histories of the Vietnam War. Each is characterized by a different form of social and cultural relationship between veterans and the world around them, which in turn organizes the veterans's storytelling around a particular perspective.

In the first, *Vietnam amnesia,* America tries to forget Vietnam. The veteran's amnesia is culturally induced through a painful and ambiguous relationship with civilian society back in "The World." The site of remembrance in these narratives is not Vietnam but the homecoming. The details of the war itself practically disappear from the main plots of these stories because the postwar experience diminishes both Vietnam as an event and the veteran as a citizen.

In the second, now *dominant* variant of memory, the veteran narrator constructs a relationship with policymakers, then and now, by articulating a powerful vision of America's destiny. The characteristic site of remembrance is not the war as such but the uniquely universal role of America as the bearer of both innocence and civilization in the world. Stories of this kind recall the Vietnam experience through certain identifiable subplots, particularly the violence of combat, and the politics of victory and defeat.

In the third, or *alternative,* variant of remembrance the narrator's primary relationship is with other citizen-soldiers. In alternative memory the site of remembrance is the Vietnam War itself and the story is based on a shared experience of trial and transformation during war.

In each type of narrative, the *site of remembrance* becomes an organizing principle of memory, providing the primary plot around which other relationships and subplots revolve, if they appear at all. For example, in the alternative variant, the memory of the war becomes the point of perspective from which the role of America in the world is, or can be, reassessed.

But it is important to remember that the site of remembrance is determined by a social or cultural relationship and context, relationships which
embed the veterans deeply within the American milieu, and make their
oral testimony representative of our popular memory and expressive of
historical and cultural developments.

The Politics of Forgetting

*I'd hoped for years that if I could just tell my story . . . I could finally get it out
. . . put it behind me . . . It didn't work that way . . . There must be another
story I have forgotten that could explain it.*

—JILL MISHKEL, *A Piece of My Heart*

When American soldiers returned home the nation confronted the living
consequences of war—and rejected them. Veterans' stories embody the
concrete and lived experience of this pervasive cultural phenomenon
called *Vietnam amnesia* which is captured most powerfully perhaps by the
single most common narrative device employed in both oral history and
popular remembrance, the image of returning veterans being spit on.
The following story is typical.

> **Frank:** I was spit on. This gang of guys walking behind me threw peanuts at
> me . . . These guys were long-haired, long-bearded . . . We went out to a
> dance that night. All I had was my Class A uniform . . . People looking at me
> like, "You scum." They'd walk by and spit on the ground. And I got this tre-
> mendous feeling that I had done something wrong. It was like I wasn't sup-
> posed to have survived.[5]

While some returning GI's actually were spit upon, the image has become
a powerful and pervasive shorthand to represent an entire range of negative ways veterans were treated. Veterans were denied job opportunities,
seen as objects of scorn, and their experiences and sacrifices were ignored
by friends and family.

> **Rose:** I refused to put down that I was in Vietnam in my applications for jobs.
> It didn't mean anything anyway: why bother trying to explain it to people?
> Vietnam was very unpopular then; you didn't want to set yourself up as being
> a Vietnam Veteran, let alone a woman who had been there. Why cause more
> trouble? Learn to keep your mouth shut about it, just do your job.[6]

> **Tom:** We got home and went into the airport. We went into the bathroom
> and there was uniforms scattered all over. Guys were just leaving them there.
> We threw ours away, put on civilian clothes and never mentioned Viet-
> nam again.[7]

> **John:** I know my family had a hard time with Vietnam. It was kind of like a
> death in the family, something you didn't talk about, and we still don't talk
> about it. Vietnam is a very embarrassing subject. It's difficult. You just don't
> talk about Vietnam over a meal.[8]

To spit on someone is to send a message of repudiation, derision, and denigration. The object of scorn is tainted, perhaps even something less than human, and may thus be regarded as subordinate, outcast, scapegoat, or victim. The impact of such behavior is to render its object socially and politically marginal. To be spit on is to be relegated to public silence, isolation, and historical invisibility.[9]

> **Bob:** It was a very scary experience. You've got to realize that I thought I was the only Vietnam veteran in this area. I could look at 100 men going by me and I would assume that none of them were Vietnam veterans. That I was the only one. I never told anybody I was a Vietnam veteran. I didn't mention it to anybody.[10]

The symbolic assault, the isolation, and the silencing all come together in this graphic passage from *NAM,*

> Somebody stabbed us in the back. The average person in the peace struggle didn't understand. We got stabbed in the back by the Army, while we were in the Army. We got stabbed in the back when we got back to the United States by the Peace people. We got stabbed in the back by President Nixon. He's talking nonsense. Henry Kissinger is talking about peace and ending the war. All this is garbage . . . I felt a guilt trip. I said to myself I can't let people know that I've been to Vietnam . . . I used to sit in my room at home and I would just drink and be quiet.[11]

Soldiers not only had to bear the burden of fighting in Vietnam, but they then became the objects through which the nation could express its unwillingness or inability to face the Vietnam War.

> **Mike:** I felt like I was being turned into an abstraction. I was an evil, immoral person. I guess I found it easier to hide and stuff my feelings, and I probably started to assimilate this. I started thinking of myself as a thoughtless or immoral person. I just stuffed a lot of feelings.[12]

Indeed, the "crazy vet" and the "baby-killer" became cultural objects, emblematic of the evils of war, for the culture of war is not a discrete set of values sealed off in military institutions. Our treatment of vets is but a domesticated version of our treatment of the Vietnamese. In the same way a "gook" or "dink" can be more easily killed than a human, so a "crazy vet" can be more easily ignored than a war hero or fellow citizen. Vietnam veterans were symbolically and culturally killed, and experienced a deeply ambiguous relationship to popular memory during the period of amnesia. Although victimized by the impact of forgetting, their narratives show that many veterans partially assimilated the amnesia by withdrawing and denying their war experience. Driven from the public realms of the popular mind, the memory of America's longest and most divisive war became personalized into private remembrances.

Vietnam amnesia privatized the burden of the war in a way consistent with the contemporary American culture of individualism. This private and individualized manner of dealing with Vietnam helps to explain the painful persistence of veteran problems which are usually written off as solely psychological. While it is beyond the scope of this essay to explore the full political, social, and psychological interconnections of post-traumatic stress disorder, one veteran summed them up concisely: "I think America's suffering from PTSD"[13]

By "spitting on vets" we repudiated the war as historical experience, hoping to exorcise it from historical and political consciousness. By attempting to banish Vietnam into the psychic worlds of those who could not forget, we tried to quarantine the contagion of the Vietnam syndrome. Ironically, it was this process of forgetting that was the primary pattern of memory between 1973 and 1979. Although Vietnam amnesia continues as a structure of memory in the present, it is being replaced, in part, by other modes of remembrance.

Remembering America

Those who opposed the war didn't realize that we were doing more for participatory democracy in Vietnam than they were doing by protesting in the United States.

—STEPHEN YOUNG, *To Bear Any Burden*

By 1980 the *dominant* pattern of memory began to appear regularly in Vietnam oral narratives. It recalls and reinstates the traditional moral vision of America, and reflects a subtle shifting of emphasis and an often unconscious revision and selection of information which occurred during the period of amnesia.

Several basic themes appear repeatedly in the dominant type of oral history accounts. Not surprisingly, they center around key areas of controversy and ambiguity. Perhaps the most consistent issues which structure the narratives concern the wisdom and outcome of American intervention. The war is justified and affirmed in several ways. Vietnamese atrocities, both then and now, are recalled and explained as failures of communism. The human costs of American involvement are usually absent from such accounts and American atrocities, such as the My Lai massacre, are seen as exceptions to the rule.

> **Michael:** You get a lot of people say, 'If you saw the movie Platoon that just confirms that American units were doing this thing on a regular basis.' No. No. The Ernest Medinas and Lt. Calleys, to the professional military people were not professionals . . . Professional military people did not support or condone that kind of behavior in any way, shape, or form. For the most part we acquitted ourselves quite well.[14]

If atrocities or abusive violence are aberrant then they are outside the meaningful experience of war. The nation-building or humanitarian aspects of United States involvement gain considerably more importance in dominant memory.

> **Michael:** The thing that used to really make me mad was to watch the evening news . . . It was just a different war you would see on television and that had such an effect on the American people . . . The humanitarian things that the American soldier did over there far outweighed any of the devastation they may have caused, or the My Lai's.[15]

In these accounts, the outcome of the war is recalled in such a way as to emphasize what went wrong in tactical or strategic terms. Criticisms of the military, media, or politicians all suggest that the substantive issue is not whether we should have been in Vietnam but how we could have won in Vietnam. Interpretations of the Tet offensive are central to this type of memory of the war; generally recognized as the key turning point of the war, the lesson of Tet becomes the fact that "we really stuck it to them. Hands down, there is no question that we really kicked their ass."[16] Focusing on the Viet Cong losses and negative media coverage, dominant memory moves America closer to victory, betrayed only by a regrettable loss of will.[17]

The question of victory is central because it responds to deeply felt cultural needs which reach well beyond the more apparent patriotic spirit Both traditional Protestant culture and contemporary consumer culture assume a strong link between outward appearance and inward nature. While victory suggests goodness, defeat implies depravity; to remember America has always been to remember victory. Thus, memories of military victory are an example of the ways that dominant memory finds an appropriate plot to lend meaning to American involvement in Vietnam. Events are recalled in such a way as to reaffirm the original cultural and moral perspective of America in all its fundamental principles. Consider this portion of testimony from *To Bear Any Burden,* revealingly entitled "Full Circle":

> From 1975 until around 1980 it seemed that everyone was trying to forget Vietnam. During that time, I decided to change my focus and try to get away from the Indochina issue. I managed to do that successfully until 1979, when I was asked by a Hollywood screenwriter to help with a script called "The Last Days of Saigon." This reawakened old memories and refocused my thinking . . .
>
> I'm sure that Vietnam will always live with me and I don't want it not to be there. Vietnam veterans experienced something that transcended ourselves. Despite the fact that we suffered a political defeat, the values for which we fought are larger than each of us and the fundamental reason for our willingness to give and to serve.

I went back to Southeast Asia in the summer of 1983, to film the Indochina refugee experience. Seeing thousands of Cambodians, Laotians, and Vietnamese still pouring out of those countries brought me back in touch again. I'd come full circle. I became aware that the struggle for the values that we fought for in Vietnam still continues in Indochina today, as it does in other parts of the world. And as long as people are living without freedom and basic human liberties, that struggle will never, never be over.[18]

The recasting of memory and the reaffirmation of original intentions have become the dominant structure of popular memory of the Vietnam War.

This process of remembrance is referred to as dominant not because it is statistically more common but because of the congruence between it and the representations of the war employed by national elites. During the period of Vietnam amnesia both Nixon and Kissinger articulated the then primary pattern by enocuraging Americans to put Vietnam behind us. Much of the scholarly historical work produced in the 1980s can be characterized as a more formal and conscious representation of the cultural process of revision and redemption of American ideals and foreign policy objectives.[19] Similarly, the dominant memory of Vietnam was championed by Ronald Reagan, who declared Vietnam a noble cause. The basic harmony of Vietnam helps to explain the political and cultural ethos of the 1980s.

The Memory of Vietnam and the Idea of America

Vietnam is when all that history changed.

–DAVE CLINE

The dominant pattern of memory does not, however, exist alone; it stands in relation to an oppositional form of remembrance which also emerges from the existing cultural landscape. *Alternative* memory centers on the events of the Vietnam War; the trauma, pain, and confusion of the war seared so deeply that these events became, for some, central to the reformation of perspective. In the alternative pattern the old worldview declines in its persuasiveness or simply collapses, and the Vietnam experience becomes seminal in the construction of a new worldview.

As early as 1966 veterans and GIs were publicly articulating their changed structures of belief based on intense personal experience and memory[20]—the opposite of amnesia. As one veteran put it, "The war is still alive today, just like it was yesterday . . . the war was yesterday."[21] In this alternative pattern, Vietnam-era events can be recalled publicly— almost relived—vividly, emotionally, persistently, and urgently.

John: Stopping the war was important to me when I got back, so I joined the street marchers; but that wasn't enough . . . so, a group of Vietnam vets got together and we started shouting on the street corners about Vietnam, showing movies like "Hearts and Minds," handing out fliers, speaking out against the draft. It was important for us to get all that gunk out in the open and try to get people to see where we were coming from.[22]

This pattern of recall perceives the impact of the war all around us and may be understood to represent the initial phase of a transformed or critical version of the older dominant worldview.[23]

Like the dominant pattern of memory, the alternative structure is constructed around characteristic themes and insights. The war is remembered in all its brutality and senseless destruction of life. A categorical critique of the war effort occurs widely in alternative remembrance and is common in the dominant memory as well; the unique characteristic of alternative memory is a transformed vision of history, identity, and values. Historical understanding becomes informed by a more critical attitude. Personal identity, particularly conceptions of masculinity, undergo alteration. This alternative pattern transforms, but generally does not repudiate, the basic value system it shares with dominant memory.

Typically in these transformed worldviews, a new critical sense of the past is employed to help explain and understand Vietnam. In his historical past, for example, an African American veteran finds a reason for his opposition to the war.

Lamont: When I got there it was almost like reliving how it must have been in antebellum times. The little value placed on Vietnamese life. Even if they were on your side.[24]

Indeed, a conception of history as a creative cultural activity and a guide to action is common among the stories of antiwar veterans. In the following passage an ex-Marine tells the story of his Vietnam experience through a new, more critical understanding of history.

Steve: The way it's sold is not unlike a book I read on women's diaries of the westward journey, about how people got suckered into going west. It's supposed to be this giant human dynamic unique to being American, the kind of people who came to America and stuff like that. If you read it they got hoodwinked man! They saw these posters . . . it was Madison Avenue at its birth. It's like a saying we had in Nam, "When you're up to your ass in alligators its hard to remember that you were here to drain the swamp." In this book women are writing: we're fucked, we don't have enough food to go back. We don't know where we're going. Everything's falling apart. We don't have enough of anything. Its hotter than hell. The locust are eating us. The Indians are fucking with us, but not hurting us. Our super-dooper scout made off with the dough and here we are . . . That predominantly seems to be the mode.[25]

The experience of betrayal and the conflict between values and reality functioned as powerful catalysts and led this veteran to create a more critical worldview which expresses and explains itself using history as an analogy to personal memory. In its sense of betrayed values, its critique of the American character and frontier mythology, this narrative gives evidence of the alternative structure of remembrance of Vietnam. More importantly, it helps us to understand the way in which experience, memory, history, and worldview interact. Identity, myth, and history all combine and recombine when viewed through the lens of the Vietnam experience.

> **Dave:** In the military the whole sexual thing is like . . . if you don't cut it you're a pussy . . . Vietnam and war calls that into question all the time. Before there was war, war becomes the definition of being tough and manhood. Then there's a war and people find there's not any glory to it. Then it passes . . . and the next generation comes along and they hype them up to it. Historically veterans have always been used to convince the next generation to fight in the next war. Vietnam should make us question that and make a break. Vietnam is when all that history changed. Now they're trying to rewrite that—Bullshit![26]

As the above narrative suggests, the relationship between opposing paradigms of memory best outlines the contours of the Vietnam legacy. Although the dominant pattern is more authoritative politically, the alternative mode has constructed a popular history which assimilates and organizes a more comprehensive body of information and thought. The alternative pattern does this by being explicitly aware of the dominant pattern of memory as a force shaping and influencing its own structure of belief and action.

> **Tom:** So, I'm feeling real good about being a veteran these days. I feel good about being out there telling people not to rewrite history, not to forget, not to let people say that Vietnam was a noble and just cause. I tell people we can't put Vietnam behind us, we have to put it in front of us.[27]
>
> **Guy:** You always feel now, ten years later, that if you can't stand up and say 'We Won' that you're some kind of a misfit. Well we didn't win and in that sense I am a misfit and in that sense I'm still against the war.[28]
>
> **Richard:** I'm very upset that history dies so quickly; in fifteen or twenty years people forget . . . The Vietnam war is not part of the upcoming generation's history. But, it is part of the legacy, and hopefully the young have met people . . . who can translate what happened then to what is happening now in Central America. As appalled as I am, it is typical of the flow of history. People forget about wars very quickly. We have to be vigilant.[29]

The alternative paradigm is also more comprehensive because it does not repudiate the original worldview or history, but transforms them and incorporates them as elements of a different sense of history and citizenship. The revolution of values that occurred in Vietnam finds its roots in the American revolution and the republican vision of the citizen-soldier.

Steve: I saw this thing on Yorktown. When the British surrendered and the tune they played upon surrendering to Washington was 'The world turned upside down.' That's the way you saw it.[30]

Jackson: Militarism is not the same thing as patriotism, in fact it's just the opposite. A critical attitude toward the foreign policy establishment which gave us Vietnam and would like to give us other wars is perfectly consistent with patriotism. It's the most patriotic gesture you can make. Our traditional values are opposed to imperial adventures.

Guy: We're not going to let the president pull that stuff on us anymore. We are not going to let Congress pull that stuff on us anymore. Whenever you go into a combat situation . . . you'd better be able to ask and answer . . . Why? Not the president, not General Westmoreland. You, you have that right as a human being, as a citizen, as a soldier to know why you are fighting. And if they can't tell you, you shouldn't be there.[32]

Dave B: I have a profound respect for the Vietnamese people. What they were saying was this, 'We are a country that is centuries old and we've always been dominated by the Chinese, the French and the Americans. All we want is the right to govern ourselves, however that may be: communism, democracy, nationalism. We just want the right to self-government.' That's the whole basis of what America was founded on . . . I'm proud I am an American and I'm proud I served in Vietnam. I wear a Vietnam Veterans of America shirt because I get pleasure shoving it down peoples throats. It's like, 'You'd all like to forget, but I won't let you.'[33]

The spirit of free inquiry, the core of the liberal tradition, is reaffirmed by analyzing anticommunism as an attack on free thought:

Dave C: I was speaking in schools the month after I had gotten out of the service. At one of the schools a guy from the V.F.W. told me I was a communist. He was yelling that I was a commie . . . I had just gotten back from fighting. He taught me something about anticommunism. If you don't understand something you can call it communist or you can argue about it and try to learn. Being called a communist ain't the worst thing. Its just something they don't understand. Its like an American code-word for 'shut your brain off'.[34]

This passage also suggests an important point of contact between the dominant and alternative patterns of memory. The dominant pattern of memory cannot recall or understand the alternative view as represented by some antiwar veterans. Veteran dissent and the cultural transformations which underlie the alternative rarely figure in dominant memory. Dominant memory handles the whole pattern of alternative memory with the same processes of amnesia or revision with which other confounding elements of the Vietnam experience were treated. But while successful on the level of power and politics, the dominant impulse to select or omit is considerably weaker as a comprehensive discourse to explain the Vietnam legacy.

The Legacy

Vietnam is not part of my past. Vietnam is part of who I am.

—PEGGI PERRI, The Women of the War

The oral testimony of Vietnam veterans suggests the existence of opposing but related patterns or structures of memory which help to define popular memory and provide an analytical framework within which most Vietnam storytelling can be located or interpreted. These distinctive patterns of memory came from a deep and undeniable crisis between experience and understanding. Indeed, the denigration of veterans as representations of the war and the pervasive forgetting about Vietnam reveal a disorientation rooted in our inability to understand Vietnam, given our perceptions of America.

> **Mike:** In addition to feeling my own personal confusion, lack of worth and stuff . . . I was also feeling like my country was going through the same thing in a way. And what was happening to us as a nation? The divisiveness was real palpable . . . I was having a hard time connecting that with my vision of America and what it stood for.[35]

Although the war experience opened a deep rift between American rhetoric and reality, individualism functioned as a ready bridge to shift the moral and political costs of war. Blame was focused on the vets as individuals, not on America as a nation or on the fundamental institutional and historical causes of the war. In *Days of Decision,* a Vietnam veteran argues that to single out individuals as representations of evil or moral depravity is in effect to see a nation's moral and political failure reflected in our own image:

> **John:** We were depicted in the press as drug-addicted, crazed killers and it was a stereotype that stuck. The naive public bought the press hype about Vietnam vets. But we weren't that way; we were just Joe-Blow citizen-soldiers that went over, did what we thought was supposed to be done, came back and found out that it was the wrong thing! So, in a sense, because people bought the press hype about the stereotypical Vietnam vet they were also buying themselves. The gods have cursed us to believe our own propaganda and so the reflection that Americans buy into is our own image. As a nation we are all crazed, drug-addicted killers. Because, if Joe-Blow, working-class American can go over to Vietnam and come back that way, then we must all be that way.[36]

We blamed the veterans but also bought into the idea that they were "our own image." By repudiating vets we showed how our culture encouraged us to understand the war as a personal moral failure, not a systemic or fundamental failure of society.

The common story of veterans being spit on may be understood as an archetypical representation which organizes and simplifies a much larger group of fragmentary motifs, and carries with it a culturally endorsed explanation for history. By "spitting on" vets we condemned them, and through this image we continue to condemn ourselves, while we shield our most sacred beliefs about American political, cultural and economic institutions from any penetrating criticism. Despite the enormous burden of guilt and responsibility we may feel over Vietnam, it is ultimately less painful than admitting to the malevolent aspects of American culture and history.

Vietnam amnesia is not always permanent. As amnesia fades, individuals gravitate toward either the dominant or alternative pattern. Amnesia seems most often to lead to dominant memory because recollection begins in a time removed from the crisis of Vietnam, which is the site of remembrance and the organizing force of the alternative mode. Alternative memory is not, however, destined to diminish as a cultural influence as Vietnam recedes in time. Current events which may signify Vietnam, such as American intervention in Central America, restate prominent elements of the Vietnam story and can give rise to, or revive, alternative memory.

The dominant and alternative patterns of popular memory are best understood as contenders in a vast cultural contest. Many oral history accounts look back to a shared worldview common in America in the 1950s and early 60s. The ways worldviews and the patterns of memory later diverge suggest the different ways in which America has digested the Vietnam War. Many of the men and women who went to Vietnam were motivated by patriotism, duty, and citizenship, values and virtues which drew strength from a shared understanding of the American character and the American past. While variation certainly exists, the oral history of the Vietnam War documents a belief in a vision of America as an exceptional nation of unimpeachable moral character. This element in the narratives is fueled by a larger, more pervasive attitude about American cultural virtue. From its origins in the earliest colonial experience, our history has been explained as the manifest destiny of a people. We have grown accustomed to viewing ourselves as a "city on the hill." America, in this view, is a beacon of freedom and progress, the innocent civilizer of wayward nations and a moral exception to the corruption and decay of the old world. Alone, America stands sometimes as the best, often as the greatest, but always as the most powerful. These are deeply felt and powerful elements of an American mythology which, like all myth and history, provides a vision necessary to understanding where we are going as a people. But this dominant understanding of America has also acted to screen us from disturbing information about our actions and motives, and it has tended to defend and preserve the existing cultural and political order.

This American mythology was sorely tested in Vietnam. The war thrust up before us deeply disturbing things. We were defeated, we committed war crimes, our intentions were suspect and our government told epic lies. The events of the war did not harmonize with and could not be easily integrated into the dominant mythology of America as a land of high moral principle. When initially confronted with such a dilemma, the boundaries of choice are clear. One could forget or deny the disturbing information or one could change one's conception of America. In such a moment of decision accepted beliefs and received wisdom may be suspended. "Fuck it, it don't mean nothin" was perhaps the most common phrase used by soldiers in Vietnam and speaks directly to this indecision and confusion.[37]

This suspension of belief can only be a brief interlude. Humans are unalterably cultural creatures, and we demand meaning in our lives. Animated by this profound cultural imperative to reconcile and understand the Vietnam experience, the opposing patterns of remembrance and cognition we have discussed arose to order and interpret history. The dominant pattern reorders the memory of Vietnam to fit the received vision of American culture and history. The alternative pattern seeks to reconstruct American history and culture to fit its memory of Vietnam. Both are attempts to make life after Vietnam more coherent and more meaningful.

These paradigms of memory are not hard and fast or mutually exclusive, but are linked and related alternatives. These deep structures of popular memory are important not because they explain all the facts, but because they indicate the nature of cultural processes which assign meaning to and reconstruct the past. Clearly much lies between these patterns and most oral narratives contain elements of differing approaches existing in tension with one another. This represents the dialectic of change within a person, much in the same way that contending cultural worldviews in our society represent the process of change that is the Vietnam legacy.

NOTES

For complete interview and publication data on the sources cited here, see the bibliography which follows.

1. For a discussion of oral history methodology on which this essay is based see Michael Frisch's "Oral History and *Hard Times,* A Review Essay." Also see

Ronald Grele's *Envelopes of Sound*. (The chapters entitled "Movement without Aim" and "Listen to Their Voices" are particularly instructive.) James Livingston and Richard Sullivan offered insightful criticisms of early drafts and helped to clarify both the theoretical foundation and stylistic execution of this essay.

2. Robert Spear, interview, 4 April 1988.

3. Santoli, *To Bear Any Burden*, pp. 211–212.

4. Jan Barry, interview, 5 June 1985.

5. Santoli, *To Bear Any Burden*, p. 109.

6. Walker, *Piece of My Heart*, p. 15.

7. Thomas Bradley, interview, 24 May 1985.

8. Gioglio, *Days of Decision*, p. 267.

9. For an excellent discussion of the Vietnam homecoming, employing a sociological perspective and based on a wide selection of oral history, memoirs, and autobiography, see Lloyd Lewis's *The Tainted War*, pp. 135–160.

10. Spear, interview.

11. Baker, *NAM*, p. 289.

12. Michael Heany, interview, 5 October 1988.

13. David Cline, interview, 1 March 1988.

14. Michael McKay, interview, 7 March 1988.

15. McKay, interview.

16. Santoli, *To Bear Any Burden*, p. 113.

17. In "Historical Memory and Illusive Victories," Thomas Paterson analyzes the current scholarly debate over the Tet offensive and related issues of victory and defeat.

18. Santoli, *To Bear Any Burden*, p. 333.

19. On the question of the Vietnam revisionism see Walter LeFeber's "The Last War the Next War and the New Revisionists," and Robert A. Divine's "Historiography: Vietnam Reconsidered."

20. For a comprehensive account of GI resistance to the war see David Cortright's *Soldiers in Revolt*. See Gerald Gioglio's *Days of Decision* for a remarkable collection of oral histories which illustrate (among other things) what I am calling alternative memory.

21. Ed Sauders, interview, 1 June 1989

22. Gioglio, *Days of Decision*, p. 266.

23. For what is still the best discussion of personal change and the transformation of identity in returning veterans, see Robert Jay Lifton's *Home From the War*.

24. Lamont Steptoe, interview, 23 February 1989.

25. Steven Shuey, interview, 14 January 1988.

26. Cline, interview.

27. Gioglio, *Days of Decision*, p. 281.

28. Guy Osmer, interview, 21 June 1985.

29. Gioglio, *Days of Decision*, p. 302.

30. Shuey, interview.

31. Jackson Lears, interview, 14 September 1988.

32. Osmer, interview.

33. Gioglio, *Days of Decision*, p. 292.

34. Cline, interview.
35. Heany, interview.
36. Gioglio, *Days of Decision,* p. 267.
37. See Richard Sullivan's chapter in this volume, "The Recreation of Vietnam," for a full exploration of this phrase and its many meanings.

BIBLIOGRAPHY

BAKER, MARK. *NAM: The Vietnam War in the Words of the Men and Women Who Fought There.* New York : William Morrow & Company Inc., 1981.

BARRY, JAN. Interview with author. Montclair, New Jersey, 5 June 1985.

BRADLEY, THOMAS. Interview with author. Asbury Park, New Jersey, 24 May 1985.

CORTRIGHT, DAVID. *Soldiers in Revolt: The American Military Today.* Garden City, New York : Anchor Press/Doubleday, 1975.

CLINE, DAVID. Interview with author. Jersey City, New Jersey, 1 March 1988.

DIVINE, ROBERT A. "Historiography: Vietnam Reconsidered." *Diplomatic History* 12 (Winter 1988): pp. 79–93.

FRENCH-LANKARGE, VICKI. "The Women of the War," *Hampshire Life,* 11 November 1988, pp. 7–10.

FRISCH, MICHAEL, "Oral History and *Hard Times,* A Review Essay," *Red Buffalo: A Journal of American Studies,* 1:2–3 (1972): pp. 217–31.

GIOGLIO, GERALD R. *Days of Decision: An Oral History of Conscientious Objectors in the Military During the Vietnam War.* Trenton, New Jersey: The Broken Rifle Press, 1989.

GRELE, RONALD. *Envelopes of Sound.* Chicago: Precedent Publishing, Inc., 1975.

HEANY, MICHAEL. Interview with author. New Brunswick, New Jersey, 5 October 1988.

LEARS, JACKSON. Interview with author. New Brunswick, New Jersey, 14 September 1988.

LeFEBER, WALTER. "The Last War, the Next War and the New Revisionists." *Democracy,* January 1981, pp. 93–109.

LEWIS, LLOYD B. *The Tainted War: Culture and Identity in Vietnam Narratives.* Westport, Connecticut: Greenwood Press, 1985.

LIFTON, ROBERT JAY. *Home From the War. Vietnam Veterans: Neither Victims nor Executioners.* New York : Simon and Schuster, 1973.

McKAY, MICHAEL. Interview with author. New Brunswick, New Jersey, 7 March 1988.

OSMER, GUY. Interview with author. Wanaque, New Jersey, 21 June 1985.

PATERSON, THOMAS G. "Historical Memory and Illusive Victories: Vietnam and Central America." *Diplomatic History* 12 (Winter 1988): pp. 1–18.

SANTOLI, ALBERT. *To Bear Any Burden: The Vietnam War and Its Aftermath in the Words of American and Southeast Asians.* New York : Ballantine Books, 1985.

SAUDERS, ED. Interview with author. New Brunswick, New Jersey, 1 June 1989.

SHUEY, STEVEN. Interview with author. Somerset, New Jersey, 14 January 1988.

SPEAR, ROBERT. Interview with author. Edison, New Jersey, 4 April 1988.

STEPTOE, LAMONT. Interview with author. Philadelphia, Pennsylvania, 23 February 1989.

WALKER, KEITH. *A Piece of My Heart: The Stories of Twenty-Six American Women Who Served in Vietnam.* Novato, California: Presidio, 1985.

PART THREE

The Re-Creation of Vietnam—and America

7

VIETNAM AND THE PRESS
MICHAEL X. DELLI CARPINI

The Vietnam War was and is a potent political symbol, a montage of discrete, contradictory, and arresting images seared into our individual and collective psyches: a Buddhist monk in flames, a South Vietnamese officer coolly blowing the brains out of a captured Vietcong, an American flag being burned. While for many Vietnam is remembered through direct, personal experiences, for most people the war was and is known only through experiences mediated by others. As the primary mediator of images of the war, the press holds unparalleled power—the power to decide what the war means.[1]

Questions about the role of the news media during the Vietnam era are as common as questions about the war itself. Was the press simply the chronicler, the unbiased eyes and ears of a nation, or did it systematically distort reality? Did the press reflect the changing national mood about the war or did it cause the shift? Did the press act as national conscience or national traitor? Was the press an independent voice or a mouthpiece for the White House, radical students, or Hanoi?

This essay presents arguments and evidence which directly address these questions. Overarching these particular concerns, however, is the more encompassing theme of how the Vietnam experience included both an extension of past press-government relations and an important turning point in that relationship. By understanding the role of the news media in our Vietnam involvement, we can reach a deeper understanding of what the role of the press is in America, and of what it should be.

The Press in America

The Conflicting Roles of the Press   What is unique about press coverage of Vietnam is not that it broke with prior traditions of press-government relations, but that because of the length and the nature of the war, it fit so many different traditions. The Vietnam experience points out the inherent contradictions that always plague the American press. Understanding these contradictions is the first step in understanding the role of the press during the Vietnam War.

Did the press accurately portray the war, or was coverage biased? One must first ask what *accurate* and *biased* mean. Each soldier's experience was different in Vietnam. The war varied by region, season, and year.[2] The war *was* different depending upon whether it was viewed from Washington or Berkeley, Hanoi or Saigon, Quang Tri or Dong Hoi. The war *was* different depending upon whether it was viewed through the eyes of an American or a Vietnamese, a private or a general, a student or a soldier, a peasant or a businessperson. Even given unlimited resources, information, print space, and airtime, the press could not present the Vietnam experience "accurately." It was impossible. Rather than ask if the Vietnam experience was covered accurately, we must ask the more modest question, were there factual errors? Instead of asking was the coverage biased, we must ask, from whose perspective(s) was the coverage biased, for what reasons, and to what end?

Most of the debate over coverage of Vietnam concerns issues of interpretation rather than fact, errors of omission rather than commission. The exception to this involves counting—how many Vietcong and North Vietnamese soldiers there were and how many of them were killed. It is clear that the United States military, intentionally or not, systematically underreported the strength of the opposition and overreported the number of "kills." It is also clear that the press corps, with few exceptions, accepted these official numbers and reported them dutifully to the American public until the Tet offensive.

The reporting of enemy strength and body counts points to important continuities with past press-government interactions. First among them is the dependency of the press on the very institutions it covers. This is particularly true for government, whose access to and control of information is superior to that of the press. It is also especially true in foreign affairs coverage (since due in part to cultural and language barriers, alternate sources are lacking), and during a war (since control of information is even more tightly maintained). Deadlines add to this dependency, since reporters and editors must depend on the more accessible, official stories and have less time to question them or check out alternate sources. Naturally, such deadline pressures are more intense in foreign affairs coverage.

Secondly, the press is restrained by its own loyalty. Reporters, editors, and producers are citizens, often even patriots. Their tendency when reporting on international affairs, especially during wartime, is to avoid sabotaging the national interest, even to aid that interest through the content and style of coverage. Hence, all other things being equal, the inclination is to report what the government wants reported.

A third factor shaping media coverage is economic interest. Even if journalists, editors, and producers are not superpatriots, they know that appearing unpatriotic does not play well with many readers, viewers, and sponsors. Fear of alienating the public and sponsors, especially in wartime, serves as a real, often unstated tether, keeping the press tied to accepted wisdom.

Why, then, is the press often blamed by politicians, academics, even journalists, for undermining the war effort, for turning the public against the war in Vietnam, and for distorting our image of the war? The answer to these questions lies in a set of traditions that conflict with those just discussed. While the press has a tradition of national loyalty, it has a competing role as "watchdog" of government. While the press is constrained by economic interests, it is also motivated by a desire to inform the public as best it can. And finally, while the media traditionally stays close to the mainstream, it also thrives on the sensational, the dramatic, the controversial. The mixed message sent out by the press concerning Vietnam resulted from the interplay of these competing pressures. At different times different traditions dominated. At any given time, conflicts over how to cover the war are evident—between mediums, among reporters, and—because of journalists', editors', producers', and owners' different perspectives—even within single stories.

The Press and Boundary Maintenance: Defining Consensus, Controversy, and Deviance   The pushes and pulls of the press's competing tendencies are bounded, however. When the topic is consensual, the media serves as advocate or celebrant of that consensus.[3] When the topic is one about which legitimate groups or individuals disagree, then the media is obliged to present those opposing views. The key, however, is the term *legitimate*. The media does not advocate or even neutrally present views that fall outside of the dominant culture. While the lines between consensus, legitimate controversy, and deviance are not written in stone, they are real, and the rules governing media coverage are different for each.

Consider, for example, national election coverage. The importance of elections in the political process is never debated. Elections as an institution fall clearly within the sphere of consensus. During the election campaign, however, the media are free to present the opposing views of legitimate political candidates—almost always defined as the Democratic and the Republican nominees. This is the sphere of legitimate controversy. The views of individuals and groups falling beyond its bounds—those of fascists, communists, socialists, etc.—are seldom covered in the mainstream press. When they are, it is usually to expose them as threats to the consensus, not to present their points of view objectively. (FCC guidelines for the Fairness Doctrine state, "It is not the Commission's intention to make time available to Communists or to the Communist viewpoints.") Since the press is the dominant source from which people learn about the political world, it is not only part of the spheres of consensus and legitimate controversy, but also "plays the role of exposing, condemning, or excluding from the public agenda those who violate or challenge the political consensus. It marks out and defends the limits of acceptable political conflict."[4]

Coverage of Vietnam, despite claims to the contrary, seldom left the spheres of consensus and legitimate controversy. When it did, it was to ridicule deviance rather than present it as a legitimate alternative. The media did, of course, criticize the war, and helped shape the debate over the war's direction. And Vietnam was covered differently than other wars. But the mainstream press never stood outside the dominant culture to criticize it. Instead, it reflected societal shifts in the boundaries between consensus, legitimate controversy, and deviance. Ultimately it continued to serve as a boundary-maintaining mechanism, preserving the status quo from serious challenges.

The Press, War, and Censorship   War both intensifies and changes the norms of press-government relations. Prior to World War I, reporters either found their own way into a war zone, or, at the discretion of the commander, attached themselves to a military unit. If found in a war zone without permission, they were often arrested. The unprecedented scale of World War I, the press's increased ability to gather and transmit information, and the growing unhappiness of everyone with the resulting chaos in press coverage led to a more formal system in which the press was granted routine access to the front in exchange for formal accreditation and censorship by the military. The threat of losing accreditation or being jailed, their knowledge that copy and film would be censored anyway, and their underlying patriotism meant that journalists often engaged in self-censorship. As Frederick Palmer of the *New York Herald* wrote, "We rarely had our copy cut. We had learned too well where the line was drawn on military secrecy. The important items were those we left out; and these made us public liars."[5]

This system of accreditation, access, and censorship, which remained largely in place through the Korean War, was as important politically as it was militarily. The mobilization of public support for a war is as critical as the mobilization of troops. From the government's perspective, the press needed enough freedom to report back frequently to the public, but enough control to assure that what was reported boosted rather than hurt morale. Often more than military secrets were the subject of censorship. During the Korean conflict, for example, the press was forbidden to make any derogatory comments about United Nations troops.

While the accrediting of journalists continued in Vietnam, formal censorship did not. The military believed it gained more by limiting the access of journalists than by giving them complete access in exchange for censorship. In addition, since the United States' involvement in Vietnam fell short of declared war, full censorship and its enforcement were politically and legally difficult. Finally, it was assumed that the combination of the threat of loss of accreditation, journalistic patriotism, the tradition of "neutrality and objectivity," and the dependence of the press on official sources of information would make voluntary guidelines workable in place of prior censorship. This assumption proved correct for most of this very long war. Eventually, however, uncensored coverage, the limited nature of the war, and a growing, vocal, legitimate opposition in the States, combined to shift the boundaries of legitimate controversy, and ultimately, of the consensus itself.

Covering the War in Vietnam

No News Is Good News: Coverage of Vietnam Prior to 1964   Prior to 1964 the only extensive coverage of Vietnam came during the 1963 Buddhist crises.[9] Networks did not assign full-time film crews and reporters until the middle of 1963, and only the *New York Times* had a full-time correspondent in Saigon during the Kennedy administration. It was in this period, however, that the context for future coverage of the war was set.

During the 1950s and early 1960s, debating the wisdom of the Cold War was taboo. For most people this acquiescence was less because they feared retaliation than because, immersed in this ideological consensus, they never thought to question it. In addition, during the Truman and Eisenhower administrations, a bipartisan consensus on national security removed most foreign policy decision making from the public agenda. Thus, neither the fact nor the method of American involvement in Vietnam was deemed newsworthy.

When, beginning in 1961, Vietnam occasionally made the news, the cold war consensus and the media's dependence on government sources combined to assure coverage supportive of U.S. policy. Consider the following quotes from the *New York Times:* "General Taylor heads a twelve-man group . . . assessing how Washington can best stop the Red advance" (1961); and, "Communist guerillas trying to subvert this country admit to having underestimated the depth of the United States intentions" (1963). Such ideological content, typical of reporting prior to 1964, was not viewed as violating the norm of objective reporting precisely because it fell within the cold war consensus. According to one NBC correspondent, "To the degree that we in the media paid any attention at all to that small, dirty war in those years, we almost wholly reported the position of the government."[7]

A typical case of government news management occurred in late 1961. General Taylor, the president's military advisor, had concluded that South Vietnam could not survive the Vietcong and North Vietnamese "insurgency" without the help of more than the 685 American advisors permitted by the 1954 Geneva agreement. While Kennedy reluctantly accepted Taylor's recommendation (by the time of his death nearly 17,000 American troops were stationed in Vietnam), he did not want public attention drawn to the escalation. The White House leaked misleading information suggesting that both Taylor and Kennedy opposed sending troops to Vietnam. This was the story reported in the press. The *New York Times,* for example, printed that "officials said it was correct to infer from this that General Taylor did not look favorably on the sending of United States combat troops at this time" and "the president and General Taylor agreed, according to reliable information available here, that the South Vietnamese government is capable of turning back the Communist threat." The story spent one day on the front page.

So the door was opened to U.S. troops fighting and dying in Vietnam while the press reported that it was still closed and locked. In December 1961, when the first U.S. troops authorized to provide "direct military support" to the South Vietnamese sailed up the Saigon River, the *New York Times* carried the story on the twenty first page. And at a televised press conference in January 1962, in answer to the direct question, "Mr. President, are American troops now in combat in Vietnam?" Kennedy simply said no and went on to the next question. He was not challenged—although the first U.S. combat death in Vietnam had occurred three weeks earlier.

Despite the predominantly cold war coverage between 1961 and 1964, some reporters did raise questions about America's Vietnam policy. As the number of combat deaths increased (from 1 in 1961 to 787 in 1963), the press found it difficult to ignore the conflict. And as the disparity between officially reported and real U.S. policy widened (for example, in December of 1961, with at least 2000 Americans in combat zones authorized to carry and fire weapons, the official count was still 685 advisors), the number of sources who questioned the honesty of government statements also increased.

While this did not mean that press coverage was consistently negative, it did result in "mixed signals." For example, in late 1961 a *New York*

Times editorial stated, "Fresh details are slowly emerging from reticent Administration sources about the expanded program of American participation in South Vietnam's anti-communist struggle." This sentence captures the complex relationship of the press to government, and the ambivalence of the press about that relationship. Its acceptance of the basic correctness of U.S. goals is evidenced in the phrase "American participation in South Vietnam's anti-communist struggle." But journalists' suspicion that there was more to U.S. involvement than met the eye, and their annoyance at government unwillingness to provide more information about that involvement shows, too, in the phrases "slowly emerging," and "reticent Administration sources."

This example also reveals the press's almost total dependence on the government for information; frustrated or not, the media can only report as much as those "reticent administration officials" will say. As U.S. involvement in Vietnam increased so, too, did the potential for official and credible sources who would provide alternative information or interpretations. Prior to 1964, however, such voices were rare and usually easily silenced. In February 1961, for example, the Republican National Committee asked the president to make "a full report to the American people" concerning U.S. involvement in Vietnam. While affirming their commitment to "any policy which will block the Communist conquest of Southeast Asia," the Republicans raised concerns that the U.S. was "moving toward another Korea which might embroil the entire Far East." This was one of the earliest attempts to redefine the boundary between consensus and legitimate controversy. Stopping the communist threat in Southeast Asia is reasserted as a consensus issue, but the Kennedy administration's strategy for doing so is gently pushed toward the sphere of legitimate controversy. The challenge was not made by the press, but by players who are considered legitimate actors within the hegemonic culture. In fact, while reporting the Republican challenge, the *New York Times* supported Kennedy in an editorial, arguing in true boundary-maintaining fashion, that "undue publicity . . . could compromise Washington's effort." Even this minor challenge quickly faded, as the Republicans conceded to Kennedy's call for a continuation of the "very strong bipartisan consensus" in foreign policy. A Democratic challenge in 1963 followed a similar pattern. A true shifting of boundaries would not occur until the Tet offensive.

Challenges most often finding their way into the press during this period originated with U.S. troops and middle-level officers. In managing the news, the government relied on its ability to control information, on the press's commitment to "objective" reporting, and on its loyalty to the U.S. cause rather than on censorship. As a result, the opinions of soldiers and officers in the field could be and were communicated directly to the public. In a traditional, declared war this would not be a problem. Vietnam, however, was a "limited" war; Americans, though shooting and being shot at, though killing and being killed, were not soldiers, but "advisors." Victory in battle and in the "pacification program" depended not only on how U.S. soldiers performed, but on how South Vietnamese soldiers and, ultimately, the South Vietnamese government performed. Moreover, just who the enemy was was unclear—was it North Vietnam? The Vietcong? The Soviet Union? Communism? The resulting frustrations and uncertainties were managed within the administration, and even, with a few exceptions, within the U.S. government and military more generally. But in the field this was more difficult. Again, most coverage was neither negative nor pessimistic. Even David Halberstam, the *New York Times'* columnist whom Kennedy wanted removed from Saigon because of his negative coverage of the war, supported the war effort, often writing in the loyal tradition of World War II correspondents:

> Here a handful of tough United States Special Forces men day after day live a precarious existence training several hundred Montagnards, or mountain tribesmen . . . The Americans . . . seem completely indifferent to danger . . . "We've got a job to do and we do it." According to Lieut. Pete Skamser of Covina, CA., . . . every man on the team is willing to die for Dak Pek. (1962)

Mixed in with upbeat reports, however, were signs of doubt and of what Hallin calls "cautious pessimism." These were not the inventions of unpatriotic journalists; they reflected the frustrations of advisors who were committed to the objectives of the war but disillusioned by the tactics. The press gave voice to frustration over the limited nature of the war, its civil/guerrilla war character, the incompetence of the South Vietnamese army, and the corruptness of the Diem regime. The result was reporting like the following *New York Times* excerpts:

> United States Army helicopters carried a Vietnamese battalion in a successful raid today . . . But as usual the main enemy force got away . . . The Government troops failed to exploit the Viet Cong state of shock. They bunched up . . . under the shade of coconut trees until an American advisor cried out in exasperation, "Let's move the thing forward." (March 9, 1962)

> The Battle of Ap Bac, in which attacking South Vietnamese troops were badly beaten by Communist guerillas, has bewildered high United States officials in Saigon. United States advisors in the field, however, have long felt that conditions here made a defeat like this virtually inevitable . . . American officers . . . feel that what happened at Ap Bac goes deeper than one battle and is directly tied to the question—whether the Vietnamese are really interested in having American advisors and listening to them. (January 7, 1963)

In reporting the soldier's perspective of the war, the media never questioned our right or our motives for being in Vietnam. Nor did they question the motives or bravery of U.S. soldiers. To the contrary, the press often championed their cause, as when in 1962 the *New York Times* criticized the government for not awarding the Purple Heart to soldiers wounded in Vietnam. Like the soldiers it reported on, the press believed in the cause; when critical, it reflected concern that bad policies put that cause at risk.

Entering the Sphere of Legitimate Controversy: The Buddhist Crisis of 1963 and the Fall of Diem   The most intensive coverage of Vietnam prior to 1964 was during the Buddhist crisis. Diem garnered much of his support from Vietnam's Catholic population. On May 8, 1963, Buddhists in Hue were prohibited from flying religious flags during the celebration of Buddha's birthday. Protests began immediately, leading to six months of dramatic, violent confrontations between Buddhists and the South Vietnamese government. Negative press coverage during this period is often used as evidence of media policymaking power, since prior to the crisis the administration supported Diem, and by its end actively supported a coup against him. More pointedly, the press is accused of undermining the U.S. war effort that depended so heavily on a stable South Vietnamese government. These accusations do not stand up under examination.

While it is true that the press criticized Diem during this period, so, too, did many American diplomatic and military officials in Saigon and Washington. Indeed, prior to May 1963 the press consistently reported the official U.S. line that, while Diem was not perfect, he held the key to success. As the *New York Times* put it in 1962:

> Official Americans here, though often impatient with some of Ngo's repressive policies and his apparent reluctance to effect reforms, appear to have concluded that his leadership . . . is an irreplaceable asset. Some Westerners who have made a specialty of studying the Vietnamese mind have suggested that a mandarin is really what most of the people want.

The administration felt Diem could be "educated" about democratic reforms and government efficiency. Most press coverage of Diem prior to May 1963, a combination of support spiked with critical nudges towards reform, reflected this view. Some members of the administration and many military personnel in Vietnam felt winning with Diem in charge was unlikely. But as long as this view remained deviant, it rarely surfaced in the media. In some cases reporters censored such criticism, seeing it as harmful to U.S. efforts (and their own careers). And when they focused on deep-seated problems in the South Vietnamese government and military, as Charles Mohr did in 1962 and early 1963 for *Time,* stories were edited back home to fall into line with government policy.

Negative press coverage increased during the Buddhist crisis, but it did so because of a growing debate over the direction of U.S. policy and not because journalists launched an anti-Diem campaign of their own. The crisis, coupled with Diem's continued unwillingness to take U.S. advice slowly turned the tables within the administration. At first this meant that the usefulness of Diem as the means to achieve victory over the communists was open to legitimate debate. By Diem's ouster in November, opposition to Diem had become the new consensus.

The media were important arenas in which the debate played itself out. Journalists who had already concluded that the Diem regime was unsalvageable were the first to give voice to the now legitimated criticism, but the words were those of military advisors and administration officials. Here the media did play an important role in the shift in U.S. policy, but not as the leader. (Indeed, when the first Buddhist monk burned himself to death in protest, the story did not make the front page of the *New York Times,* and Malcolm Browne's now famous picture of the self-immolation was not run.) Journalists did what they always do, they reported what "officials here believe." But now what officials believed was in conflict, and the press was an important weapon in the battle for a new consensus. It was, however, a weapon as likely to be used by the pro-Diem forces as the anti-Diem ones. In the midst of the crises, for example, *Time,* owned by the virulently anticommunist Henry Luce, published an editorial blasting the Saigon press corps for its anti-Diem reporting. And even as the administration position shifted away from Diem, *Time's* editorial staff insisted on so sanitizing Vietnam coverage that Charles Mohr and Mert Perry, the magazine's Saigon correspondents, resigned in September 1963.

The Kennedy administration sought to win the hearts and minds of the press corps and so the American public. Kennedy wanted minimal but positive coverage of Vietnam and the public airing of internal disputes and a stagnating war effort posed a problem. In October of 1963 Kennedy appealed to Arthur Ochs Sulzberger, publisher of the *New York Times,* to recall David Halberstam from Saigon. Sulzberger refused. But administration attempts to keep the press in line did not stop here. The White House and the Pentagon encouraged Washington-based reporters to take brief trips to Saigon, since in a short stay they could not make unofficial or dissident contacts and so would be dependent on the official government line. Reporters were also subtly pressured by the White House staff, who sought to discredit the Saigon press corp by impugning their knowledge and analysis of the war. The pressure from the Pentagon was less subtle, challenging "not just the reporters' accuracy, but their manhood and their patriotism."[8]

The tactics worked. U.S. based journalists, fresh from guided tours of Saigon and primed by White House and Pentagon propaganda attacked the Saigon press corps. Joseph Alsop called their reporting a "reportorial crusade against government," while Marguerite Higgins asserted that "reporters here would like to see us lose the war to prove they're right."[9]

Despite such claims, actual press reporting from Saigon was anything but unpatriotic. To the contrary, it helped to clearly demarcate the boundaries of consensus, debate, and deviance in a way that never challenged the status quo. At issue, for the press as for the administration, was how best to stop the communists; no journalist ever questioned that they had to be stopped. At the height of the crisis Halberstam wrote in the *New York Times:*

> The conflict between the South Vietnamese Government and Buddhist priests is sorely troubling American officials here. It has brought to the surface American frustrations of the apparently limited influence of the United States here despite its heavy investment in troops, economic aid and prestige to help South Vietnam block Communism.

The theme of television network news coverage also was that Diem was hurting the war effort. In August 1963, Chet Huntley, quoting official sources, told the ABC audience that "Diem washed eighteen months of effort down the drain." In October he reported that "we journalists have found the Diem regime guilty of serving Communism." And when Diem was assassinated Huntley spoke for all the network anchors when he said, "we can now get on with the war."

Uneasy Consensus: Covering Vietnam between 1964 and 1968   Despite a few tense periods, Kennedy and his advisors were successful in guiding coverage of the war. Conditions were optimal for this kind of news management. The cold war had been kept on ice by the Bay of Pigs and the Cuban Missile Crisis. The images of Khrushchev banging his shoe at the U.N. and threatening to "bury" the U.S. built a wall around the sphere of consensus as impenetrable as that separating East and West Berlin. In addition, although the U.S. was more involved in the war than the Kennedy administration ever admitted, the American presence was still limited.

President Johnson also wanted Vietnam downplayed; the only war he wanted to be remembered for was the one against poverty. However, the political turmoil following Diem's assassination (a constant fact of life from that point on), coupled with the inability of the South Vietnamese army to conduct the war as envisioned by the U.S., led to an escalation of U.S. involvement. Between the end of 1963 and July of 1964, the number of advisors was increased from 17,000 to 75,000, and Americans began bombing North Vietnam, first as "retaliation for North Vietnamese aggression," and ultimately, in February of 1965, as a sustained activity. Finally, in July of 1965, at the insistence of the Joint Chiefs of Staff, President Johnson dispatched 100,000 combat troops to South Vietnam. Vietnam was now an American war.

Increased U.S. involvement altered the relationship between the president and the press, as well as the environment in which that relationship played itself out. On the one hand, greater U.S. commitment meant that Johnson had to insure public and congressional support for the war. On the other, he did not want the war to dominate the public agenda. This was still a limited war and one that, like Korea, would not hold the public's loyalty if closely and constantly scrutinized. Besides, center stage belonged to the Great Society; Vietnam was an unwanted sideshow. Like JFK, LBJ walked a tightrope strung between keeping the war off the public agenda and managing media coverage so that public opinion would be supportive of the increasing U.S. involvement. As the scope of that involvement increased, however, LBJ had to build public support, and this required greater media coverage. It was a high wire act Johnson was unable to complete.

The Tonkin Gulf Resolution was President Johnson's key to unlocking public and congressional support for greater U.S. involvement in Vietnam, and the key to the resolution was LBJ's brilliant manipulation of the press. It is, perhaps, the best example of how presidential news management can shape public policy. In early August 1964, North Vietnamese PT boats and a U.S. destroyer did battle in the Gulf of Tonkin. In response, Congress passed the Gulf of Tonkin Resolution, giving the president the power to take "all necessary measures to repel any armed attacks against forces of the United States and to prevent further aggression." This vague mandate, passed unanimously in the House and with only two dissents in the Senate, gave Presidents Johnson and Nixon the power to wage an undeclared war in Vietnam, although as recently as June 1964, deliberations on a similar resolution had been deferred in Congress because of a lack of agreement on how to exert increasing pressure on North Vietnam. Why the turnabout?

Clearly the "rallying around the flag" induced by the Gulf of Tonkin incident was critical—and depended on the press. The rules of "objective journalism" allowed the president to manage the media presentation as effectively as if he had written the copy himself. The media's exclusive use of official U.S. sources, their focus on the president, the absence of interpretation, and the concentration on immediate events at the expense of historical context guaranteed that their portrayal of the incident was consistent with the administration's evolving policy of escalation in the guise of business as usual. Thus the *Washington Post* reported:

> The United States turned loose its military might on North Vietnam last night to prevent the Communist leaders in Hanoi and Peking from making the mistaken decision that they could attack American ships with impunity. But the initial United States decision was for limited action, a sort of tit-for-tat retaliation, and not a decision to escalate the war in Southeast Asia . . . The great mystery here was whether the attacks by North Vietnamese PT boats on the

American vessels were part of some larger scheme on the Communist side to escalate the war.

The network anchors, in tone and word, also supported Johnson's actions. We were committed, according to Cronkite, "to stop Communist aggression wherever it raises its head."

What is remarkable about coverage of the Tonkin incidents is that virtually every report was misleading or even false. For example, contrary to the *New York Times* report that the U.S. destroyer "was on a routine patrol when an unprovoked attack took place" and that "there was no ready explanation why the PT boats would in effect attack the powerful Seventh Fleet," the destroyer Maddox was on an intelligence gathering operation near an area where the U.S. had twice attacked North Vietnam the day before. In fact, evidence suggests that the second attack by North Vietnamese PT boats never happened. Real or not, when heavily reported in the media, it became the public rationale for retaliation and increased U.S. involvement in Vietnam—a policy change decided upon before the Gulf of Tonkin incident.

Increased U.S. military presence in Vietnam led to parallel increases in television's coverage of the war. Daniel Hallin notes five "unspoken propositions" underlying television reporting in this period. First, television in general and anchors in particular, referred to Vietnam as our war, portraying it as a national endeavor. Second, coverage often placed the Vietnam conflict in an American war tradition, in the context of World War II, and even of the U.S. frontier. For example, one 1966 NBC report closed by signing off from "the First Infantry Division, the Big Red 1 of North Africa, Omaha Beach, Normandy, Germany, and now the Cambodia border." Reporters also used the soldier's phrase "Indian country" to describe Vietcong-controlled territory. Subtly the historical context of Vietnam changes from its own history of occupation and religious and civil strife to America's "wild west" and the tradition of "great wars."

A third theme noted by Hallin is that Vietnam was a testing ground for manhood, as defined by John Wayne and Audie Murphy. Vietnam was about heroes, toughness, and professionalism:

They are the greatest soldiers in the world. In fact, they are the greatest men in the world. (NBC, February 1966)

They are Marines. They are good and they know it. But every battle, every landing, is a new test of what a man and a unit can do. (NBC, Sept 1965)

But they were bloody, and that's what they wanted. (NBC, July 1966)

Fourth, television coverage reduced the war to a game, to winning and losing. It was the language of sports and technology that, as Hallin says, purged the war of moral and political implications, as with "American and Australian forces had somewhat better hunting today," or "American soldiers captured the biggest prize so far." The enemy is reduced to dehumanized targets, to body counts, or to what Chet Huntley called "the total score."

Finally, television gave the war an appearance of order and progress where often there was none. The anchors played an important role in this structuring process, mainly through the "battlefield roundups" that introduced the film footage each night. For example, CBS viewers might see Walter Cronkite, often posed in front of a map of Southeast Asia with the words RED CHINA arching over the top, declare:

> Today, after meeting three days of desperate, almost suicidal resistance by the Vietcong, our troops find the enemy gone into sullen hiding, our firepower too powerful to face. For in the three weeks of . . . operation ATTLEBORO, the infantry has killed more than four hundred, captured scores, overrun strong point after strong point. As the fighting rages once again to preserve democracy, the GIs themselves have an eye on the elections back home. (November 1966)

This image of progress, of an enemy on the run, was based on daily press briefings by the military in Saigon. Film footage was also government influenced, as TV crews "were shunted by helicopter from one operation to another by military press officers who wanted to show off American initiative."[10] Coupled with reports from Washington and the media's inclination to close ranks around the administration in a time of war, coverage produced an image of military success. As Hallin notes, "It must have been very hard . . . for the average television viewer to imagine the possibility that American arms might not ultimately be successful in Vietnam."[11]

Television's emphasis on combat was ironic, since it is less mobile than the print media and so more dependent on news from Saigon and Washington. At times action footage was staged, since the enemy often proved too elusive. "The strangest thing about the war was we never saw the enemy, the Vietcong . . . they vanished whenever we arrived."[12] Once U.S. combat troops were committed in large numbers, the story quickly became "American boys in action," and this required having cameras in the field (nine network employees were killed in Indochina and many more were wounded). But being in the field did not mean being in battle—only 22 percent of the pre-Tet film reports from Southeast Asia showed combat, and most of these were limited to "a few incoming mortar rounds or a crackle of sniper fire."[13] When battle scenes were available, they were edited according to explicit guidelines barring the use of graphic film of wounded American soldiers or suffering civilians. According to former CBS News president Fred W. Friendly, these network policies "helped shield the audience from the true horror of the war." [14]

But while the public received positive reports about the war, a conflict brewed within the press corps. To a small but growing number of journalists, government and media accounts did not jibe with their own experiences in Vietnam. This view cut against the grain of the still-prevailing cold war consensus, however, and so was met by subtle and not so subtle censorship by editors and producers. In part, this internal censorship resulted from editors' suspicions of young reporters who were too committed to a cause to be objective. More disturbingly, it also reflected direct political intervention. For example, President Johnson intervened to stop a 1965 *Time* article by Frank McColloch revealing that U.S. troops were preparing to assume an active combat role. Such presidential involvement in press censorship was not unusual, especially at *Time,* where "any time McColloch had a particularly big story that went against the official line, somehow the Administration shot it down through the Washington bureau." [15]

Despite the stifling of occasional voices of dissent, a subtle change in coverage occurred in this period. In the print media, doubts were raised in the editorial page or buried deep in the inverted pyramid of a news story. The *New York Times,* for example, ran editorials urging stronger efforts at diplomacy, or, towards the end of news articles, referred to unnamed sources who questioned the stability of the South Vietnamese government or the competency of their military. Occasionally a soldier's quote would reveal a growing sense of confusion and frustration. But the administration was never criticized directly, and the format of newspaper reporting assured that readers could distinguish "fact" from opinion and the "important facts" from less important ones.

In television, less information is conveyed, and the distinction between fact and interpretation is blurred. Television thus limited itself to simpler and fewer themes, presenting issues in black-and-white terms. Most often this meant our good guys heroically but inexorably succeeding against the bad guys. But sometimes the norms of reporting forced the networks to make choices and present information they would just as soon not. The most dramatic example of this prior to Tet was in August 1965, when Morley Safer's crew filmed U.S. marines destroying the village of Cam Ne. Safer's report threw CBS into turmoil. While no one wanted to air footage of American boys indiscriminately burning down houses, they had the film and the norms of journalism clearly said show it. The night it aired, CBS was swamped by phone calls from viewers who were outraged that CBS would "do something like this, portraying our boys as killers, American boys didn't do things like that. Many of the calls were obscene." [16] The next day, CBS executive Frank Stanton was awakened by yet another phone call:

> "Frank," said the early-morning wake-up call, "Are you trying to fuck me?"
> "Who is this?" said the still sleepy Stanton. "Frank, this is your President, and yesterday your boys shat on the American flag." [17]

The administration's reaction did not end here. Johnson, convinced Safer was a communist, did a thorough search of his past. (Upon finding that Safer was clean, but Canadian, Johnson replied, "Well I knew he wasn't an American.") [18] Johnson also ran a check on the marine officer who took Safer to Cam Ne, and a Pentagon official tried to get the Vietnamese cameraman for CBS fired, "complaining that one of the keys to this evil story was that CBS had used a South Vietnamese cameraman, a sure sign of alien influence." [19]

The norms of newsworthiness were instrumental in a second challenge to the administration's policy in Vietnam during this period—the Fulbright hearings. William Fulbright was the senator who had, based on Johnson's promise that no U.S. ground troops would be committed to Vietnam, shepherded the Gulf of Tonkin Resolution through Congress. By early 1966 he felt betrayed and helpless, as the administration's line on Vietnam received exclusive media coverage. Thus, in late January 1966 Fulbright used committee hearings on a supplemental foreign aid bill as a platform to lambast the administration. When representatives of the administration appeared before the committee, he made Vietnam the issue. The confrontations were highly newsworthy, given the legitimate nature of the opposition (a respected senator), the stature of the forum (the Capitol building), and the confrontational nature of the issue (Congress vs. the president; a heated challenge to the president's Vietnam policy by a member of his own party and a former supporter). In fact, NBC and CBS covered much of the hearings live, despite the high cost in lost revenues. (Fred Friendly, eventually prevented from continuing coverage due to the cost, resigned as president of CBS news.) The Fulbright hearings, however, and the Cam Ne incident are most notable as exceptions during this period. Shifting the norm required changing the definitions of consensus, legitimate controversy, and deviance. This shift occurred in dramatic fashion in January of 1968.

Expanding the Sphere of Legitimate Controversy: The Tet Offensive   Coverage of the Tet offensive is among the most controversial aspects of the war. While military historians agree the offensive failed, it launched large-scale opposition to the war at home. The tenor of press coverage did change during the offensive. Prior to Tet journalists editorialized in about 6 percent of the television stories on Vietnam. During the two months of the offensive, this percentage jumped to 20 percent, subsequently dropping to about 10 percent.[20] Newspapers also editorialized more during Tet, often on the front page.

The administration's view of the offensive was *not* ignored—papers and networks dutifully reported the official line, often as the lead of the story. On February 2, for example, the *Washington Post*'s headline read: "LBJ CALLS UPRISING FAILURE—VIETCONG HOLDING ON IN HUE; THIEU ASKS MORE BOMBING—PRESIDENT SEES REPULSE OF NEW DRIVE." Now, however, "upbeat" messages were presented in ways that led one to doubt their accuracy. For example, the *New York Times* reported on February 2 that the "latest propaganda line [is] that we are now seeing the enemy's 'last gasp'." Government optimism was being reported in a way that turned it on its head. The press remained dependent on government sources, but no longer fully believed them. The result was a style of reporting that presents "facts" in a way that says these are not facts.

Television, with its tendency to blur fact and opinion, portrayed Tet even more bleakly. Again, reporters did not suggest Tet was a military defeat. Cronkite's statement of February 14, 1968—"First and simplest, the Vietcong suffered a military defeat"—was typical. Instead, the message was that such victories did not add up to winning the war. For example, CBS offered this description of prisoners captured by the U.S.:

> These pathetic-looking people may be Buddhists rather than Vietcong, and there's little record of the Buddhist's and the Vietcong working very closely together. About the only thing certain is the government hasn't won any friends here today. If the purpose of this war is to win the hearts and minds of the people, the capture of An Quang pagoda can be considered a defeat. (February 2, 1968)

An NBC report on February 20 paints a similar picture of futility:

> American Marines are so bogged down in Hue that nobody will even predict when the battle will end . . . More than 500 Marines have been wounded and 100 killed since the fighting in Hue began . . . The price has been high and it's gained the marines about 50 yards a day or less in a heavily populated part of the citadel. Still, nothing is really secure . . . Most of the city is now in rubble . . . and many Vietnamese say the fight isn't really worth it now that their city is dead.

And from the siege of Khe Sanh CBS reported:

> So there is no end in sight. The North Vietnamese out there beyond the fog show no inclination to pull back or attack. U.S. commanders show no inclination just yet to drive them back. So for the Marines and the Seabees and the rest here, there is nothing to do but sit and take it, just to wait, and hope they'll rotate out, leave before they join the roster of the wounded and dead here.

As a picture of military reality such reports may have been too pessimistic. By this time, however, reporting of individual events had become a metaphor for the war as a whole. An AP wire quoting a U.S. major in Ben Tre perhaps best captures the theme of the war coverage during this period: "It became necessary to destroy the town in order to save it." This theme was reinforced by the frequency of vivid scenes of casualties and urban destruction. Such scenes were four times more frequent during the Tet period than during the rest of the war, and scenes of military casualties were almost three times more common.[21]

Three events are particularly emblematic of the Tet coverage. The first, from early in the offensive, was the photo and film footage of Colonel Loan blowing the brains out of a captured Vietcong on a Saigon street. Putting aside the debate over whether the act was justifiable, the impact of this film on the estimated twenty million Americans who saw it was devastating. Nothing had prepared them for such a horrible, naked image of the war, and especially not for such an image of "our side's" behavior.

The second media event was Walter Cronkite's hour-long special on the Tet offensive, broadcast on February 27. Cronkite, a supporter of the war prior to Tet and perhaps the most trusted man in America presented a shocking picture of the immediate situation and of the overall war effort. He concluded:

> It seems now more certain than ever that the bloody experience of Vietnam is to end in a stalemate. This summer's almost certain standoff will either end in real give-and-take negotiations or terrible escalation; and for every means we have to escalate, the enemy can match us . . . And with each escalation, the world comes closer to the brink of cosmic disaster. To say that we are closer to victory today is to believe, in the face of the evidence, the optimists who have been wrong in the past. To suggest we are on the edge of defeat is to yield to unreasonable pessimism. To say that we are mired in stalemate seems the only realistic, yet unsatisfactory, conclusion.

These sentiments were echoed by other journalists and anchors, but as Johnson himself was purported to say, "Cronkite was it."[22]

Finally, on March 31, one day before American troops broke the seige of Khe Sanh and effectively ended this two-month offensive, LBJ told the American public on national television that

> With America's sons in the fields far away, with America's future under challenge right here at home, with our hopes and the world's hopes for peace in the balance every day, I do not believe that I should devote an hour or a day of my time to any personal partisan causes or to any duties other than the awesome duties of this office—the Presidency of your country. Accordingly, I

shall not seek, and I will not accept, the nomination of my party for another term as your president.

This speech marked more than the end of the Johnson presidency; it marked the beginning of the end of the war. When LBJ changed the opening of his address from "I want to talk to you about the war in Vietnam," to "I want to talk to you about peace in Vietnam,"[23] the idea of a military victory was gone forever. And the media, true to its tendencies, took the president's lead. As ABC telexed its Saigon personnel: "We are on our way out of Vietnam."

Never was the phrase "to win the battle but lose the war" more appropriate than with Tet. Johnson later reflected that "while the Viet Cong and North Vietnamese may have failed militarily with Tet, they did achieve the psychological victory they sought."[24] During this two-month "defeat" for the North, public opinion in the U.S. shifted dramatically. Between November 1967 and February 1968 those believing the U.S. was making progress in the war dropped from 51 percent to 32 percent. By late March LBJ's approval rating was 26 percent, a 13-point drop since November.[25] And, as the siege of Khe Sanh ended on April 1, for the first time a majority of Americans opposed the war.[26] Policy followed opinion as plans for an increase in U.S. force levels were put indefinitely on the back burner. Administration talk shifted from "the war effort" to "the peace effort." Johnson ordered another halt to the bombing of North Vietnam.

In explaining this turnaround in public opinion and public policy, many point an accusing finger at the press. Former reporters like Peter Braestrup contend that "the collective emanations of the major media [produced] a kind of continuous black fog of their own, a vague conventional 'disaster' image."[27] ABC anchor Howard K. Smith charged that the networks "just showed pictures day after day of Americans getting the hell kicked out of them. That was enough to break America apart."[28] President Johnson, in a speech to the National Association of Broadcasters on April 1, 1968, even suggested that the presence of television *might* have altered the outcome of World War II or Korea.[29] Why did coverage change during this period? Was the media responsible for the shift in opinion and policy, and for our eventual withdrawal from the war?

Answers to these questions are more complex than many critics pretend. This shift in media coverage did not occur out of the blue. Recall that since the early sixties a minority of Saigon correspondents, government officials, military personnel, and citizen dissidents had questioned the strategy and/or legitimacy of the war. When Tet shook the establishment perspective on the war, causing a momentary void, these critics stepped in to fill it. For example, during the Tet offensive Neil Sheehan published a story (cowritten by Hedrick Smith) revealing General West-moreland's request for more troops and the "stirring debate" it caused in the administration. The story would not have been in the works had Sheehan not been haunted by the war since 1962; but without Tet it would never have been published in a form capable of, according to Walt Rostow, "churn[ing] up the whole eastern establishment."[30] Tet, in short, gave those who had long questioned the war access to the agenda and control of the peg on which news is hung. Had there not been such people waiting in the wings, the Tet offensive might have produced much less journalistic chaos and might have been more easily pigeon-holed as a military victory story.

Much of the pressure for expanding the sphere of legitimate debate came from within the administration, where civilian advisors challenged the military's optimistic assessments and requests for more troops. In Congress, too, concerns were building. And the media voices that both reflected and fueled this growing debate were not deviants; they were well-known supporters of the war, like Cronkite, Reynolds, and even Howard K. Smith.

Signs of this growing debate existed prior to Tet. Beginning in the spring of 1967 with the battle for Hills 861 and 881, and continuing into the fall with the battles of Con Thien and Dak To, the North's tactics shifted to more concentrated battles, raising the level of concern within the U.S. media, public, and government. Media reports, while still over-whelmingly supportive, began to show the doubts that would dominate the Tet period:

> One high-ranking official . . . said he thought the enemy was willing to take a million casualties, which at the current ratio would mean 200,000 U.S. casu-alties, with at least 25,000 killed, and that figure may be conservative. "Will the American people accept those losses?" I wondered. "Do they have any choice?" was his rejoinder. "Then the real war out here is just beginning?" I asked. The official nodded his head in assent. (CBS, April 12, 1967)

> The battle for Dak To has now become the bloodiest of the war for American and North Vietnamese troops . . . The question every GI asks and cannot an-swer is, "Was it all worth it?" No one really knows. (CBS, November 22, 1967)

McNamara's resignation soon after a public clash with the Joint Chiefs of Staff added fuel to this smoldering fire.

This increasingly public display of doubt affected public opinion. While most indicators of support for the war remained strong, the percentage of Americans who felt getting involved in Vietnam had been a mistake and who disapproved of Johnson's handling of the war began to grow in 1966.[31] In short, the erosion of support for the war was accelerated, but not created, by Tet.

Ironically, much of the negative coverage during Tet can be laid at the feet of the Johnson administration itself. In part it was the inescapable price of previous media management. The success of efforts to make the war appear both minor and successful now came back to haunt the Pentagon and the White House with a vengeance. Film footage and stories during Tet were dramatic in their own right. Counterposed to years of exaggerated claims of U.S. and South Vietnamese control and deflated estimates of North Vietnamese and Vietcong strength, they were devastating. The American public and media were caught unaware. The Johnson administration failed to deal forcefully and directly with this dismay. Had Johnson taken control of the agenda during Tet, the void that was filled by critical, pessimistic reports might never have been opened.[32] Indeed, support for LBJ and the war increased at the beginning of the Tet offensive, providing the platform upon which he could have reestablished his leadership. Instead he retreated into brooding silence while his support plummeted, to rise again only when he announced his withdrawal from politics.

Finally, the nature of the Tet offensive and of the routines of news gathering added to the dramatic nature of the coverage. Prior to Tet most combat occurred outside the cities and therefore away from where most journalists and camera crews were stationed. Where before they depended on the military for access, during Tet "merely by stepping outside their hotels, correspondents found themselves willy-nilly in the midst of bloody fighting. There was no way that the attacks in broad daylight on such landmarks as the presidential palace could be concealed from television cameras."[33] Moreover, the frantic pace of events during Tet sped up the normal routines of filming, transporting, editing, and broadcasting. Unedited films were flown immediately to Tokyo, broadcast via satellite to New York (a rare and expensive procedure), and put straight on the air. The result was not the orderly, bloodless images to which audiences were accustomed, but raw visions of chaos, destruction, and Americans on the defensive.

It is the airing of these films that best reflects the complex interaction of journalistic norms as to what is newsworthy, the chaos of Tet, the media's distrust of the administration in this period, and the void left by the administration's failure to reestablish its authority. The war had come to the journalists, and in ways that did not fit the well established mold. Government reports were assumed to be false and were automatically questioned. As if to make up for their sins of omission and naivete, journalists gave the horror of the war free reign. Had the offensive not provided so many visually arresting images it might not have had the same effect. Had the military not so exaggerated American superiority and Vietcong inferiority, or had the press not accepted its claims so fully, the effects of the Tet offensive might have been different. But in combination, these factors loosened the grip of editors, producers, generals, and the administration on the media and offered critics of the war an opening. Even the North Vietnamese were able to occasionally get their perspective onto American front pages and into the evening news.

In the end, however, the media never questioned American motives or the policymaking system itself. They merely questioned the soundness of the tactics and whether the benefits of this protracted, bloody war outweighed the rising costs. These were precisely the questions being raised by congresspersons, senators, administration officials, and soldiers in the field. The media were no more responsible for the shift in public opinion and policy against the war effort during the two months of Tet than they were for maintaining that support and policy during the prior seven years—and no less responsible either.

A New Consensus? Media Coverage after Tet   After Tet, coverage of the war settled into a new normalcy. The networks returned to the standard operating procedure of shipping film by air freight. This delay—film would arrive in New York as much as five days after the shots had been taken—meant a return to timeless pieces designed to be non-specific. NBC, for example, ordered correspondents to "be careful about filming events that might date themselves."[34] The end of a crisis atmosphere also meant a return to sanitized images, and "the military scene was depicted as a series of orderly American actions against an unseen foe."[35]

This new consensus differed from the one preceding Tet, however. The media now portrayed the war as a stalemate. In late 1968, for example, NBC rejected producing a series showing that Tet had been a military victory because, in the words of an NBC executive, Tet was "established in the public's mind as a defeat, and therefore it was an American defeat."[36] This new view of the war is dramatically reflected in statistics on the media's description of battles as victories or defeats. Prior to Tet, of those battles journalists characterized, 62 percent were described as U.S. victories, while only 28 percent were described as defeats and 2 percent as stalemates. After Tet, the number of victories reported fell to 44 percent, the number of defeats rose slightly to 32 percent, and the number of stalemates jumped to 24 percent.[37]

Even during this last phase of the war, the media was still loyal, but Tet had changed the tenor of the coverage. Anchors and correspondents no longer portrayed the war as a national endeavor and seldom referred to "our war." They no longer invoked the memory of World War II, in effect disconnecting Vietnam from American tradition. Gone too was the macho sports image of the pre-Tet stories. "Today in Saigon," reported NBC in June 1969, they announced the casuality figures for the week, and though they came out in the form of numbers, each one of them was a man, most of them quite young, each with hopes he will never realize, each with family and friends who will never see him again. Anyway here are the numbers.

The most dramatic example of this shift to the personalization of the deaths of U.S. teenagers was the June 27, 1969 edition of *LIFE*. It simply presented the faces and names of the 242 U.S. soldiers killed during a "typical" week in Vietnam. The effect was devastating:

> The story was so plainly done, there was the air of a high-school yearbook to it; one did not know these kids, but one did—they were kids who went to high school and who, upon graduation, went to work rather than college. Nor were these photos by Karsh of Ottawa. Their very cheapness and primitive quality added to the effect, the pride and fear and innocence in the faces, many of them being photographed in uniform, half scared and half full of bravado. It was almost unbearable. It was an issue to make men and women cry.[38]

Gone was the sense of purpose, of order. Consider the following:

> The Special Forces and the enemy fought this battle to a standstill. And there was nothing left but to tend the wounded, and fight again another day. (CBS, Oct 1, 1968)

Finally, the themes of military victory, of "halting communist aggression" and "preserving democracy" simply disappeared. Instead, the policy statements read in the papers and heard on TV (made mostly by administration and congressional spokespersons) focused on how to end the war, on its costs to the U.S., and on how to protect U.S. troops and bring home prisoners of war.

The Nixon administration introduced a dual strategy of "Vietnamization," or returning the war to the South Vietnamese, and "peace with honor," or negotiating an American withdrawal without losing face. This strategy had contradictory elements, however. Vietnamization meant the removal of U.S. combat troops, but getting the North Vietnamese to negotiate required added military pressure; this, in turn, posed serious media and public relations problems.

The result was a schizophrenic relationship between the media and the Nixon administration. On issues where there was mainstream consensus—that we should withdraw, that we must negotiate for peace rather than win it militarily, that the South Vietnamese should fight their own war, that the North Vietnamese were still the enemy—the administration could count on the press's support. The media focused on relatively positive portrayals of the South Vietnamese army, and on the Paris peace talks. By 1970, consistent with U.S. policy, the main story on all three networks had become the withdrawal of American troops. When negotiations failed to produce results, the media blamed the North Vietnamese:

> President Nixon's new peace plan for Vietnam was formally offered at the Paris peace talks today, and the Communists reacted with sneers, wisecracks, and sarcasm. But actually that's about what was expected of them . . . In this country the president's plan has won wide support and approval in both parties (NBC, October 8, 1970)

Conversely, the president and the press collided when his policies most openly contradicted the mainstream consensus, and especially when they led to the war's expansion. When—as at Hamburger Hill in May 1969, the invasion of Cambodia in April 1970, and the invasion of Laos in February 1971—the war seemed to be escalating and U.S. casualties rose, the media, opposition leaders, and even the troops themselves, turned against the administration:

> The elite Special Forces have fought well and bravely as usual but for a military objective of doubtful value . . . After you've been here a while and seen all the casualties . . . you come away with the distinct impression that the principle reason these Special Forces have been ordered to take Million Dollar Mountain is simply because its there. (CBS, March 21, 1969)

U.S. casualties could no longer be portrayed in a positive, meaningful light. This shift away from military objectives made combat especially tough on the soldiers, whose morale dropped precipitously. This was not missed by the press, which reported on poor morale with increasing frequency. In one ABC report in April 1972, for example, footage of "an officer persuading reluctant troops to go out on a mission by assuring them it was not an offensive operation" concluded with the report saying "one thing does seem for sure: the average American soldier no longer wants any part of this war—even in a defensive posture." [39]

The Nixon administration also suffered in the press when its policies appeared inconsistent or deceptive. In September 1970, when the administration halted and then resumed bombing the North, the networks (echoing sentiment in parts of the government and the public) suggested that it was internally torn and lacked a clear policy. Revelations of the secret bombing of Cambodia in May 1969 further heightened tensions between the press, the administration, and the loyal opposition, as did the controversy over the printing of the Pentagon Papers in 1971.

The most important story of the post-Tet period, however, was the My Lai massacre of as many as 500 civilians. Coverage of this incident is revealing for a number of reasons. First, the failure of the press to report the massacre for an entire year after the event reflects the dependence of the media on military reports. On the day of the massacre (March 17,

1968) AP, UPI, and the *New York Times* ran stories presenting the action at My Lai as a normal-search-and-destroy action. MACV reports, which made no mention of civilian deaths, were used almost verbatim, spiced up by details that gave a more personal (though fictional) touch.[40] Second, that the press did eventually report the massacre shows how the war had shifted from a consensus to a legitimately controversial issue. In the past similar atrocities were usually ignored, and made it to the mainstream media only in unusual circumstances such as the Safer film from Cam Ne.

Third, despite the unprecedented coverage My Lai received, the media never challenged the morality of the war effort more generally. In addition, the media's focus on the trial of Lieutenant Calley, rather than on the massacre itself, pegged it as a story of individual misdeed, declining morale, and American justice rather than military atrocity.[41]

The anchors also separated My Lai from any systematic pattern or policy: "My Lai was for Americans an exceptional horror. My Lais for the other side are a daily way of life." (Howard K. Smith, ABC, May 28, 1970) Such commentary was typical of coverage throughout the war: U.S. atrocities were aberrations, the acts of individuals momentarily out of control; North Vietnamese and Vietcong atrocities were commonplace, the willful acts of irrational murderers or the application of a systematic policy of terror.

The War at Home: Maintaining the Boundary Between Debate and Deviance   Common wisdom suggests that the national media gave the antiwar movement unfettered access to the public, thus helping to turn public opinion and policy against the war and, ultimately, to bring down the Johnson and Nixon presidencies. A closer examination suggests that, while the media did cover the movement and domestic opposition to the war was influential, the media was as responsible for maintaining support for the war as for its deterioration. Moreover, during the period of declining support for the war, the media was critical in keeping antiwar, and later anti-Nixon, protest from becoming the basis for a more systematic critique of the political, social, and economic system.[42]

Like the war itself, the antiwar movement went through several phases of coverage. From 1960 to 1964, when groups like the SDS began organizing on college campuses, the mainstream media largely ignored the movement. By the end of 1965, however, SDS had grown to 124 chapters and 4,300 members. That year, with the spontaneous eruption of the Free Speech Movement at Berkeley and the March 17 march on Washington, organized by the SDS to protest growing U.S. involvement in Vietnam, the student movement became newsworthy. Reporters sought out protests and articles appeared that spring in many national magazines (for example, *Time, Newsweek, U.S. News, Saturday Evening Post,* the *New York Times Magazine,* the *Nation,* and the *New Republic*).

But greater attention from the mainstream press meant attention from inside the cold war consensus looking out. The movement was often trivialized (making light of student members' clothes, language, goals), marginalized (made to appear deviant, unrepresentative), and presented as deeply divided internally. In addition, stories almost always counterposed the movement with ultraright groups, as if to say that extremism is extremism. At the same time, the movement was presented as ineffective and so not a worthwhile political alternative.

With the Fulbright hearings in early 1966, domestic unrest became a standard news peg upon which to hang a story. From this point on, almost one in five broadcasts about Vietnam dealt with this issue. But except for infrequent criticism from "responsible" representatives such as senators and congresspersons, coverage remained largely negative. And as the number and size of protests grew (ironically, partly in response to the media's coverage of earlier protests) television began to paint the protestors with more sinister strokes:

> While Americans fight and die in Vietnam, there are those in this country who sympathize with the Vietcong. (ABC, October, 1965)

> Meanwhile, Hanoi was having paroxysms of joy over the demonstrations in this country. (NBC, October, 1965)

In a 1965 CBS broadcast on the day before nationwide demonstrations, Morley Safer showed a group of GIs in Vietnam a film of an antiwar draft-resistance lecture. He then asked one of the soldiers, "You're getting shot at. Five of your buddies were killed down the road the other day. How did you feel watching the film?" One soldier, filled with emotion, responded he wished it had been the people in the film, and not his buddies, who had been killed. The media also regularly portrayed the antiwar movement as violent. While stories occasionally addressed police brutality and overreaction, more often the theme was antiwar provocation: "The sight of the [NLF] flag was too much for some of the onlookers . . . the angry crowd along the roadway jumped in to do away with the Vietcong symbol" (CBS, 1967). The antiwar movement both attracted and repelled the media. Protests and demonstrations, especially when visually dramatic or confrontational, were perfect for television news. In addition, some of what the protestors said hit a responsive chord with some reporters. But the protests clearly fell outside the sphere of legitimate controversy, and so were presented in an almost exclusively negative light.

With Tet and LBJ's decision to not run for reelection, coverage of the antiwar movement changed. In part there was a shift in the boundary detcrmining what was acceptable—a widening of the political arena. In part, however, this shift also marked the appearance a modified version of the antiwar movement—a mainstream, middle-class version. Senators, congresspersons, and much of Middle America said enough is enough, and the media repeated their statements. The electoral process, perhaps the best barometer of what is and is not acceptable, raised the issue of the war. When Eugene McCarthy nearly beat Ed Muskie in the 1968 New Hampshire primary, the antiwar movement had crossed into the realm of legitimate controversy.

Throughout this period the media played a key role in defining the new boundaries and identifying who was to be allowed in and who remained outcast. As *Time* editorialized in 1968,

> in an era when many young Americans are turning away from involvement in the democratic process by dropping out either to psychedelia or to the nihilism of the New Left, the cool, crisply-executed crusade of Eugene McCarthy's 'ballot children' provides heartening evidence that the generation gap is bridgeable—politically at least.

This role of border guard was most evident in the coverage of the Moratorium demonstrations of October 1969. That a mass demonstration could be considered legitimate shows how far the boundaries had shifted since Tet. However, for Middle America and its media, there are good and bad demonstrations. With its connections to the political establishment (McCarthy, Kennedy, McGovern) and its middle-class support, the Moratorium was a "good" demonstration and was presented as such. Observed CBS, for example, "Today's protest was different . . . peaceful, within the law, and not confined to a radical minority" (October, 1969). Compare this to CBS's coverage of the more spontaneous, student-led protests that followed the U.S. invasion of Cambodia in 1970: "The Cambodia development set off a new round of antiwar demonstrations on U.S. campuses, and not all of them were peaceful." Again and again the post-Tet theme was the distinction between legitimate and illegitimate protest. Consider this statement, made about a student effort to lobby Congress: "earnest, clean-shaven college students, full of facts, not rhetoric, carrying well-written resolutions and legal briefs in their hands . . . These emissaries are just about as weary of high-flown oratory as their elders" (CBS, May, 1970).

As opposition to the war was first legitimated and then became the consensus, the media had to redefine and guard the nation's boundary on the right as well. The violence of pro-war protesters, hard hats, the police, the National Guard, and even the Nixon administration was increasingly denounced in much the same fashion as the radical Left. Indeed, what is most distinctive of this period is that for perhaps the only time in our history an administration occasionally found *itself* outside the sphere of legitimate controversy. The result was the ultimate demise of that administration. But here, again, the media was as important in preventing this chaotic situation from evolving into a larger questioning of the system as it was for branding Nixon as a deviant. Ultimately it was not the press that brought Nixon down. Rather it was his inability to distinguish, as the media had, between the loyal opposition and the protesters who had more fundamental grievances but posed a serious threat to the administration only in the minds of Nixon and his cadre of advisors.

The Legacies of Press Coverage of the Vietnam Era

Media coverage of the war in Vietnam has left a number of specific legacies affecting the press, government, grass-roots groups, and the general public. The press, ironically, is the least changed by the events of the 1960s. True, there is now an institutionalized adversarial relationship with the White House that is much more likely to be set in motion than before the Vietnam era. The press has also added a few more specific news pegs to its standard operating procedures. It is impossible to speak about the use of U.S. troops overseas, about protests and demonstrations, about political scandals, and so forth, without referring, explicitly or implicitly, to the Vietnam experience and its immediate aftermath. (Consider, for example, the common use of the phrase "another Vietnam," or the addition of the suffix *-gate,* as in "Koreagate" or "Contragate".) The press, in certain circumstances, is also more likely to present official information to the public with a large and cynical grain of salt.

Yet for all this, the press remains largely dependent on the government for its information about the political world. It remains an institution whose modus operandi is reporting what official sources say. And so, it remains the central institution for maintaining the boundaries of consensus, legitimate debate, and deviance. If anything, this role has fallen even more to the press, as other traditional institutions of sociopolitical hegemony have continued to decay and as the media industry has become more centralized, nationalized, and tied economically to the status quo over the past two decades.[43]

This risk-averse behavior of the press is also the result of the media becoming newsworthy in and of itself. Since the Vietnam era and the speculation that the press was unduly influential in the outcome of the war, social unrest in the United States, and the fall of President Nixon, the role of the media in covering social and political events has become part of the story. This puts the press in an unusual bind. On the one hand, becoming part of the story means challenging the myth of objectivity upon which the press depends for it credibility. On the other hand, the press's dependence on reporting what official sources say means that if those sources make the media an issue, it becomes an issue. As a result, the media will often back down from an issue rather than run the risk of becoming the story themselves.

The utility of this tendency as a tool in managing the media has not been lost on the government generally, nor on the White House in particular. While they have learned slowly, presidential administrations are now fully cognizant of two critical lessons of the Vietnam era: the press is crucial to the success or failure of an administration; in the relationship between the press and the White House, the latter holds almost all the cards. Presidential administrations now devote huge amounts of time, resources, and personnel to the management of public image. By limiting the amount and kind of information released, by controlling the press's access to people and information in government, by expanding the sphere of consensus and constraining the sphere of legitimate controversy, by exploiting those parts of the press that allow direct access to the public (speeches, photo opportunities, and so forth) and limiting those that allow the press to more freely control the spin of a story, and by intimidating the press through making it part of the story (accusing it of bias or sensationalism, threatening it with costly law suits, and so forth), government has clearly gained the upper hand in limiting negative coverage and increasing advantageous coverage.

Foreign policy is in part shaped by the lessons of Vietnam, though thus far these lessons appear limited to don't take the press along during military interventions (à la Grenada); don't use U.S. troops when engaged in limited warfare (à la Nicaragua, Angola, and Afghanistan); and, as much as possible, use covert rather than overt operations (à la the Iran-Contra affair).

Domestic policy has also been affected by the Vietnam era. The recent dismantling of many of the social welfare and civil rights programs of the 1960s and early 1970s was possible only because of the ability of the Reagan and Bush administrations to paint those programs as failed policies of a misguided liberalism. Such a representation of the Vietnam era is only possible by successfully manipulating the media environment in which our collective memory is preserved. The Reagan and Bush administrations have proven masters of such manipulation, knowing when and how to go public with certain issues (for example, tax reform, the Grenada invasion, the flag-burning controversy) and when to back off and try more covert strategies (for example, the weakening of many environmental and social regulations, the secret war against Nicaragua, arms sales to Iran). Perhaps most impressively, even when certain policies backfired (as with the bombing of the U.S. embassy in Lebanon, the attempt to roll back certain social security benefits, the incredible growth in the budget and trade deficits, and the Iran-Contra affair), the Reagan administration was able to cut off public scrutiny before much long-term damage to the administration's credibility was done. Compare the way these events played themselves out in the press with similar public issues of the 1960s and early 1970s, and it becomes clear that the lessons of the Vietnam era have thus far worked to the advantage of government.[44]

The organized public on both the left and the right have become more sophisticated in either avoiding the mainstream press through the use of direct-mail and grass-roots organizing, or in presenting themselves in ways designed to capture the attention of media. Like the government, they have learned that they can be active agents in how they are presented in the press. However, they lack the resources of government and most lack the credibility as well, making their task a much more difficult one. And, of course, how and if a group is presented still very much depends on where it is located in the spheres of consensus, debate, and deviance. The more removed from the mainstream a group is, the less likely it is to get its message heard, and the more sensational must be its actions in order to get attention. This in turn increases the likelihood that the group will be presented as illegitimate and that its agenda will be misrepresented or simplified.

And what of the larger public, for whom politics is a less central concern? Coverage of consensus and deviance, because such stories are presented from a point of view (the former is good, the latter bad), remain successful at maintaining the status quo in older generations and reproducing it in younger ones. Coverage of legitimate controversy, however, especially when it deals with problems that are both serious and seemingly intractable, lacks such a context. Presented with either disembodied facts or point-counter-points in which the logic, implications, or veracity of each side is left unexplored and assumed to be equally plausible, citizens are only able to use such information if they have their own well-developed political perspective from which to interpret the news. Such citizens are rare in our society, however, and (ironically) the way in which we expect most citizens to develop such a perspective is by being active consumers of the news.

Viewed in this way, one legacy of the Vietnam era may be an anesthetizing, alienating overload. Almost twenty-five years of uncritical images of business as usual, interspersed with tales of incompetence, corruption, violence, and destruction, have taken their toll. For the current generation of young adults, adolescents, and children such stories are the norm, not the exception. It is not that the stories are false. But presented as they are—as objectified, disembodied facts devoid of context—they can only frustrate.

In the end, however, the real legacy of Vietnam is less what has changed than what has been revealed. The role of the press in the United States is influenced by two different ethics—the libertarianism of the eighteenth and nineteenth centuries, with its emphasis on a free, diverse, adversarial press, and the social responsibility of the twentieth century, with its focus on balance and objectivity. The legacy of press coverage of the war suggests that what passes for objectivity is in fact hegemony. And, despite the cries of bias, what passes for advocacy is little more than a stenographic, relativist presentation of disputes among the powers that be. Ultimately the question raised by press coverage of Vietnam is the impact of this style of informing the public on both the form and the substance of political discourse in the United States.

NOTES

1. In this essay the terms *press* and *news media* will be used interchangeably and refer to both electronic and print media. This essay is limited to a discussion of the mainstream media, and does not explore the very different dynamic that applies to the alternative press.

2. For a detailed discussion of the experience of soldiers in Vietnam, see D. Michael Shafer, "The Vietnam Combat Experience: The Human Legacy," in this volume.

3. The following discussion draws upon Todd Gitlin, *The Whole World Is Watching* (Berkeley: University of California Press, 1980), and Daniel C. Hallin, *The Uncensored War* (New York: Oxford University Press, 1986).

4 Hallin, *The Uncensored War,* p. 117.

5. Ibid., p. 127.

6. The following section draws upon Peter Braestrup, *The Big Story* (New Haven: Yale University Press, 1978); Edward Jay Epstein, *Between Fact and Fiction* (New York: Vintage, 1975); David Halberstam, *The Powers That Be* (New York: Dell, 1979); Hallin, *The Uncensored War,* and upon my own examination of news footage and newspaper and magazine accounts. Unless otherwise noted, direct references to particular broadcasts, and newspaper or magazine stories are from these sources.

7. Cited in Epstein, *Between Fact and Fiction,* p. 215.

8. Halberstam, *The Powers That Be,* p. 627.

9. Cited in Hallin, *The Uncensored War,* p. 34.

10. NBC correspondent Ron Nesson, as cited in Epstein, *Between Fact and Fiction,* p. 217.

11. Hallin, *The Uncensored War,* p. 146.

12. NBC correspondent Lem Tucker, as cited in Epstein, *Between Fact and Fiction,* p. 217.

13. Hallin, *The Uncensored War,* p. 129.

14. Cited in Epstein, *Between Fact and Fiction,* p. 217.

15. Halberstam, *The Powers That Be,* p. 664.

16. Ibid., p. 683.

17. Ibid., p. 683.

18. Ibid., p. 683.

19. Ibid., p. 681.

20. Hallin, *The Uncensored War,* p. 169.

21. Ibid., p. 171.

22. Austin Ranney, *Channels of Power* (New York: Basic Books, 1983), p. 6.

23. Herbert Y. Schandler, *The Unmaking of a President* (Princeton: Princeton University Press, 1977), p. 273.

24. Kathleen J. Turner, *Lyndon Johnson's Dual War* (Chicago: University of Chicago Press, 1985), p. 232.

25. Roper polls reported in Braestrup, *Big Story,* and Hallin, *The Uncensored War.*

26. Epstein, *Between Fact and Fiction,* p. 224.

27. Braestrup, *Big Story,* p. 706.

28. Epstein, *Between Fact and Fiction,* p. 223.

29. Michael Mandelbaum, "Vietnam: The Television War," *Daedalus* 111 (Fall, 1982), p. 157.

30. Cited in Hallin, *The Uncensored War,* p. 169.

31. John E. Mueller, *Presidents and Public Opinion* (New York: Wiley, 1973).

32. Turner, *Lyndon Johnson's Dual War.*

33. Epstein, *Between Fact and Fiction,* p. 220.

34. Ibid., p. 225.

35. Ibid.

36. Ibid.

37. Hallin, *The Uncensored War,* pp. 146, 166.

38. Halberstam, *The Powers That Be,* pp. 676–77.

39. Hallin, *The Uncensored War,* p. 180.

40. Braestrup, *Big Story,* pp. 249–53.

41. Hallin, *The Uncensored War,* p. 180.

42. This section draws on Gitlin, *The Whole World Is Watching,* and Hallin, *The Uncensored War.* For a further discussion of the war at home, see "Vietnam, Ideology, and Domestic Politics," in this volume.

43. For a discussion of the increasing centralization of the media as an industry in the United States, see Ben Bagdikian, *The Media Monopoly* (Boston: Beacon Press, 1987).

44. For a discussion of the Reagan administration's dominance of the press, see Mark Hertsgaard, *On Bended Knee: The Press and the Reagan Presidency* (New York: Farrar Straus Giroux, 1988).

8

THE RECREATION OF VIETNAM: The War in American Fiction, Poetry, and Drama

RICHARD A. SULLIVAN

Fuck it, it don't mean nothin'.

—COMMON GRUNT EXPRESSION

The epigraph to this chapter evokes some sense of American involvement in Vietnam as a subject for recent American literature. The life of that literature is reflected in the irony and bitter, tragic frustration of the infantry soldier's response to a situation which demands meaning. The expression is at once as eloquent as it is parochial. Ironically, a world of meaning is bound up in the metaphor, which in some ways represents that activity of mind which at once dismisses as incomprehensible the immediacy of what one did with/in Vietnam and at the same time forces an intimate, procreative joining with it. It is as if relegating acts to memory or to another time will allow the gestation of understanding in a new, unambiguous form. In most cases, what got born in that later time remained a private or personal affair, rendered in public terms as the stereotypical nightmares and daylight freak-outs we at first associated with the "wacked-out" Vietnam veteran, but more recently have "come to terms with" through the clinical euphemism of post-traumatic stress disorder. In some other cases, what also got born was art.

Frank A. Cross Jr.'s "Gliding Baskets" is an effective example of such a transformation:

'Eight Six Foxtrot—Eight Six Foxtrot.
This is One One Zulu. Over.'

The woman in blue

    Carried the weight swiftly, with grace,
    Her face hidden by her
    Conical rice straw hat.

'One One Zulu—this is Eight Six Foxtrot. Go.'
'Roger Fight Six. I have Fire Mission.
Dink in the open, Grid: Bravo Sierra,
Five Six Niner, Four Six Five, Range:
Three thousand, Proximity: Eight Hundred. Over.'

    The two heavy baskets
    Balanced on tips
    Of the springing Chogi stick
    Glided close to the hard smooth path.

'Read back, One One Zulu.'
'Roger Copy, Eight Six.'
'Shot, on the way, wait.'
'Shot out, Eight Six.'

    A sighing 105 mm round slides through its parabola
    Then the explosive tearing at the steel which surrounds it,
    And the shrapnel catches the gliding baskets,
    And they crumple with the woman in blue.

The displacement to memory and eventual recreation in art of these kinds of personal, private experiences forms the core of American literature about Vietnam. For writers we will consider, most of whom were participants in the war—many of whom are combat veterans—the war was a phenomenon which was manifestly inexpressible in the moment of the experience. The letters and diaries which comprise a part of the literature, its first documentary phase, contain the facts of the experiences but are silent or at best bitterly confused where efforts to explain the experiences occur. In this sense, the second half of the epigraph—"it don't mean nothin'"—articulates worlds of meaning even in the denial of meaning. The statement is intended as both a warning and an ironic prophecy. On the one hand, such acts of witnessing shared with other combat soldiers warn against the effort to find meaning where rational and emotional understanding inevitably fail. On the other hand, the paradoxical knowledge that the event witnessed and all events tied to it do in fact mean something gives birth to one of the primary impulses out of which this literature is born.

If the experience of the phenomenon of war in Vietnam ultimately meant nothing more than the memory of obscenity, nothing other than the sensory, moral, or aesthetic repugnance associated with the individual 'war story', the viewing of the pornographic snapshots of mutilated corpses, the cliché of personal memories triggering acts of insanity and violence years after the license for violence—soldiering in war—has been revoked, then the progression to the disembodied electromagnetic voices of Cross' poem would stand as the only memory we require.

The literature we have written out of Vietnam is more than this. In "Gliding Baskets" both aspects of the event recorded have been observed, caught in memory, and recreated in such a way that the witness—the implied speaker in the poem—recognizes both an essential humanity in the woman in blue, a humanness with which he is connected, and the machine-like violence (of which he is an extension) that reduces human beings to "dinks," and "dinks" to targets. The record in the mind of the observer is all the more telling in its austerity. He is not identified as a participant on either side of the event; rather, he is a witness to the significance of two acts: the eloquent beauty of the woman moving through the field, and the routine exchange of information that triggers the destructive force of the artillery shell. Moreover, there is no effort in the poem to ask or answer questions about the reason for either action. Earlier poetic visions of war in modes of expression which are the legacy of two thousand years of culture have been reduced here to the immediacy of physiological seeing, as if no motives for this event, ironic or otherwise, can be offered. But by seeing, and in *what* is seen, the observer records his complicity in both acts—his humanity and his abrogation of it—and he assumes a measure of personal responsibility for their conjunction in space and time. In other words, the poem witnesses the observer's recognition of his own humanity and his implicit guilt in its destruction.

This immediacy of presentation, which both locates the reader in the mind of the observer and forces shared acts of evaluation and judgment—moral or aesthetic—characterizes the best literature to have come out of the American experience of Vietnam. This is not to say that this literature attempts to present its audience with unmediated experiences of the war or its consequences; it is a re-creation of the war, a function of time and memory, of experience and a return in imagination to that experience. For the writer, that return to experience serves as a form of mediation. Time and distance from actual events provide a context, throughout this literature, for the assignment of meanings which the actual experience refused to supply.

For the audience, the presentation of Vietnam as a personal or individual experience (and very little of this literature goes outside of, can go outside of the personal or individual level of experience) is mediated by the idea of the war in Vietnam as a cultural phenomenon. It reflects us, and the culture which allows us to be as we are. A national experience we have come to regard as tragically wrong, an obscene failing of moral will, obscured by ambiguity and absurdity, has assumed in our obsession to relive it the proportions of myth. We return to it, through literature, like the combat veteran relives his tour in an "anniversary year"—in meticulous, often unwonted detail but always with more vivid, more coherent and articulate versions of the war story. It is an index of the survival of the writer's identity that the memories are relived, it is a testament to his will to survive as a human being that this experience is recreated, potent with meaning, in art.

Themes and Issues

In Chapter III ("Beginnings") of *If I Die in a Combat Zone* (1973), Tim O'Brien measures the personal reasons for going to Vietnam (rather than evading the draft) against his understanding of those reasons and of the war after his return. The indecision which impelled O'Brien "by a sort of sleepwalking default" to report for induction was still there, he says, after his personal experience of war had ended. "I would wish," he writes, that "this book could take the form of a plea for everlasting peace, a plea from one who knows, from one who's been there and come back, an old soldier looking back at a dying war"; it would be equally "fine to confirm the old beliefs about war: It's horrible, but it's a crucible of men and events and, in the end, it makes more of a man of you." But for him neither of these interpretations seem right:

> Now, war ended, all I am left with are simple, unprofound scraps of truth. Men die. Fear hurts and humiliates. It is hard to be brave. It is hard to know what bravery *is*. Dead human beings are heavy and hard to carry, things smell different in Vietnam, soldiers are dreamers, drill sergeants are boors, some men thought the war was proper and others didn't and most didn't care. Is that the stuff for a morality lesson, even for a theme?
>
> Do dreams offer lessons? Do nightmares have themes, do we awaken and analyse them and live our lives and advise others as a result? Can the foot soldier teach anything important about war, merely for having been there? I think not. He can tell war stories.

Sixteen years after *If I Die* was written (and after the publication in 1978 of his second Vietnam book, *Going After Cacciato,* which won the National Book Award), O'Brien attempted to explain his telling war stories in both works. *If I Die,* he said, was nothing more than "a document . . . just a straightforward telling" of his experience. It began as a series of "little anecdotes . . . Not stories but vignettes" which were assembled in a rough chronological order. But telling stories requires the transformation of experience and memory into what O'Brien describes as "imagined events." In *Cacciato,* for example, protagonist Paul Berlin is living through the experience of being in a war while at the same time imagining the experience of escaping from war. According to O'Brien, Berlin's creation of the story of Cacciato while standing guard is his way of asking himself if the story in his imagination could be realized in the actuality of his experience. "I've imagined the events of *Cacciato*," O'Brien said, "just as Berlin imagines them." But he has also imagined the events of Berlin's war experience, and in doing so has created the composite story that is the novel. It is that composite story, those layers of imagined events, behind which there is perhaps some core exposition of actual experience, that a reader of *Cacciato* experiences, never the actual events themselves. "By going through the process of having imagined something," O'Brien considers, "one gathers a sense of the *stuff* that's being imagined, a sense of what war is and what escape from war is." [1]

John Del Vecchio, in the acknowledgments for *The 13th Valley* (1982), records an anecdote:

> A soldier on Firebase Rendezvous at the edge of the A Shau Valley during Lam Son 719 [the incursion into Cambodia], Spring 1971.
>   He said to me, "You can do it, Man. You write about this place. You been here a long time. People gotta know what it was really like.

Del Vecchio's acknowledgment of the origin of his novel is not unique; it is a story repeated in prefaces, nudged out in recorded interviews, embedded in the literature, and discussed in conferences. It occurs in connection with works as diverse in content and intention as Ronald Glasser's *365 Days* (1971), which he describes in the "Foreword" as "sketches, not finished stories," written "only to tell what I was seeing and being told, maybe to give something to these kids which was all theirs without doctrine or polemics, something they could use to explain what they might not be able to explain themselves," and John Clark Pratt's *Vietnam Voices* (1984), in which letters written from Vietnam are employed to represent, among other things, the disjunctions of understanding that existed between combat soldiers and friends and relatives at home. [2] Larry Heinemann regards himself as "one of the people who can actually tell" those who did not go to Vietnam "what happened and what it means." For Phillip Caputo, Vietnam "represented a very serious kind of psychic wound," and he senses "the same kind of wound in the country." It is his sense of that shared wounding that impels him to "keep trying to get at bits and pieces of the truth of that experience," to "universalize it so that somebody who was never there, somebody who has never even vaguely experienced battle, will see some truth about their own life in it." [3]

This conception is perhaps most recognizable in the literature in the way the war generated specific, often highly ironic sets of language to represent its events. These sets of language combine the idiom of combat soldiers with the jargon of military bureaucracy and the argot of strategic and tactical codes, and are shot through with the disembodied or redefined vocabulary of sixties and seventies popular culture. It is perhaps an index of the degree to which this language is regarded by writers and publishers alike as specific to Vietnam that a large majority of the literary works, prose and poetry, contain glossaries. (These glossaries create the sense of the language as a kind of local color necessary to the story, and it is tempting, as some literary analysts have done, to dismiss it as nothing more; but to do so is to misunderstand the nature of the literature and the experience it represents.)

The special language of the Vietnam experience is not merely a dialect with specific meaning for the participants in the war, which must be 'translated' for all others. In a more profound sense, the language operates as one of the elements in a metaphor for the war itself. Composed of elements like "angel track," "fire track," "HALO," "to lay chilly," "sky out," "bustin' caps," "ghosting," "PsyOps," "breaking squelch," "REMF," "white bird," this has a weird resonance born of a fleeting suggestion of lyric beauty constantly undercut by the inherent violence of the situation that generates it. (This particular quality of the language is captured in its most intense forms in works like Herr's *Dispatches* [1978], James Webb's *Fields of Fire* [1978], and Gustave Hasford's *Short Timers* [1979], and it runs throughout the poetry, particularly the poems of Basil T. Paquet.)

Some of the locutions (for instance, "dust off" and "willie peter") were consistent in meaning throughout the war. Others changed meaning in different phases or in different regions or with different military branches. To be "lit up," for example, could refer, early in the war, to a helicopter taking fire and exploding—the magnesium frames burned with an intense, white-green halo. At other times, the same phrase could refer to any aircraft being shot down; late in the war the phrase was used semi-officially to describe aircraft, particularly helicopters, being hit by ground fire as opposed to simply being fired on. Other idioms might be specific to a particular service—"pogues" and "REMF's," for example, were the marine and army ways of describing the same rear echelon personnel. Still other idioms were specific to units or even to individuals; "another shade of weird" for a particularly frustrating or frightening mission among maneuver battalions in the 101st Airborne Division, and a spontaneously generated expression of fear and relief, "I been *scaled,* man, I'm *smooth* now"—coined by individual soldiers and recorded by Michael Herr.[4]

When this language is fused with the dynamics of individual experience in literature its reference turns Vietnam toward something more than personal experience. Even in the compilations of oral narratives such as Mark Baker's *Nam* (1981) or Al Santoli's *Everything We Had* (1981), individuals who for fifteen or twenty or more years have managed to erect walls of normalcy around the experience of Vietnam can be seen within the limits of one recorded sentence to resume the experience and enact, in a strange kind of retrogressive process, what the movements of language and event in drama, poetry, personal narratives and fiction reveal: We all went to Vietnam. We all, in some ways, did not come back home.

The portrait of Philip Dozier, the central character in Larry Heinemann's *Close Quarters* (1974), represents one of the more incisive treatments of this theme. The novel begins with Dozier, newly arrived incountry and on station. His mind is filled with the jargon he has learned in training—"tracks," "o.d.," "Chicom claymore mines," "TC's," "CVC's"—and his expectation that his knowledge of this vocabulary of war will mark him as someone who belongs is rapidly undercut by the "ugly deadly music" of the actuality of the armored personnel carriers of his platoon and the men operating them. His preparation for Vietnam can no more translate the "jerky bitter echoes of machines out of sync" than it can interpret the way each man in the platoon, passing him, looks down at him with "the blandest, blankest sort of glance—almost painful to watch—neither welcome nor distance." Neither can Dozier understand the man (later revealed to be at the end of his tour) whose APC has broken down, climbing out, bellowing a curse, then grabbing a shovel and beating the machine, hurling profanity at it ("I'm gonna pour mogas on your asshole and burn you down to fuckin' nickles, you short-time pissant mo-gas-guzzling motherfucker!") until the shovel breaks and the anger swells into mute stasis. The event, like the language, will require the experience of combat in Vietnam before it can assume meaning for Dozier.

Eleven months later, Dozier performs his own short-time ritual. His tour nearing completion, his lieutenant has held him out of combat missions in an effort to increase his chances of survival. Consequently Dozier was absent when the "Cow Catcher" (the APC he has served in) was destroyed by a mine, killing two of the crew and severely wounding the others.

> I slapped the underside of the armor deck so hard my hand stung and started to itch . . . Atevo and Steichen and Whiskey J. and Granger and Trobridge and Walthers and Willie and the engineer and Eddie, and on down to Dano and Janecek and the Cow Catcher, and so on and so on until I couldn't remember anymore and gave up trying. The dinks were getting close, circling in on the bull's eye—walking the rounds in, and picking and choosing along the way—but getting the range; getting closer just the same. And the longer I stayed, the more chances I gave them.

The litany of attrition among the men he has served with expresses both his fear of not surviving and his guilt at surviving at such a cost. But survival, for Dozier, has been predicated on his having developed a spontaneous, almost instinctive, ability to kill. His attitudes towards killing—its morality, its necessity, his horror and revulsion in the face of it, even his fear of it—have been progressively stripped away, leaving him with only the impulse to kill. His anger at the "dinks," whose gradual whittling away at the members of his platoon or any other Americans who come in contact with him, is to him a kind of clearing of the way, a zeroing in on the ultimate target—himself.

While Dozier's ability to kill with no compunction has allowed him to survive, it has at the same time allowed him to understand those men and actions which so astonished him on his arrival. The measure of his belonging—to the unit, to the experience, to Vietnam—is evidenced in the degree to which he has come to look like all the others, to think like them, to move and act like them, and to speak like them. Almost all vestiges of his individuality, his humanity, his identity in "the World" have also been stripped away so that he is left, at the end of his tour, homogenized, differentiable only in terms of the name he has been given—"Deadeye." Whatever moral sense he might have possessed, whatever cultural values that could provide a context for questioning or understanding what he has done and become, have proven to be superficial, ultimately disposable. The residue of those values, which resurfaces with the destruction of the Cow Catcher—his sense of personal responsibility for not having been there to prevent its destruction—is easily swept away in a brief confrontation with the other short-time survivor, Quinn, who has become his de facto confidant, double, and friend:

"Who do we think we are?" I said.

"I am one bad motherfucker. Mean bad," said Quinn, thumping his thumb against his chest.

"Yeah, hey, but where are we today?"

"What the fuck ya talkin' about?"

"Shit, m'man, all's I know is, if we'd been there it woulda gone different. Tha's all. I'm tellin' ya it woulda been different."

"Aw, fuck off, *Deadeye*."

"Well, take a fucken look at it. If you 'n' me'd been where we 'uz s'posed ta be, Teddy 'n' Janecek woulda been on the back 'n' the fucken new guys woulda been someplace else. I'm sayin' you 'n' me fucked up."

"*Oh* no, m'man. I don' need ta hear it, dig? Not from you er Corso er the El-tee er anybody. People been pounding that buddy-buddy shit up my ass half a my life, an' I'm goddamn sick an' fucken tired a listenin' ta how fucked up I am."

Dozier's briefly resurrected moral sensibility is expressed initially in the language of the Philip Dozier who stood bewildered at the gates of the camp; but Quinn rejects the language as an idiom which simply does not make sense. Dozier cannot communicate with Quinn in that language any more than he can reanimate the identity and mind to which it belonged.

When he attempts then to phrase his misplaced sense of guilt in the idiom he and Quinn now share, Quinn's immediate and violent rejection of the idea makes Dozier aware that it and all other ideas like it—ideas from that other, dead life—cannot exist in the world he and Quinn now inhabit. That world is defined by the armored walls of the APC, the killing machine, and the actions and language that make the two men indistinguishable, alienated from the identities they held in "the World." "Eleven months and some in the bushes," Dozier thinks, "and it all came down to a fucked up box of junk and two stoned and mumbling, bitter drunks."

The reduction of Dozier to the archetypal survivor of Vietnam is specific to this literature; acculturated attitudes and values regarding war, death, killing, moral responsibility, personal obligation, duty, and identity are all abandoned or destroyed in the face of repeated exposure to the conditions of combat and survival in Vietnam. This primary pattern of experience is repeated in nearly all of the personal narratives from the war, and in much of the fiction, and it is the subject of intense epiphanic moments of recognition or dry, ironic exposition in the poetry. It is given comprehensive, intensified treatment in David Rabe's *Sticks and Bones* (1973). In Rabe's play, David Nelson of the "Ozzie and Harriet" television series, an ideal young American male, returns from Vietnam blinded and so altered and alien that Ozzie wants to check fingerprints and dental records to confirm his identity. The Vietnam he has been to, which he brings home in the form of his own personal narrative—an 8-millimeter home movie—is equally alien, so much so that the Nelson family, viewing it, can see only a green blur on the screen.

In *Close Quarters* Dozier survives by giving up his ability to leave Vietnam and go home. It is not simply that the old, naive Philip Dozier—the one who has died in that combat exposure—has been replaced by a new, bitter but experienced Dozier who will now see "home" with different eyes; rather, Dozier has been absorbed by his experience in Vietnam. It has become him, and he has assumed it as an identity.

In these works and others, Vietnam is represented as a place where ordinary experience merged with extraordinary experience to create a new world of meaning. We are repeatedly presented with the idea that there was something in the experience that was at once alien and bound up in the fundamental nature of American culture. Serving in Vietnam, particularly in combat, is imaged out in the literature through portraits of divided worlds of experience. On the one hand, there is that world in which the most fundamental activities—eating, sleeping, waking, talking, breathing, excreting—occur in an environment which is constantly alien in its primary sensory apprehension and in its moment-by-moment potential to erupt into spontaneous violence and death. This is "the Nam." On the other hand, the individuals who experience "the Nam" bring to it an accumulated seventeen or eighteen years of growing up in America ("the World") years of absorbing its myths, imagining its history and its dreams. The fusion of these elements into a single experience, the ordinary soldier's combat year, creates a part of the mystique of the experience, the hermetic language, the cultural analogues (cowboys and Indians, the mythology of the frontier, manifest destiny, racial stereotyping left over from the Second World War), the recourse to a redefined popular culture of the fifties and sixties, and so on.

To read this literature it is necessary to recognize the two worlds of meaning resident in it—one which speaks to the participants, like veterans trading war stories among themselves, in a language only they can properly understand—and one which is a translation for the civilians. These translations, like the meanings transcribed in the glossaries, become our lexica on the experience. They form interpretive vocabularies we can recognize, for example, in John Del Vecchio's highly stylized and artificial camp-fire sessions in *The 13th Valley,* philosophical debates which offer contextual interpretations for the equally stylized and artificial language we cannot understand: "'Quiet Rover, this is Red Rover, . . . proceed to your echo ASAP. Caution your papa Sky Devil Six is to your november one kilo. Play ball with Sky Devil.'" Or we are given other forms of translation, in the interweaving of lyric mantras on houseplants with the banter of improbably witty grunts, in Stephen Wright's *Meditations in Green* (1983), or in Tim O'Brien's fantasy of escape, which is no escape, in *Going After Cacciato.* The power of these translations can be seductive, drawing us down into the clichés of war stories which are little more than the product of tired imaginations, making us believe that we have gotten to the "truth" of Vietnam. But beyond this, there is the even more seductively attractive idea of the two worlds of meaning in the representational forms of the literature itself—the recognition that through those translations we come face to face with ourselves, become witnesses and discover that what we are looking at is a mirror reflecting our world. Creating those mirrors is what has allowed the survivors of Vietnam to begin to come home; looking into them allows us to know where they have been.

The War in Literature

If an origin for literary treatment of American involvement in Vietnam can be identified, most would agree that it would be Graham Greene's *The Quiet American* (1956). This novel stands as a significant point of origin for a number of reasons, the most obvious of which is its treatment of the shift from limited American influence in Vietnam to a more active American presense there. It is also, of course, a masterful work of fiction from the hand of an experienced and celebrated writer. In that sense, it provides an interesting context for the beginnings of American writing on Vietnam, in two ways. First, there is Greene's characteristically English sensibility, a sensibility which has recorded repeatedly the decaying remnants of English, French, and American colonialism in isolated and exotic outposts in the aftermath of the two world wars and the destruction of the old empires. Vietnam, together with the rest of Southeast Asia, was little more than an exotic setting to British and American audiences in 1956 (this, it should be noted, despite the tendency of some current histories to treat Dien Bien Phu and the Geneva Cease-Fire accord of 1954 as major events pervading the consciousness of the American public). Second, Greene's novel is a highly traditional work, bound by the functions of the mid-twentieth-century British traditional novel and the limits of taste and sensibility which allowed only so much of what one writer has termed the "information" of Vietnam to be written.[5]

The Quiet American establishes certain patterns which resonated throughout the work that follows it. In the novel, Thomas Fowler's meticulously casual fascination with Alden Pyle, his more than journalistic compulsion to document the intransigent and self-destructive innocence of the American, provides a paradigm for subsequent unwilling and unwitting movements into the metaphysics of self-discovery. Greene's epigraphs to the novel (taken from Arthur Hugh Clough and Lord Byron, respectively) establish the dynamic poles of that movement:

I do not like being moved, for the will is excited; and action
Is a most dangerous thing; I tremble for something factitious,
Some malpractice of heart and illegitimate process;
We're so prone to these things, with our terrible notions of duty.

This is the patent age of new inventions
    For killing bodies and saving souls,
All propagated with the best intentions.

This mixed mood fuels the doubling of Fowler and Pyle as central characters. The novel begins with the ultimate consequence of that fusion; Alden Pyle is dead, assassinated it seems as a result of the one action Fowler has been moved to commit through his proximity to Pyle. The narrative, circling around the events of a story which has already been acted out, is concerned with discovering what this conjunction of innocence and experience has meant. Pyle has remained an enigma to Fowler; and Fowler, in his effort to solve the riddle of Pyle, discovers instead an opacity in himself.

At the end of the novel, Fowler sees crystallized in a copy of *The Role of the West* (Pyle's erstwhile undecipherable bible) the missionary scripture which brought Pyle to Vietnam, an image which "stood out like a cabinet portrait—of a young man with a crew cut and a black dog at his heels. He could harm no one any more."

The harm in Pyle is specific to Fowler—holds no potential threat for the Vietnamese he has come with his license to save—as is made evident when Fowler asks Phuong (the Vietnamese woman they have both had as mistress) if she misses Pyle, and she responds matter-of-factly, in a statement shot through with ironic prophecy for the coming American effort to "democratize" and "save" Vietnam, "I never remember my dreams." What Americans would bring to Vietnam, of course, was an unforgettable nightmare of napalm, defoliation, dislocation, mutilation, and death. But what American literature records is the confrontation, without real resolution, of the harm we would inflict on ourselves.

Greene's novel contains all of the elements of that confrontation. Fowler and Pyle are inverted projections, mirror images of one another, and the glass that separates them is an unbridgeable gulf of difference. This doubling will be repeated, in different forms, by the characters Jake Krummel and Joe Morning in *One to Count Cadence* (1969), by Dozier and Quinn in *Close Quarters,* by Cherry Chelini and Mick Egan in *The Thirteenth Valley,* and (in more sublimated ways in implied relations) in *365 Days,* by Ronald Glasser and the broken bodies and minds he treats. Throughout fiction, poetry, and drama, doubled images will recur in connection with the war, ultimately translated from Greene's international perspective to an exclusively American set of minds, transported from the casual but deadly anxieties of Greene's opiated Saigon streets and hotels to the electric terror of the world of combat. In these works Vietnam becomes "the Nam," ambiguous, intractable, incomprehensible, a world marked more by certain psychic dimensions than by a geographical location or a people. It will be a world one learns to survive by divesting oneself of all that Alden Pyle represents, just as Fowler survives, through one dangerous act, by destroying the "harm" that is Pyle. And in this sense Greene's novel evokes the other major pattern of internal movement in the literature. Fowler is left at the end of his experience alienated, isolated, and still unable to comprehend that which the experience moved him to know. Fowler has survived the harm of Pyle by insulating himself from that knowledge; that journey into those regions of the mind or self where such insulation is possible is recorded in such works as William Pelfrey's *The Big V* (1972) and Robert Mason's *Chickenhawk* (1981).

American literature about the war has consistently appeared as a mix of documentary and fictive expression. Even the most imaginative of works—the lyricism of the poetry and the allegory of the largest part of the drama—have behind them an impulse to document the experience of the war. The more immediately authentic documentary forms—the oral histories—oscillate between artfully composed and delivered narrative renderings (which one suspects have gained much through multiple tellings) and intense moments of spontaneous memory during which all artifice falls away. Greene's novel anticipated this in its employment of historical events—terrorist bombings which can be documented to have occurred in Saigon, the arrival and early operations of Edward Lansdale's top-secret SSM mission in Vietnam (in some ways the model for Fowler and his activities), the real personage and activities of General The, and so on. On the other hand, this literature works constantly to re-interpret itself and to re-create the events that are its subject, a process which has its analogue in the circular motion of Fowler's narrative. It is as if with each re-telling, events are re-created in successive efforts to get closer to their essential reality. In that process one kind of truth—documentary realism—is abandoned for another kind of truth—the more subtle interactions of mind and event that comprise mythic reality.

The Quiet American exhibits such a translation of documentary events into mythic patterns of experience; it also represents the beginnings of a literary exploration of Vietnam. The first major work to appear after The Quiet American, Eugene Burdick and William Lederer's The Ugly American (1958), is an immediate and direct effort to rewrite Greene's novel—not, interestingly, the story, but the history behind it. The Ugly American is an interpretation of the politics and consequent human actualities of foreign policy for a politically naive American public. It sets about its objective by supplying a documentary envelope for its fiction; the writers inform their readers in a note at the beginning of the book that while it is written as fiction, "the things we write about have, in essence, happened," and they open their "Epilogue" with the expressed desire that they "would not wish any reader to put down our book thinking that what he has read is wholly imaginary."

What emerges from The Ugly American is a curious mixture of bitter self-criticism, ironic prophecy, and incipient call to arms. American policy is chastised for developing "huge technical complexes which may some day pay dividends but which at this moment in Asian development are neither needed nor wanted." What is wanted is "a small force of well-trained, well-chosen, hard-working, and dedicated professionals. They must be willing to risk their comforts and—in some lands—their health. They must go equipped to apply a positive policy promulgated by a clear-thinking government. They must speak the language of the land of their assignment, and they must be more expert in its problems than are the natives." This is, of course, Pyle's bible rewritten for a new corps of diplomatic innocents. It could also be a summary of objectives behind the transformation, in 1961, of the American Special Forces units (which had been in decline since Korea and were about to be absorbed into the Rangers) into the counterinsurgency teams that would come to be known as the Green Berets.

The Ugly American would stand as little more than a literary curiosity—a polemic disguised as an implausible fiction—were it not for its enormous, almost unprecedented popularity and success, and its equally powerful influence on the next phase of American involvement in Vietnam.[6] The "advisory" period of the war is characterized in literature primarily through a sequence of novels, including Robin Moore's *The Green Berets* (1965), Peter Derrig's *The Pride of the Green Berets* (1966), and Thomas Taylor's *A-18* (1967), which depict the training in America and subsequent adventures in Vietnam of Special Forces units. American characters in these works have taken up the challenge of Burdick and Lederer and, for the most part, have added experience and competence to their good intentions. Yet Vietnam (and Laos, in which some works are set) remains unmoved, unaffected by their activities. It is in these works that Vietnam begins to be described as a region of experience which is, for Americans who go there, incomprehensible, unpredictable. They record Vietnam as a place where, however well-trained, the external logic and values of American cultural experience are more than inadequate—they are simply inapplicable. The enemy *becomes* Vietnam in these works; more importantly, as David Halberstam's *One Very Hot Day* (1967) reports, the American mission in Vietnam shifts dramatically from the exportation of democracy to the suppression of an enemy. As the literature about Vietnam begins to emphasize this shift from applying diplomacy through manipulations of indigenous force to using ambiguous and protean American national objectives as a mandate for American military force, it also begins to portray a kind of inbreathing of violence as a characteristic of the American experience of Vietnam.

This change in perspective is represented contemporaneously in Halberstam's documentary fiction and in one of the best of the early personal narratives, Donald Duncan's *The New Legions* (1967).[7] Duncan's book, which is often overlooked in treatments of the literature and is rarely included in bibliographies, provides a realistic counterpoint to the romanticism of the Special Forces novels, and contains descriptions of the personal impact of combat which anticipate the realism of Heinemann's *Close Quarters* and the metarealism of Herr's *Dispatches*.

Later re-creations of the advisory period extend the idea of Vietnam as enemy in two directions, each focusing, as all subsequent re-interpretations will do, on the combat experience as central to whatever meaning might be discoverable in the war. Jonathan Rubin's *The Barking Deer* (1974) represents one of these interpretive directions. The novel extends the contradictions implicit in the Special Forces mission in Vietnam into a symbolic world of apocalyptic violence in which all participants in the fighting, on both sides, are ultimately destroyed, absorbed into a landscape which is immutable and mute, hiding its secrets and its dead underneath layers of impenetrable continuity. This is a variation on the concept of "the Nam," one which is played out again in John Del Veccio's *The*

13th Valley, with its symbolic constructs of spider, tree, and river acting as passive witnesses to the idea that no one gets out of Vietnam; and in Stephen Wright's *Meditations In Green,* in which James Griffin's therapeutic excursions into the symbolic texture of greenness leave him with only the intelligence that he has never gotten out of Vietnam, and the final recognition—"Who has a question for Mr. Memory?"—that all movements of the mind lead back to that territory.

The other direction, towards which James Crumley's *One To Count Cadence* (1969) moves, is a circling back to re-tell the story of Alden Pyle and Thomas Fowler. Crumley's novel, which is too often rendered the disservice of comparisons with Norman Mailer's *The Naked and the Dead* (1948), expands Fowler's collision with Pyle to include a major theme of the later literature, the recognition of the latent violence beneath the American myth of the frontier. The dangerous innocence of Crumley's Joe Morning, a young soldier to whom the older narrator, Jake Krummel, is drawn with magnetic force, becomes an idealism inextricably fused with an instinctive but unacknowledged will to violence. Like Greene's Fowler, Krummel narrates his story after the fact, in an effort to understand where his conjunction with Morning has led him.

The novel opens with Krummel recuperating in a Phillipines hospital from wounds he sustained when his signal unit, sent on a covert mission to Vietnam in late 1962, was overrun by a large Vietcong force. Although the action in Vietnam forms only a small part of the latter chapters, it is highly significant that the barely controlled violence which Krummel sees moving both himself and Morning throughout the early parts of the story is ultimately, inevitably unleashed in Vietnam. Krummel is himself a manifestation of the mythic concept of an American frontier where violence is the determinant force in moral and personal value, a descendant of a family whose sons have been mercenary soldiers for various causes for two centuries. (Krummel's great grandfather, for instance, was a hired scout during the Apache wars in Texas in the nineteenth century.) Jake Krummel was too late for Korea and, after a failed marriage, he found himself left with only "tiny wars fought with boobie traps and pamphlets and suicide . . . wars of attrition" to carry on his legacy as warrior. The novel's hospital surgeon, Gallard, who is troubled by nightmares of imaginary violence from his childhood, but has discovered that war is not "anything except stupid and evil and cruel and without honor," sees the image of his old nightmare antagonist in Krummel, an archetype of war. "All that dark, primitive nature, that dark, throbbing blood, that fogged crossroads where evil meets beauty . . . You stink of death," he tells Krummel after listening to his history, "evil murder and death."

Gallard's feelings of fascination and repulsion for Krummel are duplicated in the love/hate attraction Krummel feels toward Joe Morning. To

Krummel Morning is a man "hanging between the sun and moon, a man of great tides. Like all men without roots, direction or patience, he was a revolutionary, not a rebel but a revolutionary, a destroyer, a reacher for all or nothing for anyone." Krummel's vision of Morning, which is a reflection of himself with the restraints of idealism stripped away, fuels the relationship between them, which grows to the point where Morning actively hates Krummel, and propels the men into unrestrained psychic conflict. "His rage blossomed so wonderfully," Krummel recalls of one such confrontation, "He indulged his anger, perhaps because with something outside to hate the vague phantom-demon he hated in himself let him alone, and together both halves hated, not in an arithmetical progression of one plus one, but geometrically as dynamite adds to dynamite, so that he must explode."

The moment of that explosion of self-realization comes for Morning in the easy violence of Vietnam, which unleashes the deeper violence inside him. At the peak of the battle for the base camp, Morning erupts, running into the midst of the attackers, "firing from the hip like a hero." It is in that moment that Krummel, like Greene's Fowler moved to action by that "malpractice of the heart and illegitimate process," reaches out to destroy Morning, the image of himself. "I swung my sight across his middle and blew out the base of his spine with three quick rounds, and he folded like a waiter giving a bow, folded, fell, lay still."

Krummel's excursion into his Conradian heart of darkness (so pervasive a metaphor in Vietnam literature) leads of course to his re-telling of the story as a confession of the murder of Joe Morning. But, as in so much of this literature, confession fails to end the nightmare. Morning is resurrected in the end, discovered to have survived, a pure force of violence who goes on to operate covertly "a few miles ahead of the Army" in the wars in Laos and Vietnam, but the ghost of Morning continues to haunt Krummel: "I woke here in this bed, determined to tell someone the truth. All this leading up to the truth. But it has taken too long. I find myself trapped by my own confession. The scene, the moment of extreme truth, swept past me."

When American marine and army combat forces were committed to the war in 1965, the American soldier's experience of the war began to change in significant ways. During the advisory period, the Special Forces and other personnel who served in-country—especially in command and cadre roles—were characteristically older career or professional soldiers, many of whom had had some combat experience. By the end of 1965, with 158,000 support and combat troops added to the 23,000 in-country at the end of 1964, an increasing majority of the soldiers—especially combat soldiers—were under twenty-one years of age; their average age dropped to nineteen during the peak years of U.S. involvement, with over 500,000 soldiers in-country at the end of 1968. This reduction in age and consequent experience and maturity, combined with the peculiarities of the command and service structure in Vietnam, defined the parameters of the experience of war which service in Vietnam has come to represent for the American public.[8]

Literature which depicts the war from 1965 to the American withdrawal in 1973 increasingly focuses on the effects, for combat soldiers, of these features. In the most general sense, those effects can be summarized as a disassociation of the ordinary soldier's experience from any sense of continuity in the war. Continuity was broken by the tour (a specified time one served rather than a particular objective, apart from survival, for one's service) and by the circumstantial reduction of the combat soldier's world to long periods of time in the field with small units, platoons or squads, the composition of which was continually altered by attrition and rotation. Ambiguities about the purpose of the war, growing public disillusionment over the lack of military success and the more general social unrest at home all became a part of the baggage military personnel carried with them to Vietnam. Fear and exhaustion, coupled with the absurdity and illogic of the "grunts" or the helicopter air crews' perspectives on their actions and reinforced by a more general loss of confidence in the military's command structure, became a part of the baggage that those who survived the war, whole or in pieces, brought back home with them. The literature which followed quickly on the heels of the transition from the Special Forces war to the deployment of large-scale American forces reflects these changes and, more importantly, a growing emphasis on the complexities of the ordinary soldier's combat experience.

The major works depicting this intensification of the individual experience of the war focused on the climactic years of the fighting, 1967–1970, the years during which our national conscience and consciousness of the war came to recognize the degree to which it seemed to be consuming us. This is the period during which writers began to act as translators of the experience of the war, as the experience itself spiralled down into ever tighter loops of privacy and self-containment, of insulation and numbing against the splitting of self and the absorption into the world of "the Nam." Works like O'Brien's *If I Die in a Combat Zone* document this period, as do the poems in *Winning Hearts and Minds* (1972), which was assembled and published by the First Casualty Press, a Vietnam veteran's co-operative. The poems in this volume are arranged in the form of a tour of duty, and represent efforts from individuals who would go on to become major poetic voices of the war (John Balaban, W. D. Ehrhart, Jan Barry, Basil T. Paquet and others) and from individuals who expressed themselves this one time, and fell into silence. The vision of confrontation with "the Nam" that these works image out is re-created as nightmare in another work written contemporaneously with the war, David Rabe's *The Basic Training of Pavlo Hummel* (1969). Rabe's play, also a translation of war stories, imagines the war itself as a kind of basic training, cycles of learning death, from which it is impossible to escape. Hummel, who is killed in the beginning of the play by a Vietcong grenade, is forced in this nightmare to return to basic training and then to Vietnam, where he will go through the process of acclimation to war without understanding, until he is again killed, this time by an American grenade. Rabe describes Hummel as someone who is lost, but innocent and eager to belong. In his training and exposure to combat, Hummel's "physical efficiency, even his mental efficiency" as Rabe puts it, "increases, but real insight never comes. Toughness and cynicism replace open eagerness, but he will learn only that he is lost, not how or why or even where."

The recognition of being lost, or of having lost oneself in Vietnam, is the major new dimension that the literature of the war acquires in this phase. It is a primary subject throughout Michael Herr's *Dispatches* and is the only knowledge William Pelfrey's Henry Winstead, in *The Big V*, arrives at after his year of "training" in combat. Winstead, like Hummel, learns to be tight, efficient, absorbed in the war. But the cost of his survival is his separation from the world. When his best friend is killed, he understands that loss:

> I tried to mourn for the Anachronism, and yet realized for the first time that I didn't know what mourning was, unless it was only the purely biological reflex immediately after something happened. That wasn't enough; I wanted to feel something, some gush of emotion, the same frustration as after killing the first dink, trying to figure it out. I couldn't, I just couldn't. I lay there, all the images, everything at once, numbed.

This sense of recognizing loss without feeling, without being able to extricate oneself from the cycles of experience which have led to it, is the primary force behind Ronald Glasser's *365 Days*. The "sketches" Glasser presents of the soldiers who move through the wards of the evacuation hospital at Zama are each case studies; but it is more importantly the perspective Glasser himself acquires, as transcriber of their experiences, which registers another level of loss. As a surgeon in the military hospital in Japan, Glasser exists within the narratives as an observer of the cost, the attrition, of the war; but his experience of the region where that loss occurs comes to him only in the form of the war stories his patients and his records tell him. And he remains, as they are, trapped in the webb of fascination and despair.

During this phase in the literature, writers re-imagined and re-focused the combat experience in works like Gustav Hasford's *Short Timers,* where a bitter irony and cynicism of vision replaces Rabe's Dantesque cycles of incomprehension or Pelfry's numbed paralysis. Ironic re-creation is most acute in Heinemann's *Close Quarters,* in which the lyric intensity of vision enables an examination, in minute detail, of both the physical obscenity of the war and the psychic dimensions of being in it. What these works do, which moves them beyond Herr's or Glaser's or Rabe's closed circles of despair or dismay, is establish an interpretive distance between the war stories and the translation of those stories into exposition. They begin to restore, in other words, our sense of removal from the events. This distancing occurs in James Webb's *Fields of Fire,* through the effort to place its war stories within the social and cultural contexts of the experience, and in John Del Vecchio's *The 13th Valley,* in which the war itself and the experience of it are presented as a multifaceted texture of languages and events.

In this discussion I have concentrated on literature depicting the early phases of the war, primarily because that literature, so often glossed over, seems to represent in its internal operations as well as its historical development much of the larger body of the literature representing the war, specifically the use of the war as a ground to image through its pain and tragedy more deeply seated questions—uncertainties—about the fundamental nature of American culture. This literature is characteristically a literature of guilt and betrayal, specifically self-betrayal, placed also in the context of the failure of American cultural values, held in innocent uncritical passivity and torn brutally away in war, to sustain individual identities in the face of trauma.

The exploration of issues which are so often the subject of debate about Vietnam literature (the illegitimacy of the war, its immorality, brutality and atrocity, the failure of American political and military institutions, the conflict at home during the war, and the closing of the American mind to the loss of the war and to the individuals who fought it) often comprises the stated intentions of the writers. However, these issues are secondary to what these works repeatedly portray. The ghosts who float through the pages of these works are all allegorical figures, performing with arch, strident gestures or with slow wounding strokes a drama which finds its stage only properly within the contours of the American mind.

Literature and the Legacy of Vietnam

The legacy of Vietnam, as much of this discussion has been suggesting, is represented in our literature by the effort, at times almost a compulsion, to return to the war, its events, its facts, its images and figuration, and recreate it in different, mediated forms. Engaging and at the same time creating the legacy of the war is, in this sense of mediation, primarily an act of accommodation. But accommodation has only been possible for us through the transformation of the experience of Vietnam into myth. The ease with which, for example, we use the very word *Vietnam* to register a complex of meanings, devoid for the most part of any cultural or social referents to a particular country or nation or people we might identify with the Vietnamese, is an index of the degree to which the war has been mythologized as an American cultural phenomenon. We speak of the politics of Vietnam, the effects on our society of Vietnam, our literature of Vietnam, the legacy of Vietnam, and we have contained within that single word a compression of emotion and idea and event and identity which willfully resists the efforts of logic or analysis or explication to render its component parts. We have imagined Vietnam into something which contains, but is no longer limited to, one set of historical phenomena. Literature about the Vietnam War, then, can be regarded as a record of the extent to which our war in Vietnam was, from its very beginnings on at least one order of experience, more of a mythic confrontation than an empirical event. It is as if we went to Vietnam, in the person of Edward Lansdale and his operatives, to re-discover and re-identify some central part of ourselves. We were at first observed and recorded in that activity through the eyes of a British novelist, a latter-day Marlow, and we transformed his mode of vision to embark on our own journey into a peculiarly American heart of darkness. Unlike Marlow, though, at the deepest point of penetration into that jungle we *were* able to take that final step, to cross over "the threshold of the invisible" and see what Conrad's narrator calls "the appalling face of a glimpsed truth—the strange commingling of desire and hate" which reflects some knowledge of self welling up out of a "mysterious arrangement of merciless logic for a futile purpose." Perhaps because we were both Marlow and Kurtz at the same time we were not, as Marlow was, "permitted to draw back" a "hesitating foot," to allow restraint to keep us from self-discovery.

To describe a body of literature which responds to a legacy of Vietnam would seem in many ways to be a futile and artificial activity. The literature contains the legacy. But the war itself, as an empirical event, had an ending. It is through our returns in imagination and intellect that we have turned it into a legacy; learning to recognize that the war has bequeathed us something and working to discover the nature of that bequest is a function of time and perspective. Our culture has moved through its own cycles of accommodation—from a refusal to look at the pain and tragedy of Vietnam to a recognition that the scars left from that wounding are at least signs we can read in imagination. And the willingness to embrace Vietnam has opened the doors to another cycle of documentation, interpretation, and creation.

The literature which has emerged in this new cycle shows evidence that our translators of Vietnam have gone through their own phases of accommodation. Vietnam has of course not simply lain dormant in the memories of those who served there. Memory and imagination have shaped it into stories, and the war stories that were the subject of nightmares have been enveloped in structures of explanation. The remarkable similarity in the structure and movement of the personal accounts of the war which have appeared in oral histories—works like Al Santoli's *Everything We Had,* Mark Baker's *Nam,* and Wallace Terry's *Bloods* (1982)— speak of the degree to which the stories have been refined, focused, re-created. This is not so much a product of any conscious intent to turn the memory of experience into art. The stories in the "oral histories" remain documentary, but we must remember when we read them, as Mark Baker points out, that much of what is recorded has been shaped within the healing movements of memory and imagination. Indeed, the transformation of memory by imagination provides the distance and perspective which allows healing to occur; imagination served during the experience of the war as one mode, if not of explanation, then certainly of distillation.

The war consistently produced, for example, the kinds of anecdotal responses to violence and death which are at the heart of a work like *Dispatches*—anecdotes difficult to distinguish from experienced events. It is not surprising, then, that imagination should become, in later memories, woven into the texture of experience. In Mark Baker's *Nam,* for example, one veteran recalls his arrival, during a mortar attack, at the base camp where he would assume command:

> After the mortar attack, I got to my unit and asked to see the captain. They told me he was away from the main area of the camp. "Well, can I get to him?" "Sure, he's right out there under those trees somewhere." I walked out to meet him and to take over command. He was dead with his head blown off and his dick in the air. He had been out there masturbating when the mortars hit and got his head blown right off. Stiff as a board with his cock in his hands.

This story is one which circulated, with variations, throughout "the Nam," passed on from short-timers to FNG's (Fucking new guys) and from unit to unit. Somewhere behind it there may exist a real event, perhaps even in this particular soldier's experience. But the event has been absorbed into the collectivity of combat soldiers' experiences, has become a part of the stock property—the war stories—of Vietnam.

In another way Vietnam has become almost exclusively a product of imagination, not in the sense that it is fictive or wholly imagined, but in the way it has provided a context for imagining. Tim O'Brien, for example, described in a 1987 conference his "memories of such great stories that you can exaggerate and make even better":

> This guy . . . blown into a tree. And I remember I was ordered with another guy to shinny up the tree and get him out. I remember something kind of yellow and mush that must have been the intestines. I remember a limp arm.

The guy's name was Lemon, Kurt Lemon. That stuff wakes me up. But what really wakes me up 20 years later is the other guy in the tree with me, singing 'Lemon Tree.' That's a story I've got to write some day.

The anecdote produced knowing laughter form the other writers, and O'Brien admitted that "the guy's name wasn't Lemon. There wasn't any 'Lemon Tree' song. I didn't climb the tree. None of it's true. But it's a good story," the kind of story, O'Brien said, that "gets at the *feel* of Nam—the absurdity, the horror of death, the poignancy, the way you don't look at it. You make jokes about people who are dead. That's part of survival." It is also the kind of story that lets us see the process of converting experience into art.

Vietnam is still being written out in important accounts of the immediacy of personal experience. Charles Anderson's *The Grunts* (1976), for example, attempts to "describe the Vietnam war as it was experienced by the individual infantryman, the grunt." But Anderson's narrative is not presented as the personal experience of one individual; rather, it attempts to recreate the typical, the homogeneous experience. In an interestingly similar way, Robert Mason's *Chickenhawk* moves us through a poignant and telling reanimation of one man's encounter with the "*feel* of Nam." What makes Mason's narrative stand apart from all other personal narratives of the war is its ability to locate its readers, without art or artifice, with apparently no recourse to imaginative invention, within the mind of an individual in the war. Mason's experience, reconstructed in painfully scrupulous detail, with spare, deft strokes of language, remains essentially uninterpreted. He seems to simply record, and we merge with that record, not pushed out of it by any intrusions of voice. The narrative moves from the dream of flying of a "farm kid" so enrapt by his dream that he built "tall towers to get off the ground" to a man who dreams so hard of escaping the primal terror of Vietnam, where his childhood dream was realized, that he cannot understand the way that terror has overtaken him:

> We flew almost every day. The missions were numerous, but I don't recall them very well. I was preoccupied. Gary had received his orders to leave Vietnam, but I hadn't. . . . On a rare day off, I dragged a parachute canopy to the shore. I spread it out so that it made a circle of soft nylon fifty feet across. Carrying a towel, I walked to the center of the chute and lay down to sunbathe. I wanted to look tropical for Patience. I was trying to be healthy.

Mason's island of insulation is created to forestall the intrusions of the war on his dream of leaving it to rejoin a world where its terror cannot reach. He can defend his dream against the incursions of his commanding officer, whom he will not permit to walk across the chute to speak to him, but he cannot prevent the nightmare which his dream of flying has become. A routine flight of a maintenance helicopter, piloted by a man who "did nothing more dangerous in this war than to check out freshly repaired helicopters," floats across his field of vision. The rotor the helicopter is carrying from its cargo sling begins to swing out of control, slashing up to knock off a section of the tail rotors of the maintenance ship:

> Richards flared back, trying to slow the ship, but it was no use. As he flared, the blade knifed forward under the ship and swept up and hit his main rotor. The damaged main rotor flew off. Time seemed to stop, and I saw the ship nose down, invert, and then disappear behind some tents to smash onto the beach. It fell like an anvil. There was a brief moment of quiet after the crash and then a *whoosh*. The flattened Huey burst into flames. Orange flames first, as the fuel burned, then bright-white flames as the metal ignited. . . . People ran toward the ship, only to be driven back by the fire. . . . I was still alone on my precious beach blanket. I cried.

This displacement of dreams by nightmares provides as graphic a depiction of the mental experience of combat in Vietnam as we are likely to get. The meaning of that experience, though, we can share only by imaginative participation in the events. The functions of interpretation have been delegated to the reader.

This is the final effect of Vietnam War literature as it has thus far developed. The interchange between participant and reader requires that we witness Vietnam by imagining, then absorbing the experience. Larry Heinemann's *Paco's Story* (1987) stands as one of the best examples of this transaction. "Let's begin with the first clean fact, James," the narrative begins, drawing us into the world of Paco's experience; we are James, an identity explained in the Foreword as a compromise between the "street-corner patois" which addresses the stranger as Jim or Jack, and the higher degree of formality Paco's story "requires." And the first clean fact we are given is that "this ain't no war story"; war stories have been "denounced," we are told, as "a geek-monster species of evil-ugly rumour." What we get instead is a vision of Paco, floating through "the World" after Vietnam, out-narrated by older veterans whose stories from earlier years in the war are now more polished, better than his. His own stories are reduced to the "clean facts" that run out of his mind into the voice of the narrator, and the symbolic content of his scars.

Paco, like Philip Dozier in Heinemann's earlier novel, is a survivor whose dream of return has long since died, but who cannot resist the impulse to become a voyeur in the world that the dream portrayed. His voyeurism causes him ultimately to invade the world of the coquettish college girl, Cathy, who occupies the apartment next to his. His sortie into the girl's room is described in the language Paco understands, the language of war:

> Paco stands, . . . calmly eyeing the room, and an exquisite stillness settles over him—almost an ambush trance (that blunt and slow-motion, self-destructive death wish); a grim shiver of anticipation ripples through his feet and fingers; the hair bristles at the back of his neck and behind his ears; his back hardens; his look hardens—glistens—and his eyes sparkle. He feels enveloped in an alien ease . . . as if he's been turned inside out and rendered invisible

But it is Paco, this trip out, who is ambushed. As he reads Cathy's diary, he learns that the details of his current existence have all been recorded. She has described his "depressing room," his scars, "like purple and brown and white swirls, deep, and pinched together here and there like heavy stitches of a quilt," his movements into the crazy choreography of alcohol and drugs and memory, "holding his head with both hands . . . slapping the flat of his belly with cupped hands, making a POP POP POP sound . . . hoarsely whispering . . . 'Come on, hit me! Hit me! Hit me!' and taking time out to waive that bottle around, drinking and splashing and slurring."

Paco learns that the girl has does more than simply describe his characteristics and habits. The literal joining of his and her worlds, which Paco consistently thinks of in terms of sexual encounter, the girl has also imagined. She has written of his "pasty . . . crippled . . . honest to God ugly" body "curled up on his bed like death warmed over." And she has envisioned that juncture of war and innocence, the obscene fucking of life out of meaning. But it is only when the coupling is completed that the real nightmare beings:

> He holds himself up, stiff armed, and arches his back and reaches up to his forehead and begins by pinching the skin there, but he's working the skin loose, and then begins to peel the scars off as if they were a mask. . . . I close my eyes and turn my head, and urge him off me with my hips—but I think now that he must have thought that I wanted to fuck more. He's holding me down with that hard belly of his, and lays the scars on my chest. It *burns* . . . and I think I hear *screams,* as if each scar is a scream. . . . Then he reaches both hands behind him, as if he's going to pull off a T-shirt, grabbing and pulling the scars off his back. . . . And he lays the scars across my belly—tingling and burning—lays them in my hair, wrapping them around my head, like a skull cap. And when each scar touches me, I feel the suffocating burn, hear the scream.

Paco has "met his wraith" in his journey into Cathy's mind. He quits his job, packs his AWOL bag, and boards the bus that will take him west, to the place where "there is less bullshit." But if Paco cannot go home again, his story nevertheless has, and what is no longer a "war story" has been domesticated in the place of its origins.

Paco's Story presents us with the nightmare that results from the mingling of a mind dispossessed from home by its experience of war and a mind which departs from the familiar armed only with a dangerous innocence. Through it we can learn something of what Vietnam was and what it continues to be. But this is only one form the legacy of Vietnam assumes in our literature. Another, perhaps less Melvillian, vision concerns the rejoining of experience, not with Dozier's or Paco's dreams, but with humanity. It is eloquently contained in Bruce Weigl's poetry in *The Monkey Wars* (1985). In one poem, images of war are remembered through a return to a "Temple near Quang Tri, Not on the Map" where a "small man" was found, sitting

> . . . legs askew in the shadow
> The farthest wall casts
> Halfway across the room.
>
> One of us moves towards the man,
> Curious about what he is saying.
> We bend him to sit straight
> And when he's nearly peaked
> At the top of his slow uncurling
> His face becomes visible, his eyes
> Roll down to the charge
> Wired between his teeth and the floor.
> The sparrows
> Burst off the walls into the jungle.

These images from memory are enveloped in equally accessible memories of "A Childhood," where "only the one season of the family I remember— / The way the world is sometimes / Not inside us, / The way we turn around like children / And it is gone, and for once / It is enough to know / The wrong way of things," and of "Amnesia," where:

> You tell yourself no and cry a thousand days.
> You imagine the crows calling autumn into place
> Are your brothers and you could
> If only the strength and will were there
> Fly up to them and be black
> And useful to the wind.

NOTES

For a list of works discussed in this chapter (and publication data on these works), see the bibliography which follows these notes.

1. O'Brien's comments on his work are taken from Eric James Schroeder, "Two Interviews: Talks With Tim O'Brien And Robert Stone," *Modern Fiction Studies* 30:1 (Spring, 1984), pp. 138, 140, 148.

2. For example, see the letters from Marine PFC Chester McMullen to a friend in Gainesville, Florida, appearing throughout "Act III" of *Vietnam Voices,* in particular, the letter (p. 365) written 15 April 1968, set in the context of Tet, the battle for Hue City (McMullen was stationed at Phu Bai, the marine base camp a few kilometers southwest of Hue), the seige at Khe Sanh, and Operations Pegasus, Carentan II, and Delaware in Vietnam; and, at home, the growing student unrest on campuses, the rising racial tensions in Detroit, Newark, Watts, and other urban areas, the televised execution of a Vietcong prisoner, and the developing political campaigns that would lead to the fiasco of the Democratic Convention in the summer of 1968. McMullen's letter apparently responds to his friend having described a sniping incident on her college campus: "Gee, things went boom in the night. I'm awfully sorry to hear that. Hey, Guys, I said. Things're really rough back in the world. Listen to this. Things go boom in the night there. We all laughed and laughed. Hohoho. Really. One sniper bullet."

3. Heinemann's and Caputo's comments are taken from Marc Leepson's "Talking Vietnam," excerpts from a discussion session among writers at the 1987 Vietnam Veterans of America annual convention, printed in *Gallery,* February 1988, p. 49.

4. It should be noted that there is a tendency in the glossaries and in the development of the literature towards a homogeneity of this language, when much of it seems to have been originally heterogeneous. Its original heterogeneity was in part a function of the world it grew out of. Like the war itself, the idioms Americans created to describe it remained elusive, restricted to the concentric circles of TAC zone, unit, company, platoon, fire team, individual soldier. Everyone was conscious in some degree of coining expressions, of creating a language, much as soldiers have done in any war. But the peculiar cycles of rotation in and out of Vietnam and the general stream of veterans returning quickly to civilian life saw this language trickle back into the culture. In the postwar years it has become an integral part of our consciousness of the war in Vietnam. More importantly, the cycles of repulsion and attraction to Vietnam, which have shaped it into myth, have seen this, its idiom, become refined, regulated into a homogeneous mode of expression.

5. Gordon Taylor's article, "American Personal Narrative of the War in Vietnam," in *American Literature* 52:2 (May, 1980), pp. 294–308, measures the "fundamental differences in approach and execution" between Greene's novel and later American accounts of the war, focusing especially on *Dispatches*. Taylor considers that the "hellishly sucking vortex" that Vietnam would become for Americans in the twenty or more years following the events of Greene's novel produced a subject for writers which is "in ways still resisting treatment in established literary forms," a subject which Greene's sensibility and interests could only broach and for which American writers may still be in the process of creating a form.

6. John Hellman, in his *American Myth and the Legacy of Vietnam* (New York: Columbia University Press, 1986) documents both the political influence and the success of the book—it was serialized in the *Saturday Evening Post* and was a Book-of-the-Month Club selection when it first came out in the Fall of 1958, it went through twenty printings from July to November and was on the best-seller list for 78 weeks, and it was made into a feature film in 1962 and eventually sold over 4 million copies, becoming "one of the most popular books in the nation's history." See pp. 15–19.

7. The book contains a line of development which sees American military training as de facto training for American citizenship, an idea which is undercut by Duncan's exaggeration of it into the notion that young men who undergo military training are being programmed into a cycle of obedience to insidious government agencies. But the idea—manifestly contradicted by the Vietnam generation of military trainees—forms only a small part of the book's expository sections and is overshadowed by Duncan's exceptionally vital descriptions of the experience of that training and of subsequent combat in Vietnam. (It contains, for example, perhaps the most accurate description in all of this material of the three weeks of jump school—parachute training—at Ft. Benning, Ga.)

8. Apart from age and demographics, the training and conditions of service for the ordinary combat soldier in Vietnam contributed significantly to the nature of the experience. For example, basic and advanced infantry training were reduced from twelve weeks each in 1965 to eight weeks each by 1967, in an effort to expedite the placement of combat forces in country. And the now familiar 12 month/13 month structure of a tour of duty, coupled with frequent cycles of rotation and replacements, especially among officers (in place of the more traditional concept of unit integrity), significantly altered the nature of the combat unit in Vietnam. Undertrained and inexperienced soldiers often found themselves fighting in squad-sized units the composition and command of which were subject to frequent change. See Michael Shafer's chapters on the draft and the combat experience, in this volume, for details on these and other elements of military service in Vietnam.

SELECTED BIBLIOGRAPHY

Personal Narrative and Oral History

ANDERSON, CHARLES R. *The Grunts*. New York: Avon, 1976.

BAKER, MARK. *Nam*. New York: Morrow, 1981.

BRYAN, C. D. B. *Friendly Fire*. New York: Putnam, 1976.

CAPUTO, PHILLIP. *A Rumor of War*. New York: Holt, 1977.

DUNCAN, DONALD. *The New Legions*. New York: Berkeley, 1967.

EMERSON, GLORIA. *Winners and Losers*. New York: Harcourt, 1976.

GLASSER, RONALD J. *365 Days*. New York: George Braziller, 1971.

HERR, MICHAEL. *Dispatches*. New York: Knopf, 1978.

JONES, JAMES. *Viet Journal*. New York: Delacorte, 1974.

KIRK, DONALD. *Tell It to the Dead*. Chicago: Nelson Hall, 1975.

KOVIC, RON. *Born on the Fourth of July*. New York: McGraw-Hill, 1976.

MARSHALL, KATHERINE. *In the Combat Zone: An Oral History of American Women in Vietnam, 1966–1975*. New York: Little, Brown, 1987.

MASON, ROBERT. *Chickenhawk*. New York: Viking, 1981.

O'BRIEN, TIM. *If I Die in a Combat Zone*. New York: Delacorte, 1973.

PRATT, JAMES CLARK. *Vietnam Voices*. New York: Viking, 1984.

SANTOLI, AL. *Everything We Had*. New York: Random, 1981.

SHEPARD, ELAINE. *The Doom Pussy*. New York: Trident, 1969.

TERRY, WALLACE. *Bloods*. New York: Random, 1982.

WALKER, KEITH. *A Piece of My Heart: The Stories of Twenty-Six American Women Who Served In Vietnam*. New York: Ballantine, 1985.

Short Story Collections

KLINKOWITZ, JEROME, and JOHN SOMERS, eds. *Writing under Fire*. New York: Delta, 1978.

SUDICK, TOM. *A Few Good Men*. New York: Samisdat, 1974.

Drama

COLE, TOM *Medal of Honor Rag*. New York: Dramatists' Play Service, 1981.

GARSON, BARBARA. *MacBird*. New York: Grove, 1967.

GRAY, AMIL. *How I Got That Story*. New York: Dramatists' Play Service, 1981.

RABE, DAVID. *The Basic Training of Pavlo Hummel and Sticks and Bones: Two Plays*. New York: Viking, 1969.

————. *Streamers*. New York: Viking, 1970.

TERRY, MEGAN. *Viet Rock*. New York: Simon & Schuster, 1967.

Poetry

BALABAN, JOHN. *Vietnam Poems*. Oxford: Carcanet, 1970.

————. *After Our War*. Pittsburgh: University of Pittsburgh Press, 1974.

BERRY, D. C. *Saigon Cemetery*. Athens, Ga.: University of Georgia Press, 1972.

EHRHART, W. D. *A Generation of Peace*. New York: New Voices, 1975.

————. *The Outer Banks and Other Poems*. New York: Thunder Mountain, 1978.

————. *To Those Who Have Gone Home Tired*. New York: Thunder Mountain, 1984.

EHRHART, W. D., ed. *Carrying the Darkness*. New York: Avon, 1985.

McDONALD, WALTER. *Caliban in Blue*. Lubbock, Tex.: Texas Tech Press, 1976.

ROTTMANN, LARRY, JAN BARRY, and BASIL T. PAQUET, eds. *Winning Hearts and Minds*. Perkasie, Pa.: East River Anthology, 1972.

SHEA, DICK. *Vietnam Simply*. Coronada, Calif.: Pro Tem, 1967.

WEIGL, BRUCE. *The Monkey Wars*. New York: Viking, 1985.

Novels

BABER, ASA. *The Land of a Million Elephants*. New York: Morrow, 1970.

BRILEY, JOHN. *The Traitors*. New York: Putnam, 1969.

BROWNE, CORRINE. *Body Shop*. New York: Stein & Day, 1973.

BUNTING, JOSIAH. *The Lionheads*. New York: George Braziller, 1972.

BURDICK, EUGENE, and WILLIAM LEDERER. *The Ugly American*. New York: McGraw-Hill, 1958.

BUTLER, ROBERT OLDEN. *On Distant Ground*. New York: Knopf, 1985.

CASSIDY, JOHN. *A Station in the Delta*. New York: Scribners, 1979.

CRUMLEY, JAMES. *One to Count Cadence*. New York: Random, 1969.

DEL VECCHIO, JOHN. *The Thirteenth Valley*. New York: Bantam, 1982.

DERRIG, PETER. *The Pride of the Green Berets*. New York: Paperback Library, 1966.

DURDEN, CHARLES. *No Bugles, No Drums*. New York: Viking, 1976.

EASTLAKE, WILLIAM. *The Bamboo Bed*. New York: Simon & Schuster, 1969.

FLEMING, THOMAS. *Officers' Wives*. Garden City, N.Y.: Doubleday, 1981.

FORD, DANIEL. *Incident at Muc Wa*. New York: Doubleday, 1967.

GREENE, GRAHAM. *The Quiet American*. New York: Viking, 1955.

HALBERSTAM, DAVID. *One Very Hot Day*. New York: Avon, 1967.

HALDEMAN, JOE. *War Year*. New York: Holt, 1972.

HASFORD, GUSTAV. *The Short Timers*. New York: Harper & Row, 1980.

HEINEMANN, LARRY. *Close Quarters*. New York: Farrar, Straus and Giroux, 1977.

HEINEMANN, LARRY. *Paco's Story*. New York: Farrar, Straus and Giroux, 1986.

HUGGETT, WILLIAM TURNER. *Body Count*. New York: Putnam, 1973.

JUST, WARD. *Stringer*. New York: Little, Brown, 1974.

KALB, BERNARD, and MARVIN KALB. *The Last Ambassador*. Boston: Little, Brown, 1981.

KOLPAKOFF, VICTOR. *The Prisoners of Quai Dong*. New York: New American Library, 1967.

MASON, BOBBIE ANN. *In Country*. New York: Harper & Row, 1985.

MERKIN, ROBERT. *Zombie Jamborie*. New York: Harper & Row, 1986.

MOORE, ROBIN. *The Green Berets*. New York: Crown, 1965.

O'BRIEN, TIM. *Going after Cacciato*. New York: Delacorte, 1981.

PELFRY, WILLIAM. *The Big V*. New York: Liveright, 1972.

RUBIN, JONATHAN. *The Barking Deer*. New York: George Braziller, 1974.

SMITH, STEPHEN PHILLIP. *American Boys*. New York: Putnam, 1975.

STONE, ROBERT. *Dog Soldiers*. Boston: Houghton Mifflin, 1974.

TAYLOR, THOMAS. *A-18*. New York: Crown, 1967.

VAUGHN, ROBERT. *The Valkyrie Mandate*. New York: Simon & Schuster, 1974.

WEBB, JAMES. *Fields of Fire*. Englewood Cliffs, N.J.: Prentice-Hall, 1978.

WRIGHT, STEPHEN. *Meditations in Green*. New York: Charles Scribner's Sons, 1983.

9

THE VIETNAM WAR MOVIE
BRUCE TAYLOR

For the vast majority of Americans, film—in its various manifestations in movies and on TV—has not only assumed the proportions of literary experience, but has augmented if not replaced written history as a repository of images and information. Film has established itself as a major medium by which our culture reflects and shapes its reality with a speed and a scope previously unimagined or experienced. History becomes myth even before it has a chance to be history.

Gaylyn Studar and David Desser point out that it is particularly the controversial or ambiguous historical event that is rewritten through the use of symbols, and that the mass media, including movies and television, "have proven to be important mechanisms whereby this rewriting—this re-imaging—of the past can occur." [1]

What the Vietnam War was or was not in the American popular consciousness may be more directly related to the movies that have been made about it than to the histories written or the political or moral issues revived and debated. Much of what Americans—whether those who opposed it, those who waged it, or those who were asked to support it—knew about war during Vietnam was learned at the movies, those of the genre known as the World War II movie, and those of a new genre which has already come to be known as the Vietnam War movie.

How have American movies portrayed the historical event and the personal experience of the Vietnam War? And what does that portrayal reflect about the time period during which the movie was made?

The premise implied by these questions is an established one. Any film of a historical event is often as much about the prevalent attitudes toward that event when the film was made as it is about the historical subject itself. Consequently, as Claudia Springer concludes, "attitudes toward existing concerns are played out in . . . [an] interpretation of the past." When, as she goes on to say, "the historical period portrayed, such as the Vietnam war, contains issues directly relevant to current policy debates," an audience ought to ask itself, how does the film reveal more about its current context than about the historical issues its purports to depict?[2]

What then, within the contexts of politics, culture and genre, does a brief historical survey of some of the more popular films about the Vietnam War reveal about what we have thought and felt about Vietnam?

Joseph L. Mankiewicz's 1957 movie of Graham Greene's novel, *The Quiet American,* portrays a Vietnam of negligible importance to Americans. The movie suggests the unspoken certainty that if Vietnam became a problem, we as Americans would (with American spirit, know-how and technology) straighten things out in a hurry. By 1968 John Wayne's film, *The Green Berets,* became a litmus test for an "America—Love It or Leave It" brand of patriotism. These movies and how they were made display cold war politics and a frontier, if not colonial, mentality that reflect the causes of our escalating involvement in Vietnam.

The film version of *The Quiet American* subverts the original intention of the novel. (Graham Greene labeled it a complete treachery.) In the novel, the American of the title, Alden Pyle, works for the U.S. government. In the movie, Pyle (played by real-life war hero Audie Murphy) is employed by something called the Friends of Free Asia. In the book, Pyle attempts to establish "a third force" in Vietnam, and, in his New-World naiveté, smuggles plastic explosives disguised as bicycle parts into Vietnam, thereby adding to the chaos and destruction. In the movie, Pyle is completely innocent and becomes the victim of a jealous and corrupt Old-World reporter in conspiracy with the communists.

The novel makes clear its prophetic point: if the United States takes the place of the French in Vietnam, only suffering and death to a degree previously unimagined can result. The film, however, leaves little doubt that only America, as an alternative to decadent colonialism on the one hand and evil communism on the other, can save Vietnam.

The novel had been "corrected" to reflect the official cold war attitudes of the time in which the film was made. This transmutation from literature into propaganda, from the insight of the artist to the party line, would become the rule rather than the exception throughout the history of the filmic treatment of Vietnam. Inevitably, however, this party line would shift from time to time. Films as diverse in their view of Vietnam as *The Green Berets* (1968), *First Blood* (1982), *Who'll Stop the Rain* (1978), and *Full Metal Jacket* (1987) display, at the very least, what Terry Christensen refers to as a muting of the political message of their respective sources.

A central reason for this muting is the collaborative nature of the medium itself. It takes one painter to make a painting but a veritable army to make a movie; and, as making movies becomes ever more expensive, collaboration extends—with all its implications of compromise and cooperation—beyond the strictly aesthetic. Not only do director, author and actor collaborate, but, in financial and ideological realms, so do producers, backers, and distributors.[3]

Perhaps this is why from 1957 to 1968, as Gilbert Adair remarks, "Hollywood didn't pass the buck on Vietnam, it tried to bury it."[4] When the silence was broken in 1968 with *The Green Berets,* the film's blatant propaganda made that of *The Quiet American* pale by comparison.

In *The Green Berets,* made while the war was at its peak, John Wayne directed John Wayne, and in the movie he is still Sergeant Striker of the *Sands of Iwo Jima* (1949), although the hoards of Japanese storming the hill are Vietnamese regulars. This is still Dodge City (the name of the Special Forces outpost in the movie), where the Americans continue to be cowboys and the South Vietnamese and the Vietcong become, respectively, the "good" and "bad" Indians. The former, playing Tonto to Wayne's Lone Ranger, say lines like: "We kill all stinking Cong," and "We clobber many Vee Cee." To which Wayne replies, "Affirmative. I like the way you talk."

That it took so long for Hollywood to attempt a Vietnam movie at all betrays its reluctance to do so. The project was muscled through by Wayne himself, who went straight to Lyndon Johnson with his initial idea and an eight-page shopping list of the men and material he would need.[5] If ever any Vietnam movie could be said to directly reflect the view of the government's publicly stated foreign and domestic policy of the moment, it would be this one, in which: a soldier's job is to follow orders, not debate; there is no excuse for war protesters and draft dodgers; we are fighting world communism in Vietnam; the South Vietnamese, who are fighting for the same kinds of freedoms we fought for in 1776, want and need us there; and with American aid, South Vietnam will prevail.

As important as any of the physical battles in *The Green Berets* is the one to win the heart and mind of a cynical liberal reporter (played by David Jansen). This is won by exposing him to successively more horrific displays of the enemy's sadistic and cowardly behavior while contrasting those examples to the bravery and compassion of the American Green Berets. The message is explicit; we should support the war in Vietnam because the enemy rapes and mutilates, the enemy kills women and children, and we don't. Although the revelations concerning My Lai were yet to come, the massacre itself occurred in March of the year *The Green Berets* was released.

Many other terrible ironics lurk around this movie. *The Green Berets,* for all its clichés and stereotypes, for all its clumsy propaganda, for wrong and shameful reasons, may yet be one of the most revealing explorations of America's involvement in Vietnam. If we believed ourselves to be so morally superior, if we were as historically and culturally ignorant—as blatantly chauvinistic, racist, sexist and violent—as this film portrays us to be, if this is the way our government and military saw the war or wanted us to see it, then there is little wonder why we became involved in Vietnam or why we lost.

The Green Berets fails to provide any historical background to the war or the slightest shred of understanding of the complex social realities of the Vietnamese people; but it is only the first, not the last, Vietnam War movie to fail to do so. Some might suggest, as Loren Baritz has, that it was just such a failure to understand the war within its historical background and social realities—both American and Vietnamese—that doomed our involvement from the start and compounded that doom the longer we stayed.[6]

For nine years after *The Green Berets,* movie studios would continue to be reluctant to deal directly with the Vietnam War as a subject. Gilbert Adair observes that the studios finally got around to Vietnam in a reverse chronology; movies were first made about Vietnam veterans, then about the effects of the war upon our society in general, long before movies attempted to address Vietnam directly as a subject. Adair attributes this reluctance (in spite of what he refers to as the war's "pre-publicity" in the other media and its host of dramatic possibilities) to a self-imposed censorship.[7] No doubt much of this censorship was due to fears for the box office. The business of movies is, first and last, to make money. There also existed a real concern by filmmakers and financiers that they might be undercutting American soldiers by challenging American policy while those men were in combat. Support of the war effort was, after all, the role that the movies learned to play during World War II. For Adair the very lack of films made about Vietnam between 1968 and 1977 is deserving of study.[8]

As early as 1974, rumors that Francis Ford Coppola (direct from triumphs with *The Godfather* [1972] and *The Godfather II* [1974]) was working on a movie about Vietnam seemed to stimulate a number of projects which in turn resulted in the release of at least five major Vietnam War movies in 1978 and 1979. By this time, as Adair observes, the war had "polarized sympathies to such a degree that even the most mindnumbing adventure movies were obliged to pay lip service to at least some of the issues at stake."[9]

For example, *Go Tell the Spartans* (1978), directed by Ted Post, seems at first to be almost uncanny in its ability to focus upon and forecast some of the essential problems of the war; but the movie, though set in 1964, was made ten years after the Tet offensive, three years after American troops had been withdrawn and at a time when the problems it addressed were common knowledge to even the most casual observer of recent history. Albert Auster and Leonard Quart claim that *Go Tell the Spartans* had been "shifted from studio to studio for eight years before it was finally made."[10] Here, too, is a precedent that was followed almost without exception in regard to the Vietnam War movie: better safe and late, than sorry. (If the movie had been made eight years earlier and could have been presented, for instance, on a double bill with *The Green Berets,* this would have said something much more flattering about the courage of American movies and the workings of our culture than its release in 1978 does.)

Two other films of 1978, *Coming Home* and *The Deer Hunter,* in their respective conclusions (if not in their premises and approaches) indicate the degree to which American movies as medium attempted to take seriously the effects of Vietnam.

In *Coming Home* director Hal Ashby presents Vietnam as a horrible wound from which we must try to recover and go on. The film, part soap opera love triangle, part soft-rock video, centers on the affair between a paraplegic veteran and the wife of a career marine officer. If the hawkish husband had been portrayed with any of the sympathy or complexity of the (antiwar) lovers, or if the film had followed the husband to Vietnam, elevated him to the role of a major character, and showed us his disintegration and disillusionment, then the movie's bias might have not been so noticeable. But the husband goes to war with all the naivete of a kid wanting to be put into the big game, and returns more disappointed that he didn't get to win than changed by the horrors he tells us he experienced.

It is particularly easy to spot the disloyal opposition in a Vietnam War movie; whether "hawk" or "dove," the opposition will be drawn in grotesque caricature, as if the only way to win sympathy for one side is to make the other look as foolish as possible.

Clearly, with films like *Go Tell the Spartans* and *Coming Home,* certain filmmakers and the interests that financed them had decided there was enough antiwar sentiment across the country that it could be capitalized upon, particularly if the message of the movie was in soft focus and full of easy generalities and stereotypes. Now that the American involvement in the war was over, these movies were safe to make.

Michael Cimino's *The Deer Hunter* (1978) was the first Vietnam War movie to emphasize what its characters were before and after Vietnam in order to examine the destructive effects of the war upon a small group of friends and the community in which they live. As with *The Green Berets* (released ten years before) and *Platoon* (released ten years after), *The Deer Hunter* was the occasion of much controversy. In perhaps no other movie are Vietnam and the Vietnamese portrayed as quite so foreign and evil, or the steel mills of Pennsylvania as more idyllic. Michael Cimino was charged, often by critics who made no mention of the endemic racism present in virtually all earlier Vietnam movies, with portraying all Vietnamese as venal, sadistic killers. He was charged with revisionism and *The Deer Hunter* was said to represent a Pentagon version of the war, as if it were the first movie to do so. A case can be made that the racist portrayal of the Vietnamese in *The Deer Hunter* results from the point of view of the characters and the values of the community which they represent. If there is a general message in the movie it may be, as Gilbert Adair suggests, that "it [Vietnam] exposed America to a contamination by a continent so irredeemably mired in moral corruption that it hardly deserved to be saved."[11] Although I would substitute race for continent, there is little doubt that this is exactly the way the Vietnamese would be viewed by the community Cimino portrays.

Terry Christensen sees this process as self-reinforcing. Any mass entertainment, he suggests "cannot depart too far from the tastes and beliefs of the masses." As products, movies must entertain, not offend, "so it is safer to make movies that reinforce people's biases rather than try to change them. The content of a film may thus be at least to some extent a reflection of what its audience already believes."[12]

Practically no Vietnam combat is presented in *The Deer Hunter*. Most of the action which takes place in Vietnam (less than one-third of the movie) revolves around the infamous and almost unbearable Russian roulette scenes, with smaller sequences representing a whore trying to get an American into bed with her while her infant is crying on the floor in the same room, and the complete chaos of the fall of Saigon, full of fleeing Americans and panic-stricken hordes of stranded and abandoned South Vietnamese.

(Few critics, however, saw the aptness of Russian roulette as a metaphor for our involvement in Vietnam, but were instead quick to point out that the game itself is unknown to the Vietnamese, and that the actors portraying Vietnamese were themselves Chinese and speaking Chinese. Vietnam War movies, which are, after all, narrative fiction not non-fiction, which are art not history, though not necessarily any less subjective, are held to a stricter sense of realism than most other movies. While praising *Platoon* (1986), in *The Nation,* Terrence Rafferty, speaking of both *The Deer Hunter* and *Apocalypse Now,* says "neither of those big deal movies was about Vietnam at all they were about the shape the war took in our imaginations . . . We've had the war as metaphor for moral chaos, and the war as rock-and-roll hallucination."[13] Rarely is a point missed in such a revealing fashion. In the first case, the shape the war took in our imaginations is exactly what is important. In the second, it was moral chaos and a rock-and-roll hallucination that were used as metaphors for the war, not the other way around.)

The last scene of *The Deer Hunter* was also a matter of controversy; in it the surviving characters sing "God Bless America," presenting an image many critics found to be offensively jingoistic, while others saw it as representing America's healing. Though Cimino claimed that his characters were supporting nothing except each other, it was impossible, as Albert Auster and Leonard Quart observe, for the film not to have a political resonance: "The war is finally too charged and partisan a subject to be treated in ahistorical terms."[14] Indeed the controversy over *The Deer Hunter* (as is the case for many Vietnam movies) makes the movie, as Gilbert Adair notes, "less about the Vietnam War . . . than a part of it."[15]

Apocalypse Now, directed by Francis Ford Coppola, appeared in 1979. The movie is a highly stylized vision of Vietnam as rock-and-roll nightmare, an acid flashback to an existential hell. Curiously, a case can be made that *Apocalypse Now,* like *The Deer Hunter* before it, can be viewed as having everything or nothing at all to do with the subject of America's involvement in Vietnam. Coppola himself stated his purpose was "to go further, [beyond Vietnam] to the moral issues that are behind all wars."[16] Many audiences and critics were not ready for Vietnam to be so universalized. Though critically acclaimed for artistic excellence, the high style of Cimino and Coppola was, for many, too bookish and fancy to apply to Vietnam.

Coppola, who is often cited as the one director of his time who might have been a great film writer, employed methods suspiciously literary. In Joseph Conrad's *Heart of Darkness,* Coppola's source for *Apocalypse Now,* nineteenth-century European colonialists, thinly masquerading as religious pilgrims, pretend to "civilize" (Christianize) Africa, while plundering the continent, enslaving and murdering the populace.[17] In Coppola's movie the American army, as the policy-enforcing strong arm of the United States government, is in Southeast Asia to "win the hearts and minds" of the Vietnamese even if the military has to "destroy the country to save it."

Until *Gardens of Stone* (1987) and *Hanoi Hilton* (1987), two films that unabashedly attempt to glorify a military tarnished by Vietnam, a pattern seems to have been established within the genre of the Vietnam War movie of portraying as foolish, cowardly, hypocritical any figures above (and often including) the rank of sergeant. This attrition of authority, an abandonment and betrayal of the individual by any kind of reliable authority outside that of the self has, according to the modernist tradition, been an informing plight of modern existence itself.

Willard, the protagonist of *Apocalypse Now,* is a quester knight who must face and test the shadowy civilian/military authorities that give him his mission to travel upriver into off-limits Cambodia and "terminate with extreme prejudice" the command of Colonel Kurtz. He encounters the outrageous Lieutenant Colonel Kilgore, whose Air Cavalry helicopters are equipped with loudspeakers to play Wagner because "it scares the hell out of the slopes," and who chooses his military objectives depending upon the availability of good beaches for surfing. If Kilgore is innocent, what, Willard imagines, can Kurtz be guilty of?

As Terry Christensen observes, *Apocalypse Now* is particularly successful in communicating "the war's other-worldliness, its confusion of good and evil, and its contagious, destructive madness." [18] The farther up the river Willard goes the more meaningless and morally vacant a nightmare Vietnam becomes. "Charging a man with murder in this place [Vietnam]," Willard says, "was like handing out speeding tickets at the Indy 500."

The case against Kurtz is the case against the surreal and ultimately paradoxical nature of America's military involvement in Vietnam. Colonel Kurtz has, as those who accuse him claim, "gone too far." First of all, he is in Cambodia, a location which assumes its own special significance of illegitimacy and transgression. Too far also means that he has killed— not just Vietnamese (that is the job of the American soldier in this particular war)—but the wrong ones. Or has he? Great care is taken to suggest if not confirm that the South Vietnamese officials Kurtz is explicitly charged with killing were in fact North Vietnamese agents, that perhaps Kurtz has been able to do what the American army in Vietnam could not, tell the good guys from the bad guys and act appropriately.

Kurtz commands a tribe of Montagnards to whom he has become a god, endowed with total authority and blindly obeyed. Kurtz's methods, which the general judges unsound (not immoral or illegal), are in question, but his results are not, for he has simply established the situation of command and popular support that the American military and government desired but never enjoyed.

The two major Vietnam War movies of 1978 and 1979, *The Deer Hunter* and *Apocalypse Now,* present Vietnam as an event of immense proportion and consequence and represent it as catastrophe or tragedy. By the mid-eighties, however, any pretense of seriousness in the treatment of Vietnam as a subject for popular film pales in the face of *First Blood* (1982) and *Missing In Action* (1984) and their ilk, films whose makers found it politically expedient and financially rewarding to exploit the stereotype of the Vietnam veteran (solidified in one B film after another about street gangs and psychotic losers) by inflating the vet into a cartoon hero. In these films Americans finally get to win the war or at least feel as if they have, although they have to become Vietcong to do it.

The implausible circumstances and convolutions of plot used by these movies to get their respective protagonists into the appropriate situation indicate just how uncomfortable the filmmakers feel about America in the role of the technologically advanced invading superpower and how much they long for our traditional posture of the underdog jungle fighter. Perhaps this attitude also accounts for the mythologizing of the enemy which occurs throughout later Vietnam War movies, an enemy (as Roger Ebert points out) now portrayed as an "elusive collective myth . . . who lived in tunnels, subsisted on a few grains of rice, and was nowhere and everywhere at the same time."[19] In films as diverse in their approach as *Apocalypse Now* (1978) and *Hamburger Hill* (1987), there is a stern respect, even admiration, displayed by the American fighting man for the enemy (perhaps a grudging nod to the military outcome of the war), which was not shown the Japanese in the majority of World War II movies. But in the Sylvester Stallone and Chuck Norris macho male adventure fantasy films, the enemy functions merely as cannon-fodder. These movies are cartoons made from real human suffering, American and Vietnamese, and those Vietnamese are treated with a degree of racism shocking even within the long history of the way Asians have been stereotyped by American movies, from Charlie Chan to the "yellow hoards" and sadistic prison camp commanders standard in World War II movies.

For all the firepower expended in *First Blood,* which takes place here in the United States, we are supposed to believe that the only person who actually dies is the sadistic deputy who deserved to. If, however, the hero is in Vietnam, as he is in *Rambo II* and the Chuck Norris movies, then he is free to kill as many people as possible; his victims are, after all, Vietnamese, the enemy, and that makes their slaughter in such hyperbolic numbers not only, one fears, acceptable to the filmmakers, but also admirable. Like the endlessly expendable faceless robot storm troopers served up to Luke Skywalker during the *Star Wars* series, wave after wave of the "yellow hoard" are like so many pins in a bowling alley when faced with the great American war hero as portrayed by Sylvester Stallone or Chuck Norris.

It is too easy to dismiss this cycle of movies as a Reagan-era phenomenon; they are more insidious than mere nostalgia and their strategy is too odious. Vietnam and the Vietnam veteran are trivialized by a stultifying simplicity. By presenting themselves so unabashedly as lightweight action adventures, these movies are allowed to get away with unloading unlimited political and emotional propaganda upon audiences that have been consciously set up to receive it. As Terry Christensen sees it, "movies may be a particularly powerful medium of political socialization" because "we go voluntarily, often for social reasons, with a positive, receptive attitude. We expect to be entertained, so our guard is down. We do not go to learn, yet any teacher will tell you that the first problem in teaching is getting the student's attention, and that's what movies are designed to do." [20]

The most popularly successful of these movies, *Rambo: First Blood Part II* (1985), directed by George Cosmatos and timed for release on the tenth anniversary of America's withdrawal from Vietnam, was based upon two premises: first, that the American government knows there are men missing in action being held as prisoners in Vietnam but does not want the public to know; and second, that the United States military could have won the war if the government and American public had let them.

In this sequel, Rambo is released from jail and promised a pardon for the carnage of the last movie if he will return to Vietnam. "Do we get to win this time?" Rambo asks sarcastically. The mission is to find out if there are any MIA's still being held prisoner. There are, but as Rambo tries to drag one out as evidence, both are abandoned on the order of the shadowy civilian authority in charge of the mission. Rambo must then fight his way (with, it seems, atomic tipped arrows) through the Vietnamese and their Russian advisors back to the American who betrayed him and whose life he contemptuously spares (though he guns down the computers). At the movie's end he is taunted with a request to reenlist, "Don't you love your country?" Rambo replies that all the vets love their country but that what they want is for their "country to love them."

As least as important as the movie itself is the emergence of Sylvester Stallone, widely, if not often hysterically, self-promoted to be "The Spirit of America" as this generation's John Wayne. The two Rambo movies and the Rocky movies combined to make Stallone the top box office attraction in the world. Among the most recognizable icons of this era would be the photos of Stallone as Rocky the boxer stripped to the waist and wearing red, white, and blue trunks in front of an American flag, or as Rambo the Vietnam vet, again stripped to the waist, with weapons ablaze.

The second Rambo film had the third largest opening gross of any movie up to that time—more than $3.25 million in tickets sales in its first six days of release—and was the second only to *Back to the Future* in profits for the year. It spawned a phenomenon dubbed Rambomania along with the requisite spinoffs: war toys, bubble gum trading cards, Halloween costumes, candy, at least one nightclub (Rambose, in Houston), "Rambo-grams" (delivered by a bare-chested messenger carrying a toy automatic weapon), and an entire line of camouflage designer wear. Eventually the politics and the marketing promotion become self-referential. When Ronald Reagan, referring to a solution to the problem of Libyan terrorists, was quoted worldwide as saying "I saw Rambo last night and now I know what to do," it was estimated that fifty million dollars were added to the movie's domestic profits alone. What was inestimable was the damage done to America's image throughout the world.

In the later 1980s, twenty years after *The Green Berets* and a dozen years after the fall of Saigon, another group of Vietnam War movies has appeared—five within two years. As with the group of films released in 1978, the similarities shared by the movies of 1987 and 1988 demonstrate attitudes important to our survey. Not only did America lose in Vietnam, but we shouldn't have been there in the first place, and while there we acted in ways insane, brutal and devious even by the usual standards of warfare. Studlar and Desser identify the realization of these circumstances as a "cultural trauma" which has set forces in play within post–Vietnam America similar to those in Japan and Germany after World War II, including a "desire to rewrite history and to repress collective guilt and responsibility."[21]

Each of the movies released in the late 1980s attempts to establish itself as beyond politics and even history. In all of these movies, whether or not Americans should have been in Vietnam is not supposed to be an issue; how the men who were there suffered and what they sacrificed are the primary concerns.

As David James maintains, the "presentness" of a movie can transform "the movie theater into the theater of war," a condition which depends on the effectiveness with which the "audience can be made to experience the textures and terrors of the phenomenal experience of battle." In such a film, James goes on to say, "the GI is our surrogate and intermediary between us and Vietnam" and represents an "authenticity of knowledge upon which the war can be evaluated and validated." The very intensity of his sacrifice and suffering is often "not only its justification, it is its own explanation."[22] Claudia Springer notes, however, the danger of such a strategy: "Being there seems a prerequisite for formulating a valid opinion about an event . . . Viewers may be convinced of their own inability to hold an opinion because they are not validated as experts."[23]

Any literature about war is to some degree about the people (individually and collectively) who fought that war, the societies that involved themselves in it, the history that preceded it and that which will follow, as well as about the war itself, the actual hostilities, the killing and the dying. But literature that deals as specifically with combat as do these movies is usually, as Frederick Karl states, "removed from ideological concerns . . . placed . . . outside a political stance that both transcends and falls beneath politics."[24] What is particularly interesting about this group of films—*Platoon, Hamburger Hill, Full Metal Jacket, Gardens of Stone,* and *Hanoi Hilton*—is that at the same time each places itself beyond criticism of the policy and politics of Vietnam, each also carries its own political agenda. Each is quick to lay the blame on one group or the other—be it the rich, the liberal press, the peace movement at home, or a corrupt and crippled armed forces—for America's loss in Vietnam.

The most popular and critically acclaimed of these movies, *Platoon* (1988), was directed and written by Oliver Stone, one of the few Vietnam combat veterans to make a movie about Vietnam. *Platoon,* which according to Stone, was delayed ten years before a studio would attempt it, is not the first major American movie concerning Vietnam that is unabashedly from the "grunt's" point of view, but it is the first to set aside, at least on the surface, any debate about national policy in favor of attempting to come to terms with the reality of men being there.

Like *The Green Berets* in 1968 and *Apocalypse Now* in 1979, *Platoon* was heralded not so much as a movie, but as an event; inherent in its publicity was a claim of realism and of the film's supposed symbolic value to the Vietnam veteran (to whom the film, in the World War II movie tradition, is dedicated). Special showings, often free or at reduced rates, were scheduled for veterans, who were advised to bring along a friend in case they found the movie too real to handle. These showings were covered as news on all the national networks. Stone himself, accepting the Oscar for his film, claimed (somewhat self-servingly many felt) that America had finally "welcomed home" her Vietnam vets. The phrase "Vietnam-guilt chic" began to be bandied about by film critics.

Avoiding the grandiose visual metaphors of *Apocalypse Now* and *The Deer Hunter, Platoon* does seem to get some details right, particularly those that would remain central to the infantryman's experience—the heat, the bugs, the fear and horror of night combat. It is also one of the few major films to deal at all (never mind as powerfully as it does) with the fact of atrocities committed by American troops. In addition, blacks appear in significant numbers and in central and even sympathetic roles. Yet any special claim to realism in *Platoon* (beyond the claim that it may make the viewer feel as he or she imagined it must have felt to be in Vietnam) flounders as the film consumes itself in a style one reviewer referred to as "literary preppie," replete with allusions to hero archetypes and Herman Melville.

The movies of 1986 and 1987 also establish a populairst fatalism and a glorification of the "grunt." In *Platoon* the protagonist is instantly recognizable as the young naif out to find and test himself. Chris Taylor (Charlie Sheen, whose father played Willard in *Apocalypse Now*) plays an upper-middle-class white kid, disaffected with family and college, who drops out and volunteers for combat in Vietnam because it does not seem fair to him that only the poor be sent to fight—an attitude which, as one of the black draftees points out, one must be rich to afford: "The poor is always gettin' fucked over by the rich. Always has. Always will." Chris later establishes what might be called "the grunt's creed":

> These are guys no one really cares about. They come from the end of the line, towns nobody has ever heard of . . . Two years of high school is about it. Maybe, if they're lucky a job waiting for them in a factory when they get out. They are the poor and the unwanted yet they are fighting for our society, our freedom. They are the bottom of the barrel and they know it. That's why they call themselves Grunts because a Grunt can take it, can take anything.

Each of these movies attempts with varying degrees of integrity and depth to address matters of guilt and innocence, both personal and national. "The first casualty of war is innocence," announced the major promotion for *Platoon*. Indeed, as bleakly ironic as it may be, these mid-eighties Vietnam War movies portrayed the major tragedy of Vietnam as a loss of American innocence rather than as the loss of both Vietnamese and American lives.

(Any exploration in these films of our innocence or lack of it seems to require that someone else be guilty. *Hamburger Hill* was supposed to make anyone who didn't fight in Vietnam feel guilty, while *Hanoi Hilton* condemned anyone who didn't support the war completely and unequivocally. It is important to note that these movies as a group spend as much or more time and energy assigning blame for our having lost the war as they do worrying about our being in Vietnam at all or about what we may or may not have done there.)

John Irvin's *Hamburger Hill* (1987), written by Vietnam veteran James Carabatsos, was released shortly after *Platoon* (though it had gone into production long before) and takes as its subject the assault of Hill 937 in the A Shau Valley in May of 1969 by one thousand men of the 101st Airborne Division.[25] The title of the film refers, of course, to a Korean War battle and the film *Pork Chop Hill* (1959). The Korean battlefield got its name from the shape of terrain itself, but Hamburger Hill is named for the condition of the men who stormed it over and over again. This curious film seems to make a virtue out of being cannon fodder. Watching it, we are never completely sure how much we ought to admire and respect the bravery and persistence of the men as they try repeatedly to take the hill, suffering massive casualties; or whether we should question the criminal stupidity of their being there at all. The answer is that we are supposed to do both at the same time.

Hamburger Hill is full of references to the "hairheads" at home who protest the war (insulting vets, for example by throwing dog shit on them at the airport), who love everyone and everything in the world (including "Luke the Gook") except the "grunt," and who are imagined rolling around in bed with the girls the GIs left behind.

Such polemics, no matter how accurately they may reflect the view of many soldiers, abound in the film and, as Jack Kroll suggests in a *Newsweek* review, "not only dilute the whole political problem of Vietnam, but also undercut the film's scrupulous depiction of the soldiers' heroic behavior under the most horrific conditions fighting men could possibly face." [26] Stanley Kauffmann adds that no recognition was made of the fact that "most of the peace movement was trying to get these men out of the deathtrap they were in." [27]

There are probably more Vietnamese shown in this movie than any other. Most, of course, are the enemy (hoards of them) but others are civilians milling around in and out of the movie's non-combat moments, relegated to a backdrop. The enemy is shown either firing maniacally at the Americans who assault the hill or swarming, chattering, into underground bunkers to avoid (unfairly, we are somehow led to believe) air barrages of white phosphorus and napalm. One notable scene features an appropriately fierce character named Han, a demonstration Vietcong who, we are told, "gets his rocks off" killing. As is often the case, the only dialogue given any Vietnamese is spoken by prostitutes.

It is probably true that more blacks are portrayed in central roles (though none is an officer) in *Hamburger Hill* than in any other movie under discussion, and that more attention is paid to the racial tensions between white and black soldiers, though the resolution of those tensions seems overly simplistic. As he is carried away on a stretcher, the black spokesman, Doc, tells the white sergeant, "We are all niggers on this hill."

Mostly, it is this "no one cares about us but us" camaraderie that is the central focus of the movie. After one soldier dies, another angrily contends he didn't die for America and apple pie, but for his fellow "grunts." As was traditionally the case in World War II movies, the men have no one and nothing else to depend upon except each other; amidst the senselessness of war this is the only thing that makes sense.

Martha Bayles has observed that this is "a devilishly clever trick, . . . that focuses narrowly on the emotional bonds between fighting men while disparaging the cause for which they are fighting as evil or absurd." [28] The result, as Bayles concludes, is films like *Platoon* and *Full Metal Jacket* (I would also add *Hamburger Hill, Hanoi Hilton* and *Gardens of*

Stone), which "shrink the moral component of the Vietnam tragedy to the unproblematic morality of buddy helping buddy." [29] These films begin a re-glorification of the American fighting man, and a re-romanticizing of war that had been interrupted by the consequences of atomic capability, by Korea, by the 1960s and by Vietnam itself

Perhaps it is because they concern a loss of innocence, the traditional theme of stories about young men going to war, that these movies hearken back as much to World War I for their resonances as to World War II. Like many World War I movies, *Platoon, Hanoi Hilton,* and *Gardens of Stone* are unabashedly elegiac in tone. By 1988 Vietnam seems a tragically futile war in which the "flower of our youth" was lost. In World War I this image applied to a generation of English leaders, statesmen, poets. In Vietnam, it more likely refers, as in *Platoon,* to the "bottom of the barrel" with democratic connotations of a nobility which is earned, not conferred. It is always the young who suffer the most in these movies; who, depending on the point of view, are sacrificed (*Platoon*), consumed (*Hamburger Hill*), or disposed of (*Full Metal Jacket*). It is the young who have been betrayed and abandoned and in that context it may be possible to view much of what we see in the Vietnam War movie as the culmination of the alienation of youth and resultant nihilism and distrust of authority that dominated the films of the late fifties and early sixties. This was a war, we must remember, fought by a generation who warned that "you can't trust anyone over thirty." Precious little in most of these movies contradicts that advice.

At least one film seems to turn the tables and make youth itself, particularly American youth, into the villain, not the victim. Stanley Kubrick's *Full Metal Jacket* of 1987, was as eagerly awaited as *Apocalypse Now.* To those familiar with Kubrick's vision as displayed in movies such as *Dr. Strangelove* (1964) and *Clockwork Orange* (1971), his Cyborg-Punk treatment of Vietnam may have come as a disappointment, but as no surprise.

The movie makes the point stridently and repeatedly that the Marine Corps—and by macroscopic implication, American society and its attitudes about masculinity, sex, and violence—creates killers and that this is exactly what is needed in war. Auster and Quart conclude, "Kubrick has never been clearer about the connection between sex, aggression, and death . . . [Still] blaming it all on the innate brutality and corruption of man may aptly describe a great deal of behavior of all sides in Vietnam, but it is an evasion of the political issues and culture surrounding the war and its specific historical context." [30]

As we watch young men become harder and more cynical in *Full Metal Jacket,* neither we nor they seem to care very much; not knowing how or even if they feel, we don't know what to feel about them. Is this then the point? Is this a movie about not feeling and about which we are not supposed to feel anything? According to Auster and Quart, "there is some-thing essentially disturbing about it [Kubrick's remote style] used in as passionate and immediate a universe as Vietnam."[31]

The movie concludes with a panorama of young marines marching as shadowed automatons against a backdrop of the city of Hue burning. They sing in unison, as if it were a drill corps cadence, the theme song of the "Mickey Mouse Club." This is a chilling and accusatory vision, one which Auster and Quart suggest "fuses the murderousness of Vietnam with the synthetic innocence of the pop culture that helped shape the sen-sibilities of the young marines."[32]

The number of movies about the Vietnam War seems to increase the further we get in time from the war itself. At least seven such films were released in 1988, at least three more in the first half of 1989.

In all this increased interest in Vietnam as a setting if not a subject for movies, is something of a winding down and exhaustion of the genre. In *Off Limits* (1988), plainclothes criminal investigators roam Saigon in 1968 searching for a serial killer of prostitutes who may be a high-ranking army officer. Vietnam is treated as an exotic backdrop to the meaning-lessness and corruption of an unspeakable evil which can be found and conquered. The investigators' superior informs them that Vietnam is a "gigantic toilet" from which they have dedicated themselves to remov-ing "one big turd." This is not Willard of *Apocalypse Now,* the "assassin of assassins" lost in the moral complexities of an existential hell, but a "salt and pepper" cop movie in which the good guys may not be able to save Vietnam, but can make the streets of Saigon safe for Vietnamese bargirls. In other movies, such as *Platoon Leader* (1988) and *Siege at Firebase Gloria* (1989), it is obvious that the Vietnam War movie has become so estab-lished as a genre that it has become self-reflexive, feeding on itself in the manner that all genres do. A Vietnam War movie at this point may have about as much connection to the war as most Western or private eye movies do to the periods and subjects they are supposed to depict.

However, Vietnam War movies continue to reveal much about the era in which they were made. The issues of the war have become the obliga-tory iconography of the Vietnam War movie, but some changes are re-vealing. In 1988 and 1989, only the bad soldiers smoke dope, or no one smokes it at all. Racial tensions are nonexistent. Atrocities are once more committed only by the other side. In these films of the late eighties, we may indeed have lost the war, as we seem finally to admit, but we lost it for all the right reasons. These movies promote what Terry Christensen refers to as "traditional values, . . . individualism, self-sufficiency, com-petition, courage, pride, and patriotism in a conveniently simplified world." These are values common to other Reagan-era films such as *Red Dawn* (1984), *Invasion U.S.A.* (1985), and *Top Gun* (1986).[33]

In the Vietnam War movies of this period, our awareness as audience that the war *was* lost is intended to impart a nobility to the fighting itself. The awareness of the American soldiers in these movies that the war is being lost even as they are fighting it, that the war will be lost no matter what they do, is supposed to impart to their actions the gravity of tragedy. America is likely to be seen as dug in and defending itself bravely though hopelessly as (at least according to other movies) it did at Fort Apache or the Alamo.

Most of these movies are shamelessly nationalistic. The re-glorification of the American fighting man, particularly of the professional and the volunteer at the expense of the draftee (quite the reverse of the situation in the mainstream World War II movie) continues the refurbishment of the military's image. The tough but lovable old sergeant is back. The war is no longer fought exclusively by leaderless nineteen-year-olds. Appearances are made by officers who are not always madmen and/or cowards. War itself is once more being glamorized and romanticized in a manner not seen since the 1940s.

The word *communist* is being thrown around again in these movies. The American flag ends its fifteen-year absence from films about this particular war; it is center stage against the rear wall of the quarters of the new lieutenant in *Platoon Leader,* providing a backdrop for all his lonely and important decisions. The flag fills the frame against a blue sky in *Siege at Firebase Gloria.* Though it also quite literally droops at appropriate places, the flag is displayed prominently during battle scenes, which are accompanied by swells of elegiac music. Vietnam is no longer the rock-and-roll war. It is, as *Platoon* and *Hamburger Hill* taught us, where we lost our innocence, our youth.

Perhaps because America lost, these movies continue to mythologize the enemy, going so far as to portray individuals almost as major characters, though they are still drawn broadly and melodramatically. A "Terry and the Pirates" view of all that is Asian still dominates most of these movies. *Iron Triangle* (1989), which purports to be based upon the diary of a Vietcong soldier, does devote almost half of the film to the enemy, but this enemy is depicted as either saintly and heroic or unspeakably cruel and savage. In *Bat 21* (1988), an aging air-war expert is shot down and must spend days on the ground behind enemy lines, experiencing the devastation he was responsible for. At one point he tries to avoid killing a Vietnamese peasant to whom he must have appeared as a demon dropped from the sky; the peasant will not relent and the downed pilot must kill him with his bare hands. At least part of the plot of this movie has to do with the effect of the suffering he witnesses on the main character. Yet the film itself is primarily an action-adventure buddy film which stresses individual initiative over the cohesive action of a group, a hallmark and legacy of the World War II movie. Group consensus and cooperation, as well as single-mindedness (if not purity) of purpose, seem by now conceded to the enemy.

In *Siege at Firebase Gloria* the enemy is saluted and eulogized, at least on the surface. The Chinese saying, "The courage of your enemy does you honor," is repeated throughout this movie, but only by the enemy. The Vietnamese (or some of them) are admired for their courage and complimented on their strategy. At one point the main character even explains their willingness to die in such staggering numbers as not exclusively due to the supposed Asian disdain for the individual; he imagines we might do the same thing if someone had invaded North Carolina. Yet when asked by a nurse what distinguishes the American from the enemy, another character responds that the Vietcong would "rape her to death," but would have to "kill me to do it." "I am not an animal," he asserts; which, of course, means that the enemy is.

Sometimes the love/hate relationship with the enemy that began as a "grunt"-to-"grunt" recognition in the films of 1986 and 1987 goes so far as to imply politics indistinguishable from those of movies like *The Green Berets* (1968), or even *The Quiet American* (1957). In *Siege at Firebase Gloria* the Tet offensive, which is called "the greatest PR stunt of the war," is directly portrayed as not only the beginning of the end for America's involvement in Vietnam, but also as the end of any national identity or territorial sovereignty for the Vietcong. Depleted as they are from their Pyrrhic victory, the Vietcong, we are told, will now be swallowed up by the North Vietnamese; if we have to lose in Vietnam, then everybody loses.

Two major movies of 1989—versions of Bobbie Ann Mason's *In Country* and Ron Kovic's *Born on the Fourth of July*—amply demonstrate that, whatever the movies have done with or to Vietnam, they have not put it behind them. At this point, however, it is necessary to ask a few questions.

What should we have expected from a medium as reliant on consensus and money as the American movie when it took as its subject a war as contemporary, complex, and divisive as the Vietnam War?

Vietnam War movies are, after all, narrative fictions. But popular and critical reactions indicate we have been applying standards to them more appropriate to non-fiction documentaries. Claudia Springer clearly delineates these two different sets of expectations: "Questions brought to narrative fiction films include, 'What is this story about?' 'What happens to the characters?' and 'Will I be entertained?' Questions brought to documentary films are, 'What will it teach me?' and 'Do I agree with it?'" If the expectations we bring to documentaries are, as Springer suggests, particularly naive because they are based upon the premise that "immediate access to reality without imposition of the filmmaker's perspective

[is] a possibility," then they are particularly inappropriate and self-defeating when applied to fictional narratives.[34]

Yet it is a testament to the degree of trauma that Vietnam continues to inflict upon our culture that we as an audience persist in our expectation that a movie about the war in Vietnam will not only give those of us who were not there some idea of what it was like, but that it will also address why we were there and what went wrong. Movies about the Vietnam War are put under a special pressure to reflect and/or interpret "the real Vietnam," a phrase that increasingly eludes consensus.

If it is true that we have often asked too much from Vietnam War movies, it is also true that these movies have often delivered far too little. It is difficult not to agree with William Palmer, who concludes that "the majority of the Hollywood portrayals of the Vietnam War or of the effects of the war on Americans involved have been misguided, insensitive, exploitative, clichéd, unauthentic and just plain stupid."[35] "Hollywood," according to Gilbert Adair, "has always traded in the most artless kinds of myths, consistently managing to palm them off on the same intelligent paying customers who would scorn such shoddy wares if offered them in literature or theater."[36]

Of course no one film can capsulize a war that lasted so long, killed so many while wounding and maiming the lives of so many countless others, which destroyed the American economy, divided our nation, and shook America's very faith in its image of itself. That is not what movies, even good movies, do best; their truths are more apparently subjective than those available to history.

No matter what expectations we may bring to it as a body of literature or as a social phenomenon, the Vietnam War movie cannot be ignored because movies are not ignored by the public. Over half of today's filmgoers are under twenty-one years of age. A new generation, for all intents and purposes, will know little about the war in Vietnam beyond what these movies will show them. World War II heroes, John Wayne and Audie Murphy, led us into Vietnam. We should tremble to think where Sylvester Stallone and Chuck Norris may lead us if we let them.

NOTES

1. Gaylyn Studlar and David Desser, "Never Having to Say You're Sorry: Rambo's Rewriting of the Vietnam War," *Film Quarterly* 42: 1(Fall 1988), pp. 9–10.

2. Claudia Springer, "Vietnam: A Television History and the Equivocal Nature of Objectivity," *Wide Angle: A Film Quarterly of Theory, Criticism, and Practice* 7: 4 (1985), p. 60.

3. "In short, the very nature of the film medium complicates the task of political filmmakers. Add to this the limits placed on films by audience expectations and the need to make a profit and it's easy to see why the messages of political films are muted." Terry Christensen, *Reel Politics: American Political Movies from "Birth of a Nation" to "Platoon"* (Cambridge, Mass.: Basil Blackwell, 1987), p. 218.

4. Gilbert Adair, *Vietnam on Film* (New York: Proteus, 1981), p. 32.

5. Julian Smith, *Looking Away: Hollywood and Vietnam* (New York: Scribner, 1975), pp. 126–127.

6. Loren Baritz, *Backfire: A History of How American Culture Led Us into Vietnam and Made Us Fight the Way We Did* (New York: Morrow, 1985).

7. Adair, *Vietnam on Film,* p. 10.

8. Ibid., p. 12.

9. Ibid., p. 31.

10. Albert Auster and Leonard Quart, *How the War Was Remembered: Hollywood and Vietnam* (New York: Praeger, 1988), p. 52.

11. Adair, *Vietnam on Film,* p. 140.

12. Christensen, *Reel Politics,* p. 7.

13. Terrence Rafferty, "Platoon," *The Nation* 244 (17 Jan 1987), p. 54.

14. Auster and Quart, *How the War Was Remembered,* p. 61.

15. Adair, *Vietnam on Film,* p. 142.

16. William M. Hagen, "Apocalypse Now: Joseph Conrad and the Television War," in *Hollywood as Historian,* ed. Peter Rollins (Lexington: The University Press of Kentucky, 1983), p. 230.

17. I use the word *source* more loosely than in almost any other instance. Most recent scholarship stresses Michael Herr's *Dispatches* as a source for *Apocalypse Now* since that author was brought in late in the movie's making to write a voice-over which ties the movie together, and because many scenes in the movie have correlatives in the book itself.

18. Christensen, *Reel Politics,* p. 154.

19. Roger Ebert, "At Vietnam War Films, The Strangers Met," *Centerviews* (January–February 1989), p. 4.

20. Christensen, *Reel Politics,* p. 5.

21. Studlar and Desser, "Never Having to Say You're Sorry," pp. 9–10.

22. David James, "Presence of Discourse/Discourse of Presence: Representing Vietnam," *Wide Angle: A Film Quarterly of Theory, Criticism, and Practice* 7:4 (1985), pp. 42–44.

23. Springer, "Vietnam: A Television History," p. 58.

24. Fredrick Karl, *American Fictions: 1940–1980* (New York, Harper & Row, 1983), p. 95.

25. Four hundred South Vietnamese were also involved in the assault, though no mention is made of them in the film.

26. Jack Kroll, "Remembering Hamburger Hill: On The Point in Vietnam," *Newsweek* 110 (14 Sept 1987), p. 83.

27. Stanley Kauffmann, "Don't Mean Nothin'," *New Republic* (14 September 1987), p. 32.

28. Martha Bayles, "The Road to Rambo III," *New Republic* (18 and 25 July 1988), p. 33.

29. Ibid., p. 34.

30. Auster and Quart, *How the War was Remembered*, p. 143.

31. Ibid., p. 142.

32. Ibid., p. 144.

33. Christensen, *Reel Politics*, p. 199.

34. Springer, "Vietnam: A Television History," pp. 53–54.

35. William J. Palmer, *The Films of the Seventies* (New Jersey: Scarecrow Press, 1987), p. 181.

36. Adair, *Vietnam on Film*, p. 45.

PART FOUR
FACING THE FUTURE

10

BLACKS AND THE VIETNAM WAR

PETER B. LEVY

Civil rights as an issue is fading. The poverty program is heading for dismember-
ment and decline. Expectations of what can be done are receding. Very possibly,
our best hope is seriously to use the armed forces as a socializing experience for the
poor—until somehow their environment begins turning out equal citizens. . . .
History may record that the single most important psychological event in race rela-
tions in the nineteen sixties was the appearance of Negro fighting men on the TV
screens of the nation. Acquiring a reputation for military valor is one of the oldest
known routes to social equality.

–DANIEL PATRICK MOYNIHAN, *1965*

> *In the light beyond lies*
>   *we shall see*
>   *how long we have killed*
>   *for our master enemy*
>   *how long we have died*
>   *to purchase our death.*
>
> *And there shall be rage,*
>   *not tears,*
>   *a blazing black rage*
>   *shall possess us*
>   *to turn*
>   *to turn on them*
>   *with all the fury of battle they have taught us*

with all the guns they have bought us
with all the roasting, searing flame
from Freedom's furnace door . . .

—VINCENT HARDING, *1966*

Was Daniel Patrick Moynihan right? In the 1960s was black America's best hope the use of the Vietnam War as a means to a better and more equal place in America? Or was Vincent Harding more prescient in suggesting that Vietnam was just the most recent war in which blacks were falsely promised equality in exchange for risking their lives on the battlefield? What was the impact of Vietnam on African Americans? What was its legacy for them?

The Vietnam War had and is still having a profound effect on African Americans. They were among the war's greatest heroes and victims. Young black men in disproportionate numbers fought and died, or returned to the United States with the physical and emotional scars of combat. Black veterans continue to live in the shadow of the war. Vietnam alienated and further radicalized large numbers of blacks in the 1960s and continues to color African American politics and thought. The war contributed to the dissipation of the civil rights movement and the unravelling of liberalism in the 1960s. It wasted an opportunity to reform America, to create a Great Society; it sparked a resurgence of conservatism that undercut black efforts to achieve equality. Indeed, contrary to Moynihan's expectations, Vietnam did not make a bad situation better. For many black Americans, things have gotten worse.

Despite the fact that blacks played a central role in the fight in Southeast Asia and in the protests at home, they have received little attention in either historical or commercial works on Vietnam. The typical antiwar activist is still seen as the young white college student; the characteristic soldier and veteran, a southern white or blue-collar ethnic. We need to recognize the role that blacks played in the war and the long-term impact that it has had on their community, politics and thought. Not to do so is not only ethically wrong but will condemn us to misunderstand the nature of the problems that confront the black community today.

The Black Soldier

By the time Lyndon B. Johnson escalated the war in 1965, the military stood as the most integrated institution in American society. Black Americans had implored George Washington and Abraham Lincoln to employ them in the fight against colonialism and slavery, and had volunteered in vast numbers during World War I and World War II, fighting in segregated units to protect freedoms abroad that they did not enjoy at home. In the midst of the Cold War President Truman desegregated the armed forces and during the Vietnam War no special effort was made on the part of either blacks or whites to enroll young black men in the armed services. By the time the first American ground troops were sent to Southeast Asia, blacks constituted 10 percent of the armed forces, roughly equivalent to their percentage of the population at large.

Blacks enlisted in the military because they saw it as an avenue of advancement or as a way to escape the ghetto or the rural South. Thomas Johnson explained, "To the ordinary Negro fighting man, Vietnam means not only integration but also an integral role in American life," something not readily available at home. Like millions of whites, many blacks enlisted out of a sense of patriotic duty; unlike whites, their patriotism was mixed with a feeling that in war they still needed to prove themselves as individuals and as a race. Blacks in previous wars shared this belief. (In the mid-1960s, Defense Secretary Robert McNamara initiated Project 100,000, which lowered entrance standards for the poor [largely minorities] to get into the armed forces. McNamara did so because he believed [like Moynihan] that the military was a time-tested means to social advancement.) Thousands of blacks who did not enlist, of course, ended up in Vietnam as draftees.[1]

With respect to actual combat service in Vietnam, blacks fought and died in numbers disproportionate to their percentage of the population at home. In 1965, blacks made up almost 20 percent of the combat troops and more than one quarter of elite and more dangerous fighting units, such as the paratroopers. One report claimed that 45 percent of the soldiers in the airborne units were black, 60 percent in the airborne rifle units. Up through 1966, blacks were three times more likely to reenlist than whites. In 1965 and 1966 black soldiers suffered 25 percent of the U.S. battlefield deaths; from 1967 to 1968 their casualty rate remained high; as of 1970, even after the Army and the Marines undertook specific measures to decrease the battlefield exposure of blacks—in reaction to protests at home—they still suffered 12.8 percent of the casualties. By comparison, blacks were 11.1 percent of the total population and 10.9 percent of the population eligible for the draft (males between the ages of eighteen and twenty-six).[2]

What explains these figures? Why did blacks serve and die disproportionately in Vietnam? More than any other factor, social class determined the likelihood of service. The lower and working classes of America were more likely to fight in Vietnam than the middle or upper classes. As a result, blacks faced a high likelihood of being sent to Southeast Asia. They did not benefit from student deferments and other mechanisms that might have kept them out of Vietnam. In 1967, at the height of the draft, 98.5 percent of 17,123 persons on the nation's draft boards were white. Not a single black served on the boards of the states of Alabama, Arkansas, Louisiana or Mississippi. Not surprisingly, blacks found it harder to enlist in the branches of the service that were least likely to see action, the Coast Guard and the National Guard, which were largely comprised of white college-educated youths, the sons of the upper and upper middle class.[3]

Once in the military, blacks faced a higher casualty rate than whites of similar class background for two reasons. First, though officially integrated, neither the Navy nor the Air Force had large numbers of blacks, and they were the "safest" branches of the military, at least until the waning years of the war. In contrast, infantry units had a disproportionate number of blacks. Blacks served in the dangerous elite units for the same reason that they reenlisted at a higher rate than whites: dangerous duty paid. For example, paratroop volunteers received an average of $55 extra a month, a 50 percent boost in their earnings; as one Army spokesman explained, "Army pay probably is the most money a lot of these people ever made." In addition, the elite corps in the Army and the Marines offered prestige and status lacking in civilian life.[4]

Discrimination at home (which had played a role in sending them to Vietnam) and a growing sense of the immorality of the war increasingly alienated and politicized black soldiers. By 1970, wrote Wallace Terry, black soldiers returned from Southeast Asia "fed up with dying in a war they believe is a white man's folly." "They feel," Terry added, "they have no business fighting in Southeast Asia." This was in marked contrast to Terry's impression of the black soldier of several years earlier, "who was out to prove himself in the most integrated war in U.S. history."[5]

Air Force historian Bernard Nalty's study of blacks in the military supports Terry's views. He found "ominous developments, such as the appearance in rear areas of Confederate flags." In spite of the Department of Defense's efforts to eradicate racism in the ranks, racial tensions worsened following the assassination of Martin Luther King, Jr. Nearly every branch of the service experienced a spate of racially motivated outbreaks of violence, including one in Long Binh, South Vietnam, where U.S. Army prisoners, mostly black, battled with white military police for days. In addition, drug use, particularly prominent among black soldiers, reached unprecedented proportions.[6]

For some black soldiers alienation came slowly and was never complete. For instance, years after the war, Sergeant Major Edgar Huff, the first black sergeant in the Marines, proudly recalled his term of service and defended America's role in Indochina. Yet Huff remembered his journey up the ranks with bitterness and exploded when describing the treatment he received when he came home to Gasden, Alabama. Shortly after his return from Vietnam, three white Marines threw a hand grenade into his station wagon and he and his family barely escaped alive. "I've fought for thirty years for the Marine Corps. And I feel like I own part of this ground that I walk on every day," Huff explained, "these guys . . . [tried] to destroy my family and myself." The local Marine camp officer responded that the perpetrators "told him they didn't understand how a nigger could be living this way, sitting out there eating on a nice lawn under the American flag." (The three white Marines were discharged from duty but never prosecuted.)[7]

Huff's anger was mild in comparison to that of many of his compatriots, especially young blacks who were drafted into the Army after 1967, many of whom were influenced by the Black Power movement. While it would be incorrect to stereotype the black soldier as a rebel in arms, subtle and not-so-subtle rebellion in the ranks became a reality that even the Department of Defense acknowledged. Wrote Colonel Robert D. Heinl Jr., "Racial conflicts . . . are erupting murderously in all services." Likewise, military expert Charles Moskos found that "near mutinous actions of black servicemen in the early 1970s reached such proportion as to undermine the very fighting capability of America's armed forces." One officer declared that Vietnam "made his once taut unit divide up like two street gangs."[8]

The case of Billy Dean Smith shows the degree to which Army morale could and did break down. Smith, a young black, was the first soldier tried for "fragging" and although he was eventually acquitted, his experience in Vietnam was not considered unusual by either Army brass or antiwar advocates. (According to the Department of Defense there were 161 cases of fragging in 1969, 271 in 1970, and 238 in the first eight months of 1971.) Smith entered the service in 1967. He did so primarily out of respect for his family's wishes, not because he favored the war. He quickly gained a reputation as a soldier with a "bad attitude." Within six months of duty in Vietnam, he received three summary company punishments (Article 15) and was being processed for dishonorable discharge when he was arrested for fragging. Smith never disputed the prosecution's claim that he was not fit for duty, nor that he was a poor soldier. He maintained his innocence in regards to the fragging charges, however, contending that he was being persecuted for his open defiance of Army etiquette and his occasional refusal to accept dangerous combat assignments. Like many other black soldiers in Vietnam, Smith sported an Afro haircut and frequently greeted his fellow black soldiers with a clenched-fist salute or other signs of solidarity (such as the "dap," an elaborate handshake). The jury evidently agreed, though it convicted him on lesser assault charges.[9]

The antiwar movement championed Smith's case, as well as those of other openly defiant black soldiers, such as the Fort Hood Three; the military prosecuted Smith and others to the fullest extent of the law. Studies revealed that in addition to court-martials, blacks were dishonorably discharged from the service and received Article 15 punishments far out of proportion to their numbers in the military. Out of approximately 3 million Vietnam-era veterans, the majority of the 792,000 who received bad conduct or less-than-honorable discharges were black. June Wilenz observed that for those who received less than honorable discharges, the war worsened their prospects; it crippled them for life. They were disqualified from all GI benefits and marked with a social stigma that left them virtually unemployable.[10]

In addition to condemning their treatment by white officers, many black soldiers criticized the war itself as racist. From their first combat training, which taught them to dehumanize their foes by calling them "gooks," to press releases that explained high enemy casualty rates in terms that stated that the Vietnamese valued human life less than Americans did, black soldiers found American racism replicating itself abroad. Many considered their government hypocritical for demanding that blacks fight for freedom abroad even if they did not enjoy freedom at home. "Mother fuck America!" the main character in "Soldier Boy" declared, "My man Thompson gets blown away because he's out here trying to save his country. Ha! He can't even piss in the right places in his country. And this is 1972." Moreover, in many cases black soldiers identified with the Vietnamese as "brown brothers." Almost half of all black soldiers held positive feelings toward the Vietnamese; only one in ten held negative ones. In contrast, white Vietnam veterans were more likely to hold negative than positive attitudes toward the Vietnamese.[11]

Cognizant of the alienation of black soldiers and veterans, antiwar activists established coffeehouses near army bases, supported underground military-base newspapers, championed the causes of insurgent soldiers and enlisted returning veterans in the crusade against the war. While these activists never succeeded in achieving their goal of undermining the war effort from within, they clearly added to a weakening of the war effort and to America's eventual withdrawal. "Never before in modern history have the armed forces been so shaken by internal turmoil and disaffection," wrote David Cortright.[12]

At the same time, combat duty and military service in general placed blacks and whites in much closer proximity and dependence on one another than they were accustomed to in civilian life. As a result, relations between whites and blacks improved, at least on an individual level. As Thomas Johnson put it, Vietnam produced "the closest thing to real integration in U.S. history." Yet, a black sailor wryly added, "it's the kind of integration that could kill you."[13]

All in all, the war reinforced blacks' sense of institutional or systemic racism. Black soldiers came to understand, if they had not before, that their color sent them to Vietnam in the first place and would limit their opportunities upon their return to the United States. "The brothers thought that because they fought and saw their buddies die it would make a difference," stated one black veteran, "but they came back to SOS—the same old stuff . . . It's business as usual in America, and business as usual means black people are going to catch hell."[14]

The Civil Rights Movement and Vietnam

Every major civil rights organization was affected by the Vietnam War. Some immediately denounced it; others avoided taking a public stance for or against it until the bitter end. All became increasingly drawn into the quagmire at home that tore the nation apart.

Prior to adopting Black Power as an ideal and a slogan, the Student Nonviolent Coordinating Committee (SNCC) and the Congress of Racial Equality (CORE) put themselves at odds with the older and more conservative civil rights organizations (the NAACP and National Urban League), white liberals, and President Johnson by condemning the Vietnam War. SNCC leaders saw America's involvement in Indochina as hypocritical. Why could the government send troops to protect freedom abroad but not to the South to protect the rights of American blacks? At a memorial service for Michael Schwerner, James Chaney and Andrew Goodman in Philadelphia, Mississippi in the summer of 1964, SNCC stalwart Robert Moses held up the headlines of the Jackson, Mississippi newspaper that simultaneously announced the Gulf of Tonkin Resolution and the slaying of the three civil rights workers. Signs at an August 6, 1964 peace demonstration in New York City made the intent of Moses' gesture clear: "UNITED STATES TROOPS BELONG IN MISSISSIPPI, NOT VIETNAM." Less than a month after Johnson announced the commencement of bombing of North Vietnam, SNCC chairman John Lewis, who had just been bashed in the head by an Alabama state trooper, likewise declared, "I don't understand how President Johnson can send troops to Vietnam, to the Congo, to Central America and he can't send troops to protect black people who want the right to register to vote." A little more than a month later, Robert Moses delivered one of the keynote addresses at the first national anti–Vietnam War protest, organized by SDS; again he emphasized the government's hypocrisy.[15]

Several of SNCC's leaders devoted themselves to antiwar activity. Robert Moses participated in massive teach-ins at the University of California at Berkeley and served as a cochair of the Assembly of Unrepresented People, an early antiwar coalition and a predecessor of the National Coordinating Committee to End the War in Vietnam. The Assembly staged major demonstrations in Washington, D.C. in the summer of 1966, adopting the tactics of nonviolent direct action which civil rights activists had used so well in the South. After leaving SNCC (in large part because of disagreements over its separatist tendencies), John Lewis spoke at several large antiwar demonstrations. Julian Bond became one of the first political candidates to denounce the war in his campaign for a seat in the Georgia State Assembly. All three drew on SNCC's historical commitment to nonviolence along with a growing identification with the Third World in articulating their antiwar stances.

On January 6, 1966, SNCC formally declared its opposition to the war. The decision to do so was sparked by the murder of Sammy Young, Jr., a black twenty-one-year Navy veteran and SNCC activist, at the hand of a white Alabama restaurateur. Moving beyond early criticisms of the government's hypocrisy, SNCC announced its sympathy with draft resisters. In place of fighting in Vietnam, SNCC called for the government to allow individuals to work for civil rights organizations in the struggle for equality in the South.[16]

CORE's stance on the war essentially paralleled SNCC's. CORE's more militant chapters denounced America's policy in Indochina prior to 1965. For example, in March 1964, Columbia University's CORE chapter urged President Johnson to support French peace efforts in Vietnam. In 1965, Lincoln Lynch, president of the Long Island branch of CORE, argued vehemently within CORE for a sharp break with the president. In January 1966, CORE directors James Farmer and Floyd McKissick issued a joint statement declaring that the "escalation of the war is wrong" and that "the war which must be escalated is the war against poverty and discrimination." In April, the Northeast Regional Action Council of CORE denounced the war as a "racist and diversionary effort to stifle civil rights protest." And in July 1966, CORE ratified this position and pledged its support for draft resisters, reversing a decision made a year earlier to avoid adopting a formal policy because of the political imprudence of doing so.[17]

Newcomers to the civil rights movement, most notably the Mississippi Freedom Democratic Party (MFDP) and the Black Panther Party, along with independent black activists, joined SNCC and CORE in condemning the war, offering some of the sharpest attacks on the government made during the entire Vietnam War era. MFDP's July 1965 newsletter suggested that blacks should not fight in Vietnam as long as freedom was denied to them in Mississippi. MFDP leader Fannie Lou Hamer questioned why black Mississippians should risk their lives abroad only to return to oppression and threats of lynching at home. One of the Black Panther Party's demands, stated in its ten-point manifesto, was that blacks should be exempt from military service. The manifesto stated that blacks would not fight and "kill other people of color in the world who, like black people, are being victimized by the white racist government of America." Explained Eldridge Cleaver, cultural minister of the

Black Panthers, the freedom of black Americans was directly linked to that of the Vietnamese. "Once the white man solves his problem in the East," Cleaver warned, "he will turn his fury again on black people in America."[18]

Such sentiment resembled the arguments of one of the earliest critics of the war, Malcolm X. Before his assassination in 1965, Malcolm had railed at the United States' involvement in Southeast Asia as a continuation of an archaic and racist French colonial policy. He also used the war as a mechanism to defend the right of self-defense by blacks at home. "If it is right for America to draft us, and teach us how to be violent in defense of her," he declared, "then it is right for you and me to do whatever is necessary to defend our own people right here in this country."[19]

Malcolm's admirers went even farther. He encouraged black radicals to concern themselves with people of color around the globe; they announced their solidarity with Ho Chi Minh and the National Liberation Front and other nonwhite colonial people. Julius Lester argued that the war was polarizing the world into two camps, the "West (white) versus everybody else (colored, black, yellow)." James Baldwin asserted that the war represented the West's attempt to "hold on to what they have stolen from their captives." And George "General" Baker, a young black nationalist from Detroit, informed his local draft board, "UHURU, LIBERTAD, HALAGUA AND HARAMBEE! When the call is made to free South Africa . . . to liberate Latin America . . . to free the black delta areas of Mississippi . . . to FREE 12TH STREET HERE IN DETROIT!: When these calls are made, send for me," but that he would not fight "my oppressed brothers."[20]

Unlike SNCC and CORE, Martin Luther King, Jr. maintained "friendly" relations with white liberals, moderate civil rights leaders and organizations, and President Johnson until 1967, largely because he did not identify himself with the antiwar movement. Even though he expressed sentiments akin to those of John Lewis during the Selma campaign and criticized Johnson's policy before his congregation and in private, this was not his main thrust. Instead, faced with the prospect of ostracizing liberal supporters, and desiring to concentrate on the needs of poor blacks in the North, King maintained a safe distance between himself and the foes of LBJ's foreign policy. As Andrew Young recalled, King chose to limit his antiwar criticism and activity, to chart a middle course between those who continued to support Johnson and those who did not.[21]

The war continued, however, and so did the pressure from antiwar activists and friends, such as William Sloan Coffin and James Bevel, to take a stronger stance. King's turning point came in January 1967 with his reading of a *Ramparts* magazine article, "The Children of Vietnam," a story which portrayed the devastating impact of American bombing on the people of Southeast Asia. On February 25, 1967, with a speech at a fund-raising dinner for the *Nation* magazine, King took his first step toward joining hands with the antiwar movement. "We are engaged in a war that seeks to turn the clock of history back and perpetuate white colonialism," stated King. "The bombs in Viet Nam explode at home and they destroy the hopes and possibilities for a decent America," he continued, "We must combine the fervor of the civil rights movement with the peace movement. We must demonstrate, teach and preach, until the very foundations of our nation are shaken." Soon thereafter, via participation in an antiwar demonstration in Chicago, a major speech on the war delivered at Riverside Church and another at the Spring Mobilization demonstration in New York City, King became one of the most prominent antiwar spokespersons in America.[22]

King's objections to the war went well beyond pacifism and a moral revulsion to the carnage pictured in *Ramparts*. His "Beyond Vietnam" address, delivered at Riverside Church and then again in abbreviated form at the Spring Mobilization rally, presented a multi-faceted attack on President Johnson's policy in Southeast Asia and America's cold war foreign policy in general. Paradoxically, King noted, the war placed America, a nation founded on the right of self-determination, on the side of colonialism. As a Christian, a preacher, and a Nobel Prize winner, King explained, he felt a special duty to speak out. And as an American, King exclaimed, he felt compelled to denounce a war that was poisoning America's soul.

While King's claim that protest was patriotic swayed some liberals—for example, the Labor Leadership for Peace, an organization of antiwar trade unionists, heralded King's stance—most moderates, black and white, denounced his position. They did so primarily for two reasons. First, they felt it was strategically wrong for a civil rights organization or leader to venture outside affairs central to the concerns of blacks at home. Second, they considered it suicidal to break with President Johnson, not just because of the impracticality of breaking with a president during wartime, but also out of a feeling of loyalty to the leader who had delivered so much to blacks. (It should also be remembered that until the Tet offensive many liberals agreed with Johnson's policies in Indochina; they saw the war as right and winnable.) "You cannot serve the civil rights struggle at home by involving it in a struggle abroad," asserted NAACP president Roy Wilkins. King "has done grave injury to those who are natural allies," wrote *Washington Post* columnist Carl Rowan (perhaps the most influential black journalist in the country), "Many who have listened to him with respect will never accord him the same confidence. He has diminished his usefulness to his cause, to his country and to his people. And that is a great tragedy." Bayard Rustin's criticism of King was more evenhanded, but coming from a long-time pacifist, advisor and friend, probably stung more than those of Rowan or Wilkins. Rustin defended King's right to speak out as an individual, but he agreed with those who saw it as politically imprudent.[23]

In contrast, black radicals and the white New Left applauded King's action. *Ramparts* reprinted the Riverside address in full, advertising it as the official version of King's "declaration of conscience." *Guardian* heralded King's stance and predicted that he would generate even greater opposition to the war. Others noted that the Spring Mobilization marked the first time since the James Meredith march in 1966 that King (SCLC), Floyd McKissick (CORE) and Stokely Carmichael (SNCC) had gathered on the same platform, and predicted that a left-of-center, black-white coalition was in the making.[24]

Although King's break with Johnson was welcomed by the student Left and perhaps legitimized "dove" sentiment among working- and middle-class Americans, its more immediate impact was to reinforce the divisions within the civil rights movement and to bolster conservative backlash. Put another way, along with the rise of black nationalism and the urban uprisings of the latter half of the 1960s, the war broke the back of the civil rights movement, transforming a loose coalition of divergent organizations into competing and antagonistic camps in a context in which liberal reform was becoming increasingly unpopular.

Most clearly, the Vietnam War sharpened SNCC's, CORE's and SCLC's critiques of America. At the least it prodded them to see America as hypocritical for fighting for freedom abroad while it shortchanged the freedom movement at home. More drastically, Vietnam radicalized blacks, including King, leading them to question America's institutions, rather than just the performance of these institutions. As King noted, the war was symptomatic of a much greater illness in American society. It symbolized the white majority's priorities, a preference for fighting communism abroad to combating poverty at home. Every dollar spent in Vietnam was one dollar less spent on social programs. How could a nation founded on the belief in equality for all choose such a course?

In contrast, the NAACP and the National Urban League continued to insist that it was possible to have both guns and butter, to fight a war in Vietnam and one on poverty in America at the same time. Rather than blaming the war for the shortcomings of existing social programs, they blamed Johnson's Vietnam War critics for undercutting his support. Even when and if they disagreed with Lyndon Johnson's actions in Southeast Asia, they did not feel that the war was so important that it mandated a break with the president. "The choice is clear," stated Bayard Rustin in an endorsement of Hubert Humphrey in the waning days of the 1968 presidential election, "It would be a national tragedy if these assets [Humphrey and the Democrats] were lost to us because of the divisions among progressive forces over Vietnam—especially when the alternative is a Republican 'solution' in Southeast Asia." Rustin added, "The war in Vietnam will end before long, but our problems at home will haunt us for generations if we do not act now." [25]

Black Opinion on the War

Implicit in Wilkins's and Rustin's denunciations of King and other black activists who broke with Johnson was the belief that an antiwar stance was strategically impractical and not representative of the views of the black masses. As the moderates saw it, the majority of blacks supported their president's policy, or in the least agreed that it was imprudent or unpatriotic to criticize him. Militant blacks, of course, felt the opposite. Martin Luther King, Jr. delayed taking a strong public stance in part because he felt that the black masses would not follow his lead, although several of his close associates insisted that it was not only morally incumbent upon him to denounce the war, but also strategically practical. Who was right?

While public opinion polling remains a far from exact science, it provides us with a reasonable estimate of the sentiments of black Americans toward the war in Vietnam. Early in the Johnson administration, surveys showed that blacks supported the president's "conduct of the war." For instance, from April 1965 through April 1966, Louis Harris found that 51–59 percent of blacks felt that Johnson was conducting the war in an excellent or pretty good manner, 18–29 percent felt he was doing only a fair or poor job, and a large contingent remained unsure. By 1967, however, a higher percentage of black Americans felt that the war was a mistake and favored quick disengagement than of any other group of Americans. Despite the contemporary and historical characterization of the antiwar activist as a white college student (usually a male with long hair), the typical dove was a black (table 10.1).[26]

A battery of polls taken in the wake of the invasion of Cambodia in 1970 displayed even further the depth of black opposition. Much more than whites, blacks distrusted President Nixon's policy, disapproved of the invasion, and felt that the U.S. should withdraw from South Vietnam as quickly as possible. For instance, 42 percent of whites approved of Nixon's decision to send troops to Cambodia; only 9 percent of blacks did.[27] And although the event received very little attention, just as four white Kent State students were killed during an antiwar demonstration, two black students were also shot and killed and fourteen others seriously wounded during demonstrations at Jackson State College in Mississippi.

Election results show a similar pattern of beliefs. With the exception of Senator Edward Brooke of Massachusetts (whose support was not largely black), nearly every black politician who was elected in the late 1960s and

Table 10.1: Black vs. White Views of the War (Select Polls)

	BLACK (%)	WHITE (%)
What policy do you prefer? (10/67)		
a. total victory	19	22
b. negotiated peace	14	27
c. get out quick	56	43
The war is immoral. (12/69)		
a. agree	55	35
b. disagree	27	55
U.S. should withdraw all troops by		
end of year. (4/71)		
a. yes	81	71
The war was a mistake. (12/74)		
a. agree	80	76
b. disagree	13	17

Source: Elizabeth Martin et al., *Sourcebook of Harris National Surveys* (Chapel Hill, N.C.: Institute for Research in Social Sciences, 1981).

early 1970s opposed the war. Perhaps the most famous black candidate to oppose the war was Julian Bond. A founding member of SNCC, Bond ran for the Georgia state assembly in 1965 on a platform that supported SNCC's antiwar position. He won, becoming the first black elected to the state house of representatives since reconstruction. Because of his war stance, the assembly refused to allow him to take his seat. With the support of his constituents, Bond took his case to the U.S. Supreme Court, eventually winning reinstatement.

One further gauge of the black population's opinion was its support for black celebrities who opposed the war. Harry Belafonte, Dick Gregory, Diana Ross and Jimi Hendrix were just some of the black stars to denounce the war and retain a following among blacks. Probably the most noteworthy figure to do so was the heavyweight boxing champion of the world, Muhammad Ali. Ali's refusal to be inducted into the army, based upon his religious beliefs, brought upon him public and private wrath not seen by a black celebrity since that experienced by Paul Robeson during the early years of the Cold War. The World Boxing Association stripped Ali of his title; the government filed charges against him; and the mainstream press vilified him as a hypocrite and traitor. (Even most of the black press refused to recognize his name change, continuing to refer to him as Cassius Clay.)

To foes and friends alike, Ali symbolized the growth of black militancy through his opposition to the war and his identification with the Muslim faith. Much to the chagrin of the mainstream press and the government,

Ali did not back away from a fight. Not only did he maintain his opposition to serving in Vietnam, he fueled the fire of dissent. "I ain't got nothing against them Viet Congs," Ali announced, "No, I'm not going ten thousand miles from here to help murder and kill and burn another poor people simply to help continue the domination of white slavemasters over the darker people the world over." The Left, both black and white, made the most of Ali's opposition to service in Vietnam. For example, *Freedomways,* a radical black journal, observed that in the 1960 Olympics Ali fought for the United States as a boxer and was heralded for bringing back the gold medal, yet on his return to his home town of Louisville, Kentucky, he was refused service at a lunch counter. "Where was the Federal Government then, to uphold human rights?" the editors rhetorically inquired, "And where is the Federal Government today as civil rights workers in Louisville face screaming mobs, throwing rocks and bottles at them as they peacefully march to end housing discrimination?"[28]

Blacks and the Antiwar Movement

Despite black opposition to the war, neither civil rights leaders nor the rank and file were integrated into the mainstream antiwar movement. Most of the national antiwar organizations, from the National Coordinating Committee to End the War in Vietnam to the New MOBE were run primarily by white leftists. Blacks had only token representation on their boards and did not play a major role in organizing the most noteworthy demonstrations of the era. Just as important, these protests were largely white. For example, the countless mass demonstrations that took place in Washington, D.C., from SDS's April 1965 protest to the Pentagon affair to the massive New MOBE march in November 1969, failed to enlist the participation of much of the large local black population of Washington, D.C.

Several overlapping explanations can be offered for the absence of large-scale black participation in the antiwar movement. First, as noted, the antiwar movement came of age at the same time that Black Nationalism reached a high water mark. SNCC, CORE and the Black Panther Party advocated a separatist position that precluded coalition with whites. Not that members of these organizations did not participate in antiwar protests, but they did not throw their energies behind the antiwar movement. Of course there were exceptions. Eldridge Cleaver ran for president as part of a black–white coalition Peace and Freedom ticket. Bobby Seale showed up in Chicago during the 1968 convention demonstrations, which were tangentially antiwar demonstrations. But in neither case did these occurrences reflect the main impulse of Black Nationalism, which since the Mississippi Summer of 1964 had turned away from coalition.

The tendency of black leaders was to focus their energies on domestic concerns. Aside from his burst of antiwar activity in the spring of 1967, from 1965 until his death in 1968, King concentrated on the social and economic needs of urban blacks. Before the spring of 1967, his main priority was his foray in Chicago. After the spring of 1967, he focused on developing the Poor People's Campaign. Likewise, the Black Panther Party, SNCC and CORE became engulfed in fights for community control of various institutions—the schools, police and city hall—and took part in antiwar protests only sporadically.

Second, the emphasis or focus of the mainstream antiwar movement ran counter to the strategy followed by civil rights activists in the early 1960s and by some militants in the latter part of the decade. In general, the antiwar movement did not build up local constituencies against the war except among students on or around college campuses. Rather the movement focused on large single-day media-grabbing events. In contrast, SNCC had flourished by building grass-roots community-oriented movements in Mississippi, southwest Georgia, and Alabama. Martin Luther King's greatest triumphs came in campaigns in which he galvanized the black communities of Birmingham and Selma around the fight for their rights. The Mississippi Freedom Democratic Party, the Black Panther Party of Lowndes County, Alabama and that of Oakland, California achieved their greatest successes when they maintained a local base.

Where branches of the antiwar movement did orient themselves to community opposition, such as in GI coffeehouses, they were successful in melding with local black opposition. For example, the GI coffeehouse Oleo Strut and the *Fatigue Press* (a GI newspaper) were instrumental in bringing the cause of the Fort Hood Three (and later the Fort Hood Forty-Three) to the nation's attention. Coffeehouses like the Oleo Strut provided space for politicized black soldiers to gather. In addition, when protest erupted the coffeehouses utilized their connections with the larger antiwar movement to mobilize support behind a local affair.

Third, beyond tactical or strategic differences, ideological factors inhibited the formation of a mass black-white antiwar movement because the black and white communities arrived at their antiwar convictions from different directions. For whites, criticism of the war grew out of abstract and moral concerns. They came to the antiwar movement through teach-ins, the media and draft notices (more often than not evaded through a student deferment). The views of blacks, in contrast, developed out of firsthand experiences. "Black and white opposition to the war has been different," wrote Clyde Taylor, "Majority opposition grows largely out of frustration and fatigue . . . Black opposition . . . arises as a natural extension of a personally felt concern for human rights." Blacks felt the sting of war via high casualty rates, lost federal funds for domestic programs, and the hypocrisy of being called to fight for rights that they did not enjoy at home. Whites did not.[29]

Repercussions

While Roy Wilkins misjudged the opinion of the black populace, he did not misunderstand the repercussions of opposing President Johnson. If anything, he underestimated them. The most blatant form of punishment or retribution that black activists faced was government harrassment. In 1974, the Church committee revealed that in the mid-1960s the Johnson administration launched a counterintelligence operation (COINTELPRO) aimed at dividing and debilitating the black and white Left in the United States. Upon assuming the presidency, Richard Nixon not only continued the program, he expanded it. In the mind of the nation's top law enforcement official, FBI director J. Edgar Hoover, opposition to the war was tantamount to treason or at least confirmed connections with the communists and qualified a group or organization for surveillance. This was a view that did not change over time, even as public opinion turned against the war.

The FBI infiltrated and tapped the phones of CORE, SNCC, the Black Panther Party and SCLC. It sent damaging letters to the press, fostered suspicions within organizations by floating false rumors and may even have provoked acts of violence in order to further discredit the militant wing of the civil rights movement. After the Tet offensive, with at least the implicit consent of President Johnson and subsequently President Nixon, the FBI did everything possible to keep various radical forces from coalescing. For instance, in June 1968 the FBI embarked on a campaign to expose the membership of various "pacifist type organizations" as de facto segregationists. The Bureau encouraged informants to spread the idea that the Students for a Democratic Society, a leading antiwar organization, was racist, in spite of the Bureau's full knowledge that such charges were utterly false.[30]

David Garrow documents the importance that the Vietnam War played in prodding the government to take such extraordinary measures. The FBI had followed King and tapped his phones since the early 1960s, but its interest in him had waned in the mid-1960s—until King publicly denounced the war. After King's Riverside Church address, "hostility towards him in the Bureau and throughout the executive branch emerged more starkly than at any time since late 1964." Hoover reported to the White House, "Based on King's recent activities and public utterances, it is clear that he is an instrument in the hands of subversive forces seeking to undermine our nation." Presidential advisor John Roche declared that King's "Beyond Vietnam" address proved that he had "thrown in with the commies." Subsequently, the FBI and the White House encouraged reporters to confront King with hostile questions and pressured liberal and moderate politicians and organizations to ostracize King.[31]

Criticism of the war also contributed to a drastic change in the fund-raising capabilities of various civil rights organizations. Those that opposed the war—SCLC, SNCC and CORE—watched their contributions plummet in the latter half of the 1960s. In contrast, the NAACP and the National Urban League, both of which either supported President Johnson's foreign policy or abstained from criticizing him, watched their funds skyrocket. In 1964 the NAACP raised $388,000 from outside sources, SCLC $1.64 million, CORE $678,000 and SNCC $638,000. Three years later, the NAACP raised $1.9 million, SCLC $1 million, CORE $250,000 and SNCC $150,000. And in 1970, the NAACP raised $2.6 million while SCLC, SNCC and CORE combined raised $635,000. Although the war alone did not produce these results, clearly it played a significant role. (A switch to a Black Power philosophy might explain SNCC's and CORE's loss of funding but this does not apply to SCLC's financial woes.)[32]

Legacies

In what ways does Vietnam continue to affect African Americans? Did the war have positive impact, as Daniel Moynihan predicted it would? Or are blacks justified in feeling anger and bitterness over having once again fought their "master enemy's" war to their own detriment? How has Vietnam affected blacks as individuals, especially veterans and their families? What has been the war's legacy for the black community, including the damage to the Great Society and other social programs? And in what ways has Vietnam shaped recent black politics and thought?

While many Vietnam veterans experienced great difficulty integrating themselves into American society, black veterans have had the most difficult time. Richard Strayer and Lewis Ellenhorn observed that "being Black or Chicano . . . exacerbated the problems of re-entry into civilian life; the black and Mexican American veterans suffered greater unemployment, were more decidedly against the war, and felt less able to control their situation" than white veterans. In 1969, for instance, black veterans faced an unemployment rate three times as high as that of white veterans and an even higher underemployment rate. As of 1978, 25 percent of all Vietnam veterans had been arrested at least once, 40 percent of these were black. Over one fifth of the veterans spent one out of five years out of work following their return to the United States, with black veterans three times more likely than whites to fall into this category. In addition, many black veterans suffered and continue to suffer emotionally from the war. Partly because of their identification with the Vietnamese, black veterans are more likely to feel guilty and demoralized about their service than whites and are thus more likely candidates for post-traumatic stress disorder. Charles B. Howell, who retired from the U.S. Air Force in 1969 following twenty-two years of service, summed up many black veterans' unfavorable feelings toward the war: "I think I'd shoot one of my kids before I let them fight for this country."[33]

Some have suggested that in spite of their experiences in the war, or perhaps because of them, blacks gained a greater sense of pride and unity than they had before. Black soldiers from diverse backgrounds congregated in Vietnam, partly because of the discrimination they faced from white soldiers, and collectively woke up to their oppression. To paraphrase one black veteran, "I was such an ignorant fuck before I got to the Nam, but then . . ." Yet if black soldiers gained a sense of unity in Southeast Asia, it largely dissipated on their return to the United States. Observes James Creedle, Secretary of the National Association of Black Veterans (NABV), most black veterans became isolated and ended up dealing with the war as individuals. Even though organizations such as the NABV were established to bring black veterans together, they have not had nearly as much success as have white veteran groups. Recent celebrations involving Vietnam veterans have had a hollow ring to most blacks; these celebrations have been lily-white and have not addressed the specific needs and concerns of the black community.[34]

Since the Vietnam War, black enlistment in the armed services has increased substantially. Some contend that this is a sign of progress, that blacks have learned the benefits of military service, but the evidence does not bear out such a conclusion. During the war about one out of every ten soldiers was black. As of the mid-1980s, this figure stood at nearly one in three. With this increase has come a growth in the number of black officers, and the naming of blacks to the top post at West Point, the National Security Council and the Joint Chiefs of Staff. Yet social and economic forces have produced the higher enlistment rates, not the advantages accruing from military service. The options for many young black youths have narrowed since Vietnam. Even though the armed services offer status and stability lacking for blacks in much of civilian life, they cannot be considered as a true avenue of opportunity. As Earl Graves, publisher of Black Enterprise put it, "Our armed forces is the exception that proves the rule . . . Most Americans with decent economic prospects in civilian life, by far, prefer these to a military career." The armed forces have not provided blacks with the training and skills they need to move up upon the end of their army term. Writes Alvin Schexnider, they are "overrepresented in support activities . . . and greatly underrepresented in technical fields." Moreover, the *Wall Street Journal* reported, "even black senior officers with a wealth of managerial experience cannot find jobs in the civilian community worthy of their ability," a problem not suffered by their white counterparts.[35]

Furthermore, black soldiers have not benefited from the recent wave of "new patriotism." In the 1950s and 1960s, blacks in the military received a great deal of attention and acclaim in the black press. *Ebony* and *Sepia,* for instance, regularly featured black soldiers and veterans alongside other black heroes such as sports and entertainment stars. But recent editions of *Ebony* and other bastions of the black media do not usually exalt the black GI. For example, *Ebony's* recent listing of the one hundred most influential black Americans contained five sorority leaders but not a single black military officer, not even Lieutenant General Colin Powell, the National Security Advisor to President Reagan.[36]

Some conservatives blame black political leadership for the lack of respect that black soldiers and veterans receive. "How a sorority leader could be considered more influential than Lt. General Colin Powell . . . defies logical explanation," writes Harry Summers. Only the antimilitary bent of the black leadership can account for this, Summers continues. Yet, as we have seen, Summers's attempt to blame blacks themselves rather than the war, which was begotten and run by individuals like Summers, misses the point. Insofar as black politics and thought is antimilitary, it is a result of the cumulative effect of the war and not of some illogical bias.[37]

In a variety of ways, Vietnam has left the black community with a deep and unhealed scar. Most obviously, the black community has had to grapple with the problems, physical and emotional, that accompany the black veteran. Most recently, this has included a disproportionate number of black veterans who are homeless or who suffer from AIDS. While not the cause of the many problems that beset the so-called black underclass, the existence of large numbers of veterans clearly contributes to the incidence of crime, drug addiction, broken families, and unemployment in the inner city.[38] Moreover, opportunities for the black underclass have been diminishing ever since the Vietnam War and partly due to it. Few in the midst of the war foresaw the long-term impact that it would have on the American economy. Yet it marked a turning point, leaving in its wake stagflation and a diminished manufacturing sector, which had provided a modicum of opportunity for thousands of unskilled and semi-skilled blacks.

Blacks have been hurt still more by the lack of a concurrent revival of social programs. Lyndon B. Johnson's Great Society collapsed under the weight of the Vietnam War; so, too, did the liberal consensus that had increased the welfare state and leaned toward a policy that favored redistribution of wealth. Not only did a left-of-center coalition fail to replace the old New Deal coalition, the void was filled by conservatives, who historically opposed civil rights legislation and the welfare state. Hence, government "tax and spend programs," which could have been expected to ameliorate the conditions faced by the poor, have not been forthcoming. For example, during the Reagan years, Aid to Dependent Children payments declined 25 percent, while higher Social Security deductions cut into the funds available to the working poor. As pessimistic as Moynihan was about the prospects of the Great Society in 1965, he probably could not have imagined the sea change in political attitudes that has taken place since. Not only have liberal social programs experienced "dismemberment and decline," no substantial new programs have taken their place.[39]

A final legacy of the war has been its long-term effect on black politics. Black political gains since the escalation of the Vietnam War have been phenomenal. Blacks have taken control of city hall in many of America's largest cities, and in the South once disenfranchised blacks have become a major force on the political scene. The civil rights movement, the Voting Rights Act of 1965 and demographics account for much of this change. But the impact of Vietnam should not be discounted.

Although the war initially drove a wedge between various civil rights groups, it ultimately reinforced black solidarity. Since Vietnam, internal differences among black organizations have lessened, especially with regard to foreign affairs. Vietnam hammered home a lesson that blacks had learned before. Historically, American statesmen had promised blacks that service in war could be used as a means to gaining freedom and equality. Yet the promised land was never achieved and, in the case of Vietnam, blacks were asked to pay disproportionately for the belief that it would. Angered by this fact, the majority of blacks turned against the war and as long as the physical and emotional wounds of the war remain, it is unlikely that the black community will alter its disapproval of American militarism and intervention abroad.

Evidence of black distaste for American militarism and aggression abroad abound. Jessie Jackson stresses both the urgent need to address the ills of the inner city and the need to cut defense spending. Like his mentor, Martin Luther King, Jr., he presents a picture that casts foreign and domestic policy together. Writes Arch Puddington, Jackson holds views "sharply at variance with both the Reagan administration and the declared views of many leading figures of his own party." In his 1984 and 1988 presidential campaigns, Jackson opposed aid to the Contras, favored increased sanctions against South Africa, endorsed the nuclear freeze and advocated a reduction of American troops aboard. Puddington adds that the line from the black militants of the 1960s to Jackson is clear; he has consistently criticized the values and direction of American policy since World War II and refers to himself as "a Third World Resident in the first world."[40]

Most black politicians who gained power in the late 1960s or since also stand to the left of center on foreign policy. The Black Congressional Caucus unanimously condemned America's invasion of Grenada. Following the invasion, five members of the caucus, joined by two white Democrats, sponsored a measure calling for the impeachment of President Reagan. At the 1983 March on Washington (commemorating the 1963 March) the Coalition for Conscience, including the NAACP, which had not opposed the Vietnam war, denounced America's "militarization" of various internal conflicts around the globe, from the Middle East to Central America, called for a drastic reduction in defense spending, and demanded a concurrent boost in social spending.

Paradoxically, the conduct of American foreign policy is dependent on those who most oppose it. What if blacks refuse to fight in the next war? What if blacks take their guns and training and turn with vengeance on their "masters"? At the start of the Cold War, when blacks constituted a much smaller part of the United States' fighting forces, American policymakers understood this potential dilemma—as evidenced by the treatment accorded to Paul Robeson, who suggested that blacks should not or would not fight in the Cold War. Today, when blacks make up a much larger part of the military, one can only imagine the nightmares of some defense experts. The fact that black officers and commanders would play a role in ordering blacks into battle only further complicates such a scenario and perhaps reflects the dilemmas that face the American and African American communities as we approach the twenty-first century.

This is not to argue that blacks are unpatriotic. On the contrary, black criticism of American policy grows out of a conviction that it is patriotic to dissent against that which is un-American. Martin Luther King, Jr. saw the United States' support of colonialism in Vietnam as un-American. John Lewis considered the American government's presence in Southeast Asia but not in the Deep South as hypocritical because he believed that the United States stood for freedom for all. Whereas Daniel Moynihan saw the war socializing blacks, Vincent Harding (a friend of King and Lewis alike) hoped the war would have a socializing effect on whites. While he noted the potential for black retribution and vengeance, Harding hoped that blacks would rise above the war, that Vietnam would ultimately have a redemptive effect, and that blacks would lead all on to a better day:

I pray for the dead,
>   I pray for the living
>   that a new Master may arise
>   and call us to His way
>   beyond the darkness and terror
>   and the blood of all our brothers
>   (with our own)

To Light
And Freedom
And Joy
Then the long achieved march shall end
And the dirges heard no more
And the weeping will be silenced
>   by the wind
And the mourners shall break out
>   to a Bantu jubilee
And the ashes shall awaken
>   in the mourning.[41]

NOTES

1. Thomas Johnson, "The U.S. Negro in Vietnam," *New York Times,* 29 April 1968, pp. 1, 16.

2. Robert W. Mullen, *Blacks in American Wars* (New York: Monad, 1973), pp. 61–67; John Willis, "Variations in State Casualty Rates in World War II and The Vietnam War," *Social Problems* 22:4 (April 1975), pp. 558–568; Harry G. Summers, Jr., *Vietnam War Almanac* (New York: Facts on File, 1985), p. 98.

3. Lawrence M. Baskir and William A. Strauss, *Chance and Circumstance* (New York: A. Knopf, 1978), pp. 5–9; Gilbert Badillo and David G. Curry, "The Social Incidence of Vietnam Casualties: Social Class or Race?" *Armed Forces and Society* 2:3 (1976), pp. 397–406; Bernard C. Nalty, *Strength for the Fight: A History of Black Americans in the Military* (New York: Free Press, 1976), pp. 296–298. See D. Michael Shafer, "The Vietnam-Era Draft: Who Went, Who Didn't, and Why It Matters," in this volume.

4. Willis, "Variations," pp. 558–568; Baskir and Strauss, *Chance and Circumstance,* p. 8.

5. Introduction to Wallace Terry, *Bloods* (New York: Ballantine, 1984).

6. Nalty, *Strength for the Fight,* pp. 296–298, 305–320.

7. Terry, *Bloods,* pp. 143–154.

8. Colonel Robert D. Heinl, Jr., "The Collapse of the Armed Forces," *Armed Forces Journal* 13 (June 1971); Charles Moskos, Jr., "The American Combat Soldier In Vietnam," *Journal of Social Issues* 31:4 (Fall 1985), pp. 25–38.

9. Mark Allen, "The Case of Billy Dean Smith," *Black Scholar* 4:2 (October 1972), pp. 15–17.

10. June Wilenz, "Other-Than-Honorable Discharge," *Crisis* 81:8 (1974), pp. 275–280.

11. Sam E. Anderson, "Soldier Boy," in *Vietnam and Black America,* ed. Clyde Taylor (Garden City, N.Y.: Doubleday, 1973), pp. 195–196; Ellen Frey-Wouters and Robert S. Laufer, *Legacy of A War* (London: M. E. Sharpe, 1986), pp. 136, 333–340.

12. David Cortright, *Soldiers In Revolt* (Garden City, N.Y.: Doubleday, 1975), pp. 210–211.

13. Johnson, "The U.S. Negro In Vietnam," pp. 1, 16.

14. Thomas Johnson, "Negro Veteran Is Confused and Bitter," *New York Times,* 29 July 1969, pp. 1, 14.

15. Clayborne Carson, *In Struggle* (Cambridge: Harvard University Press, 1981), p. 183; Nancy Zaroulis and Gerald Sullivan, *Who Spoke Up?* (Garden City, N.Y.: Doubleday, 1984), p. 24; Lewis quoted in Joan and Robert K. Morrison, *From Camelot to Kent State* (New York: Times Books, 1987), p. 32.

16. James Forman, *The Making of a Black Revolutionary* (New York: Macmillan, 1972), pp. 445–447; SNCC press release, 6 January 1966, in Taylor, *Vietnam and Black America,* pp. 258–260.

17. *New York Times,* 11 March 1964, p. 18; August Meier and Elliot Rudwick, *CORE* (New York: Oxford, 1973), pp. 401–415.

18. Carson, *In Struggle,* pp. 185–186; "Life in Mississippi: An Interview with Fannie Lou Hamer," *Freedomways* 15:12 (Spring 1965), pp. 231–242; Eldridge Cleaver, *Soul on Ice* (New York: McGraw Hill, 1968), pp. 121–128; Philip Foner, ed., *The Black Panther Speaks* (New York: J. B. Lippincott, 1970).

19. Malcolm X quoted in Taylor, *Vietnam and Black America,* pp. 59–60.

20. Julius Lester, *Revolutionary Notes* (New York: Grove Press, 1969), p. 16; James Baldwin, "The War Crimes Tribunal," in Taylor, *Vietnam and Black America,* p. 102; General G. Baker, Jr., "Letter," in John Bracey Jr. et al., eds., *Black Nationalism In America* (Indianapolis: Bobbs-Merrill, 1970), pp. 507–508.

21. David Garrow, *Bearing the Cross* (New York: Wm. Morrow, 1986), pp. 429–430; Stephen Oates, *Let the Trumpet Sound* (New York: New American Library, 1972), pp. 373–376, 380–382.

22. Garrow, *Bearing the Cross,* pp. 543–545, 549–559; Oates, *Let the Trumpet Sound,* pp. 431–443.

23. Wilkens, "Civil Rights Must Stand on Own Merits," *Justice,* 15 April 1967, p. 12. Rowan quoted in Garrow, *Bearing the Cross,* p. 553; also see Adam Fairclough, "Martin Luther King Jr., and the War in Vietnam," *Phylon* 45:1 (March 1984), pp. 19–39; Bayard Rustin, *Down the Line* (Chicago: Quadrangle, 1971), pp. 166–170.

24. *Ramparts* 5:11 (May 1967), p. 33; *Guardian,* 25 March 1967, p. 1, and 15 April 1967, p. 13.

25. Rustin, "The Choice," in *Down the Line,* pp. 242–243.

26. Elizabeth Martin et al., *Sourcebook of Harris National Surveys* (Chapel Hill, N.C.: Institute for Research in Social Sciences, 1981). A breakdown of the poll data was obtained directly from the Institute.

27. Louis Harris and Associates, *The Harris Survey Yearbook of Public Opinion, 1970* (New York: Louis Harris, 1971), pp. 110–121.

28. G. Marine, "Nobody Knows My Name," *Ramparts* 5:12 (June 1967), pp. 11–16; "Muhammad Ali—The Measure of A Man," *Freedomways* 7:2 (Spring 1967), pp. 101–102.

29. Introduction to Taylor, *Vietnam and Black America*. One might even extend this reasoning to a class analysis of the antiwar movement. Most simply, class divided blacks and whites. Most white antiwar activists were of the middle class; most black opponents came from a working-class or lower-class background.

30. Kenneth O'Reilly, *Racial Matters: The FBI's Secret File on Black Americans, 1960–1972* (New York: Free Press, 1989), pp. 285–295.

31. David Garrow, *The FBI and Martin Luther King Jr* (New York: W. W. Norton, 1981), pp. 180–207; Carson, *In Struggle,* p. 262; Garrow, *Bearing the Cross,* p. 554–559.

32. The figures are from Herbert Haines, *Black Radicalization and the Civil Rights Mainstream, 1954–1970* (Knoxville: University of Tennessee Press, 1988), pp. 77–128.

33. Richard Strayer and Lewis Ellenhorn, "Vietnam Veterans: A Case Study Exploring Adjustment Patterns and Attitudes," *Journal of Social Issues* 31:4 (1975), pp. 81–93; James Fendrick and Michael Pearson, "Black Veterans Return," *Transaction* 7:5 (March 1970), pp. 32–37; Howell quoted in Johnson, "Negro Veteran Is Confused and Bitter." (See n. 14, above.)

34. James Creedle, interview with the author, Newark, New Jersey, 7 July 1989.

35. Earl Graves, "The Military and Our Fair Share," *Black Enterprise,* July 1980, p. 7; Morris Janowitz and Charles Moskos, Jr., "The Military Establishment: Racial Composition of the Volunteer Armed Forces," *Society* 12:4 (May/June 1975), pp. 37–42; The *Wall Street Journal,* quoted in Harry G. Summers, "Red Badge of Courage: Earned and Ignored," *Los Angeles Times,* 5 November 1987, Part II, p. 7; Alex Schexnider, "Blacks in the Military and the Challenge," in *The State of Black America, 1988* vol. 12 (Washington, D.C.: National Urban League).

36. "The Hundred Most Influential Black Americans," *Ebony* 43 (May 1988), pp. 138–139. *Sepia* ran a monthly column on the black soldier in Vietnam and did not criticize the war until after the Tet offensive.

37. Summers, "Red Badge of Courage."

38. James Creedle, "Death: A High Price for Approval," *Sepia* 31 (July 1982), p. 16; also see the NABV's newspaper, *Eclipse.*

39. Peter Passell, "Forces in Society, and Reaganism, Helped Dig Deeper Hole for the Poor," *New York Times,* 16 July 1989, p. 1, 20.

40. Arch Puddington, "Jesse Jackson, The Blacks and American Foreign Policy," *Commentary* 77:4 (April 1984), pp. 19–27.

41. Vincent Harding, "To the Gallant Black Men Now Dead," in Taylor, *Vietnam and Black America,* pp. 7–20.

11

THE DAY THEY BURIED TRADITIONAL WOMANHOOD: Women and the Vietnam Experience

RUTH ROSEN

The Burial of Traditional Womanhood

On January 15, 1968, a remarkable thing happened. A group of young women symbolically buried "Traditional Womanhood." A large coalition of women's peace groups, loosely organized as the Jeanette Rankin Brigade, traveled to Washington, D.C. to present a petition to the United States Senate and to stage a peaceful march and rally that called for the immediate withdrawal of American troops from Vietnam. The coalition included such traditional women's peace groups as the Women Strike Peace (WSP) and the Women's International League for Peace and Freedom (WILPF). The style and discourse of the demonstrators reflected American women's traditional participation in antiwar campaigns; they carried banners and gave speeches emphasizing women's special nature and ability to create, rather than destroy, life. Sprinkled among the coalition, however, were small contingents of young feminists who, in a rebellious and controversial act, carried a dummy of a passive woman to Arlington Cemetery and there buried "Traditional Womanhood."

This ritual was hardly spontaneous. A group of New York radical feminists had spent "a lot of energy and a good few months of our early formation period preparing an appropriate action for the Brigade peace march." [1] After months of consciousness-raising, they had come to disagree with a women's demonstration that played "upon the traditional female role . . . as wives, mothers and mourners; that is, tearful and passive reactors to the action

233

of men rather than organizing as women to change that definition of femininity to something other than a synonym for weakness, political impotence, and tears." [2] As one of the first women's liberation groups in the nation, they were fueled by new revelations of their subordinate status. For weeks, the women threw themselves into building a larger-than-life dummy on a transported bier, "complete with feminine getup, blank face, blonde curls, and candles. Hanging from the bier were such disposable items as S & H Green Stamps, curlers, garters, and hairspray. Streamers floated off it and we also carried large banners, such as 'DON'T CRY: RESIST!'" [3] The funeral entourage sang songs specially written for the occasion, accompanied by a drum corps with a kazoo. A long funeral dirge, written by Peggy Dobbins, lamented "woman's traditional role which encourages men to develop aggression and militarism to prove their masculinity." To the other five thousand women of the Jeanette Rankin Brigade, they issued black-bordered invitations, "joyfully" inviting them to join the torchlight burial of Traditional Womanhood, "who passed with a sigh to her Great Reward this year of the Lord, 1968, after 3,000 years of bolstering the ego of Warmakers and aiding the cause of war. . . ." Their invitation was snubbed. Later that evening, five hundred young women split off from the main convention of women and held a counter-congress, which, because it lacked direction and coherence, they later judged a failure. Though they failed to gain many new recruits, the counter-congress helped consolidate and publicize the rapidly expanding women's liberation groups of cities across the nation. At the same time, the militancy, theatrical antics and separatism of the young women enraged quite a few older peace activists. [4]

Kathie Amatniek (who later renamed herself Kathie Sarachild), a member of the New York group, wrote and delivered a "Funeral Oration for the Burial of Traditional Womanhood." It is worth examining in some detail, for her rhetoric and her concerns reveal some of the underlying reasons these early feminists departed from traditional women's peace discourse.

Amatniek's oration begins with a critique of the "feminine mystique" of the 1950s, the unquestioned belief that women's biology destines them to devote their lives exclusively to the care of husbands and children:

> You see here the remains of a female human being who during her . . . lifetime was a familiar figure to billions of people in every corner of the world. Although scientists would classify this specimen within the genus species of homo sapiens, for many years there has been considerable controversy as to whether she really belonged in some kind of sub-species of the genus. While the human being was distinguished as an animal who freed himself from his biological limitation by developing technology and expanding his consciousness, traditional womanhood has been recognized, defined and valued for her biological characteristic only and those social functions closely related to her biological characteristic. [5]

As daughters of the 1950s, these young women felt particular hostility towards domestic life,[6] and had already discussed their anxieties of being trapped by traditional marriage and childcare. Fearing adult repetition of their own childhood experiences, they insisted that "our children will not become victims of our unconscious resentments and our displaced ambitions." Determined to avoid the plight of their mothers, they had largely avoided marriage and modeled themselves after their male counterparts.

Who were these young women? Like their male counterparts, they were the best-educated generation in American history, brought up by families who expected both their daughters and their sons to receive a college education. At the same time, they had one foot rooted in the fifties, a decade that taught young women to find fulfillment exclusively within marriage and motherhood. Many had rebelled. As veterans of the civil rights and antiwar movements, they had gained considerable experience and skills as organizers. From these movements they had learned to question received authority and traditional hierarchies, and to decipher how the powerful exploit the oppressed. They had also learned how the subordinate learn to internalize negative images of themselves. Sexism within both movements, however, had often excluded them from leadership, occasionally kept them from being heard, and sometimes led to their being treated as revolving bodies in male leaders' beds.[7] In their group, they had questioned the sexual revolution and criticized men's treatment of them as sexual toys even as they prepared to participate in the Jeanette Rankin Brigade.[8] Their break from the New Left would come later, in fits and stages. Meanwhile, new women's liberationists organized their own groups at the same time that they continued to participate in antiwar activities.

Born during the peak of the Vietnam War, the women's liberation movement frequently combined a radical critique of America's involvement in the Third World with an analysis of women's subordinate position in society. At the time, these young women could not have imagined how much their feminism would influence future women's peace movements. In 1979, NATO decided to deploy U.S. Cruise and Pershing II missiles in several European countries during the 1980s, igniting resurgent women's peace movements in both Europe and the United States. After fifteen years of feminism, women now possessed a greater self-consciousness about how to engage publicly in peace protest. The women's movement was an irreversible and incontrovertible fact of history and women now had a clear choice about whether to reject or incorporate a feminist critique of society into peace protest. During the 1970s, moreover, feminists had questioned their original ideal of equality—being treated as if they were men. They had celebrated their difference as women and even advanced the provocative thesis that men should reassess and adopt women's experiential history of preserving rather than destroying the race. It was in such an atmosphere of reconsideration and reassessment that the women's peace movement of the late 1970s and 1980s was conceived, amidst the realizations that to imitate men, their institutions and values, was wrong-headed, and that "women's values" were needed to transform the culture.

Women moved in many directions to stem the rise of militarism and the nuclear threat. In most cases, the Vietnam experience—especially women's subjective experience of "the movement"—remained the frame of reference. Many women, for example, after a decade of separatism now felt the time was ripe to rejoin men in what feminists called "mixed" movements. Reports of these efforts were also mixed. At feminist meetings in Europe and the United States, women publicly described their disappointment and disgruntlement. Men still claimed automatic leadership and women still did the routine and invisible maintenance that sustained peace organizations. Other women joined organizations which, avoiding the legacy of Vietnam, also tried to avoid feminist criticism. Instead, they resurrected an idealization of women's role as mothers or some form of traditional womanhood. Still other women, especially those in direct-action groups and peace encampments, took up the symbolic and countercultural politics of the Vietnam era and, in a dramatic feminist critique of society, tried to demonstrate what they had learned about women's values since the late 1960s.

The Vietnam Era

The "Funeral Oration for the Burial of Traditional Womanhood" expressed the rage of civil rights and antiwar activists who had gradually come to recognize the power men held over their lives. The oration, filled with anger, expressed the power which male approval still exerted in these women's lives:

> For some reason, man said to woman: you are less sexual when you participate in those other things, you are no longer attractive to me if you do so. I like you quiet and submissive. It makes me feel as if you don't love me, if you fail to let me do all the talking . . . When you confront the world outside the home . . . the world where I operate as an individual self as well as husband and father, then for some reason, I feel you are a challenge to me and become sexless and aggressive.[9]

The masterful male voice then goes on to threaten that if he is turned off he'll simply find another woman—leaving yet another woman divorced, without a man, and almost certainly with children. Sadistically, he describes her descent to poverty as she attempts to live on "women's wages." The fear of appearing uppity, silly, and unattractive haunts these young women. Not surprisingly, the need for female solidarity is forthrightly yoked to the need to organize any woman who might become a "scab" and replace an uppity woman: "We women must organize so that for man there can be no 'other woman' when we are expressing ourselves and acting politically, when we insist to men that they do the housework and child-care, fully and equally, so that we can have independent lives as well."[10]

Having played out future possibilities, the oration moves onto the subject of women's false consciousness, a common theme in the women's liberation movement:

> And so traditional Womanhood, even if she was unhappy with her lot, believed that there was nothing she could do about it. She blamed herself for her limitations and she tried to *adapt*. She told herself and she told others that she was happy as half a person, as the "better half" of someone else, as the mother of others, powerless in her own right.[11]

Rejecting "the so-called power of wives and mothers," the oration insists upon women's autonomous right to act for themselves as well as against the war.

It was no easy matter to bring up women's subordinate position in society in the midst of a shooting war. These women knew their issues would be ridiculed by men in the antiwar movement. Anticipating the trivialization of their feminist issues, Amatniek preemptively asks: "Why should we bury traditional womanhood while hundreds of thousands of human beings are being brutally slaughtered in our names . . . when it would seem that our number one task is to devote our energies directly to ending this slaughter or else solve what seems to be more desperate problems as home?" The answer is that women's problems are not merely personal, but social and political: "We cannot hope to move toward a better world or even a truly democratic society at home until we begin to solve our own problems." Peace without sexual equality, she insists, will only be temporary. "If men fail to see that love, justice and equality are the solution, that domination and exploitation hurt everybody, then our species is truly doomed; for if domination and exploitation and aggression are inherent biological characteristics which cannot be overcome, then nuclear war is inevitable and we will have reached our evolutionary dead end by annihilating ourselves."[12]

The oration ends with an explanation and a plea for a new beginning:

> And that is why we must bury this lady in Arlington Cemetary tonight, why we must bury Submission alongside Aggression. And that is why we ask you to join us. It is only a symbolic happening, of course, and we have a lot of real work to do. We have new men as well as a new society to build."[13]

Embedded in this funeral oration are some of the most basic assumptions and premises of the early women's liberation movement. Apprehension, even terror, of becoming victims of the feminine mystique, is key to the thoughts of the women who staged the burial. The ghost that haunts them wears an apron and submissively serves a husband and children. Fear that men won't like uppity women, that feminists will be replaced by more compliant women, is a pervasive and, as it turns out, wholly justifiable anxiety. Rejecting the biological determinism of the 1950s, they assume that men and women are more alike than unlike and that traditional manhood, like traditional womanhood, can be buried along with aggression and submission.

During the first years of the women's movement (from 1967 to 1971), most young feminists, then in their early twenties, tried to articulate ways in which women resembled rather than differed from men. Partly because of their youth and their fear of being trapped in a domestic future, they renounced their moral superiority as mothers (which most weren't) and proclaimed an independent right to denounce the American government's role in Vietnam. Like their male counterparts, they would fight against war with strength and might, not with the tears and weakness of traditional women.

No doubt they were influenced by the growing militancy of the antiwar movement, which since the fall of 1967 had frequently renounced non-violence in favor of "shutting the system down" by any means possible. As the antiwar movement moved from protest to resistance, the macho style of both GI antiwar and Black Power activists prodded young men and women to step up their militancy.

No longer, then, would young women encourage men to make war, nor would they fight against war as the relatives of men. As they buried traditional womanhood, they declared their right to resist war as autonomous beings, not merely as contingent appendages of men. As we shall see, this position was not to last very long.

Motherhood and the American Women's Reform Tradition

When young feminists buried traditional womanhood, they probably knew too little history to realize how far they had strayed from two centuries of the American women's reform tradition. It had been motherhood which had always justified women's desire to advance their rights, as well as their public efforts to reform society. After the American revolution, women had used the need for an educated "Republican Motherhood" to support their demand for female education. In their campaigns against prostitution, liquor and other assorted vices, nineteenth-century women had always protested that, as mothers, they had a special right and responsibility to protect their families and homes. During the Progressive Era, female reformers justified their public campaigns for women's suffrage, prohibition, child labor laws and peace by arguing that their mothering and housekeeping skills should be extended to the public arena.[14]

Women's use of "motherist" rhetoric to justify their engagement in reform has a long and honorable tradition in American history. In 1915, when Carrie Chapman Catt and Jane Addams founded the Woman's Peace Party (which subsequently merged into the Women's International League for Peace and Freedom), they also argued that women's special morality—derived from the their life-giving and life-preserving role as mothers—provided them with a unique capacity to join women all over the globe in seeking disarmament.[15] Until the Vietnam war, in fact, American women (with the exception of those attached to socialist or communist parties) had traditionally based their opposition to war—and nuclear weapons—on their biological difference as mothers. Claiming a special aversion to violence, they emphasized their biological specificity as a way of legitimizing their participation in public protest and peace organizations.

The Women Strike for Peace: A Recent Example of a Motherist Movement

The Women Strike for Peace of 1961 is exemplary of motherist peace efforts. As a radioactive cloud from a Russian nuclear test hung over the United States, fears of nuclear fallout intensified some citizens' desire for a test ban treaty. Suddenly, seemingly out of nowhere, an estimated fifty thousand women in over sixty cities walked out of their kitchens in a one-day nation-wide strike on November 1, 1961. The strike had been organized by five women who had met in SANE, grown weary of that group's ineffective bureaucratic and lobbying tactics, and determined to take direct action against the nuclear threat. They spread the word of the strike through female networks: local PTAs, the League of Women Voters, WILPF and SANE, even Christmas card lists.[16]

After a decade of containment and cold war, with dissent silenced by McCarthyism, the Women Strike for Peace stunned the nation. Where had they come from? Who had organized them? What sinister force did they represent? They looked so deceptively commonplace. As *Newsweek* explained, the strikers seemed like "perfectly ordinary women, with their share of good looks, the kind you would see driving ranch wagons, or shopping at the village market, or attending PTA meetings." Their slogans, moreover, sparkled with motherist rhetoric designed to appeal to ordinary women. Worried about strontium 90 contaminating their children's milk, the women carried placards demanding such modest goals as "Pure Milk, Not Poison," and "Let the Children Grow." From the neck of a little girl in a baby buggy hung a sign expressing the motherist beliefs of the strikers: "I want to grow up to be a mommy some day."[17]

In fact, the strikers were not as innocent as they looked. Some had been members of the Communist party, radicals, fellow travelers, union sympathizers or peace activists in the forties. At the very least, they constituted a relatively liberal, educated, and civic minded group of women who had absorbed the feminine mystique and left jobs or educational dreams to raise their children throughout the 1950s, but retained an interest in civic affairs. Over 61 percent worked as housewives; most still had children at home.[18]

The WSP's maternal imagery was extremely effective. During the 1950s cold warriors had argued that America needed to protect women's domestic role in the home. Patroitism became equated with "the American Way of Life," which specifically included traditional gender roles.[19] Now the WSP women used the same domestic imagery as a basis for a radical critique of the cold war, nuclear tests and the madness of cold war containment. They impressed many people, including President Kennedy. At a 1962 press conference, he recognized their sincerity and praised them for their work. Shortly before his death, he made an appeal for more such maternal activism: "The control of arms is a mission we undertake particularly for our children and our grandchildren, and they have no lobby in Washington. No one is better qualified to represent their interest than the mothers and grandmothers of America."[20] Jerome Wiesner, President Kennedy's science advisor later "gave the major credit for moving President Kennedy toward the Limited Test Ban Treaty of 1963, not to arms controllers inside the government but to the Women Strike for Peace and to SANE and Linus Pauling."[21]

The WSP women made very effort to avoid framing their strike in terms that challenged traditional gender relations. Dagmar Wilson, who became the spokesperson for the strike, described herself as a housewife, even though she was employed as a successful freelance graphic illustrator. To a reporter from the *Baltimore Sun,* Wilson reassured the public, "Our organization has no resemblance to the Lysistrata theme or even to the suffragettes. We are not striking against our husbands. It is my guess that we will make the soup that they will ladle out to the children on Wednesday."[22]

Amy Swerdlow, the historian who has studied the WSP in greatest detail, argues that WSP women chose to use a simple language, "the mother tongue," because they believed in their motherist ideals and also because they wanted to avoid imitating male forms of political discourse. "Convinced that professional politicians, scientists, and academics were, for the most part, leading the world to extinction, they gloried in their own exclusion from the system," argues Swerdlow. In other words, they gloried in the purity and saintliness of their status as mothers. Swerdlow also explains that most WSP women simply were "unable to offer a feminist critique of the bomb and the war. We in WSP, and I include myself, had neither language nor the analytical tools to make a connection between woman's secondary status in the family and political powerlessness or between domestic violence and state violence."[23]

Such maternal purity, however, did not prevent HUAC from investigating WSP one year later. Refusing to grant the investigation legitimacy, the women brilliantly employed a politics of "humor, irony, evasion and ridicule." They brought cribs, suckled babies, and did everything possible to emphasize that their patriotism, the defense of children, was far superior to the cold war arms race. Their effective but unconventional organization turned HUAC's inquiry into a circus. Opposed to membership lists, central organization, and hierarchical leadership, the WSP quickly made HUAC's arcane search for leadership and communists an exercise in futility. The press, sympathetic to the WSP, turned the inquiry into a battle between the sexes, which the WSP won decisively.[24]

In many ways, argues Swerdlow, the motherist campaign of WSP was superbly effective:

> It helped to change the image of the good mother from passive to militant, from silent to eloquent, from private to public. In proclaiming that men in power could no longer be counted on for protection, WSP exposed one of the most important myths of the militarists, that wars are waged by men to protect women and children. By stressing international cooperation among women rather than private family issues, WSP challenged the key element of the feminine mystique; the domestication, privatization, of the middle-class white housewife. By making recognized contributions to the achievement of a test ban, WSP also raised its participants' sense of political efficacy and self esteem.[25]

Swerdlow adds that in creating a nonhierarchical, decentralized, participatory and playful style of politics, the WSP also prefigured the political culture of the New Left and the radical wing of the women's liberation movement.

Only seven years later, as we have seen, young women rejected the motherist rhetoric of the WSP for a discourse that attempted to ignore biological difference and especially women's role as mothers. By then, some WSP women were also ready to exchange motherist rhetoric for the language of a radical feminism that proclaimed women's independent right to oppose war. This is not surprising. As we shall see, women's peace discourse has often mirrored, consciously or not, the feminist or antifeminist atmosphere of the period in which it is conceived.

The Women's Liberation Movement Rediscovers Difference

Like other revivals of feminism, the women's movement had to confront a serious conundrum—the problem of defining woman's nature, position and condition in a society dominated by male perspective and experience. In her brilliant explication of this ontological problem, Simone de Beauvoir described woman as the 'other,' and used the term 'otherness' to describe woman's social and cultural marginality. It is precisely women's 'otherness' that sets the intellectual agenda of any feminist revival; first, because women must address maleness as the norm; and second, because women must analyze their own positions, as well as the society in which they live, from the distinct perspective of the 'other.'[26] Both the perspective and nature of the questions raised by feminists are profoundly influenced by women's 'otherness.' The feminist discourse of the late 1960s and 1970s can be understood as a sustained confrontation with how women resembled or differed from the normative ideal of maleness.

The ghost of the feminine mystique, the 1950s emphasis on biological determinism, the widespread acceptance of Freudian psychology—all influenced early feminists to move in a direction that stressed similarity rather than difference. From the beginning, women in the National Organization for Women (NOW), a more traditional civil rights group, committed themselves to formal legalism, maintaining that women gained more by stressing women's resemblance to men than by stressing their difference. They advocated legislation that provided women the same rights and responsibilities as men, sometimes forcing women to squeeze their biological experience and cycle into a male model of success. Biological difference, argued NOW advocates and attorneys, had too long been used as a basis for exclusion. Younger radical feminists similarly tried to underplay the significance of difference. Shulamith Firestone even went so far as to suggest that women free themselves from the material oppression of bearing children by having them born from test tubes.[27]

By the mid-1970s, however, the atmosphere in the younger and radical part of the movement began to shift. The growth of the draft resistance and GI movements in the late sixties and early seventies gradually shifted antiwar work to men and excluded by grass-roots participation large numbers of female activists (except in GI coffeehouses). The macho style of the GI movement turned off many feminists who were criticizing the growing violence and combativeness of the antiwar movement itself.

As the war began to wind down in the mid-1970s, many women entered the women's movement without having had prior involvement in either the civil rights or antiwar movements. Concerns of race, American imperialism, or the Third World were not part of their political background. Moreover, the trendy human potential idea that one had to change oneself before changing the world justified women's exclusive focus on themselves. Many feminists, therefore, became absorbed in discovering and battling the many hidden injuries and problems experienced by women—rape, sexual harrassment, battering, incest, and the medicalization of women's natural bodily processes. The list seemed infinite. The focus on women's problems inevitably challenged the idea that women were indeed so similar to men. Some writers and activists toyed with the ideal of androgyny. But increasingly, radical feminists began exploring, even celebrating, women's difference.[28]

From the beginning, the civil rights movement exerted an enormous influence on the radical wing of the women's movement. The pull towards separatism and the search for a separate women's culture had its seeds in the Black Power and Black Nationalist movements of the late 1960s. Efforts to change men, to convince them to see the political dimensions of personal life, had largely failed. Movement men trivialized and ridiculed feminist demands and in so doing, often became identified as the enemy. To be like men, then, implied adopting the very privilege and arrogance that feminists condemned. As in the civil rights movement, integration—this time, with men—seemed a hopeless task. In a separatist mood, lesbian and other feminist separatists began creating a vibrant women's culture—coffeehouses, bookstores, musical festivals, rural communes—which they associated with the superiority of women's values. Like advocates of Black Nationalism, they stressed their own cultural heritage, a heritage that now seemed filled with rich experiences that men had devalued.

By the late 1970s and the 1980s, a burst of feminist scholarship and polemic had launched a fairly devastating critique of the "male culture" that produced the institutions, values and attitudes under which women had lived. Feminist intellectuals began reevaluating women's experience from a female perspective. Adrienne Rich distinguished between the patriarchal institution of motherhood and the actual joyful process of creating and preserving life. Carol Gilligan reassessed women's moral values, while Susan Griffin and Carolyn Merchant compared male and female attitudes towards nature. Sara Ruddick and other feminist theorists reconsidered the value of "maternal thinking," a cognitive style seen as stemming from the experience of preserving rather than destroying life. Evelyn Fox Keller analyzed the ways in which scientific knowledge mirrored men's attitudes toward thought and emotion. Mary Daly reinvested positive meaning in the spinster, the crone, the hag. An endless list of authors tried to resurrect mythical matriarchies in which women, as peaceful nurturers, had reigned before the onslaught of "patriarchal barbarism." [29]

Personal experience also drove radical feminists to reconsider the value of their "difference." As young feminists aged, the terror of the 1950s retreated and their respect for motherhood grew. As some feminists entered male professions, they also discovered, with considerable disappointment, a world shaped by men's biological rythymns, linguistically depicted by men's bodily metaphors, described by mystified abstractions, and enacted in an adversarial and combative interpersonal style. Sociologist Arlie Hochschild criticized academic life for maintaining a tenure cycle that ignored women's need to bear and raise children during their intellectually formative years. Feminist lawyers complained of the adversarial nature of their profession and argued for better means of conflict resolution. Legal scholars like Catherine MacKinnon persuasively argued that the law, like the rest of society, simply didn't fit women's needs. When feminist lawyers argued women's causes on the basis of protectionism, they created precedent for exclusion. But to argue cases based on women's similarity to men meant ignoring important female biological differences, especially those associated with pregnancy and maternity. [30]

Increasingly, the dominant tone in the movement—with the exception of NOW and other mainstream civil rights organizations—reflected a search for "a woman-centered" approach that could challenge the normative values of a patriarchal culture. How, such feminists asked, can we achieve a kind of equality that incorporates difference? The answer, increasingly voiced, was that only a critical mass of women—and men—could successfully challenge the assumptions, premises and values of the culture, and that such a critical mass had not yet surfaced. As a perfect example, it was one thing to force men or institutions to provide childcare; it was quite another matter to invest such work with prestige and reward it with decent monetary compensation.

The Emergence of the Women Peace Movement in the 1980s

As the need for a renewed peace effort emerged in the late 1970s, women once again, as during the Vietnam war, entered and indeed often led resistance to nuclear deployment in Europe.

Women's efforts to join "mixed" groups in both the United States and Europe reminded many of their experiences during the Vietnam War. They complained of the bureaucratic and abstract wrangling in the Campaign for Nuclear Disarmament, of men's combative style in the Livermore Action Group. They watched men obey the letter but not the spirit of feminist process. [31] Unlike the WSP women just emerging from the 1950s, women who joined mixed groups no longer lacked a language with which to express their resentment. Whether they chose to use it was quite another matter. Thus, when they entered mixed peace groups, they did so with apprehension, but with the hope or belief that mixed groups provided the most effective and strategic means for mobilizing people to protest the bomb, war, or interventionism.[32]

Motherist Campaigns

In addition to joining mixed groups, some women revived motherist campaigns for peace, but few really tried to resurrect the traditional womanhood that young feminists had buried in 1968. Some used motherhood tactically, believing that women held greater legitimacy as mothers than as feminists; some members of the Women's International League for Peace and Freedom and the WSP had never relinquished their belief that women ought to organize as mothers.

Motherist campaigns and rhetoric had considerable appeal. Mothers Against Drunk Drivers, after all, had scored important victories. In the United States, groups like Women's Action for Nuclear Disarmament (WAND), founded by Helen Caldicott, happily exploited Mother's Day and other symbols of motherhood to promote women's organization for peace. In Germany, Petra Kelly, a leading figure of the Greens, held a placard "Father State Makes Mother Earth Kaput" at a blockade of U.S. army bases. In San Diego, Mothers Embracing Nuclear Disarmament (MEND), founded in 1986 by Linda Smith, adopted motherist rhetoric and drew on the traditional respectability of mothers to organize women against the nuclear threat. Mother's Day became an annual occasion for mothers to gather at the Nevada test site to protest nuclear weapons. In general, those movements that wholly or occasionally employed motherist rhetoric tried to avoid associating their goals with a feminist critique of women's condition or of patriarchal culture in general. Women for Survival, for example, scrupulously avoided all association with the women's movement. In the age of Reagan, with the defeat of the ERA in 1982, feminism, along with any echo of the Vietnam experience, had become another "f word," better left unsaid.[33]

Another reason women found motherist campaigns appealing is that a variety of maternal protests during the 1970s proved effective in challenging established authority and focusing world attention on the madness of violence and the violation of human rights. In Argentina the Mothers of the Plaza of Mayo demonstrated enormous courage when, in 1977, they began invading the traditionally masculine space of the government plaza every Thursday. Silently they circled the plaza, demanding information of their missing children.[34] Wearing scarves on their heads, they signaled their acceptance of their subordinate role, but inverted the symbol by embroidering the names of the disappeared on the cloth. Around their necks hung photos of their children. Nonviolence, they argued, was essential. Even their use of silence, they felt, was an accusatory, not passive statement.[35] In South Africa, motherist groups played an important role in nonviolent resistance. South African Women's Resistance to Pass Laws cast their opposition in terms of the laws' infringement of their rights as mothers.[36] In August 1976, when Irish violence resulted in the killing of three small children, a group of housewives, later called the Irish Peace Women, instigated a movement of Protestant and Catholic mothers who staged a peaceful and nonviolent march of ten thousand women to protest the violence that was decimating whole families. For their effort, they would win the Nobel Peace Prize.[37] In 1979, Danish and Finnish women, sitting around the perennial kitchen table which looms so large in the histories of women's peace movements, formed Women for Peace in recognition of the fact that mothers all over the world care about their children's future. Demanding "Food Instead of Arms," they managed to gather half a million women's signatures on peace petitions. In 1981 they staged a dramatic peace march from Copenhagen to Paris, where the press either ignored them or interviewed the few men who accompanied them.[38]

The Women's Direct Action Movement and Peace Encampments

In the 1980s, other women moved in a third direction, one that integrated feminist analysis with nonviolent protest of the bomb and war. These were groups of women who adopted a specifically anti-masculinist discourse and proclaimed their unique moral claim as women to protest violence and the nuclear threat. Their campaigns included an acknowledgment of the importance of mothers, but, more significantly, emphasized the moral superiority of women per se and revived—even invented— female cultural rituals for protesting world violence. Among these groups were the Women's Pentagon Action of 1980 and 1981, the Greenham Women's Encampment (1981 to the present), the Seneca Encampment for a Future of Peace and Justice (1982 to the present) and the Puget Sound Encampment in Seattle (1983 to the present), as well as various women's peace encampments and movements in Italy and Australia.[39]

Consider how far these feminist groups had moved away from the young women who in 1968 thought they had buried traditional womanhood. At the Women's Pentagon Action, for example, posters decried male violence and called for women to "disarm the patriarchy." One of the most popular placards urged women to "Take the Toys Away from the Boys."[40] The protest, designed as a four-part theatre piece, gloried in enacting rituals that distinguished women from men. The protesters began mourning, chanting and weeping (something Kathie Amatniek swore women would never again do). Next, the women entered into a period of rage, denouncing male violence against women and the planet. During the third stage, in an image meant to convert domesticity into defiance, the women spun yarn across the doors of the Pentagon. In the fourth and final stage, called an encirclement, women used scarves to form an interweaving web encircling the five points of the Pentagon. At the Seneca and Puget Sound encampments, such four-part outpourings of emotion became a tradition.

The Women's Pentagon Action typified the atmosphere and discourse of peace encampments. Once again, women reveled in using symbols that declared their pride in the moral superiority of being women. Indeed, the camps themselves were supposed to provide a prefigurative peek at how a cooperative, nonsexist, nonhierarchical society could be run without violence. During the late 1960s, many activists in the anti-war movement had believed that people must live "as if" their goals had been achieved. This emphasis on cultural politics had deeply influenced the women's movement throughout the 1970s. At the camps, women shared the endless chores required to maintain the camps and stressed participatory democracy and consensus as the only means to reach decisions. During acts of civil disobedience, they festooned the fences surrounding missile silos with flowers and pictures of their children or female lovers, and spun yarn and scarves to "reweave the web of life" all over the world.[41]

Like the explicitly motherist groups, the Women's Pentagon Action and the women's peace encampments implicitly presumed the moral superiority of women. The difference was that they de-emphasized motherhood and contrasted women's intrinsically peace-loving, life-preserving, nonviolent manner against men's violent, exploitative and plundering nature. One possible reason for the relative lack of motherist rhetoric is that the participants, many of whom were young and/or lesbians, were not (yet) mothers; another is that these women took feminism for granted, no longer feared the feminine mystique and felt free and proud to publicly value women's tradition of seeking peaceful conconciliation. At the Pentagon Action, for example, women raged against those men "who destroy our lives" and declared "A Feminist World is a Nuclear Free Zone."[42]

The Women's Pentagon Action grew out of an April 1980 conference at Amherst, Massachusetts, entitled "Women and Life on Earth: Eco-Feminism in the 1980's." Eco-feminism does not necessarily promote "essentialism," the belief in innate differences between men and women. Simply put, eco-feminism argues that the particular patriarchal culture which has developed in the West has been characterized by a mind/body split that associates men with spirit and rationality and women with nature and intuition, and that men, who have held greater power in this culture, have developed patriarchal culture, along with its exploitative views of nature and women, and its violent responses to conflict and difference. For an eco-feminist, the dangers of this worldview are clear—violence against both women and nature and the terrifying prospect of ecological or nuclear disaster; both men and women have colluded in this construction of reality and both remain responsible for creating a new vision of harmony with nature, equality between the sexes, and global cooperation. From the eco-feminist perspective, present differences between the sexes are regarded as being the result of men's and women's different historical and social experiences. Virginia Woolf's conviction that men's mental liberation from daily cares (housekeeping and childcare) is dangerous and makes them too detached from the facts and exigencies of life is often quoted to support this point of view.[43]

Yet in practice the eco-feminist discourse—symbols, slogans and protests—at least as expressed by separatists at peace encampments, often implies that men are the violent partners of the species. Participants portray women as the saviors of the earth, the caretakers of the planet, while men destroy the earth through ecological rapaciousness and nuclear weaponry. The "Unity Statement" written for the Pentagon Action, for example, sentimentally describes how "the earth nourishes us as we with our bodies will eventually feed it. Through us our mothers connected the human past to the human future." Rejecting the liberal feminist idea that women should join men in the military, they explicitly state, "We do not want to be drafted into the army. We do not want our young brothers drafted. We want *them* equal to *us*."[44]

In this view, women in effect have a moral responsibility to wrest control of the earth from men. At Greenham Common a similar perspective presided. "For many women," explained two participants, "the issue is about reclaiming power for ourselves, and not remaining victims of a male-defined world characterized by violence."[45] At the Seneca Encampment the women created a new pledge of allegiance that emphasized their view of the earth as a female living organism: "We pledge allegiance to the earth, And to the life which she provides, One planet interconnected, With beauty and peace for all."[46] In visual terms, the participants compare the planet to a woman's body, repeatedly raped and plundered by male violence. Male violence toward women and the threat of nuclear holocaust are seen as originating from the same source, a patriarchal culture that devalues nature and employs violence at every turn. In *Reweaving the Web of Life: Feminism and Nonviolence,* a popular collection of essays, such articles as "Patriarchy: A State of War," "Patriarchy is a Killer: What People Concerned About Peace and Justice Should Know," "The Future—if There is One—is Female," and "Fear of the Other: The Common

Root of Sexism and Militarism," contrast men's violent and aggressive culture with that of women's nonviolence.[47] The Unity Statement of the Puget Sound Encampment explicitly states that "we are ordinary women: mothers, daughters, sisters and workers who see the relationship between use of U.S. militarism and the violence women experience on the street, on our jobs and in our home." Both domestic violence and war, they argue, legitimize "use of violence to resolve conflicts . . . A nonviolent, feminist way of living seeks cooperation, not domination, and includes respect for peoples' physical and spiritual well-being and a love of the earth and her creatures." Men's use of weapons is likened to their need to dominate, master, and control those around them, whether it be women or other nations. To make these connections some of the women at Puget Sound distributed leaflets against pornography to try to link the exploitation and degradation of women with male plundering of the planet. During the Vietnam War, feminists had distributed similar pamphlets linking imperialism to the exploitation of women.[48]

The idea that men make war on women—and the world—had its roots in the women's movement of the mid-1970s. Susan Brownmiller's influential *Against Our Will* (1975) convinced many feminists that rape, an act of terror against women, exerts enormous social control in keeping women in their place. A 1976 poster from the American women's movement stated in no uncertain terms, "RAPE IS WAR!" The following explanation appeared below:

> It is the tradition of the patriarchy to conquer and possess. The capacity for dehumanization, the equation of manhood with the domination of another's body, is carried over from sex into war. War is the ultimate act of coercion inflicted on a people and a country. Rape is the ultimate act of coercion inflicted on women by men. Rape is war.[49]

To counter the influence of patriarchal culture, peace encampment participants valorize everything female. Emotionality—excessive displays of weeping, raging, chanting, and mourning—are honored and favorably compared to men's sublimation of feeling into violence. Traditions inherited—or newly invented—from women's past are used to glorify women's magical healing powers. Wicca practices, worship of various goddess figures, new feminist spiritualist rituals, and Gaia (Earth) Consciousness have all, at one time or another, appeared as ritualistic observances.[50]

The idea of the web, reweaving the seam of life, gradually took on symbolic importance in the peace encampments. It was not a new idea and had its roots in the women's movement of the late 1970s. In 1976, feminists in Amherst, Massachusetts celebrated International Women's Day with a poster that compared women to spiders, who, by creating a world-wide web, could "entangle the powers that bury our children."[51]

To those who participated in the peace encampments, the weaving of webs became symbolic of women's potential power to enforce peace, to tie together women's protests—from the Boeing Aerospace construction site in Puget Sound, to the nuclear depot at Seneca, to the actual missile silo at Greenham Common. As the authors of *Greenham Women Everywhere* explain,

> Each link in a web is fragile, but woven together creates a strong and coherent whole. A web with few links is weak and can be broken, but the more thread it is composed of, the greater its strength. It makes a very good analogy for the way in which women have rejuvenated the peace movement. By connections made through many diverse channels, a widespread network has grown up of women committed to working for peace."[52]

But peace is not simply the absence of war. For women in the peace encampments and their sympathizers, redefinitions of peace, security and defense are all necessary: "To oppose nuclear weapons requires a fundamental change in our attitude to life." Imagination, suggests one Greenham participant, is essential: "What we want to change is immense. It's not just getting rid of nuclear weapons, it's getting rid of the whole structure that created the possibility of nuclear weapons in the first place. If we won't use imagination nothing will change. Without change we will destroy the planet. It's as simple as that."[53] At Puget Sound, the women made the connection between male supremacy and war explicit:

> Feminism implies a total world view rather than simply positions on traditional women's (biological/reproductive) issues . . . The Feminist resistance to war and nuclear weapons challenges the system of male supremacy at least as fundamentally as these struggles. War is a structural aspect of male supremacy, and a particularly deadly one. Since war is one of the areas in and through which men have most effectively consolidated and extended their power over the world, challenging militarism is essential for a feminist revolution.[54]

Unlike motherist groups, women in peace encampments encountered considerable derision and ridicule. During the first months, Greenham Common women received some positive press. Soon, however, critics chastised women who had left their husbands and children to join the peace encampment, calling them neglectful mothers and wives. Eventually, those women who were freest to remain at Greenham or at other peace encampments tended to include young lesbians whose commitment to a countercultural woman's community was essential. Hence, they had little interest in seeking male approval. Their independent and feisty spirit, their disregard for feminine demeanor or clothing, threatened local townspeople and even generated violence against them. The consequences of invading conservative small towns could be serious. At Seneca, marchers were stopped by local men wearing T-shirts emblazoned with the slogan "Nuke the Dykes." The press, to put it mildly, was largely hostile, except in Seattle, where some liberal journalists treated the peace camp with greater respect. In England, journalists repeatedly discredited them as "strident feminists," "burly lesbians," "hefty ladies," "the harridans of Greenham Common" and "Amazon waifs and strays."[55]

The Implications of Women's Peace Protest

How one argues for peace matters. Discourse not only shapes strategy but reveals participants' construction of reality, sense of purpose and projected identity. In the late 1960s, in the midst of the Vietnam War's slaughter, the young feminists who tried to bury traditional womanhood understood their personal stake in antiwar discourse. In the 1980s, the possibility of apocolyptic war forced women to consider how best to preserve peace.

Women peace activists are currently debating how women should advocate peace. Some radical feminists have written diatribes against the peace encampments, arguing that the peace movement has drained feminist energies away from the more important peace project of ending male violence against women.[56] Other radical feminists have argued that women's issues are simply too petty to consider when compared with the immediate threat of nuclear war. Women in mixed groups have expressed considerable discomfort with the moral supcriority expressed by both motherist groups and women's encampments; separatists have argued that only women can make peace; motherist campaigns have carefully skirted feminist issues that otherwise effect their lives.

Let us take a brief look at some of the social implications of women's peace protest. The advantages of motherist campaigns are easy to spot. They receive great press, appeal to women who fear being associated with feminism and are perfectly suited to a patriarchal culture that welcomes women's efforts to seek change in the name of their traditional status as mothers and their maternal right to protect their children. In other words, in the short run, motherist campaigns have considerable potential to attract a sympathetic audience. As Amy Swerdlow and others have argued, moreover, motherist campaigns can alter women's consciousness. As mothers engage in public protest, they often perceive ways in which their power as women is limited. They also gain valuable political experience. Over time, motherist campaigns can therefore radicalize women into demanding rights for themselves.[57]

Because the short-term effects are so obvious, advocates of motherist campaigns sometimes ignore the long-term disadvantages of maternal protests. In the long run, motherist rhetoric may reinforce the culture's gender system by reifying women's biological role as mothers. Further, motherist rhetoric no longer accurately reflects the complexity of women's lives. In the 1990s, the vast majority of women will be doing many other things in addition to mothering. It might help if men also argued against nuclear weapons or war as fathers, but usually they don't. When they *do* speak of future generations and emphasize their paternity, their words do not carry the same social significance as motherist campaigns. In short, they don't reinforce a societal belief that men's lives should be shaped by their biological capacity to father. By emphasizing mothers' moral superiority, moreover, motherist rhetoric tends to place women on pedestals, where, as feminists have long observed, women are worshipped but rarely granted equal rights. In other words, a conflict of interest may exist between the strategy of using motherist rhetoric and the feminist goal of transcending an exclusively biological role. The women who tried to bury traditional womanhood in 1968 thought so. Were they then right overall?

The peace encampments also have advantages and disadvantages. On the positive side, they are among the few strains in the peace movement to make connections between a feminist critique of the culture and militarism. Their expressive politics, so reminiscent of the countercultural politics of the Vietnam era, suggest an alternative way to resolve conflict; their "bearing witness" draws attention to the production, storage and presence of missiles, making the abstract idea of nuclear holocaust more concrete.

Strong criticism can also be made of the peace encampments. Some feminist peace activists argue that separatists may in fact reinforce the gender system.[58] By emphasizing women's culture, peace encampments may reify traditional gender roles. The logic of their biological determinism can also lead to political paralysis. If men are so hopelessly violent, then why bother to protest at all? Why not go home and simply live out one's remaining days in peace? Further, the emphasis on male violence demonizes and alienates most men, who, in the final analysis, truly do have the power to make peace. Because lesbians and feminist separatists have so dominated the encampment movement, they have strengthened the association of feminism with exotic rituals and alternative lifestyles. As a result, they have frightened local townpeople and often alienated the very public they wish to convert. They receive a great deal of press, but most of it is negative.

The Vietnam Legacy and the Women's Peace Movement

In many ways, the women's peace movement is one of the most profound legacies of the Vietnam War. Although women's peace protest began long before the 1960s, the Vietnam era introduction of feminist consciousness forever altered the frame of reference for women involved in peace movements.

Yet two decades after the women's movement began, women in the 1990s still face the same conundrum that is an integral problem of feminism itself—the fact that women's discourse about themselves—and peace—inevitably turns on how much women do or do not resemble men. That this has been a problem during all feminist revivals is well understood by historians.[59] What historians have ignored, however, is that female peace activists face the same dilemma, though not always with the same intellectual self-consciousness. The central problem is that within a male-dominated culture, men remain the frame of reference and women have not successfully moved beyond this limitation. Either they emphasize the similarity of the sexes—thereby negating their special needs and biological processes—or they emphasize their difference and claim a moral superiority based on maternalism and relative powerlessness. In either case, they remain the 'other' and their intellectual discourse about themselves—and peace—remains imprisoned within a paradigm that fails to transcend women's contingent relationship to men. This was true during the Vietnam War; it remains true today.

Within this very brief history of women's peace protest, we have seen women swing back and forth between two tendencies. One emphasizes women's difference, and condemns the world men have made. A common feminist adage best expresses this position: "The woman who strives to be the equal to men lacks ambition." The other tendency emphasizes men and women's similarity, knowing that difference has too often been used as the basis of exclusion. During the Vietnam War, Betty Friedan, like the women who buried traditional womanhood, argued that "my own revulsion toward the war in Vietnam does not stem from the milk that once flowed from my breast, nor even from the fact of my draft-age sons, but from my moral conscience as a human being and as an American." A few years before her death, Simone de Beauvoir expressed her firm conviction that "women should desire peace as human beings, not as women. And if they are being encouraged to be pacifists in the name of motherhood, that's just a ruse by men who are trying to lead women back to the womb. Besides, it's quite obvious that once they're in power, women are exactly like men. Women should absolutely let go of that baggage."[60]

To expand a discourse that is limited by, refers to, and is judged by a dominant patriarchal culture is no easy task. Still, there are now some female peace activists attempting to create a feminist, rather than feminine, analysis of war, the bomb, and interventionism in the Third World. Around the globe there are signs that a variety of individuals are trying to make feminism and human social welfare, not women's special nature, the basis of peace protest.

One example of this tendency in the United States is the effort to educate more women in the technical langauge of arms control and weaponry and to advance peace and social welfare through the electoral process. Sometimes the goal is to put more women, not always or necessarily with a new worldview, at the negotiating table. Whatever its limitations in promoting feminist concerns, and they are sometimes considerable, such efforts succeed in creating an important female presence within mainstream discourse and politics. Women for a Meaningful Summit, which grew out of the 1985 United Nations Decade of Women conference in Nairobi, has attempted to infuse summit meetings with women's voices thoroughly informed about "throw weights, verification and security issues." Trying to create and document a gender gap about war and military expenditures provides women with potential political clout. Such disarmament specialists as Alva Myrdal and Randall Forsberg have promoted important and viable negotiating formulas adopted by political constituencies. Forsberg's role in creating the Nuclear Freeze, to cite just one example, was instrumental in the formation of a national movement. Weapons and arms control experts such as Mary Kaldor and Jane Sharp have helped transform strategic debate. Attacking the military budget, as Sheila Tobias and others have done, is another tactical way of demonstrating that national security involves meeting women and children's needs.[61]

Elsewhere, women are searching for ways of transcending the sameness/difference limitations of their peace discourse. Senator Susan Ryan, the Australian Minister of Education, expressed this vision in 1982:

> The biological imperative alone is not enough to defeat militarism. Rather than assuming that women as women will end war, I suggest that it is the relationship between feminism and disarmament that provides hopes for change . . . Contemporary feminism, whose ideology includes the replacing of aggression, authoritarianism, discrimination with reason, democracy, tolerance and an acceptance of all possibilities in life for women and men provides the best starting point for a popular and effective disarmament movement.[62]

In Italy, one group of feminists, trying to link the "micro" level of women's lives to the "macro" level of international conflict have argued that they are pacifists not because they are women, but because they are feminists. Feminism, they argue, unmasked the fragility of women's security and men's protection when it exposed domestic violence and rape. In the same way, feminism can unmask the fragility of a security built on mutually assured destruction, as opposed to security built on mutual cooperation.[63] In a similar vein, Sister Julianna Casey, I.H.M., a member of the ad hoc committee to draft the U.S. Bishops' pastoral letter on nuclear war, criticized what passes for normal discourse on nuclear arms from a feminist perspective:

> One has only to listen carefully to the language used to speak of the nuclear reality to realize that abstract theories and pronouncements cover up death-

dealing facts. The testimony of experts and of former and present governmental and military officials . . . brought this home to me in brutal ways. I learned about "anticipatory retaliation" and "serendipitious fallout" . . . Perhaps most telling was the number of times disarmament or nuclear freeze were referred to as the "emasculinization" of American defense policy . . . As women we are painfully conscious of the power of language and of abstract rationalization to oppress, to hide, to make invisible. It has happened to us.[64]

Carol Cohn, in her brilliant deconstruction of defense language, similarly concluded that "the dominant voice of militarized masculinity and decontextualized rationality speaks so loudly in our culture, it is difficult for any other voice to be heard." Still, she called for a reconstructive effort:

We must recognize and develop alternative conceptions of rationality, we must invent compelling alternative visions of possible futures, and we must create rich and imaginative alternative voices—diverse voices whose conversations with each other will invent a future in which there *is* a future.[65]

Can feminism provide one of those rich and imaginative alternative voices? The feminist project of renaming, redefining and deconstructing the dominant culture has been immensely successful. What women used to call (with a sigh) "life," is now correctly labeled rape, sex discrimination, sexual harrassment, and wife battering. The most successful aspect of the feminist movement, in fact, has been to expose and re-name experiences that once remained carefully guarded private secrets. Acts once considered natural have been redefined as acts of exploitation and domination, incompatible with peace, equality and justice.

The burial of traditional womanhood offered women a brief glimpse of an autonomous moral right to criticize the culture and its dominant discourse about war. The effort was premature. Women had not yet gained the economic independence for making such autonomous moral pronouncements. Twenty years later, many more have the means to make their voices heard.

The strength of feminism grew from women's ability to derive simple truths from personal experience, and the bold willingness to puncture received wisdom. Just as feminism helped redefine women's lives, can it help expose the euphemisms, mystifications and paradigms that threaten the planet with nuclear destruction and ecological devastation? What voice will best advance the interests of *both* women and peace? Put another way, can feminism help inform the way we think about peace, the way we go about arguing for disarmament, the way we imagine a global community that respects, rather than seeks to dominate and conquer, difference?

And what would such a feminist discourse sound like? It is premature to know, and particularly difficult to imagine at a time when pro-natalism and antifeminism have regained cultural dominance. Among feminist peace activists, moreover, there is also a great divide between those who stress equality and those who emphasize female difference. One can imagine, however, that such a discourse could go beyond the motherist and peace encampment movements, thereby creating an inclusive atmosphere that can embrace men's participation. It might also incorporate the values promoted by eco-feminism, thereby including a feminist critique of the culture's relation to the environment. As an expanding global feminism encounters an expanding global militarism, disparate voices are suggesting that the feminist vision of an egalitarian and nonviolent society—one that refuses to demonize men, is unwilling to be constrained by women's role as mothers but draws upon women's historic role as preservers of life, and respects the need to live in harmony with nature— *may* challenge and redefine some of the dominant culture's most deeply held beliefs about peace, security and defense.

Already, such voices can be heard. In *Rocking the Ship of State: Toward a Feminist Peace Politics* (1989), a group of feminist activists and theorists, many veterans of Vietnam-era movements, point to new ways of making feminism the basis of peace protest.[66] But can a feminist discourse ever compete for legitimacy or gain a hearing? Can a critique and vision that cuts so deeply to the core of the culture be anything more than utopian?

Historians are neither soothsayers nor theorists. They know only that the future, in its predictably inscrutable way, will somehow be shaped by the past. Jeanette Rankin, who outraged her male colleagues by voting against both world wars, once wisely observed the obstacles facing women dedicated to peace protest:

> The individual woman is required . . . a thousand times a day to choose either to accept her appointed role and thereby rescue her good disposition out of the wreckage of her self-respect, or else follow an independent line of behavior and rescue her self-respect out of the wreckage of her good disposition.[67]

As women's lives continue to change, however, they may discover a new language that reflects the greater complexity of their lives. They may also discover that the burial of traditional womanhood, a seemingly trivial event in the midst of a shooting war, helped free women to discover feminism as the basis for peace protest.

NOTES

The author gratefully acknowledges a grant from the William Joiner Center of the University of Massachusetts, Boston, a Rockefeller Foundation Gender Roles Fellowship and a faculty research grant from the University of California, Davis, all of which helped support this project. Todd Gitlin offered challenging suggestions, editorial advice, and inspired encouragement during the development of this paper.

1. Shulamith Firestone, "The Jeanette Rankin Brigade: Woman Power?" New York Radical Women, *Notes From the First Year,* published pamphlet, New York, June 1968, p. 22.

2. Ibid.

3. Ibid.

4. Gerda Lerner, personal interview with author, Berkeley, California, 15 March 1988.

5. Kathie Amatniek, "Funeral Oration for the Burial of Traditional Womanhood," reprinted in *Notes From the First Year,* p. 24.

6. See for example, Kathleen Gerson, *Hard Choices: How Women Decide about Work, Career, and Motherhood* (Berkeley: University of California Press, 1985) and Ruth Rosen, "Daughters of the Fifties," Chapter 3 of *The Second Wave* (forthcoming).

7. Sara Evans, in her *Personal Politics: The Roots of Women's Liberation in the Civil Rights Movement and the New Left* (New York: Vintage, 1980), makes these points in her analysis of the origins of the women's movement.

8. Interviews by the author with members of New York Radical Women between 1985 and 1987.

9. Amatniek, "Funeral Oration," p. 24.

10. Ibid., p. 26.

11. Ibid., p. 24.

12. Ibid., p. 26.

13. Ibid.

14. See, for example, Barbara L. Epstein, *The Politics of Domesticity* (Middletown, Connecticut: Wesleyan University Press, 1981); Ruth Bordin, *Women and Temperance: The Quest for Powerful Liberty, 1873–1900* (Philadelphia: Temple University Press, 1981); Ruth Rosen, *The Lost Sisterhood: Prostitution in America, 1900–1980* (Baltimore: Johns Hopkins University Press, 1982), just a few of the dozens of books and articles that have explored this tradition. I also thank Kathryn Sklar for providing me with part of her unpublished manuscript on the life of Florence Kelley, which eloquently describes this female political tradition in the United States. See also her article "Jane Addams's Blessings as a Peace Activist, 1914–1922, Are What Women Peace Activists Need Today," the keynote address to Women and Peace, an international conference at the University of Illinois at Urbana-Champaign, 13 March 1989. For an analysis of the trajectory of women's peace activities and ideologies in California, see Joan Jensen, "Helen Marston and the California Peace Movement, 1915–1945," *California History,* June 1988. The other major tradition of female protest that has excluded a presumption of female moral superiority has been that of American Socialist and Communist parties.

15. See, for example, Linda Schott, "The Woman's Peace Party and the Moral Basis of Women's Pacificism," in a special issue on women and peace of *Frontiers: A Journal of Women's Studies* 8 (1985), pp. 18–25; Jill Conway, "The Woman's Peace Party and the First World War," in *War and Society in North America,* ed.

J. L. Gramatstein and Robert D. Cuff (Toronto: Thomas Nelson and Sons, 1971), pp. 52–65; Barbara Steinson, "The Mother Half of Humanity: American Women in the Peace and Preparedness Movement in World War I," in *Women War and Revolution,* ed. Carol Berkin and Clara Lovett (New York: Holmes and Meier, 1980), pp. 259–84; Marie Lousie Degen, *The History of the Woman's Peace Party* (New York: Garland Publishing, 1972)

  16. Amy Swerdlow, "Ladies' Day at the Capitol: Women Strike for Peace Versus HUAC," *Feminist Studies* 8 (Fall 1982), pp. 493–521.

  17. Swerdlow, "Ladies' Day" (quoting *Newsweek,* 13 November 1961, p. 21).

  18. Amy Swerdlow, "Pure Milk, Not Poison: Women Strike for Peace and The Test Ban Treaty of 1963," paper presented to the Berkshire Conference on Women's History, Wellesley College, June 1988; Elise Boulding, *Who Are These Women?* (Ann Arbor, Michigan: Institute for Conflict Resolution, 1962).

  19. This analysis is brilliantly made in Elaine May, *Homeward Bound: American Families in the Cold War Era* (New York: Basic Books, 1988). I thank Elaine May for allowing me to read the unpublished manuscript.

  20. Swerdlow, "Ladies' Day," p. 497 (quoting "Transcript of the President's News Conference on World and Domestic Affairs," *New York Times,* 16 January 1962, p. 18).

  21. Ibid. (quoting *Science* 167 (13 March 1970), p. 1476).

  22. Ibid. (quoting *Baltimore Sun,* 29 October 1961).

  23. Swerdlow, "Pure Milk," p. 16.

  24. Swerdlow, "Ladies' Day," p. 505.

  25. Swerdlow, "Pure Milk," p. 17.

  26. Simone de Beauvoir, *The Second Sex* (New York: Vintage, 1974) and Ruth Rosen, "Reclaiming the 1970's: Feminist Intellectual History Revisited," paper presented to the Sixth Berkshire Conference on the History of Women, Smith College, 3 June 1984.

  27. Shulamith Firestone, *Dialectics of Sex,* (New York: Morrow, 1970).

  28. This shift in intellectual orientation is documented in Hester Eisenstein, *Contemporary Feminist Thought* (Boston: G. K. Hall, 1983). For the development of a women's culture, see Gayle Kimball, *Women's Culture: The Women's Renaissance of the Seventies* (New Jersey: The Scarecrow Press, 1981).

  29. Adrienne Rich, *Of Woman Born: Motherhood as Experience and Institution* (New York: W. W. Norton and Company, 1976); Carol Gilligan, "In a Different Voice: Women's Conceptions of Self and Morality," in *The Future of Difference,* ed. Hester Eisenstein and Alice Jardin (New Jersey: Rutgers University Press, 1985), pp. 274–818; Sarah Ruddick, *Maternal Thinking: Toward a Politics of Peace* (Boston: Beacon Press, 1989); Susan Griffin, *Woman and Nature: The Roaring Inside Her* (New York: Harper and Row, 1978); Carolyn Merchant, *The Death of Nature* (San Francisco: Harper and Row 1980); Evelyn Fox Keller, "Gender and Science," *Psychoanalysis and Contemporary Thought* 1:3 (1978) pp. 409–43; Mary Daly, *Gyn/Ecology: The Metaethics of Radical Feminism* (Boston: Beacon Press, 1978); Jean Baker Miller, *Toward a New Psychology of Women* (Boston: Beacon Press, 1976); Charlene Spretnak, ed., *The Politics of Women's Sprituality* (New York: Anchor Press, 1982). For the best overview of debates on the issue of difference see *The Future of Difference,* mentioned above.

30. See, for example, Catherine MacKinnon, *Feminism Unmodified: Discourses on Life and Law* (Cambridge, Mass.: Harvard University Press, 1987).

31. This is especially evident in Lynn Jones, ed. *Keeping the Peace: A Women's Peace Handbook* (London: Women's Press, 1983), which contains articles on women's groups for peace in various parts of the world.

32. For critiques of mixed movements see, for example, Birgit Brock-Utne, *Educating for Peace: A Feminist Perspective* (New York: Pergamon Press, 1985); and Alice Cook and Gwyn Kirk, eds., *Greenham Women Everywhere: Dreams, Ideas and Actions from the Women's Peace Movement* (London: South End Press, 1984), p. 44. Another of my sources was Barbara Harber (member of Livermore Action Group), interview with the author, Berkeley, California, March 1988.

33. William Droziak, "West German Protesters Blockade Unites States Bases," *Washington Post,* 2 September 1983; Hugh Mehan and John Wills, "Mend: A Nurturing Voice in the Nuclear Arms Debate," paper presented at the Institute on Global Conflict and Cooperation of the University of California conference on the discourse of the nuclear arms debate, Ballyvaughn, Ireland, 9–16 August 1987; Jones, *Keeping the Peace,* p. 4.

34. Brock-Utne, *Educating for Peace,* p. 50.

35. Marjorie Agosin and Marysa Navarros, "The Mothers of the Plaza de Mayo: A New Form of Politics in Argentina," paper presented at the Berkshire Conference on Women's History, Wellesley College, June 1988; Marjorie Agosin, "Metaphors of Female Political Ideology: The Cases of Chile and Argentina," *Women's Studies International Forum* 19 (1987) pp. 570–77.

36. Julie Wells, "An Infringement on Motherhood: South African Women's Resistance to Pass Laws," paper presented at the Berkshire Conference on Women's History, Wellesley, June 1988.

37. Brock-Utne, *Educating for Peace,* p. 47.

38. Ibid., p. 48. For a more theoretical and historical analysis of motherist campaigns, see Temma Kaplan, "Female Consciousness and Collective Action: The Barcelona Case, 1910–1918," *Signs* 3 (1981) pp. 545–66.

39. Some of the sources I found most useful for these actions and encampments are Brock-Utne, *Educating for Peace,* chap. 2; Cook and Kirk, *Greenham Women Everywhere;* Caroline Blackwood, *On the Perimeter: A Vivid Personal Report from the Front Line of the Anti-Nuclear Movement* (New York: Penguin, 1984); Tacie Dejanikus and Stella Dawson, "Women's Pentagon Action," in *Fight Back/ Feminist Resistance to Male Violence,* ed. Frederique Delacost and Felice Newman (Minneapolis: Cleis Press, 1982) pp. 282–291, 282–290; Ann Snitow, "Holding the Line at Greenham," *Mother Jones* 10 (February 1985) pp. 30–47; Grace Paley, "The Seneca Stories: Tales from the Women's Peace Encampment, *MS.,* December 1983 pp. 54–62; Mima Cataldo, Ruth Putler, Byrna Fireside, Elaine Lytel, *The Women's Encampment for a future of Peace and Justice* (Philadelphia: Temple University Press, 1987). Two collections that have important descriptive and analytic essays on these events are Cambridge Women's Peace Collective, *My Country is the Whole World: An Anthology of Women Work on Peace and War* (London: Pandora Press, 1984) and Jones, *Keeping the Peace,* especially Ynestra King's "All Is Connectedness: Scenes from the Women's Pentagon Action USA," pp. 40–64.

40. Undated poster from the Women's Pentagon Action, the Aouon Archive: An Archive of Community Political Posters, Berkeley, California. I thank Michael Rossman, the curator of this archive, for giving me access to the collection and for spending months analyzing the posters with me.

41. For pictures, slogans, and discussions of the encampments see the books and article mentioned above, n. 39.

42. Undated poster from the Women's Pentagon Action, Auoun Archive.

43. Susan Griffin, interview with the author, Berkeley, California, 30 March 1988; Irene Diamond, interview with the author, Berkeley, California, 16 March 1988; "The Artist and Natural Imagery: An Intimate Discussion of Eco-Feminism," Susan Griffin and others, San Francisco, California, 10 April 1988. It is Virginia Woolf's *Three Guineas* (London: Hogarth Press, 1937) in particular that is often quoted in articles and books on women and peace. Also see Ynestra King, "Feminism and the Revolt of Nature," *Win*, February 1983, pp. 11–15; Michael Zimmerman, "Feminism, Deep Ecology, and Environmental Ethics," *Environmental Ethics* 9:1 (Spring 1987); Karen Warren, "Feminism and Ecology: Making Connections," *Environmental Ethics* 9:1 (Spring 1987); Jim Cheney, "Eco-Feminism and Deep Ecology," *Environmental Ethics* 9 (Summer 1987).

44. Leaflet of Women's Pentagon Action reprinted in Cambridge Women's Peace Collective, *My Country is the Whole World*, p. 242.

45. Cook and Kirk, *Greenham Women Everywhere*, p. 87.

46. Cataldo et al., *Women's Encampment*, p. 29.

47. Pam McAllister, ed., *Reweaving the Web of Life: Feminism and Non-violence* (Philadelphia: New Society Publishers, 1982).

48. Participants of the Puget Sound Women's Peace Camp, *We Are Ordinary Women: A Chronicle of Puget Sound Women's Peace Camp* (Seattle: Seal Press, 1983), p. 33.

49. Poster from Women's Graphics Collective, Chicago, 1976, Aouon Archive.

50. Barbara Epstein, "Feminism and Direct Action Groups," presentation at the Conference on Gender, Science, and Technology at the University of California, Davis, 10 April 1988.

51. Poster from Amherst Mass, 8 March 1976, Aouon Archive.

53. Cook and Kirk, *Greenham Women Everywhere*, p. 126.

53. Lesley Boulton, June 1982, quoted in Cook and Kirk, *Greenham Common Everywhere*, p. 127.

54. *We Are Ordinary People*, p. 17 (see n. 48, above).

55. Cook and Kirk, *Greenham Women Everywhere*, quoting the British press; *We Are Ordinary Women*, pp. 45, 96; Cataldo et al., *The Women's Encampment*, pp. 71, 87.

56. Brenda Whisker, Jacky Bishop, Lillian Mohin, and Trish Longdon, *Breaching the Peace* (London: Only Women Press, Ltd., 1983).

57. Swerdlow, "Pure Milk," and Kaplan, "Female Consciousness," are just two of the many historical works that are currently reassessing motherist campaigns in the past. A panel was devoted to this subject at the Berkshire Conference on Women's History, Wellesley College, 7 June 1988.

58. See Swerdlow, "Pure Milk" for a statement of these arguments. For a more positive view of the Greenham project, see Ann Snitow, "Holding the Line at Greenham" *Mother Jones*, Feb/March 1985.

59. See, for example, Nancy Cott, *The Grounding of Modern Feminism* (New Haven: Yale University Press, 1987).

60. Betty Friedan, *It Changed My Life* (New York: Random House, 1976), p. 101; Alice Schwartzer, "Simone de Beavoir Talks about Sartre," *MS.*, August 1983, p. 37.

61. Suzanne Gordon, "From Earth Mother to Expert," *Nuclear Times,* May 1983; Sheila Tobias, "Toward a Feminist Analysis of Defense Spending," *Frontier* 7:2 (1985); "Women Convene Peace Summit," *New Direction for Women* 17:2 (March/April 1988); Galia Galan, "Israel's Gender Gap," paper presented at the International Congress in Women, Dublin, Ireland, Summer 1987; Marjorie Lansing, "The Gender Gap in America on the Force Dimension," Department of Political Science, Eastern Michigan University unpublished paper, 1987.

62. Brock-Utne, *Educating for Peace,* p. vi.

63. Elizabeth Addis and Nicolette Tiliacas, "Conflict, Fear and Security in the Nuclear Age: The Challenge of the Feminist Movement in Italy," *Radical America* 20 (1980), pp. 7–15.

64. Mary C. Segars, "The Catholic Bishops' Pastoral Letter on War and Peace: A Feminist Perspective," *Feminist Studies* 11 (Fall 1985), p. 632.

65. Carol Cohn, "Sex and Death in the Rational World of Defense Intellectuals," Center for Psychological Studies in the Nuclear Age, 1987, p. 34. Republished in *Science* 12:4 (1987): 685–718.

66. In addition to the Italian and Australian examples mentioned above, two feminists reconsider the presumption of female moral superiority in Michaela di Leonardo, "Review Essay: Morals, Mothers, and Militarism: Antimilitarism and Feminist Theory," *Feminist Studies* 121 (Fall, 1985), pp. 598–617 and Jean Bethke Elshtain, *Women and War* (New York: Basic Books, 1987). One very important example of women creating a feminist discourse about peace, emphasizing women's needs but not their moral superiority, is "Israel Women's Alliance Against the Occupation," unpublished paper by Dr. Lillian Moed, P.O. Box 4319, Jerusalem, Israel. Also see the range of arguments presented in Adrienne Harris and Ynestra King, eds., *Rocking the Ship of State: Toward a Feminist Peace Politics* (Boulder: Westview Press, 1989).

67. Prologue and Chapter 8 of Hannah Josephson, *Jeanette Rankin: First Lady in Congress* (1974), cited in Elaine Partnow, *The Quotable Woman* (New York: Anchor, 1978), p. 175.

12

INDOCHINESE REFUGEES:
A Challenge to America's Memory of Vietnam

JAMES W. TOLLEFSON

The only way to be human is to be human together, and the only way to survive is to survive together.

–BISHOP DESMOND TUTU

Since 1975 more than 900,000 refugees from Vietnam, Cambodia, and Laos have resettled in the United States. In 1988 and 1989, approximately 3,000 refugees continued to arrive each month, while more than 400,000 others remained in holding centers in Thailand, Malaysia, Hong Kong, Indonesia, and the Philippines.[1] Moreover, Vietnamese arrivals in first asylum camps increased dramatically during spring and early summer of 1989, with more than 2,000 per week landing in Hong Kong alone.[2]

Almost fifteen years after the end of the Vietnam War, the continuing refugee crisis in Southeast Asia and the long struggle of resettled refugees to create new homes in the United States have largely slipped from America's consciousness. Even though millions of Americans live in communities with Indochinese, most continue to rely upon stereotypes formed during the war and its tragic aftermath. To many Americans, Vietnamese remain deadly guerrillas moving silently through dense jungles at night, pitiful "boat people" washing up on beaches in leaky crafts, or "economic migrants" taking jobs from hard-working Americans; Cambodians are emaciated victims dying by the millions under the Khmer Rouge or spindly figures living forever in border encampments for long-forgotten reasons. In a less precise image, Laotians seem to be identified with the Hmong highland group known mainly for its detailed handicrafts sold in markets in urban America. During a generation of involvement with Indochina, Americans have seen Southeast Asians as creatures to be killed, pitied, or saved, but rarely as human beings.

Official analyses of the refugee problem are equally subject to simplistic thinking. Former Secretary of State George Shultz claimed that "the root cause of the refugee problem in Southeast Asia . . . is . . . the imposition of communist oppression on the people of those countries."[3] In an effort to blame Vietnam for refugees, the State Department wistfully recalled the Thieu regime in South Vietnam:

> The Thieu government was sensitive to and restrained by public opinion both at home and abroad . . . The South Vietnamese people under Thieu were generally free to travel . . . abroad without restriction . . . Since 1975, as many as 1 million refugees have fled their native homeland to escape the brutal and repressive totalitarian regime.[4]

Such simplistic statements ignore the economic and social consequences of a generation of warfare, bombing, and chemical defoliation, as well as the successful U.S. economic embargo designed to strangle the Vietnamese economy. The official version of history—that communists create refugees while Americans save them—disguises the U.S. role in creating and sustaining the ongoing refugee crisis.

Elsewhere in this volume, Michael Shafer discusses the changing images of America's Vietnam veterans as baby-killers, guilt-ridden psychopaths, and, more recently, heroes victimized by weak politicians, changes reflecting America's shifting memory of the Vietnam War. Stereotypes and simplistic interpretations of refugees which dominate U.S. rhetoric also contribute to the revision of America's memory of the Vietnam War. Unlike the changing images of veterans, however, the changing images of refugees have not contributed to reconciliation and healing.

Yet more is at stake than memory, for memory becomes history, and history is one source for current policy decisions. Thus America's images of the refugees, like its images of the veterans, have important consequences for foreign policy in Southeast Asia as well as for domestic policies that affect almost one million Southeast Asians and countless other immigrants living in the United States.

Responses to Asian Immigration

The Indochinese refugees are not the first large group of Asian immigrants to come to the United States, nor are they the first to suffer from discrimination in education, employment, housing, and health care. From 1820 until the end of the wave of immigration that took place between 1880 and 1920, the U.S. Immigration and Naturalization Service counted more than seven hundred thousand Asian immigrants, though the actual number was probably much higher.[5] Chinese immigrants were subject to particular harrassment, including special taxes in several states. In violent riots, mobs in major cities in the West burned the homes of Chinese immigrants, killing dozens. Anti-Chinese sentiment culminated in the Chinese Exclusion Act of 1882, which banned most immigration from China (though business leaders and students were still permitted to enter, as were children of Chinese-American citizens).

Such sentiments were not expressed only toward the Chinese. In 1905 the Japanese, for instance, were forced into separate classrooms in the San Francisco public schools. The formation of the Asiatic Exclusion League in 1905 further legitimized racist attitudes, which gained increasing influence on public policy in the next decade. This influence led to the Asiatic Barred Zone, a large area in Asia from which the 1917 Immigration Act banned immigrants, and the Oriental Exclusion Act of 1924, which banned all immigration from Asia, except from the Philippines, then an American colony.

Arguments against Asian immigrants were both economic and racist in character. White workers on the railroads and in the mines claimed that Chinese were willing to work for lower wages and therefore lowered the standard of living of white communities. Others complained that Asians could not be assimilated due to their race, that they had inferior moral standards, that they were criminals, or that they lacked a commitment to American democracy.[6] Most critics attacked them for being unskilled, un-Christian, and of an inferior culture, in contrast to European immigrants, who were described as skilled in crafts, committed to democratic traditions, and able to contribute their culture to the development of the New World. It is worth noting that similar criticisms were directed against immigrants from southern Europe, who were described as being inferior to northern Europeans who had arrived in the mid–nineteenth century.[7] Such hostility led to the Americanization Movement of 1890–1920, which required new immigrants to complete educational programs designed to transform them into "true Americans."

Today, critics of Indochinese immigration, as well as many State Department officials in the resettlement program, express similar views—that today's refugees present a particular threat to American culture and economic life because they are from peasant backgrounds, may have little or no education, and may not be literate.[8] Of course this fear of diversity is not limited to Southeast Asian refugees, but extends particularly to immigrants from Central and South America. The growing rejection of the principle of diversity, which for so long had been part of the myth of American immigration, is manifest most clearly in the movement to declare English the official language of the United States. The result of such fear of difference is that refugee education programs today, like those for immigrants at the turn of the century, assume that a change in the culture, values, and attitudes of Southeast Asians is the key to their successful resettlement in the United States.

Indochinese Refugees and America's Vietnam Veterans

This concern with differences between Asians and Americans is an important undercurrent in the American debate about Vietnam. It explains in part the insignificant role that Indochinese played in the American debate over the war. For policymakers as well as most concerned citizens, the people of Indochina were not important. The consequences of the war for them were largely irrelevant to American war policy. Even in the present-day discussion of the tragedy of Vietnam, Americans often forget that Southeast Asians were the real victims of the war. In 1987, on the ABC News program "Nightline," Ted Koppel began a discussion of the Soviet war in Afghanistan by asking, "Is the war in Afghanistan doing to the Soviet Union what Vietnam did to us?" Like so many discussions of the effects of the war, this question focused on America's suffering, while ignoring the millions of dead and wounded Indochinese and the awesome destruction which the American war inflicted upon their societies.

The assumption that Asians are different from Americans—despite the fact that decendents of people from Asia have been in the United States for 150 years—seemed to unite Americans who were otherwise divided by the war. Although the Vietnam War polarized the country, at the center of the argument was the feeling among both supporters and opponents of the war that those who disagreed with them had betrayed their country's ideals. Beneath the arguments over national policy and purpose was the universal concern with what it means to be an American. This concern excluded Southeast Asians from the debate over the morality of the war.

But there is another, more fundamental question: What does it mean to be human? In the historical trauma over Vietnam, this question has rarely been asked, yet the difference in perspective is profound. While the first concern encourages us to focus on the differences between Americans and Indochinese, the second focuses on our common ground.

One thing Americans and Indochinese have in common is shared suffering in the war and its aftermath, and no two groups symbolize that shared suffering more than the Indochinese refugees and America's Vietnam veterans. Le Thi, recalling the Vietnam War in an essay written in an English class at a refugee camp in the Philippines, spoke for refugees and veterans alike: "I can still remember the hot smell of war. It made me cry 'Daddy, Mommy' in the din and disorder."[9] An analysis of the refugee experience reveals striking similarities between refugees and veterans.

Life in the Refugee Camps   For all refugees, the flight from home is a shattering experience. For Vietnamese, flight usually meant (may still mean) a harrowing journey on an overcrowded boat with inadequate fuel, food, and water, across the South China Sea toward Malaysia, Hong Kong, or the Philippines. Many boats, perhaps more than half, are attacked by Thai pirates, who steal belongings, rape or kidnap girls and women, and often murder entire boatloads of refugees. Survivors may drift for weeks as their family and friends die one by one. Some survive by eating the flesh of their dead companions.

Although Vietnamese are perhaps the most well known refugees, the flight from home is no less traumatic for Laotians and Cambodians. Most refugees from Cambodia fled to Thailand after years of brutality at the hands of the Khmer Rouge. To reach the border, many crossed mountain passes by walking for days or weeks with little food. At the border, they encountered minefields and armed troops from several armies—the Vietnamese, the Khmer Rouge, the non-communist Khmer forces, and the Thais. Most reached Thailand malnourished, suffering from malaria and other diseases, and desperately in need of medical care. Laotians flee across the Mekong River or the poorly marked border between Laos and Thailand further north. Many are members of resistance groups who fought the Pathet Lao during the Vietnam War and then spent years struggling to survive after their American suppliers abandoned them. For some, reaching Thailand means the end of months, even years, of hiding from Lao government soldiers.

But arriving in one of the first asylum camps does not end the refugees' problems. For many, especially on the Thai-Cambodian border, life in the first asylum camps is life in a war zone. Some camps are shelled and occasionally attacked. Military guards steal belongings and commit more serious crimes, such as rapes, beatings, and murders with little chance that they will be disciplined. Armed gangs invade camps at night as guards retreat to safety rather than risk their lives to defend refugees. In some camps, competing groups battle for control of trade, territory and people. Even in the safest camps, refugees undergo the petty humiliations suffered by prisoners everywhere: loss of belongings, mandatory haircuts, curfews and confinement to barracks after hours, verbal and physical abuse, and lack of any due process. Commenting on his confinement in the Lantau Island camp in Hong Kong, one middle-aged man described the feeling of betrayal that remains with some refugees for many years: "It is beyond my imagination, really, that we have to flee a communist country to be detained later in . . . a concentration or closed camp . . . People in the camp are really detainees. We are treated as criminals."[10]

In their study of American soldiers in Vietnam, Brende and Parson found that these soldiers had a constant sense of having been "uprooted, transplanted and dislocated to a strange planet."[11] Similarly, the central unifying experience among Indochinese refugees is the feeling of having been suddenly and violently uprooted and then placed in a bewildering world controlled by individuals from foreign cultures. Like soldiers in the military, people in refugee camps have no control over their daily lives. Decisions about housing, food, arrival and departure, even where and when to sleep and with whom, are made by officials rather than refugees themselves. Refugees newly arrived in camps, like the American FNGs (Fucking New Guys) in Vietnam, are frantic to gather information that might aid their survival. Camps fill with rumor and tension as new arrivals struggle to overcome their anxiety by gathering information from any available source, trying to anticipate and prepare themselves for their uncertain future.

But with all the tension and uncertainty, there is also endless boredom. Nearly everyone worries constantly about family members left behind. Like the FNGs who sat for days in the heat, showing up for roll calls while waiting to be sent to their units, refugees have little to do but wait, often for years marked only by periodic denial of their resettlement appeals. As one mother with three children wrote in her English class: "I hope that when I will be in the U.S., I will feel less sad than now because I will be very busy."

Like soldiers, refugees develop ways to cope with the violence, fear, and extreme inner disorganization associated with life-threatening circumstances, long-term dislocation, and loss of autonomy. Because the struggles of refugees and veterans are so similiar, it is not surprising that their coping mechanisms are also similar. Both veterans and refugees have two initial strategies for survival, *numbing* themselves and *denying* the psychotic reality around them.

An essential tool for survival in extreme circumstances, psychic numbing is found in concentration camp survivors, soldiers, and refugees. The function of the deadening of surface emotions is to enhance the ability to act; it is a focusing of resources for the struggle at hand, as intelligence, physical strength, and will are harnessed and directed toward survival. The task is to survive today without thinking too much about tomorrow.

Most refugees, particularly those whose applications for resettlement have been repeatedly turned down, also deny their circumstances by maintaining unrealistic hopes of being resettled or reunited with their families. For many, denial becomes intensified as more and more refugees find themselves turned down by every resettlement country. As the camps gradually fill with people who have no hope of leaving, depression, tension, and violence increase; for many refugees, the camps become prisons in which they serve an endless sentence.

In such circumstances, many refugees deny the awful reality of a hopeless future and numb themselves against its pain. Yet, paradoxically, most refugees clearly understand their current situation and whenever possible act decisively to try to gain some control over it. The result is a numbed yet precisely accurate assessment of their reality. Thus Thue wrote of her life in the Philippine camp: "I'm just a Vietnamese refugee whose past was a time of great hardship and difficult decisions, whose present is crowded by emotional distress and anxiety, whose future is full of uncertainties."

There is a price for prolonged numbing and denial. Many soldiers in combat reported that they became "like the walking dead," their normal range of emotions blunted, replaced by the overwhelming imperative to remain alive through it all.[12] Refugees themselves recognize a similar consequence of years in asylum camps. One Vietnamese man described people he met in the Pulau Bidong camp in Malaysia: "Many people lived there for a long time . . . They told me that they were afraid to be a person. They became more and more withdrawn. No smiling."

Refugees who are fortunate enough to be accepted for resettlement eventually escape camp conditions, but they quickly discover, like American soldiers returning from war, that their new world in the United States is just as difficult as the one they left behind. For both refugees and veterans, the journey to America is not an end, but instead a new chapter in the struggle to survive.

Refugees in the United States   America generated a tremendous outpouring of sympathy for refugees during 1978 and 1979, but the continuing crisis in Southeast Asia and refugees' lengthy adjustment to living in the United States has led to "compassion fatigue." What official attention refugees have been given increasingly focuses on their high rate of unemployment and public assistance, much as the early attention to veterans focused on violence, drug abuse, and unemployment. Though refugees share both the trauma and the struggle of the veterans, there is little evidence that they are being welcomed as equal members of the American community.

Many combat veterans felt like strangers when they first arrived back in the United States. In his oral history of Americans in Vietnam, Mark Baker quotes one soldier, just off the plane in San Francisco, who said that sitting in the airport restaurant eating eggs was like going to Disneyland.[13] For these soldiers, it was difficult to reconcile the simultaneous realities of war in Vietnam and daily life in the United States. Those who have lived in the refugee camps of Southeast Asia also feel the contradictions between life in the camps and life in America's towns and cities. Although many Americans work hard to help resettle refugees, others have attacked Indochinese children in schools, burned their fishing boats, and vandalized their cars. For many refugees, resettlement in the United States requires a difficult psychological reorganization.

Though research on the psychological adjustment of refugees in the United States is inadequately funded, what little has been done shows that many refugees suffer post-traumatic stress disorder. Hyperalertness, extreme startle reactions, fear of the sounds of airplanes and other noises, flashbacks, and recurrent dreams are well documented.[14] Health care specialists and Indochinese community leaders are increasingly concerned about high rates of depression, paranoia, uncharacteristic aggression, and drug abuse.[15]

The disruption of family life is particularly severe, especially among those who lost family members in war or flight. Even intact families undergo great stress. Children usually learn English more quickly than their parents, and so take on major responsibility for contact with American society. Thus they gain great power even as they adopt values and patterns of behavior which the parents find offensive—particularly lack of respect for teachers and elders and loss of religion. So while children gain power, adults deeply resent their own loss of authority and the dramatic changes they seem unable to resist.

The struggle to find employment also contributes to seriously disrupted family life. Males from traditional Southeast Asian families lose prestige when they are out of work or when their wives must work to support the family. Women have formed support groups and economic cooperatives to market their crafts, deepening the conflict between traditional economic roles and the reality of life in the United States. Many adolescents take jobs to help out, often leaving school to do so. Even those in school feel pressure from American students not to speak their own language, which isolates them further as they are unable to communicate fluently either in English or their native language. As in some veterans' families, children and adolescents facing isolation at school and their child-as-parent role at home may become "symptom bearers" for the family.[16] Increasing numbers of children, unable to tolerate the pressures of disintegrating traditional families and inadequate economic resources, turn to other children for support. The result in many urban areas is an increasing number of youth gangs, especially among the thousands of Vietnamese males who were resettled as "free cases"—individuals alone without other family members.

The collapse of family structure is part of a larger breakdown in traditional culture, particularly among refugees from rural areas resettled in large American cities. In many cases, people arrived without their extended families, who had provided support and security in Southeast Asia. Religious organization also weakens, particularly among children and young adults. Yet many refugees live in areas with a high concentration of other Indochinese, who may exert pressure in the form of gossip and community censure against anyone who violates traditional community standards. Older refugees may try to reimpose religious practices, further alienating the young. Though community structures may exert traditional authority, they are largely unable to provide traditional security.[17]

The result of such economic and social pressures is an extraordinary rate of depression. In one study, 52 percent of Vietnamese refugees were found to be depressed after they reported to clinics complaining of physical symptoms such as stomach pain and headaches.[18] In counseling, Southeast Asians are often reluctant to talk directly about emotions; therefore limited Western therapeutic processes that rely on talking about one's problems are often ineffective. Some innovative programs have sought to provide psychological counseling within traditional Southeast Asian paradigms.[19]

One of the major challenges to people in these innovative programs is refugee guilt, which is a major source of psychological and social conflict. Robert Lifton, who has studied survivors of Hiroshima, concentration camps, and Vietnam combat, found that survivors feel a powerful bond with those who died and guilt for having lived.[20] Cambodians who lived through Khmer Rouge rule and Vietnamese survivors of attacks against their boats may feel contaminated by contact with evil, just as Brende and Parson found veterans who felt "vitiated by an evil presence."[21] Some of these refugees feel responsible for the deaths of others, as if their survival were made possible by those deaths, and so they come to believe that they too should have perished. They may even envy the dead. As Tran wrote about her father, who died after six years in a reeducation camp: "I hope he's resting somewhere in the sky, not to be involved in the struggle for life here any longer. Truly I say that I haven't any plans for the future. Why do I want to do? What can I do?"

For a few refugees, the feeling of being linked to evil and to death leads them to avoid intimate personal contact, and so they become further alienated, which can lead to apathy, further numbing of emotional life, and even greater fear of involvement with others. Unless this process is reversed, the result is a loss of purpose, a loss of hope, and a terrible inability to find meaning in the experiences of daily life.[22]

While veterans must reconcile their prewar vision of themselves and their country with the reality of war and their postwar feelings of betrayal and guilt, refugees must reconcile their vision of America with the reality of resettlement. Some respond by staying in their homes, afraid to go out, unsure what will happen and unable to speak English. Even those who familiarize themselves with their new city or town, find jobs, and make friends inevitably feel isolated, lonely, and depressed. Barry Stein, a noted authority on the process of adjustment, describes refugees' inner tension between fear and rage, dream and reality: "In pursuing their rose-colored expectations of their ability to recover what they have lost, refugees can become aggressive, demanding and suspicious. Behind these behaviors, though, is confusion, uncertainty, and a need for guidance." [23]

Among policymakers, there is a tendency to emphasize success stories that are not representative of refugees generally. For instance, in a "State of the Union" address, President Reagan introduced Jean Nguyen, a Vietnamese who had graduated from West Point, telling Nguyen's inspiring story of success less than ten years after leaving Vietnam. Such stories not only set an unrealistic standard that contributes to frustration among both refugees and resettlement officials, but they also serve to absolve Americans of their responsibility to provide funding for programs to aid in resettlement. If hard-working refugees become valedictorians, college graduates, and successful owners of restaurants and grocery stores, then those who are not successful must be guilty of failing to try hard enough. In this view, Americans do not need to support programs for people unwilling to help themselves.

Yet the continuing challenges facing resettled Indochinese have not overwhelmed most refugees; like the veterans, most refugees have refused to succumb to the cycle of trauma, rage, and withdrawal. In San Diego, where Vietnamese account for about 6 percent of the school population, they account for a quarter of the speakers at high school graduations. Others have started successful businesses, initiated private schools, and organized art and performance groups. Within Southeast Asian communities the thousands of successful refugees provide a source of pride and inspiration.

For many, the effort to reconstruct their lives means forming ties with other Indochinese to care for each other. Tens of thousands have moved to California and other areas where they can live with relatives and friends and rely upon them for employment. Small businesses operating with razor-thin profit margins have clustered in formerly decaying areas of San Jose, Houston, and a dozen other cities, leading to a new wave of refugee-led urban renewal. Dozens of Vietnamese newspapers, radio broadcasts, and television shows reach families from California to Washington, D.C. A committee of former refugees in San Diego has collected hundreds of thousands of dollars to fund a rescue ship that picks up refugees in the South China Sea. Like the veterans, Southeast Asians in America have sought to reconstitute their community. For a nation that seems to have lost its sense of commitment to community, the refugees offer a compelling vision of mutual cooperation and support.[24]

Images of Community and Bureaucracy

Refugees in flight, like soldiers in combat units, depended on each other for their survival. Recalling a terrifying journey to Malaysia that cost the lives of seventeen other Vietnamese, Tho Van expressed the life-saving value of community: "I had trouble and problem, but had small happiness from friends [who] shared together. I will never forget them in my life." Many refugees in the United States form new households and businesses, sharing expenses, incomes and responsibilities. Increasingly, Vietnam veterans' groups are reaching out to Southeast Asians, inviting them to their meetings, forming Scout troops for Indochinese children, and sponsoring rallies for shared political concerns. These veterans are beginning to acknowledge what they have in common with Indochinese in the United States.

Yet many Americans, especially the country's policymakers, have not been able to form connections to refugees or to welcome them into the American community, in part because America has not yet confronted its dehumanizing images of them. Significantly, the dehumanizing process has been easier to overcome with regard to the "enemy." Veterans describe North Vietnamese and National Liberation Front soldiers as good fighters, fellow warriors, as tough as the Americans; some American veterans, including former prisoners of war, have returned to Vietnam and formed bonds with their former enemies. A much more difficult task for most Americans is to give refugees back their humanity and to form connections with them. Many are from South Vietnam, whose soldiers Americans described as ineffective, corrupt, and weak. To many Americans, they lost the war, and in memory remain "slants" to this day. In the United States, Indochinese are often seen as mysterious people speaking unintelligible languages and wearing odd clothing, nameless victims of communism, faceless peasants lost in modern society, or welfare dependents draining the public coffers.

These stereotypes influence policy by justifying America's continuing power over Southeast Asians. Resettled refugees have little involvement in deciding what new arrivals must learn in special pre-entry training programs. Government officials criticize refugees for moving from state to state, claiming without evidence that they are relocating to increase their welfare benefits, when in fact they do so to reunite divided families and to reconstitute communities. The State Department complains that refugees are ungrateful and uncooperative, blames unemployment on their eagerness to be dependent on welfare, and concludes that the resettlement program has done everything it can for them.[25] Some taxpayers feel that refugees are obligated to make major life decisions in a way that meets America's budgetary needs. The resulting pressure on refugees increases enormously their sense of isolation. In large part, all of this is a result of the bureaucratization of the resettlement program.

Most bureaucracies are moved by efficiency and cost-effectiveness, and therefore evaluate their work according to technical measures which may be irrelevant to the real impact of programs. In the war, the classic bureaucratic measure of effectiveness was the body count. Though it was precise and quantifiable, it was based upon the false assumption that North Vietnam's leaders shared the standard of progress which the body count claimed to provide. Thus predictions about the outcome of the war based on the body count failed miserably, since body counts did not measure the intensity of human commitment to struggle. In 1966, Pham Van Dong asked Harrison Salisbury of the *New York Times* how long Americans would be willing to fight. "How many years would you say? Ten, twenty—what do you think about twenty?"[26] Without a national consensus about the war, twenty years was unthinkable. Instead, the U.S. government explicitly tried to avoid arousing the nation's passions. Thus Secretary of Defense Robert Macnamara boasted that "the greatest contribution Vietnam is making—right or wrong is beside the point—is that it is developing an ability to fight a limited war, to go to war without the necessity of arousing the public ire."[27] The Vietnam War showed that irrelevant measures of progress combined with ignorance of history and other cultures can lead to tragic failure of policy.

In the refugee program, the body count is the primary measure of America's commitment to refugees: how many refugees pass through processing, how many classes are offered for them, how many end up living in the United States on welfare. Little effort is made to understand the experience of being a refugee or the effects of the war on the societies of Southeast Asia. The Americans in charge do not critically examine the impact of their policies upon Indochinese, though they claim to be acting in their interests. Thus, the refugee program recapitulates the relationship between Americans and the Vietnamese in Vietnam. Though the Vietnam War showed that America can be wrong, in the refugee program Americans are once again acting as though they know what is best for the people of Southeast Asia.

This confidence in America's ability to care for Southeast Asians is ironic in light of the fact that most Americans know little about the cultures, histories, and personal lives of these refugees. For three decades, policymakers who do not speak the languages of Indochina or understand the cultures and peoples of the region have made life-and-death decisions affecting millions of Southeast Asians. Few Americans know any-thing about the process by which Vietnamese, Cambodians, and Laotians left their countries or how they ended up in towns and cities across the United States.[28] Apart from knowing that something horrible happened in Cambodia, few people know anything about events inside the coun-tries of Indochina. Teachers in schools cannot tell which of their students are Vietnamese, Cambodian, or Laotian. Most public school curricula ig-nore the history of U.S. involvement in Indochina. The U.S. educational program overseas is little known outside the small circle of Americans who work in social services, and even these people are unaware of most of what refugees are taught in those classes.

During the war, such ignorance made it difficult to understand Viet-namese perceptions of American actions. Frances Fitzgerald described the gulf between Americans and Indochinese: "For the Americans in Viet-nam it [was] difficult to . . . understand that while they saw themselves as building world order, many Vietnamese saw them merely as the pro-ducers of garbage from which they could build houses."[29] Something like this persists today in the resettlement program. While Americans see their work as redeeming tragic victims, refugees see Americans as camp guards and indifferent bureaucrats.[30]

Despite official confidence in the success of the program based on the body count, there is overwhelming evidence that the resettlement pro-gram leaves resettled refugees in the United States with long-term eco-nomic, social, and psychological problems.[31] Contrary to popular opin-ion, most refugees experience significant downward mobility by coming to the United States, as measured by their comparative economic posi-tion, the social and psychological problems they face, and/or their long-term prospects for resolving their difficulties.[32] Despite the glowing picture of America they are given in the overseas training centers, most refugees learn soon after their arrival that the reality of resettlement is frustration and unemployment, poverty and welfare, unrelieved stress, and longing for a distant homeland. Thus, like the war, the refugee pro-gram demonstrates the consequences of America's reluctance to give up its virtuous self-image. Indeed, the program reconstructs and fosters the mythic vision of virtuous America which was at the root of the war.

Some refugees adopt this vision as their own. They expect Americans to welcome them to the United States as partners from a long war. They expect coworkers to be interested in their language and culture and to be eager to help them learn English. Their faith in America mirrors that of Vietnamese who believed, right until the very end of the war, that the United States would continue to fight for them and then protect them in case of defeat. Yet while some officials and soldiers escaped in 1975, many more were left behind to face reeducation camps and economic hardship. Even today, refugees are surprised to learn that many peace activists work in overseas camps and domestic resettlement agencies, while interest groups that supported the war oppose large federal expenditures for resettlement. The images of America and Southeast Asia that were behind the war persist today in the refugee program.

Listening to Veterans and Refugees

The difficulties facing Indochinese in the United States show that prosperity is not related to virtue and that finding a home in the American community is not the simple result of bureaucracy at work. Building community and addressing the problems facing Indochinese in the United States requires that America begin to listen to all refugees—not just those who are successful.

America's refusal to listen helps to sustain simplistic analyses of resettlement, such as the belief that refugees' unemployment is due to their values and attitudes, that unemployed refugees have no one to blame but themselves, and that the bureaucracy must force refugees off public assistance for their own good. Also, refusal to listen excludes refugees from the American communities in which they live. Although their stories are remarkably similar to the stories of America's Vietnam veterans, refugees remain stigmatized by the war and its aftermath without enjoying the release of being heard and the human connections which result. Of course, some Americans in the private agencies that offer resettlement aid work generously with little or no public reward. Yet, although the United States has resettled nearly one million Indochinese and provided hundreds of millions of dollars in special resettlement aid, most Americans are not willing to see the refugees as being able to offer guidance or to participate in the process of reconciliation and healing from the war. Fewer still are willing to see the Vietnam War through the eyes of the people of Indochina.

In contrast to America's ability to ignore Southeast Asians, a great deal of media attention has been given to Vietnam veterans since the dedication of the Vietnam Veterans' Memorial in 1982. Oral histories of the war have become best-sellers, while television and film vividly depict fictionalized versions of the soldiers' experience. Veterans' groups have been organized across the country, while countless newspaper articles, television reports, books, and films focus on the veterans' experience and resettlement. Although this attention has not translated into adequate funding for health, education, and employment, it is no longer true that veterans have been abandoned to their personal isolation. This profound shift in public awareness and response reflects a growing sense of the Vietnam veterans' importance to America. Their suffering has come to represent the nation's suffering, and their reintegration into the American community symbolizes the nation's hope for healing from the war. Though the process has only just begun, the willingness to listen to veterans expresses a willingness to recover the bonds that connect those who fought with those who did not. By listening, America acknowledges that the vets are us.

In contrast, America's response to refugees, particularly among federal policymakers, has gone from generosity and concern in 1978 and 1979 to indifference, compassion fatigue, and, more recently, open hostility. Although the United States has been involved with Southeast Asian refugees since the first large refugee movements in 1954, and America's veterans and these refugees share the most intimate life-and-death experiences, for most Americans the refugees are not us.

America's response to Southeast Asian refugees represents the nation's refusal to acknowledge the awesome suffering the war inflicted upon the people of Indochina. To understand the scope of death during the war, imagine a wall forty times the size of the wall at the Vietnam Veterans' Memorial. That is the size needed to include the names of all the dead Indochinese.

The Legacy of the Refugees

Personal reconciliation and healing from the war—for both veterans and refugees—will ultimately depend not upon sympathy, but upon the resources available to them. As Americans, the veterans have personal, cultural, and political resources available for this task. Though they have often been alienated from America, they are nevertheless *of* America. They understand in a deeply personal way the rhythms of life around them. Although some veterans suffer family disruption and loss, others have the support of intact family groups, still others reconstruct new relationships. Though veterans' programs are underfunded, political action within a familiar and sympathetic political system provides hope for change. Although the Vietnam Veterans' Memorial was long overdue and President Reagan refused to attend its dedication, nevertheless it was finally built and has become one of the most visited sites in the nation's capital. All of these resources and the process of healing are made possible by the fact that the veterans are home.

Most Indochinese refugees do not have a deep, personal, or immediate understanding of the culture, the people, or the language around them. They do not have access to the same therapeutic processes as the veterans, and they experience daily the hostility of Americans who resent their presence. It is in their prospects for reconciliation and healing from the war and its aftermath that refugees differ so much from America's veterans.

But the refugees' struggle for recovery is no less important than that of the veterans. Like the vets, they have an overpowering need to belong. In order to gain their rightful place in American society, some have become politically active. Former refugees have run for city council positions in California, and the National League of Vietnamese American Voters works to increase refugees' political clout in local elections. Others have formed interest groups that lobby for programs and laws serving Indochinese communities. For instance, the National Association for Vietnamese American Education supports programs that benefit Vietnamese in schools. In California, the Vietnamese Fisherman's Association has challenged as unconstitutional federal rules that limit ownership of commercial fishing vessels to U.S. citizens, arguing that the two-hundred-year-old law should not be enforced against refugees who must wait seven years for their citizenship applications to be processed.

Increasingly, refugees are speaking up, arguing that they need material support such as emergency housing, employment opportunities and services, education, and training, but that they do not need a new identity; that they deserve safe and sanitary living conditions in camps free from humiliation; and that they have a right to make their own decisions about their lives, and to not be kept for months or years in prison-like conditions by officials who claim to be acting in their interests.

The relationship between refugees and America's Vietnam veterans is much deeper than the similarities of shared experiences and the indifferent or hostile reaction of many Americans toward their arrival in the United States. As reminders of the Vietnam war and its aftermath, they continue to raise fundamental questions: What happened in Indochina? What did America do, or fail to do, there? In what ways have America's actions since the war forced refugees to make the difficult decision to leave home? How did they survive? What do they hope to find in America? Do they want to go home? Through these questions, the refugees, like the veterans, present a deep and disturbing challenge to America's vision of itself and its changing memory of Vietnam. Until America confronts the story of the Indochinese refugees, it will miss altogether their profound understanding of the value of community, the traditional ties that guided them this far, and the hope that community provides. Nevertheless, the refugees and the veterans will continue to symbolize our common humanity. In this way, they offer America a legacy of hope.

NOTES

1. This figure includes approximately 180,000 refugees under the protection of the United Nations High Commissioner for Refugees, and roughly 250,000 "displaced persons," assisted by the UN Border Relief Operation, who are not eligible for resettlement.

2. See *Refugee Reports* 10:5 (19 May 1989), pp. 10–11.

3. Secretary of State George Shultz, statement before the Subcommittee on

278   JAMES W. TOLLEFSON

Immigration and Refugee Policy of the Senate Judiciary Committee, 17 September 1985, in *Department of State Bulletin,* November 1985, p. 21.

4. "Vietnam under Two Regimes," *Department of State Bulletin,* September 1985, p. 55.

5. David M. Reimers, *Still the Golden Door: The Third World Comes to America* (New York: Columbia University Press, 1985), p. 2.

6. For a summary of anti-Chinese actions, see Reimers, *Still the Golden Door,* pp. 4–6.

7. For a discussion of parallels between early twentieth-century attitudes toward immigration and current attitudes, see James W. Tollefson, *Alien Winds: The Reeducation of America's Indochinese Refugees* (New York: Praeger, 1989), pp. 39–60.

8. For instance, see Kathleen M. Corey, "ESL Curriculum Development in the Overseas Refugee Training Program: A Personal Account," *Passage* 2 (Spring 1986), pp. 5–11. Also see Kathleen M. Corey, "The Cultural Assimilation of Indochinese Refugees," *Passage* 2 (Winter 1986), pp. 41–43.

9. This quote and others from refugees are taken from class essays, transcripts of classes, and interviews conducted by the author at the Philippine Refugee Processing Center between 1983 and 1986.

10. Refugee interviewed in *The Camp on Lantau Island,* a documentary film produced for the United Nations High Commissioner for Refugees (Oxford, England: Oxford Ethnographic Films, 1984).

11. Joel Osler Brende and Erwin Randolph Parson, *Vietnam Veterans: The Road to Recovery* (New York: New American Library, 1985), p. 42.

12. See Brende and Parson, *Vietnam Veterans,* pp. 47–49, and Arthur Egendorf, *Healing from the War: Trauma and Transformation after Vietnam* (Boston: Shambhala, 1986), pp. 65–67.

13. Mark Baker, *Nam: The Vietnam War in the Words of the Men and Women Who Fought There* (New York: Quill, 1981), p. 278.

14. See Carolyn L. Williams and Joseph Westermeyer, eds., *Refugee Mental Health in Resettlement Countries* (Washington: Hemisphere Publishing, 1986).

15. See Joseph Westermeyer, "Migration and Psychopathology"; Keh-Ming Lin, "Psychopathology and Social Disruption in Refugees"; and Jean E. Carlin, "Child and Adolescent Refugees: Psychiatric Assessment and Treatment," all in Williams and Westermeyer, *Refugee Mental Health in Resettlement Countries.* Westermeyer estimates that 20–25 percent of all refugees are at risk of suffering disabling mental illness. The incidence of paranoia and schizophrenia among immigrants generally is as much as double that of the U.S. population. For a discussion of the consequences for refugee education, see J. Donald Cohon, Moira Lucey, Michael Paul, and Joan LeMarbre Penning, *Primary Preventive Mental Health in the ESL Classroom: A Handbook for Teachers* (New York: American Council for Nationalities Service, 1986), p. iv.

16. Brende and Parson, in *Vietnam Veterans,* discuss this phenomenon among children of veterans, pp. 148–51.

17. See Julia Menard-Warwick, "Addressing the Resettlement Needs of S. E. Asians: Three Seattle Programs" (unpublished paper, University of Washington, Department of English, 1987).

18. Elizabeth Hiok-Boon Lin, "An Exploration of Somatization Among

Southeast Asian Refugees and Immigrants in Primary Care" (M.A. thesis, University of Washington, School of Public Health and Community Medicine, 1984).

19. For details about such programs, see Susan C. Peterson, Amos S. Deinard, and Anne List, *An Annotated Bibliography on Refugee Mental Health* 2 (Minneapolis: Refugee Assistance Program, Mental Health Technical Assistance Center, University of Minnesota, 1989).

20. Robert Jay Lifton, "The Survivors of the Hiroshima Disaster and the Survivors of the Nazi Persecution," in *Massive Psychic Trauma,* ed. H. Krystal (New York: International Universities Press, 1968), pp. 168–89. Also Robert Jay Lifton, *Death in Life: Survivors of Hiroshima* (New York: Basic Books, 1967).

21. Brende and Parson, *Vietnam Veterans,* p. 126.

22. In refugee camps and in the United States, the suicide rate among Indochinese is much higher than among the U.S. population generally.

23. Barry Stein, "The Experience of Being a Refugee: Insights from the Literature," in Williams and Westermeyer, *Refugee Mental Health in Resettlement Countries,* p. 16.

24. Nguyen Ngoc Bich and Dao Thi Hoi, "The New Americans: Vietnamese Refugees in the United States," unpublished MS, 1989.

25. See Tollefson, *Alien Winds,* pp. 121–26.

26. Quoted in Harrison E. Salisbury, *Behind the Lines—Hanoi* (New York: Harper and Row, 1967), pp. 196–97.

27. Quoted in Loren Baritz, *Backfire: American Culture and the Vietnam War* (New York: Ballantine Books, 1985), pp. 319–20.

28. Similarly, virtually all accounts of returning veterans emphasize the unwillingness of family and friends to ask questions about Vietnam or to talk about soldiers' experiences there, yet the ability to talk about Vietnam is crucial for healing from the war. The importance of telling one's stories in the process of healing is examined by Egendorf, in *Healing from the War,* pp. 69–74. The role of telling one's personal stories in the process of building community is explored by M. Scott Peck, *The Different Drum: Community Making and Peace* (New York: Simon and Schuster, 1987). See "The Vietnam Combat Experience: The Human Legacy" and "Talkin' the Vietnam Blues: Vietnam Oral History and Our Popular Memory of the War," in this volume.

29. Frances Fitzgerald, *Fire in the Lake* (New York: Vintage, 1972), p. 6.

30. John Knudsen, *Boat People in Transit: Vietnamese in Refugee Camps in the Philippines, Hongkong, and Japan* (Bergen, Norway: University of Bergen Occasional Papers in Social Anthropology, no. 31, 1983).

31. For an example of official praise for the resettlement program, see James N. Purcell, Jr., "Refugee Assistance: Overseas and Domestic," address before the Subcommittee on Immigration, Refugees, and International Law of the House Judiciary Committee, 17 April 1985, in *Current Policy* 693 (Washington: Department of State, 1985). For evidence that the program is not effective, see Tollefson, *Alien Winds,* pp. 87–102.

32. *Southeast Asian Refugee Self-Sufficiency Study: Final Report* (Ann Arbor: University of Michigan, Institute for Social Research, 1985).

13

COUNTERCULTURE AND OVER-THE-COUNTER CULTURE: The 1960s and the Legacy of Protest

BARBARA TISCHLER

The idea of an American culture challenges precise definition, and raises the possibility of fruitful debate on issues of consensus and the nature of democracy. Regional, ethnic, racial, gender, and class differences lend diversity to any portrait of the national character, and efforts to define or impose "American" values or cultural patterns often confront the absence of national consensus that such efforts assume. In the 1980s, voices from the so-called new conservative perspective have claimed title to traditional American values that proponents feel need to be restored after a period of neglect and decay which presumably began in the heyday of contemporary liberalism in the 1960s. At the same time, there are calls for flexibility with respect to the variety of values that can be subsumed under the American rubric.

As we enter the 1990s the concept of national culture remains a subject for heated, often acrimonious, debate over such issues as censorship, patriotism, and individual freedom. Attempts to suppress unpopular art, the recent furor over flag burning as a form of protest, and attempts to control private behavior, all resonate with the cultural and political debates of twenty years ago. As we have seen in a previous chapter, the period of the 1960s was marked by a broad range of overlapping changes that make it possible to argue that the sixties made a difference in the lives of a significant number of Americans.[1] The nature of that difference is still a matter of serious disagreement, however. To understand the contested terrain of American culture and values in the late eighties and 1990s, it is useful to explore some of the challenges to consensus posed in the 1960s. The culture of protest that emerged then clearly had its philosophical roots in the broad spectrum of American history, but it was during the sixties that the concept of cultural, political, and artistic protest reached a wide public and bequeathed a legacy of questioning and struggle.

For many Americans the sixties connote cultural extremes, with excesses of style and substance that were shocking and exciting enough to make culture itself news from locations as far-flung as New York and San Francisco, Woodstock and Altamont. Pop art, American flag patches for torn jeans, nudity, protest music, public use of marijuana and LSD, electronic music, strobe lights, the blues and soul, long hair and short skirts, and "filthy" language were the subject of much analysis as reporters of the youth culture scene sought be au courant with "what was happening."

As we approach the end of the twentieth century, many of the manifestations of a colorful youth culture that began in a spirit of protest against the political and social status quo have become commonplace for today's young people. Children of 1960s protesters sing Beatles music, wear tie-dyed shirts, and express bemused curiosity at the activities of their elders "twenty years ago today."

Cultural commentators of the 1960s, not known for an emphasis on the long view, focused their attention on what seemed to be contemporary and avant-garde, with little reference to previous cultural vanguards. The times seemed to be changing rapidly, and popular media accounts of the newly labeled youth culture asserted that it was the young and the new that held sway over the older and more established. Even the word *establishment* had pejorative connotations for young people who mistrusted the wisdom of their elders. These were the actors on the historical stage who took as an imperative the popular warning not to trust anyone over thirty. Madison Avenue understood the importance of this emphasis on the moment as it pitched to the "Pepsi Generation" of Baby Boom children on the verge of adulthood.

The culture of the United States in the sixties can be analyzed in terms of challenges to authority and the search for a better community which could be achieved only through a struggle with established ideas and social structures. Antiestablishment movements and ideas were presumed to reject hierarchy and conformity as they challenged the legitimacy of traditional authority. When they transcended simple nihilism and rejection, antiestablishment views also represented a search for a more humane and morally correct community that would maximize individual freedom in ways that American society as then structured had not.

The rejection of America's war in Southeast Asia, which grew into a powerful if loosely-structured protest movement, emanated from this challenging of established authority and the struggle to find alternative cultural patterns. For many Americans in the 1960s, Vietnam became a symbol of misguided policy and outright betrayal, and protest against the war was a central aspect of the decade for many middle-class young Americans. The spirit and strategy of protest against the war emerged out of the struggle for civil rights and African American identity which, for many black Americans, was more important to the development of a culture of protest than the war itself. These two struggles converged, and two decades later the slogan "No More Vietnams" connotes for many Americans resistance to militarism, racism, and the politics of passivity that led the nation into its crusade against communism abroad at the expense of meaningful reform at home.

Many of the cultural patterns that define both mainstream and oppositional culture in the 1960s had been formulated in the previous decade. While it is true that much of the protest of the sixties was directed at the cultural conformity demanded by the political imperatives of the Cold War, many of the cultural rebels of the decade grew up in the standardized milieu of suburban culture, with its TV dinners and shopping centers and public schools that taught prayer and consensus values along with history and geometry.

The explosion of prosperity and consumerism that would soon become the target of sharp cultural criticism during the 1960s was the subject of popular but uncritical discussion in the previous decade. As early as 1949, Russell Lynes had written on the subject of "Highbrow, Middlebrow, and Lowbrow" for *Harper's,* and the following year *Life* published a chart based on Lynes's research, against which Americans could measure their status. For those who cared, music composed before Bach and avant-garde literature were highbrow, membership in the P.T.A. and "his and hers" bath towels were middlebrow, and the jukebox, beer, and coleslaw were decidedly lowbrow.[2]

The relatively new commercial use of television contributed to both the popularization and the trivialization of traditional cultural values. The tenor of the decade was profoundly anti-intellectual, and, in spite of the presence of some adventurous dramatic and live comedy productions, television of the 1950s was emblematic of the "vast wasteland" that FCC commissioner Newton Minnow would decry in the early 1960s. The conflicts and tensions exhibited on a typical family television show were personal ones; resolutions came not as a result of debate or rational discussion but because of the intercession of an authority figure, usually a parent, whose wisdom went unchallenged. The lives of television families were far removed from those of real Americans, even those whose affluence had brought them to the suburbs. Thus, TV represented an escape from the cares of the less-than-idyllic real world of work.

The absence of serious issues in entertainment programming coincided with political and social censorship of television. Following in the wake of *Red Channels: The Report of Communist Influence in Radio and Television,* published in 1950 by a group known as Counter-Attack, commercial sponsors responded by blacklisting the actors, writers, and announcers named as subversive. One result was a tendency toward banal and inoffensive programming, as sponsors who paid the bills were themselves driven by product sales to provide wholesome, "family" entertainment. For television producers, the need to keep sponsors happy contributed to entertainment that portrayed nuclear families in happy suburban homes with no visible bathrooms and separate beds for mom and dad, solving problems that no one off the screen really cared about.

By the mid-1960s, television offered contradictory messages to the American public. The unreality of commercials and situation comedies prevailed, but television was also the medium through which Americans learned about the civil rights movement and the Vietnam War. The nightly news presented images of police dogs and fire hoses turned on children in Birmingham, Alabama in 1963, the drama and power of Martin Luther King, Jr.'s "I Have a Dream" speech at the March on Washington in the same year, the horror of body counts in Vietnam, and the uncomfortable reality of demonstrators protesting the war and often becoming the targets of police violence. America's "television war" set the standard for future reporting, making the visual image as important as the written word for post-Vietnam generations that had never known a world without TV.[3]

From the vantage point of the political Left and the counterculture, the decade of the 1960s was a time of protest, and the art, rock music, and fads of the period represented a search for identification with a current that ran outside of the mainstream of American life. This culture of protest has retained a measure of its vitality in the late 1980s. Disarmament may have replaced the particular war in Vietnam, and acid rain may now occupy our attention as the rain of bombs from B-52s once did; nevertheless, Abbie Hoffman's exhortation to resist lives on as a legacy of political activism of the sixties.

In the 1950s, rebellious voices contributed to the adventurous spirit and experimentation of the counterculture in the following decade. A new romanticism featured lone heroes who struggled against the system and the conformity it demanded as a price for acceptance. J. D. Salinger's Holden Caufield escaped with the cry "Sleep tight, ya morons" as he looked for something better from life. The characters in Jack Kerouac's *On the Road* never struggled for change because they remained constantly in motion, never lighting on a problem long enough to engage it, let alone solve it. Ralph Ellison's invisible man played society's game on the surface while the "real" person remained insulated from engagement, challenge, or failure. These literary voices remind us of the primacy of the romantic individual who remains committed to a search for happiness. Romanticism and self-absorption remained in many of the social and cultural movements associated with the 1960s, but the politics of the period demanded a broadening of vision and purpose as art came to be perceived as existing not only for its own sake but also for the sake of society.

The culture of the Beats represented an alternative to the conformist expectations of the 1950s not only in terms of the challenges that the poets, writers, artists, and musicians posed to the conventional cultural canon, but also in terms of how the creative rebels and those who followed them in the 1960s chose to live their lives. They publicly challenged materialist values, propriety, and respectability and emphasized a spontaneity and an individuality which denied the ethos of responsibility that pervaded middle-class life in the 1950s and early sixties. Allen Ginsberg's critique of modern America in *Howl* offered no pleasant visions of suburban homes. Instead, the poet used dramatic imagery to portray the loss of "the best minds of my generation" to the god of materialism. Themes of madness, homosexuality, and drug use, while not new in Ginsberg's work, were regarded as scandalous, especially when the Whitmanesque "I" spoke so directly to young people. Even if the general public was not receptive to Ginsberg's poetic song in the fifties, by the early 1960s his work had begun to "turn on" a generation to the uses of art for powerful social commentary.[4]

The banning of *Howl* in San Francisco made Ginsberg a symbol of rebellion for artists and students throughout the sixties, but his was not a lone voice. The critiques of mainstream American society offered by Salinger and Ellison reached an educated and potentially critical audience, and lesser-known works, such as Kurt Vonnegut's *Player Piano* (written in 1952 and set in a post-industrial future), offered an alternative to the decade's message that all was right with America. These critiques, along with those of Herbert Marcuse in works like *One-Dimensional Man,* and Paul Goodman in *Growing Up Absurd,* helped to provide a philosophical underpinning for voices of protest in the 1960s.

The Beat poets and writers were joined in their quest for individual expression by musicians who also placed themselves self-consciously outside of the mainstream of public attention and acclaim. Among the musical rebel voices whose legacy informed the styles of the sixties were BeBop musicians, performers of astounding virtuosity who had challenged the aesthetic of the highly-orchestrated swing music of the 1940s and were established, by the 1950s, as experimental creative artists. They pushed instruments and voices to the limits of their physical and emotional capabilities, creating music that demanded attention and could not be used simply as background to conversation in a nightclub. Bop musicians were mainly black, young, and rebellious, and they were accorded little esteem, even by other jazz musicians. Louis Armstrong called Bop "Chinese music," indicating how far-removed from the mainstream was the Bop aesthetic that valued rhythmic drive and improvizational virtuosity over singable melody and regular meter.

The musical perspective of the Bop virtuosos, Charlie Parker, Dizzy Gillespie, Max Roach, Curly Russell, and many others, had much in common with the experimental bent of composers who utilized extended harmonies, noise, tone clusters, "prepared" instruments, non–Western melodic and harmonic structures, and electronic sound and computers to generate music. The governing idea behind musical experimentation of the early sixties was Edgard Varese's concept, articulated in the 1920s, that music was nothing more or less than organized sound. The goal for John Cage and other experimental composers working in the 1960s was to liberate music from the restraints of form, style, and critical judgment, as it was possible for *any* combination of sounds to be considered music.

The experimenters of the fifties and sixties reached a small but eager audience, often located in university communities. Indeed, much musical experimentation took place in laboratories large and small, from the Columbia-Princeton synthesizer and the electronic music studios at the University of Illinois to small rooms on small campuses equipped with little more than a Buchla or Moog synthesizer and a few tape recorders. Soon, the tape recorder, stopwatch, and speakers became integral to performances of the "new music." It is difficult to measure the impact of new ideas in musical composition on the larger public, but technical virtuosity, expanded capabilities of instruments and voices, ideas of randomness in musical structure, and a greater acceptance of environmental sounds as part of musical performance eventually appeared in the popular music of such diverse performers as Eric Clapton, Janis Joplin, and Jimi Hendrix. The idea that it was possible to liberate culture from its earlier canonical fetters, freeing audiences from the constraints of order and rationality, was clearly in the air.

In modern art, the times began to change even before the 1960s, as post–World War II individualism began to blur boundaries between artist and inspiration, painting and public. As early as 1947, the painter Jackson Pollock had strayed far from traditional artists' tools and techniques to create massive canvases that were a reflection of himself as much as they were about any particular subject. Foreshadowing one aspect of the new visual aesthetic that would turn everyday subjects and materials into "high art," Pollock used sticks, brushes, broken glass, knives, trowels, dripping paint, sand, and other unlikely implements to convert his unstretched canvases into art.

Pollock's work anticipated the "happenings" of the 1960s, in which the process of creating art was as important as the final product. Artistic happenings became multimedia events, often with audience participation. Members of the audience could paint, sing, or dance as they crossed the boundary between themselves and art. The Living Theater encouraged the blurring of distinctions between audience and performer, often creating their dramatic events from within the audience, and the San Francisco Mime Troupe brought their art to antiwar demonstrations as well as to more conventional performing situations. The happening could even involve the audience in antiwar protest, as at the Destruction in Art Symposium at New York's Judson Memorial Church in 1968. At one event, Yoko Ono's clothing was cut to shreds by audience members, in a symbolic enactment of the violation of an innocent Vietnam.[5] With the new aesthetic came questions of artistic quality that were to haunt creative experimentation of the 1960s, as canonical standards often no longer applied to works whose inspiration, materials, and technique came from unfamiliar sources.

One of the most unlikely sources for art in the early 1960s was familiar commercial culture, and it was from everyday objects that many new, soon to be called Pop, artists took their subjects as part of a rebellion against abstract expressionism. Pop artists presented a realistic, almost photographic, style that raised the same cry of "Is this art?" that had been used to denigrate the work of abstract painters. Instead of retreating from the world of commercial culture, Pop artists, according to Andy Warhol, "did images that anybody walking down Broadway would recognize in an instant—comics, picnic tables, men's trousers, celebrities, shower curtains, refrigerators, Coke bottles—all the modern things that the Abstract Expressionists tried so hard not to notice at all."[6]

But the public did notice the new images of car crashes, electric chairs, Campbell's soup cans, Marilyn Monroe, even Warhol himself, silkscreened and produced as multiples resembling film frames or photographic negatives. Even the name of Warhol's studio, the Factory, was emblematic of the spirit of detachment with which the artist approached his work. Warhol and his fellow Pop artists immersed themselves in the culture of the modern urban environment and took from it everything they could to create provocative art. While at first it was difficult to discern a political statement in the works of the Pop artists, points of connection between art and politics were provided when artists such as Claes Oldenberg, Dan Feigin, Tom Wesselmann, Roy Lichtenstein, James Rosenquist, and Robert Rauschenberg made antiwar statements on and off the canvas.

As the decade of the sixties began, there seemed to be little connection between politics and popular music. The United States was not without its musical social commentary, from the union songs of Woodie Guthrie and Hudie Leadbetter (Leadbelly) in the 1940s to the eclecticism of the

Weavers in the 1950s. The Beat gestalt welcomed not only poetry and BeBop, but also folk music. But the folk music of protest did not reach young people in the United States on AM radio stations. The rebel voice in music in the late 1950s and early 60s was that of the rock-and-roll musician whose songs began to reflect a youth culture whose values diverged from the priorities of the adult world.

Early rock-and-roll music represented a challenge to the status quo of the popular music world because it represented two previously marginal cultures, black America and young America. The phrase "rhythm and blues" denoted a particular treatment of the blues genre, one in which the blues, an integral aspect of African American musical expression in the urban environment throughout the twentieth century, was played faster and with a steady rhythmic articulation from drums and bass. This treatment turned the vocal blues into dance music that featured voices and instruments in a style that obscured the melodic twists and turns that had emanated out of the African roots of the blues. The new popular style retained little but the poetic form of the twelve-bar blues, a rhymed couplet in iambic pentameter.

> You ain't nothin' but a hound dog, just crying' all the time.
> You ain't never caught a rabbit and you ain't no friend of mine.

Remnants of the original call and response of singer and instrumentalist remained, but the ragged melodic edges and emotional content were transformed by white cover artists into music that was generally free of the sexual innuendo and double meanings of earlier blues pieces.[7] The blues continued to be sung and played, but this music remained confined to black communities until it was transformed again by British and American rock musicians in the late 1960s.

As the "black" characteristics of rhythm and blues were de-emphasized, adults worried about the sexuality (vague or explicit) in rock music lyrics and overtly sexual images cultivated by performers like Elvis Presley, which were seen as a challenge to parental norms and authority. When Presley appeared on television's "Ed Sullivan Show," he was shown to millions of American viewers from the waist up. For viewers, this only high-lighted Presley's risqué image as a sensuous, gyrating performer, dancing in tight pants as he hugged his guitar. Coming out of the country and western tradition of songs that expressed overt emotionality and performers who cultivated an outlaw image, Presley brought the music of the blues, hillbilly, and western American cultures into the mainstream of popular American music.

The rock-and-roll which emerged by the mid-1950s and remained popular throughout the following decade articulated the personal concerns of young people and contributed to the creation of a cultural form in which adults had little specific interest except to decry the moral decay of youth or to exploit the market value of music that appealed to young people. Songs about the search for the perfect, if unattainable, girl ("Chantilly Lace," "Teen Angel"); the non-conformist, and therefore attractive, boy ("He's a Rebel," "Leader of the Pack"); the angst of boy-girl relationships ("Teenager in Love," "Will You Still Love Me Tomorrow?" "Breaking Up Is Hard to Do") and the imperative of female fidelity ("Heartbreak Hotel" and "Run Around Sue" from the perspective of the jilted male, "My Boyfriend's Back" and "Soldier Boy" from the faithful female point of view), all reflected an idealized youth culture. But as much as this music seemed to baffle adults, it represented only a minimal critique of adult society. As a result, the vague sexuality and superficially rebellious quality of much rock music of the late 1950s and early 1960s, could be dismissed as relatively harmless, in spite of the occasional sermon or editorial that asserted a direct connection between this music and juvenile delinquency or worse.

Many adults smiled at the folly of their children screaming over Elvis, and they wondered why early 1960s dances like "the Twist" and "the Mashed Potato" were so popular. The argument that rock lyrics were just bad poetry was strengthened by David Susskind's derisive television reading of a song that began,

> I met him on a Monday and my heart stood still,
> Da doo run run run, da doo run run.
> Somebody told me that his name was Bill,
> Da doo run run run, da doo run run.

Its less-than-elevating lyrics notwithstanding, rock music was here to stay by the early sixties. Indeed, in its myriad forms in the following years, rock would communicate a number of the messages, from the frivolous to the near-revolutionary, to a diverse and eager young audience.

Television, the dramatic growth in the record album industry, and the emergence of FM radio as a significant source of cultural inspiration for young people encouraged three distinct but related varieties of musical expression: the so-called British invasion that pervaded not only music but fashion as well; the revival of folk music and the emergence of folk-rock as a vehicle for social commentary and protest; and the development of black American music out of the blues and gospel traditions into Motown and soul music. Audiences had long been accustomed to seeing their favorite musical performers on television, and the "Ed Sullivan Show" had helped to make Elvis Presley famous. It was not surprising that the Beatles appeared on the same program in early 1964, accompanied by much fanfare and audience screaming. Other groups, from the Dave Clark Five to Peter, Paul, and Mary, appeared before the cameras, and, by the mid-1960s, television programs such as "Shindig," "Hulla-baloo," and "Hootenanny" captured respectable week-night market shares, as sponsors discovered the value of music in appealing to a youth market. Just as important was the use of television to cover events in the musical world. From the arrival of the Beatles in this country to the per-formances of famous musicians at antiwar rallies to John Lennon and Yoko Ono's "lie-in" for peace in 1969, the cameras brought youth culture into American living rooms.

Shifts in the recording industry and in broadcasting also brought mu-sic to the forefront of the American consciousness in the 1960s. Until the middle of the decade, most music played on rock-and-roll radio stations had been pressed on 45-RPM records. Album production increased dra-matically in the 1960s, as major recording companies signed rock artists to appeal to the youth market, and as independent record producers en-tered the field. For a time, the Beatles made news with their own com-pany, Apple Records, which produced their own music and that of lesser-known musicians. The new artists and new companies created in-ventive designs for album covers, and psychedelic images in Day-Glo colors decorated music which increasingly reflected the values of ques-tioning and often rebellious youth. The release of "Sgt. Pepper's Lonely Heart's Club Band" by the Beatles and the Who's rock opera, "Tommy," showed the creativity that was emerging in "concept" albums that dis-played an integral relationship between music, lyrics, and cover design which previous albums, collections of ten or twelve unrelated songs, had not shown.

The standard AM radio format, consisting of 45-RPM records, each about two-and-a-half-minutes long, separated by commericals, commu-nity announcements, and mindless chatter, proved inappropriate for the new music, but even in the midst of some fundamental changes in broad-casting, AM radio remained popular and lucrative for sponsors and sta-tions. Fortuitously, the Federal Communications Commission changed the sound of young people's radio by administrative ruling. In an attempt to provide greater access to the airwaves for smaller, less powerful sta-tions, the FCC ruled that as of January 1, 1967 AM and FM stations owned by the same companies and bearing the same call letters would have to have different programming for at least half of the broadcast day. This new rule meant that there was a lot of air time to fill, few sponsors to fill it with commercials, and many innovative announcers and pro-grammers willing to experiment. The new format allowed announcers to play entire albums. Station breaks complied with the legal requirements, but otherwise typical AM patter rarely disrupted the music and the low-key conversation of new radio personalities (some of whom, like Murray "the K" and Scott Muni, had recently made the transition from the AM pop music band). With fewer sponsors to dictate standards for play lists, it was possible for programmers to include songs with lyrics that were more sexually explicit or were evocative of the emerging drug culture. Recording artists, attuned to both the commercial reality of AM air play and the aesthetic possibilities of recording longer songs on albums that would receive FM play, sometimes recorded two versions of the same song. For teenagers, it was possible to listen to the commercial version of The Doors' "Light My Fire" on their car's AM radio and enjoy the longer, more musically innovative version on an FM station. FM became the radio of choice for high-school and college students by 1967; programmers called their medium "underground radio," and the FM dial was the place to experience the newest and most provocative music.

Just as underground radio offered a more flexible approach to programming and aired songs that commercial sponsors would never approve for AM stations, independent writers and editors, students on college campuses and, as the Vietnam War dragged on, military personnel, developed their own "underground" press. From the *LA Free Press* and the *Berkeley Barb* to the *East Village Other* and Chicago's *Seed,* alternative newspapers printed more articles about drugs and antiwar activities than one could find in any other source. Many papers tested the limits of the First Amendment and local obscenity laws by printing articles and art work that were graphically sexual. Student papers provided alternatives to the "politics of the sandbox" that prevailed on many college campuses. GI antiwar papers with names like *FTA* (nominally *Fun, Travel, and Adventure* but more often *Fuck the Army*), *Harass the Brass,* and *Fragging Action,* thrived, although not with difficulty, on many bases. Poetry, cartoon art, and letters from individuals expressing their opposition to the war in Vietnam represented the creation of a spontaneous popular culture. Such expression was often met with local or military police harassment and the infiltration of newspaper staffs. While it could be extremely difficult to sustain a newspaper, many small groups persevered and were successful.[8] The GI antiwar papers became a critical organizing tool in the antiwar movement and they often provided articles that linked American militarism with racism and oppression, thus helping to bring together GIs with a variety of protest agendas.

While they were not at first considered a part of the counterculture, the Beatles were mildly exotic when their music was first heard here in 1963, and their arrival was accompanied by a fascination with things British. Fashion consciousness emanated for a time from London's Carnaby Street instead of from the salons of Paris; short skirts and Nehru jackets that took their "British" identity from the fact that the Beatles wore them, became all the rage. Young women teased their hair and young men grew theirs to Beatle length.

Musically, the Beatles dominated the airwaves and the pop music charts, but they were joined by groups that cultivated decidedly different images. If the Dave Clark Five at first appeared to be cut from the same cloth as the "fab four," the Rolling Stones projected a much less clean-cut, more agressive and overtly sexual image. Their music was more raucous and down to earth than that of the early Beatles, and "Satisfaction" became an anthem of youthful restlessness long before the Beatles popularized a rebellious spirit in their music. A gentler spirit pervaded the ballads of Chad and Jeremy and Peter and Gordon, while Herman's Hermits sang songs just for fun. In fashion and in music, the excitement of the youth culture penetrated the adult world of marketing; the "Twiggy look" was touted as the "mod" image of the mid-1960s and it became acceptable in many circles to wear a miniskirt or long hair. Before too long, popular Beatles songs were recorded by entertainers whose main audience was over thirty, and you could hear "I Want to Hold Your Hand" recorded by 101 Strings in the supermarket.

By the mid-1960s, a different musical genre was being rediscovered by young people and turned into an expression of countercultural values and commercial success. Folk music, never completely out of style, had experienced a revival in the 1950s, with relatively complex arrangements of traditional and contemporary songs performed by groups like the Weavers and the Kingston Trio. This music was exciting but somewhat removed from original folk sources and the causes, including labor organizing and civil rights, that had given rise to social commentary and protest in song. The civil rights movement revived religious songs like "We Shall Overcome" and "We Shall Not Be Moved" which helped to articulate the goals of the movement. American folk music reached the public in a variety of ways in the 1960s. As older singers and their music were rediscovered, contemporary performers and composers created new music using older folk music forms, and folk protest and social commentary were combined with rock music to create a popular hybrid style. Eventually, rock music itself became a vehicle for social commentary and protest.

When Bob Dylan came to New York from Hibbing, Minnesota, his music expressed the dissatisfaction of young people with many aspects of American society, ranging from government military policy ("With God on Our Side") and civil rights ("The Lonesome Death of Hattie Carroll") to the cry for change ("The Times They Are A-Changin'"). But Dylan also came to New York to find singer-composer Woody Guthrie, who spent the last years before his death from Huntington's chorea in an institution. The younger composer visited Guthrie often and found inspiration in the simple, strophic folk songs and in talking blues pieces which expressed the spirit of poor and downtrodden people during the Depression. The straightforward quality of Dylan's early narrative songs resembles the "sit down and let me tell you a story about America" quality of Guthrie's music. Even later pieces like "Subterranean Homesick Blues," with its electric instruments and rock beat (heretical to folk music purists), are like Guthrie songs in which the story is spoken as well as sung.

Tom Paxton's early sixties songs "Daily News," "What Did You Learn in School Today?" and "Standing on the Edge of Town" are all examples of contemporary social commentary in traditional musical styles. His later "Talkin' Viet Nam (Pot Luck) Blues" harkens back to Guthrie and other talking blues performers. Pete Seeger and Malvina Reynolds also wrote new songs in old styles, songs that reflected the growing dissatisfaction of many Americans, especially young people, with the state of their world. Seeger's "Where Have All the Flowers Gone?" became a classic antiwar statement and was recorded all over the world, while Reynolds's "Look What They've Done to the Rain," about the damage done to the environment, and "It Isn't Nice," about the need for direct action in the civil rights movement, were sung on college campuses all over the United States as folk music became fashionable. Phil Ochs wrote with an often satirical tone. His antiwar songs, such as "I Ain't Marchin' Anymore" and "Draft Dodger Rag," were popular, sobering, and occasionally funny; in contrast, his songs about civil rights such as "Here's to the State of Mississippi" were extraordinarily serious and angry. Arlo Guthrie adapted his father's narrative style in "Alice's Restaurant," a lengthy monologue on the Vietnam War with many memorable lines. As contemporary folk music found its causes and its voice on college campuses and in coffeehouses and small clubs, the genre found its way into record company catalogs. Relatively affluent young people chose to buy albums by all these performers, as well as Judy Collins, Joan Baez, Peter, Paul and Mary, and many others, even as they continued to purchase the music of British and American rock artists.

The folk-rock genre synthesized, to a limited extent, the social commentary of contemporary folk music with the electric instruments and percussion of rock music. Less direct in its narrative and performance style, folk-rock was softer in its approach to the listener. The Byrds' recording of Pete Seeger's "Turn, Turn, Turn" (with a text from Ecclesiastes), Judy Collins's "Both Sides Now," "Circle Game" by Buffy Saint-Marie, and Simon and Garfunkle's "Sounds of Silence" and "Dangling Conversation" are examples of this style.

Eventually, the various "sounds" of rock music were effective transmitters of protest and specific calls for social change. The Rolling Stones were among the first in the early 1960s to articulate youthful frustration, and they continued throughout the decade to express the rage of the period in pieces such as "Paint it Black," "Sympathy for the Devil," and

"Salt of the Earth." The Beatles remained eclectic and somewhat enigmatic. If the message of "Give Peace a Chance" seems to be a call for change, then "Revolution" (in its various forms on the "White Album") makes it clear that change is not to come through radical political action.

Some performers dealt with the issue of the Vietnam War directly in their music. Country Joe (McDonald) and the Fish recorded "Fixin' to Die Rag," and their performance at the Woodstock Festival in 1969 (at which two hundred thousand people in the audience were exhorted to sing louder to end the war) offered an exciting combination of the optimism of folk protest music with the sound of rock. After the murders of four students at Kent State University in May of 1970, Crosby, Stills, Nash, and Young recorded "Ohio," an angry denunciation of the government, its war policy, and the Ohio National Guard. Rock protest music has continued to thrive among contemporary musicians, who utilize the sounds of reggae, rock, and rap.

Specific denunciations of the Vietnam War and calls for social change were less common in music than allusions, veiled or specific, to the emerging drug culture. References to "mellow yellow," life "within you and without you," "turning on" and "getting high" were familiar and reflected a fascination with heightened states of consciousness. Drugs of all types were the subject of controversy, as the counterculture became increasingly identified with finding consciousness through a drug experience. In this context, Eastern musical traditions, specifically the music of the Indian subcontinent, influenced American popular music. Some college students plumbed the complexity of the sitar music of Ravi Shankar or the tabla playing of Ustad Allah Raka, while other young people listened to Beatles songs with sitar solos by George Harrison or popular rock songs with riffs played on an electric sitar, music that could be heard on AM radio. The Beatles also created unusual effects by playing tapes backwards and/or at different speeds.

Throughout the 1960s, popular rock-and-roll that eschewed a social message was generally an escape from the real world, except when the reality created in song was the social scene of teenage dating and relationships with parents. Music about surfing and cars in Hawaii or California was a real escape from reality for young people in Iowa or New York City, and the Beach Boys ("Surfin' Safari," "Fun, Fun, Fun," "Surfer Girl"), Jan and Dean ("Surf City"), and their imitators captured the imaginations of eager young AM listeners. Love songs were still in style, and songs sung by the Four Seasons ("Sherry," "Rag Doll") differed from their 1950s predecessors very little. Patriotism and adherence to traditional values were encouraged on popular radio stations in songs like "Only in America" (Jay and the Americans) and "Be True to Your School" (the Beach Boys).

As music that called critical attention to the Vietnam War began to receive air play, songs also emerged that praised American soldiers and asserted that it was un-American to dissent from government policy or traditional societal norms in style or opinion. Staff Sergeant Barry Sadler released "The Ballad of the Green Berets" in 1965, when opposition to the war was not yet widespread beyond college campuses. The song was heard frequently on AM radio and reached the top of the charts. Glenn Campbell recorded "The Universal Soldier," a paean to the American man serving his country. In direct opposition to the popularity of the hippie style, Merle Haggard recorded "I'm Just an Okie from Muskogkie," an attack on the long-haired protesters who didn't appreciate America. The airwaves and record store shelves were crowded with competing messages, some representing mainstream American views and others emerging as strands of various countercultures.

The music of African Americans made its way into the mainstream culture, and, in doing so, began to reflect the tension between the white version of the American Dream and the reality of life in black America. The blues had evolved in the country in response to the vicissitudes of a hard life; in the cities, women blues singers offered their own perspective on life in songs that expressed their joy, sorrow, sexuality, and toughness. The blues that Americans heard on recordings of the 1950s had many of its rough edges smoothed and much of the directness of its poetry submerged. Indeed, the early rock-and-roll of white cover artists sounded happy rather than soulful. Black blues artists, Chuck Berry, Muddy Waters, B.B. King, and many others, continued to record their own earthy versions of the blues that would become popular with a mainstream white audience in search of authenticity later in the decade.

The expressive music of the black churches was transformed into a popular genre known as Motown, for Detroit (the "motor city") and after Berry Gordy's record company, which brought many black groups to center stage. In a synthesis of gospel music (with its call-and-response style derived from African music), the blues, and the big-band style, the "Detroit sound" was popularized by so-called girl groups such as Diana Ross and the Supremes, the Shirelles, and the Angels, and by male groups, including the Four Tops, the Temptations, and Smokey Robinson and the Miracles. These groups sang about life and love, and their music seldom reflected the conditions in black communities which had sparked civil rights activism, urban violence, or the call for Black Power. Motown groups were popular with white audiences, and their performance style, featuring fancy hair styles, tight dresses and slick suits, and choreographed stage moves, made it clear that commercial black music was not intended to communicate a message of protest or social commentary. By the late 1960s, some popular black artists turned to a social message; for example, the Supremes sang "Love Child" (about illegitmacy) and the Temptations recorded "Cloud Nine" (with its references to heroin) and "Papa Was a Rolling Stone."

When James Brown sang "Say It Loud, I'm Black and I'm Proud," he asserted the message of black pride that was in the air. The era of civil rights marches and calls for slow reform had given way to polarization within the civil rights movement over strategies for change, and the demand for "Black Power for Black People" was heard throughout the country. At the 1968 summer Olympics in Mexico City, the awards ceremony for the 200-meter dash became a political event, as winner Tommy Smith and bronze medalist John Carlos, members of the United States Olympic team, publicly raised their fists in a Black Power salute, using the occasion of their victory to show solidarity with the cause of black nationalism in this country and throughout the world.

Assertions of black cultural uniqueness and rejection of white norms of beauty and fashion were challenges to the ethos that had told black Americans that change would come slowly and only if they stayed "in their place." Uncropped and unstraightened hair, African clothing, and the adoption of African or Muslim names sent a message to white America that black was indeed beautiful. Gil Scott Heron's 1970 recording of "The Revolution Will Not Be Televised" powerfully asserted that the commercial messages of white television culture would be inadequate for the coming of the new age of black consciousness. But these powerful messages of the strength of black culture came at a time when that culture itself was divided. Black Power appealed mainly to younger black Americans eager to demand their rights rather than ask politely for them. By the end of the 1960s, black culture was diverse and reflected the tensions of the time; wearing a dashiki or an Afro hairstyle became a political as well as a cultural expression.[9]

Fashion and style were also vehicles for expressing broader cultural dissent and specific opposition to the Vietnam War. The hippie image that included casual clothing, long hair, flowers, beads, headbands, and other accoutrements was at first an expression of individuality and rebellion against the dictates of early 1960s fashion. The spirit of cultural rebellion was also identified with specific places which connoted a bohemian image. The Haight-Ashbury neighborhood of San Francisco and New York's East Village were two such famous localities, although hippie enclaves could be found in cities across the country where young people, some of them runaways from middle-class respectability, found kindred spirits. Drugs, especially marijuana, mescaline, and LSD, flourished in a street culture which trusted those who appeared to be "hip" and held in contempt these (such as parents or the police) who represented authority.

While relatively few people under thirty actually "crashed" in the Village or the Haight, these neighborhoods symbolized the free-spirited nature of life as a hippie. The popular media focused on San Francisco and dubbed 1967 the "summer of love," as young people listened to the Doors sing "Light My Fire" and the Jefferson Airplane's "White Rabbit," the latter evoking images of drug-induced hallucinations that young people found liberating and their parents saw as threatening, "Psychedelic" became the term of the period, one that implied an expanded consciousness found through the use of drugs. Like many other facets of hippie culture, the word was soon applied to interior design, clothing, or anything else that advertisers could think of to capture the youth market which, in spite of the impoverished image of many hippies, was thriving.

If hippie culture represented a revolt from the conformity and middle-class conventionality that still predominated in American society, it also was infused with a collective spirit. Sharing, giving away food and money (as in the case of San Francisco's Diggers), smoking dope, listening to music, even sleep and sex, were all activities that could be engaged in together. Among these, listening to music, especially when the sound was accompanied by drugs, strobe lights, and other atmospheric devices, was especially important. Concert halls like Bill Graham's Fillmore in San Francisco and the Fillmore East in New York provided a forum for rock bands and the light shows that became obligatory for many performers.

In 1967, John Philips of the The Mamas and Papas organized the Monterey Pop Festival, which brought together many of the most popular musical groups of the day. This outdoor festival was an opportunity for young people to share music and the experience of being together. The festival is documented in D. A. Pennebacker's "Monterey Pop," and the release of this film allowed million of Americans to experience the music and the effect vicariously. The Woodstock Festival, in August of 1969, made famous by the news photos of nude swimmers, lovers, and drug takers, was also captured on film. Performers included Joan Baez, Jimi Hendrix (whose version of the "Star Spangled Banner" impressed some listeners with its inventiveness and technical virtuosity and horrified others because it turned the national anthem into nothing more or less than the material for musical invention), Country Joe and the Fish, and many others, some of whom used the opportunity to show their disapproval of the war in their music. The spirit was one of peace and enjoyment of the music and each other, in spite of the traffic on the way to and from Max Yasgur's farm.

The Woodstock high did not last long. In November of 1969, the Rolling Stones gave a concert at Altamont, near San Francisco. Never the nice boys of rock-and-roll, the Stones had a reputation for challenging propriety and presenting discomfiting images in their songs (their current hit was "Sympathy for the Devil"); Mick Jagger's portrayal of the embodiment of evil was charged with excitement and tension, and the presence of the Hell's Angels, who had been hired to provide security, was hardly calming. A young man who appeared to be carrying a gun was stabbed by one of the motorcyclists. The spirit of peace and love that had pervaded Woodstock was gone. The mass concert could never again be an informal, peaceful affair. After Altamont, security was as important to concert promoters as the quality of the performers.

The message of Altamont was confusing to proponents of countercultural values: music no longer brought people together to work for peace, if it ever really had; in fact, song lyrics could convey harsh realities and even inspire violence. When Charles Manson claimed to have been influenced by the Beatles' song "Helter Skelter" in his 1969 murder spree, the response was shock and horror, not only at the violence of the killings, but also at the possibility that popular music might have influenced the killer. Manson's crime seemed to vindicate critical disapproval of the youth culture. Twenty years later, the fear of a connection between violence and popular culture has been exploited by many who have proposed to label, if not actually censor, the contents of rock music and music videos.

Other cultural developments also seemed more confusing than enlightening as the 1960s drew to a close. The release of Peter Fonda's and Dennis Hopper's *Easy Rider* in 1969 brought current popular music to the silver screen, but the message of the film was anything but hopeful or redemptive. The bikers in the film, including Fonda's "Captain America," are going nowhere even before they are killed. Was "Captain America's" companion Billy's fateful line "We blew it" the final sigh of resignation for a decade that had gone sour? Even Bob Dylan seemed to be abandoning the cause of music that inspired thought and cries for reform, if not revolution. (After he abandoned his acoustic guitar and "plugged in" at the 1965 Newport Folk Festival, Dylan continued to place images in his songs that made his admirers think. His voice, never his strongest attribute, was nevertheless appropriate to the task of sending musical messages.) The release of the "John Wesley Harding" album in 1969 revealed a new Dylan, one who sang love songs and left his revolutionary message in the old acoustic guitar case. The new Dylan really could sing, but did he still have anything to say?

Many aspects of hippie garb and style that were referred to as underground or countercultural had permeated the larger youth culture as early as 1966. The "look" was appropriated and marketed by the fashion industry itself; the miniskirt became an international fashion cause célèbre, and stores everywhere began to sell mass-produced replicas of clothing that young people had originally made themselves or found in Salvation Army stores. By the late 1960s, fashion-conscious Americans could

purchase faded jeans, bell-bottom pants, jewelry, and ersatz Army surplus clothing for high prices in an attempt to "dress down." The look
and style of the counterculture had truly become, in Susan Sontag's
phrase, "over-the-counter" culture.

The Vietnam War became the most important cultural symbol in this
country from the mid-1960s until the withdrawal of American forces in
1973, as dress and style increasingly represented views on the war itself,
the government, and authority in general. Beyond the stereotypical images of hippies against the war and "straight" young people and their
parents supporting it, lay a growing consensus on the part of artists that
the war was wrong. As early as June of 1965, when the student movement was just organizing its teach-ins and massive Washington demonstrations against the war, the *New York Times* printed a full-page adver-
tisement against the American intervention in both Vietnam and the
Dominican Republic signed by five hundred painters, sculptors, writers,
editors, musicians, and theater artists, including Philip Roth, Betty
Friedan, Tony Randall, Mark Rothko, and Elie Siegmeister. Reflecting a
basic confidence in American democracy, the statement declared that
American artists "wish once more to have faith in the United States of
America. We will not remain silent in the face of our country's shame. We
call on citizens of our nation to join with us." [10]

Artists sometimes expressed their antiwar views collectively, as with
the erection of the Los Angeles Peace Tower in February of 1966. With
the aid of artists Robert Rauschenberg, William Copley, Judy Chicago
and others, more than four hundred painters from all over the United
States and Europe contributed works which were affixed to the 58-foot
structure. The mosaic effect was powerful; the tower melded the various
images and styles into a unit that included messages such as "Murder No
More" and "Make Love and Not War." The installation of the paintings
was covered by Los Angeles television stations, and the site attracted visi-
tors, some who came to sign antiwar petitions and others who threatened
to tear down the structure. When the owner of the property on which the
tower stood refused to renew the lease and no suitable home could be
found for the work, the individual paintings were sold by lottery, with
the proceeds benefitting the Los Angeles Peace Center. The collaborative
effort, more in the spirit of a mass demonstration or a rock concert than
of the isolated artist competing for individual recognition, reflected a
spirit of rebellious community inspired by the mindless authoritarianism
that the war represented to many. [11]

The war became a subject of literary debate. Joseph Heller's *Catch 22*
gained a popular following for its antiwar message, and the antiauthoritarian, surreal spirit of the period was also reflected in such works as John
Barth's *The Sot-Weed Factor,* Thomas Pynchon's *V* and *The Crying of Lot*

49, Philip Roth's *Portnoy's Complaint,* Kurt Vonnegut's *Slaughterhouse Five,* and Thomas Wolfe's *Electric Cool-aid Acid Test.* These works are not bound together by common themes but by a willingness to challenge literary, social, and political contentions. The result is a literary art that reflected the spirit of the times for a mass audience.[12] The Vietnam War and the role of the artist were the subjects of a newspaper debate between Soviet poet Yevgeny Yevtushenko and American writer John Steinbeck in July of 1966. In the *New York Times,* the poet declared that

> Some other writer's "Grapes of Wrath"
> Are still to come,
> But is it possible that yours
> Are only in the past?
> You always were able to hear
> the voice of time
> Do you hear
> From far-off Vietnam?
> Through the jungles to New York and Moscow,
> There flies
> The cry for help.
> "Mama, Mama"
> Is it not dreadful for you these nights
> When a pilot flies to bomb children,
> And perhaps
> Is carrying with him your book about Charley?
> The winter of our discontent is now . . . .[13]

The publication of the poet's attack on Steinbeck's support for the war and acceptance of the government position that Americans were fighting for a good cause made it clear that, in 1966, Americans were divided on war. Steinbeck responded in *Newsday,* noting that he was against all wars, especially the "Chinese-inspired" war in Vietnam. Steinbeck accepted the official view of Lyndon Johnson that if North Vietnam would agree to negotiate, the war would end. He implored the poet

> to use your very considerable influence on your people, your government, and on those who look to the Soviet Union for direction, to stop sending the murderous merchandise through North Vietnam to be used against the South.
>
> For my part, I will devote every resource I have to persuade my government to withdraw troops and weapons from the South, leaving only money and help for rebuilding . . . And do you know, Genya, if you could accomplish your part, my part would follow immediately and automatically. . . . the bombing would stop instantly. The guns would fall silent and our dear sons could come home. It is as simple as that, my friend, as simple as that.[14]

Steinbeck died in 1968, by which time it had become clear that finding a way out of Vietnam was anything but simple.

Visual images were important to countercultural rebellion and antiwar protest, and artists often appropriated images from popular culture for their expressions of antiwar sentiment. The peace sign was a symbol of resistance that appeared on clothing, books, luggage, buttons, bumper stickers, and anywhere else that its message against the war would fit. The use of the American flag itself as a transmitter of the antiwar message caused considerable tension between those who viewed the flag as a patriotic symbol whose alteration represented the defamation of the United States itself and those who viewed the use of the flag to protest the Vietnam War as an appropriate, even patriotic, expression of legitimate political views.

In 1967, art dealer Stephen Radich was convicted of publicly displaying an American flag that was "defiled and mutilated" (in the words of a 1903 New York state statute). At issue was the showing in Radich's gallery of a three-dimensional construction by ex-Marine artist Marc Morrell of an abstract but vaguely human figure with a penis wrapped in a tiny American flag. Three years later, as Radich continued to fight his case in court, the organizers of the People's Flag Show at New York's Judson Memorial Church were arrested and briefly detained. According to *Arts Magazine,* in its "Political Scene" column: "The opening of the show was a six-hour affair: a flag was burned in the courtyard, six dancers performed almost in the nude, and Abbie Hoffman, Kate Millet, and a representative of the Black Panthers spoke. About 250 artists and their friends were present."[15] Art and politics had indeed converged, as tempers and passions rose over the issue of whether the flag could legally or morally become a tool of the artist.[16]

As debate over the flag continued, groups espousing patriotic values and support for the Vietnam War effectively used the American flag to promulgate their own messages. Lapel pins, bumper stickers, flag decals in bags of potato chips, and the holiday display of a sixty-by-ninety-foot flag from the George Washington Bridge reinforced the "Our Flag: Love It Or Leave" message of those who opposed seeing Old Glory on bed sheets, bathing suits, and torn clothing. In the small suburb of Midlothian, Illinois, residents flew American flags twenty-four hours a day. One resident commented:

> I don't think it's political. It's the simple fact that the majority of people in the U.S. are pretty damned proud to be here. And they're tired of seeing pictures of people with beards hanging down to their navels with love beads on, pulling down the flag or urinating on it or some other damned thing. It's our flag. Thousands of guys died for it.[17]

The use of the American flag as a weapon in the cultural war over Vietnam raised the issue of the extent to which freedom of speech was a protected right. Ironically, commercialization of the flag violated its sacred status. The American flag, the peace symbol, psychedelic images, and Day-Glo colors all became part of the commercial iconography of the 1960s. By the end of the decade, as the war raged on and the society was only minimally closer to healing the wounds of its recent struggles on the road toward equality for all, those symbols could be purchased anywhere, just as it was possible to buy bell-bottom jeans, beaded jackets and headbands in Woolworth's or Sears Roebuck. As the United States entered the "Me" decade of the 1970s having raised but not resolved the conflicts of the 1960s, the counterculture in many, but not all, important respects had lost its critical edge. It had truly entered the mainstream.

While the shock value of many of the trappings of 1960s culture has diminished and the counterculture of twenty years ago has been appropriated to an extent by the consumerist main stream, the culture of protest itself has left a legacy of resistance to normative patterns that contributes to the creation of countercultural currents. It is these currents that will produce major challenges to the new status quo and constitute a real cultural legacy of the 1960s.

NOTES

1. See "Promise and Paradox: The 1960s and American Optimism" in this volume.

2. Russell Lynes, *The Tastemakers, The Shaping of American Popular Taste* (New York: Dover Publications, 1980), pp. 348–9.

3. See Michael X. Delli Carpini, "Vietnam and the Press," in this volume.

4. See Morris Dickstein's discussion of Ginsberg's importance in his *Gates of Eden: American Culture in the Sixties* (New York: Basic Books, 1977), chap. 1.

5. Edward J. Adler, "American Painting and the Vietnam War," (Ph.D. dissertation, New York University, 1985), p. 122.

6. Ibid.

7. On the issue of censorship of blues lyrics, see Carl Belz, *The Story of Rock* (New York: Harper & Row, 1969), p. 58. See also Giles Oakley, *The Devil's Music: A History of the Blues* (New York: Harvest/Harcourt, Brace, Jovanovich, 1978).

8. See Abe Peck, *Uncovering the Sixties: The Life & Times of the Underground Press* (New York: Pantheon, 1985).

9. See "Blacks and the Vietnam War," in this volume.

10. "End Your Silence," *New York Times,* 27 June 1965, p. 18.

11. See Adler, "American Painting and the Vietnam War," pp. 93–96.

12. For a more detailed discussion of literary currents and specific works, see Dickstein, *Gates of Eden.*

13. *New York Times,* 8 July 1966, p. 6.

14. John Steinbeck, "An Open Letter to Poet Yevtushenko," *Newsday,* 11 July 1966, p. 3.

15. "The Political Scene," *Arts Magazine,* December 1970/January 1971, p. 16.

16. In March of 1971, the Supreme Court split four to four on Radich's appeal, with Justice William O. Douglas abstaining. On 1 November 1973, the case was re-heard in Federal District Court in New York. See Carl R. Baldwin, "Art and the Law: The Flag in Court Again," *Art in America,* May/June 1974.

17. "Who Owns the Stars and Stripes?" *Time,* 6 July 1970, p. 14.

14

VIETNAM, IDEOLOGY, AND DOMESTIC POLITICS

MICHAEL X. DELLI CARPINI

Politics has been called the art of the possible, but a more apt description is the art of the imaginable. What we see as politically possible is largely determined by our collective political imagination. This collective imagination, or *ideology,* is shaped by a set of shared beliefs, some centuries old and others periodically added to our national consciousness.

While shared beliefs are important for a sense of national community, they also set ideological boundaries beyond which the general public never ventures. These boundaries determine both what is open to public debate and the rules of that debate. As a result, they play a key role in determining the political agenda and in making public policy. In the United States, the contours of our national consensus are shaped by the tenets of liberal democracy. Historically, however, periodic challenges to these tenets occur. While not replacing our core values, they have altered the boundaries of political debate, changing our sense of what is imaginable or possible. Vietnam was such a boundary-altering event, the effects of which are still with us.

Vietnam was the catalyst for a period of unusually intense politics, the energy of which was enough to melt the boundaries of "normal politics," but not to recast the core values of American society. As the red-hot politics of the 1960s cooled, several new ideological amalgams were formed—the new Right, neoconservatives, neoliberals, even a new New Left. While combining beliefs, strategies, and tactics in new ways, these ideologies are composed of the core values that have shaped U.S. politics since the founding.

The Roots of Ideology in the United States

Ideology is the perceptual screen through which we interpret the world and translate our thoughts into action. Since an individual's ideology evolves in part from personal experiences, one person's worldview is somewhat different from the next person's. However, people raised in the same political, economic, and social environments share experiences, cultural myths, and so on. The result is an overarching national ideology. In the United States this consensus ideology is liberal democracy.

John Locke (1632–1704) greatly influenced the framers of the U.S. Declaration of Independence and the Constitution. He also influenced Adam Smith (1723–1790), whose theory of free market capitalism shaped American economic theory and practice. For Locke, liberalism meant a respect for individual freedoms, particularly the inalienable rights to life, liberty, and the pursuit of property. Without rules, however, chaos is inevitable. To counteract this harsh reality, rights and obligations must be clarified, and laws established to assure that rights are protected and obligations met. Government's role is limited, serving mainly to assure that one person's pursuit of self interest doesn't interfere with another's inalienable rights. This system need not result in an equitable distribution of material goods; for Locke, Smith, and their American disciples, class differences were the natural consequences of differences in ability, motivation, and even divine selection. Locke's philosophy was not democratic. Except in forming and breaking the social contract, mass participation played no part in his theory. Government did consist of representatives acting in the public interest, but the selection process did not require majority input.

The role of citizen participation received increased attention in the eighteenth and early nineteenth centuries. For Jeremy Bentham (1748–1832) and James Mill (1773–1836), popular selection of representatives assured that government served the public, rather than private, interest. Both, however, doubted whether suffrage should be granted to the uneducated, the propertyless, or women.[1]

The framers of the U.S. Constitution, influenced by the writings of Locke and anticipating those of Bentham and Mill, designed a system that stressed individual freedoms and rights, the rule of law, the protection of private property, and limited, representative government. Underscored by the sensibilities and work ethic of Protestantism (especially Calvinism) and free market capitalism, the ideology of liberal democracy became institutionalized.

For over two hundred years liberal democracy has remained *the* ideology in the United States. The partisan divisions that characterize political discourse, elections, and so forth reflect different applications of liberal democracy. Liberals (in the modern sense) advocate using government to *extend* inalienable rights to less popular or disadvantaged groups, while conservatives place greater emphasis on *preserving* these rights (especially to property) for those who have already attained them. But both views revolve around interpretations, not rejections, of liberal democracy.

The liberal democratic consensus normally confines competing ideologies to the periphery of American politics, where they are either ignored or viewed with hostility. Periodically, however, movements arise that challenge this arrangement. At such moments, ideas normally considered illegitimate are afforded a more serious appraisal. Peripheral groups momentarily wield disproportionate influence, often by pointing out inconsistencies in the logic or practice of liberal democracy. Eventually these challenges are overcome or co-opted, but not before they change the nature of "legitimate" debate in significant ways. While unable to dismantle the liberal consensus, they redefine it. As a result, the meaning of left and right has changed over time. In addition, alliances between specific groups often shift, leading to unusual, if temporary, political bedfellows.

Religious communities such as the Puritans and the Society of Friends; the utopian experiments of Emerson and Thoreau; the Anti-Masons, Ku Klux Klan, and Nativists of the mid-1800s; populist and progressive movements of the late nineteenth and early twentieth century; socialist movements of the 1930s; the communist witch hunts of the 1950s— these are all, to varying degrees, examples of periodic challenges to the liberal democratic consensus.[2] So too, in ways that often draw on these earlier movements, was the New Left movement of the 1960s.

The Politics and Culture of the 1950s

Much of the cultural and political tumult of the 1960s was an extension of or a reaction to the preceding decade.[3] What were the boundaries of ideological consensus, debate, and deviance in the 1950s? Since the New Deal, limited social welfare had become a consensus issue. Democrats, influenced by democratic, progressive, and communitarian tendencies, advocated the expansion of government regulation and entitlements; Republicans were wary of these, but the days of true laissez faire economics were gone. Liberal emphasis on individualism and property remained at the core of New Deal reforms. Government programs did not challenge these tenets but, in a growing economy, simply helped guarantee them. Into the 1950s both parties remained anchored to classic liberalism, evidenced by Eisenhower's indecision, only months before being nominated for president, whether to run as a Democrat or a Republican.

The line drawn between limited social democracy and socialism or communism is seen in the cold war consensus of the 1950s. International and domestic communism were being fought, the former by way of Korea and the latter with McCarthyism. Even unions, the acceptance of which was a clear rethinking of liberal democracy, were largely anticommunist. When it came to communism, liberal beliefs in individual rights and limited government often gave way to more authoritarian tendencies.

Alternative Definitions of Left and Right   Outside of the Democratic and Republican parties, less consensual ideas were percolating. On the left were organized parties with roots reaching back to the 1860s. The League for Industrial Democracy (LID), for example, was a pro-union, anticommunist organization founded in 1905 (then called the Intercollegiate Socialist Society) by the progressive muckrakers Upton Sinclair and Jack London. The Prohibition Party, despite its emphasis on the evils of drink, was, from the 1860s, in the forefront of many populist and progressive causes (women's suffrage, black civil rights, child labor laws, and social welfare). Coming from a southern populist tradition were black organizations like the National Association for the Advancement of Colored People (NAACP), the Congress on Racial Equality (CORE), and the Southern Christian Leadership Conference (SCLC). The advent of the nuclear age led to the Committee for a Sane Nuclear Policy (SANE). Further to the left were the Communist Workers Party, the Progressive Labor Party (PLP), the Socialist Party, and the Socialist Labor Party, some with roots as far back as the Workingmen's Alliance of the 1850s, and others tied more directly to the Russian Revolution of the early twentieth century.

On the far right were conservative populism, racism, authoritarianism, and anticommunism. Building from the fundamentalist populism of the South and rural Midwest, groups like the Ku Klux Klan, experiencing its third reincarnation after the *Brown v. Board of Education* decision in 1954, and the John Birch Society, founded in 1958, preached a philosophy of white supremacy, anti-Catholicism and anticommunism. In the South, White Citizen's Councils (a middle-class version of the Klan) also developed in the 1950s.

The Rise of Middle America and Its Critics   It was not until World War II that the U.S. economy recovered from the 1929 collapse. The optimism generated by the postwar boom fed a desire for larger families. This personal decision was encouraged by the belief that more children now meant a stronger economy in the future as the number of consumers and producers increased. Corporations awarded shares of stock to employees who had babies. *Time* magazine heralded the addition of millions of new consumers. Public-service signs proclaimed "Every day 11,000 babies are born in America. This means new business, new jobs, new opportunities." A *Life* magazine cover story was titled "Kids: Built in Recession Cure."[4] The baby boom, beginning in 1944, had by 1962 resulted in an unprecedented number of young, middle-class adults.

The economic and population growth of the 1950s spurred a growth in public education, increasing the number of students attending college. The college campus served as both the fertilizer and the incubator of the student movement. College introduced the young to new ideas, traditions, and values, which demonstrated the relativity of values they had held as incontrovertible, and pointed out the inconsistencies between social norms and values taught to them as children, and those actually practiced all around them.

Higher education also provided a forum for interaction among different cultures and subcultures. Individuals who had rarely stepped outside their own subculture (a city neighborhood, a rural community, or an upper-middle-class suburb) found themsleves face to face with people literally and figuratively foreign to them. This intermingling offered new options in lifestyles and challenged the inherent logic of ideas upon which this generation was raised. College campuses became not only places to learn sciences and the liberal arts, but laboratories for personal and social experimentation. Students could try alternate lifestyles in an environment where the costs of such experimentation were minimized and in which the influx of new blood and new ideas was constant.

Ironically, many of the ideas that this largely middle-class generation was exposed to were critical of Middle America and its values. European social criticism had a great impact on the American campus in the 1950s, especially since many European intellectuals, fleeing the Nazis during World War II, emmigrated to the United States. While some of these thinkers espoused conservative ideas (for example, Joseph Schumpeter), for the most part they came from a neo-Marxist perspective that emphasized the debilitating, alienating effects of modern mass culture. Intellectual roots of this criticism included the Frankfurt school, the Eurocommunism of Gramsci, and the existentialism and nihilism of German philosophy and literature.

Among the most influential works of the period were C. Wright Mills' *The Power Elite,* David Riesman's *The Lonely Crowd,* and Eric Fromm's *The Sane Society,* each arguing that modern society was creating a generation of powerless conformists, manipulated by a loosely affiliated, vaguely conspiratorial "political-military-industrial complex." The literature and philosophy of such existentialists as Camus, Sarte, Brecht, and Pinter, as well as the nihilism of Nietsche (all of which were popular at the time) expressed a sense of alienation from and displeasure with the modern world.

This combination of politics, philosophy, sociology and literature led some to a schizophrenia between dropping out and becoming politically active. By 1953 the leaders of the "beat generation"—Jack Kerouac, Alan Ginsberg, Kenneth Rexroth—had established a rapidly spreading counterculture. While not politically active, the beats disdained social conformity and indicted Middle America for its "materialism, conformity, and mechanization leading to war."[5] Jazz, sex, drugs, and eastern mysticism all acted as stimulants to jar oneself out of the lethargy of contemporary America

While the beatnicks provided the new generation with an alternative cultural lifestyle, a number of student organizations were setting the stage for the activism of the decade to come. In the 1950s, most of these were politically amorphous (such as the National Student Organization) or were affiliated with liberal or old Left parent organizations; for example, Students for Democratic Action (the student wing of the liberal Americans for Democratic Action), Student SANE, and the Young People's Socialist League (the student arm of the Socialist Party). The campus affiliate of the League for Industrial Democracy, Students for a Democratic Society (SDS), would play a major role in the politics of the 1960s.

Student organizations were greatly restricted in their agendas by parent organizations. Neither the SDA, Student Sane, or the SDS could advocate policies or associate with organizations that had even vaguely communist connections. While their ideologies varied from the most mainstream SDA and Student Sane to the most radical YPSL, they were very much a part of the old Left. A few unaffiliated student organizations were emerging, however. The Student Peace Union's (SPU) ideological roots were in the British antinuclear peace movement. And the largely black Student Nonviolent Coordinating Committee (SNCC), while having ties to CORE, NAACP, and especially to the SCLC, refused to affiliate itself with any of them. Many of the early leaders of the radical student movement in the 1960s would come from these independent organizations.

The Early 1960s and the Formation of a New Left Agenda

Since the mid-1950s a civil rights movement in the South had attempted to win social and political equality for blacks.[6] The strategy was nonviolent but confrontational civil disobedience designed to point out racial inequities and so have them redressed by the legislatures, courts, and the public. Economic boycotts and public demonstrations were also employed. At the forefront of this movement were three groups: black religious leaders and their congregations organized through SCLC; black community leaders organized through the NAACP and CORE; and black students, mainly members of the SNCC.

Though a Southern phenomenon, the civil rights movement did draw attention in the North, especially on college campuses. Some Northern schools had chapters of SNCC and others had civil rights activists speak on campus. Encouraged by the rhetoric of John F. Kennedy's presidency, the cause caught on with idealistic students. In the summer of 1963 Northern students, both white and black, made the long "freedom ride" into the deep South, demonstrating for racial equality. While the movement had drawn some national media attention prior to the arrival of these students, the sight of white middle-class kids being beaten, hosed, attacked by dogs, and arrested by local law enforcers made the story much more "newsworthy," and so a much hotter political issue.

In exchange for their services, Northern students gained experience in political organizing, and an eye-opening lesson in the realities of power and justice in America. They also returned with a new consciousness concerning inequities in their own part of the country. Soon boycotts and demonstrations were organized in the North. Campus political groups such as the SDS translated the Southern racial issue into a national and economic one.

The SDS (known as SLID, the Student League for Industrial Democracy, until 1959), had been on college campuses for decades, though it was largely inactive. Like its parent organization (LID), it was strongly influenced by the policies of the New Deal and the cold war philosophy of Joe McCarthy, accepting the tenets of corporatism, industrialism, militarism, and anticommunism. More radical campus views came from student wings of the Socialist Labor Party (SLP) and the Communist Workers Party (CWP), or from independent organizations like Berkeley's SLATE (a campus political party) or the University of Chicago's Student Peace Union.

In the early 1960s, however, encouraged and educated by the experiences of the civil rights movement, a new generation of SDS leaders at a handful of campuses rethought the goals, strategies, and tactics of the organization. In a series of statements culminating in the 1962 Port Huron Statement, the SDS elucidated a new vision of American society, drawing on several of the historical traditions described above. Consistent with past democratic experiments, the SDS argued for a participatory society in which citizens are directly involved in all aspects of political decisions, from setting the agenda to choosing particular policies. Their model of politics was the New England town meeting. The SDS also drew on the populist tradition, emphasizing decentralized decision making and the wisdom of the common citizen.

The SDS's ideological perspective was also influenced by socialist thought. Though not advocating an end to private property (true to the populist vision, they were enamored of the yeoman/artisan image of the citizen), the SDS saw the necessary connection between economic and political equality. They advocated programs for improving the economic conditions of the poor and the working class, while diffusing the concentration of wealth of the "power elite." Finally, given its middle-class base, the SDS was also strongly influenced by the progressive tradition. A belief in the liberating power of education, and in rational and moral decision making permeated its rhetoric and agenda.

These traditions formed the raw material from which the SDS crafted its political agenda, along with the more contemporary ideas of the beat generation (with its anarchistic tendancies), the intellectual critics of Middle America and mass culture, and the civil rights movement. While often vague on details, it did articulate a political vision that was distinctive from either the liberal or radical old Left. In a stance that angered its parent organization, the SDS argued that economic gains made through a growing military establishment were morally and rationally unacceptable, as were those made at the expense of the environment or the health and safety of workers. Instead the SDS advocated a nonmilitary, noncorporatist economy; as part of this critique they argued against the growing involvement of the U.S. in Southeast Asia. They also argued that economic change was not enough, and that the good society required economic equality in conjunction with social, sexual, racial and political equality. In short, they advocated a radical transformation of society that was consistent with some liberal tenets, but that also built on more esoteric ideological strains.

This description of the SDS serves as a reasonable approximation of the New Left more generally. More socialistic and antimilitary than mainstream liberals, more capitalistic and middle-class than communists, and more decentralized, participatory, and egalitarian than either variants of the old Left, the New Left often found itself in conflict with its ideological stepparents. For example, LID viewed the Port Huron Statement as naive at best and subversive at worst, and claimed that by not specifically condemning communism, the SDS was as good as supporting the red menace. The New Left, by combining participatory democratic socialism, concern over economic and civil justice, resistance to militarism and a military economy, and social, environmental, and cultural issues, was expanding the nation's political imagination.

The initial forays off campus by the SDS had been with SNCC and the Freedom Riders. The next were into white working-class neighborhoods and black inner city ghettos of the North. Summers were spent in Oakland, Chicago, Detroit, Philadelphia, and Newark, establishing "indigenous leadership" and political agendas tailored to the particular needs of the community. These attempts (known collectively as the Economic Research and Action Project, or ERAP) uniformly failed, often leading to frustration on the part of both the students (who despite warnings hoped for more immediate, tangible results), and the community (which resented the intrusion of young outsiders spouting radical, if somewhat appealing, rhetoric for three months and then leaving to return to school). Nevertheless ERAP was part of a far-reaching strategy designed to address a number of interrelated social, economic, and political problems.

While the New Left was essentially a local, grass-roots phenomenon, its philosophic and policy orientations were not out of step with the more mainstream politics of the Kennedy administration. It was JFK, after all, who spoke of passing the political torch to a new generation of Americans, and much of his rhetoric and policy initiatives (e.g., the Peace Corps and Vista) focused on volunteerism, activism, and social conscience. The Kennedy administration also put solving the problems of racial, sexual, and economic inequality firmly on the political agenda, even if this was often more rhetorical than substantive. Initially, at least, the New Left, while perhaps a little more extreme and a little less patient than the administration, embodied much of what the administration itself exposed.

This compatability extended to the first years of the Johnson administration's Great Society. The Civil Rights and Voting Rights Acts, and the policies of the War on Poverty, while not identical to the New Left's agenda, were cut from the same ideological cloth. All this changed in 1965, however, as the war in Vietnam became a more central part of LBJ's foreign policy, and as opposition to the war became a more central part of the New Left's agenda.

The New Left and the War in Vietnam: Reform or Revolution?

Opposition to U.S. involvement in Vietnam was an early plank in the New Left's platform, but not a central one.[7] For most New Left organizations, the ultimate concern was over economic, political, and societal inequities, and the primary strategy was grass-roots organizing in off-campus communities. As U.S. involvement in Vietnam escalated, however, the war became *the* issue for the New Left.

U.S. involvement in Vietnam was both a catalyst and an emblem for the domestic political upheaval of the 1960s. For the liberal Left it raised questions about the United States' role in world affairs and whether good intentions justified such prolonged carnage. These questions eventually drove a wedge between the Democratic administration of LBJ and many of its strongest supporters. For the radical old Left Vietnam was a natural outgrowth of U.S. capitalism and imperialism, as well as a rare opportunity to have access to the national political agenda. For conservatives Vietnam was initially an example of the United States' willingness to stop the spread of communism, and eventually an example of the lack of such will. Caught as they were between liberalism and a more radical critique of liberal democratic politics, proponents of the New Left were forced by Vietnam to "choose sides."

The Emergence of Vietnam as the Defining Issue for the New Left   The earliest opposition to the Vietnam conflict came from a decentralized network of old Left organizations and students. For example, twice in 1964 the May Second Movement, consisting of representatives from the SDS, the Young People's Socialist League, the Young Socialist Alliance, and the Progressive Labor Party, as well as unaffiliated students, organized public protests around the country. This alliance argued that U.S. involvement in Vietnam was representative of a larger policy of militarism and imperialism and that universities, by supplying "managers, technicians, and apologists" for the war, were complicit in this war effort. They advocated resistance to the draft and pledged solidarity with Third World communist, socialist, and anarchist movements.

By 1965 opposition to the war was the dominant issue in student politics. In March, students and faculty at Michigan and Columbia held the first teach-ins about the war. Within a month thirty other colleges and universities followed suit. While many administration spokespersons participated (ironically providing the legitimacy needed for media attention), the message of the teach-ins was hostile to the administration's policy.

The first mass protest against the war was on April 17. The central protest was in Washington, D.C., but numerous activities around the country were coordinated with it. The march caused considerable debate within the New Left, in part because of the SDS's decision to allow groups with socialist and communist affiliations to participate. The march brought together opposition to the war from the liberal to the radical Left. Close to 25,000 people, students and nonstudents alike, marched on Washington.

Like the April march on Washington, protests in October demonstrated a surprising ability to mobilize the public, this time nationally. The demands of the protest's organizers were extreme: U.S. withdrawal from Vietnam, recognition of the NLF, and the impeachment of Johnson. As a result, they drew the administration's ire. Citing pamphlets giving ways to "beat and defeat" the draft, U.S. Attorney General Nicholas Katzenbach publicly advocated an investigation of the New Left.

The reaction to the antidraft pamphlets by the government was telling. By mid-1965, though a majority of the public still supported administration policy, it was clear that the war could become the central issue in domestic politics. The movement was being taken seriously by the administration, whose strategy was to drive a wedge between the relatively small radical leadership and its growing, largely liberal following, by redefining the debate from pro– or anti–Vietnam War to pro- or anti-America. Ironically, New Left leadership was also trying to shift the debate from the war itself to the institutions and processes that allowed it to occur.

The Factionalization of American Politics   The years 1966 and 1967 were marked by the Vietnam War's increasing dominance of the domestic political agenda. By this time the war had all but eliminated any possibility of a New Left–Democratic party alliance, despite the significant overlap in their political agendas. Ironically, the war was also dissolving the connections among groups within the New Left itself.

The rapidly expanding base of support was a mixed blessing for the New Left. A new type of member/supporter was filling the movement, slowly filtering up to leadership positions. These new radicals, accounting for 85–90 percent of SDS membership, were described by the vice president of SDS as follows:

> They are usually the younger members, freshmen and sophmores, rapidly moving into the hippy, Bobby Dylan syndrome . . . staunchly anti-intellectual and rarely read anything unless it comes from the underground press syndicate. They have never heard of C. Wright Mills or even Bob Moses, nor do they care to find out. In one sense, they have no politics . . . they turn out regularly for demonstrations. They are morally outraged about the war, cops, racism, poverty, their parents, the middle-class, and authority figures in general. They have a sense that all those things are connected somehow and that money has something to do with it. They long for community and feel their own isolation acutely, which is probably why they stick with the SDS.[8]

The changing membership led to a shift in emphasis away from the traditional focus of the Left—the poor and working classes. This shift did not sit well with black activists. The ERAP projects and the Vietnam War were the only common denominators in what was becoming two distinct movements. With the demise of ERAPs, the increasing attention to campus issues by the white New Left, and the growing frustration of black student leaders with the slow pace of tangible gains in the North, a split was inevitable. In July 1967, following the Newark and Detroit riots, the first national conference on Black Power was held in Newark. While the political views of the participants varied, it is significant that integrationists such as Roy Wilkens of the NAACP, Whitney Young, Jr. of the National Urban League, and Martin Luther King, Jr. did not attend. It was at this meeting that H. Rap Brown stated, "Black people are going to be free by any means necessary." By this time, Brown, in his position as chair of the SNCC (and despite its name), had begun to endorse violence as a means of achieving freedom and equality for blacks. At the Newark meeting, resolutions such as one calling for the establishment of a black militia to teach self-defense were passed. At meetings in which both blacks and whites participated, the tension was apparent.

During this period, the Vietnam War played a paradoxical role in domestic politics. On the one hand, the almost exclusive attention being paid to the antiwar effort by the New Left was largely responsible for its growing factionalization. On the other hand, as disputes among factions (blacks vs. whites, old Left vs. New Left vs. new New Left, liberal reformers vs. revolutionaries) and over strategy and tactics (a centralized party vs. a decentralized movement, violence vs. nonviolence, electoral politics vs. mass demonstrations vs. active resistance) increased, the one unifying theme remained opposition to the war in Vietnam. Much of this opposition focused on the draft, with almost all the various New Left groups vowing to resist the draft.[9]

Different segments of the New Left chose to resist the draft in different manners. The SDS, fearing the loss of student support if they boycotted the Selective Service examinations in May 1966, instead distributed a "counter-examination" designed to educate potential draftees about the war. At Berkeley, the Vietnam Day Committee ran an antidraft candidate for Congress (significantly, the VDC candidate lost to a less radical opponent of the war). And at numerous campuses around the country, antidraft protests took place, including attempts to prevent the sending of grades to the Selective Service and the harrasement of military recruiting tables.

As draft quotas increased in late 1966, so did antidraft activities. Growing numbers of students sought legal protection from the draft. Others opposed the draft by openly or secretively breaking the law. The SDS leadership increasingly viewed mass demonstrations and marches as counterproductive and superficial. They saw the induction center as the key battleground and the organization of antidraft unions for counseling and education as the best strategy. And, while denouncing the 2-S deferment, SDS leaders felt actions leading to surrendering those deferments would do nothing but destroy their capability to organize a larger antidraft movement.

In opposition to this approach was "the Resistance." Made up largely of students (some of whom were also members of the SDS), the Resistance believed the way to end the draft was to disrupt the system. They advocated mass demonstrations, draft-card burning or returning, and "complete and open non-cooperation with the draft." They also advocated the open surrender of 2-S deferments (including their own), thereby forcing the government to act, clogging the legal system, and causing a national furor over the draft, the war, and ultimately, the U.S. system in general.

The first public act of the Resistance was a march against the war, held in New York in May 1967, during which about 175 students burned their draft cards. The SDS did not endorse the protest. Similarly, a massive march on Washington in October 1967, organized by the National Mobilization Committee and supported by the Resistance, was not supported by the SDS national council. While some loose coordination of activities was still possible, by the end of 1967 even opposition to the war in Vietnam was not enough to keep the New Left together.

Distinguishing Reform from Revolution: Middle America against the War   The seeds for the dissolution of the New Left, sown in 1966 and 1967, took root in 1968 and 1969. Ironically, but not coincidentally, this demise coincided with the largest, most visible antiwar demonstrations, and with the legitimation of antiwar sentiments in the eyes of the loyal opposition, Middle America, and the media.[10] Suffering from continued intra- and inter-organizational fighting, the New Left became less ideologically and programatically coherent, decreased its local organizing, and increased its dramatic, uncoordinated, and violent rhetoric and actions. At the same time, government tolerance of the radical New Left decreased, leading to frequent confrontations and systematic attempts to discredit the movement. The net effect was to expand the antiwar movement while at the same time distinguishing between "legitimate" opposition that questioned the policy without questioning the system that produced it, and "illegitimate" opposition that threatened the basic institutions of liberal democracy.

Within the New Left, old cleavages became chasms and new fissures developed. Disagreements between the PLP and the SDS national council, centering on the former's desire to forge a working class–student alliance and the latter's interest in campus and antiwar activities, led some local chapters to support the national council's "Ten Days That Shook the Empire" (a period of disruptive protests ending in a student strike in April 1968), some to support the PLP's program to educate students on working-class issues and form a revolutionary party, and others to simply go their own way.

New groups, some rising from the ashes of failed organizations or SDS chapters, others coming to national prominence after years of local notoriety, began to proliferate. The Black Panther Party, a local Oakland organization advocating policies such as the arming of blacks to protect themselves from white brutality, exemption of blacks from military service, and comprehensive welfare, had existed since 1966. In 1967 it gained brief national exposure when twenty-six Black Panthers, toting loaded guns, walked into a meeting of the California State Legislature in the hopes of reading a political statement. They were also known for their practice of following the police in Oakland (again armed), acting as a rather unusual neighborhood watch group. In 1968 the Black Panthers became a more national phenomenon, rivaling the SNCC as the most visible Black Power organization. After an aborted attempt to merge, the SNCC, split over whether to endorse the Panthers' policies and tactics, gradually disintegrated, leaving the Black Panthers as *the* black militant organization. The SDS national council, in an attempt to reach out to nonstudent radical movements, endorsed the Panthers, thereby further alienating their less radical members, who saw the Panthers as too violent, and the PLP, who saw them as undisciplined and unprogramatic.

In this period many women began to formally disassociate themselves with the male New Left, forming their own radical feminist organizations. Since Martin Luther King, Jr.'s reference to "the sons" of former slaves and slave-owners, the status of women in the New Left had been precarious. Despite their critical role in the New Left, women were consistently derided, even pelted with tomatoes, when issues of sexism were raised within both SDS and SNCC. Stokely Carmichael's infamous statement, "The only position for women in SNCC is prone," reflected the implicit attitude of much of the male New Left. By 1966 and with the formation of the National Organization for Women (NOW), a viable middle-class women's movement had evolved, and by 1967 radical feminists were breaking away from both this liberal movement and the New Left. As the New Left self-destructed in the late sixties, the feminist movement emerged as one of the few viable remnants to survive, indeed to thrive, in the seventies and beyond.[11]

Meanwhile, campus protests were taking on the look of guerrilla warfare, though often occurring spontaneously, with little formal direction or strategy. Even campuses with few organized New Left groups were still vulnerable to disruption. In April 1968, for example, Columbia SDS, boasting fewer than 150 members, occupied several buildings for a week in a demonstration that ended with police clearing the campus, arresting 700 students and injuring another 148.

The increasingly confrontational nature of campus protests was forcing people to choose between revolution and reform, between violence and nonviolence, between governance and anarchy. In the first five months of 1968, ten bombings or burnings occurred on campuses, the first concerted use of violence by the student Left. The last three months of that year had forty-one bombings and cases of arson on college campuses. Both the Black Panther and the Progressive Labor parties endorsed at least the rhetoric of violent revolution, with the Panthers involved in several shootouts with the police. The SDS, the third national force of the Left, was as usual split on this issue, with a majority still favoring peaceful protest but a growing minority pushing more strongly for physical confrontation. Increasingly, however, the ideological and strategic battles between the SDS national council, the PLP, and the Black Panther party were being fought exclusively among a small and shrinking number of leaders—mass membership was declining and mass support was becoming almost nonexistant.

Meanwhile, mass support was increasing for the more moderate elements of the antiwar movement. The Tet offensive crushed any hopes for a quick end to the war. While the New Left had been protesting the war since 1963 on the grounds that it was immoral and symptomatic of more fundamental weaknesses in the U.S. system, this new mass protest had more pragmatic concerns—the inability of the U.S. to win the war quickly and the uncertain benefits to be reaped from the very high and visible costs in American lives. Whether the issue was morality or winnability, the war was viewed as an isolated bad policy and not as symptomatic of imperialism or capitalism or any of the other evils attributed to the U.S. by more radical protestors.

The Tet offensive also raised doubts among the loyal opposition and the media. Leaders of the Democratic and Republican parties in Congress spoke out against the war. Returning vets refused their medals and organized against the war. Dissident administration officials began to question the war openly. Newspaper editorials and television commentaries spoke of the "bloody stalemate in Vietnam." Prior to 1968, such concern was limited to isolated and sporadic voices, seldom taken seriously and relatively easy to silence or explain away. Now they were a growing chorus. By the end of March 1968, when LBJ announced his decision to not run for reelection and his desire to talk about peace, it was clear that the U.S. was on its way out of Vietnam.

The last large-scale gasp of the radical Left was the protest of the Democratic Convention in August of 1968. The SDS, the Resistance, the National Mobilization Committee, and the newly formed Yippie Party came together to protest the war and force the Democratic party to address the issue. The emergence of the yippies was symptomatic of the new turn the Left had taken, now representing as much a cultural as a political movement, and fully immersed in media-event politics. It also shows the anarchistic, nihilistic turn of a large part of the movement. According to Abbie Hoffman:

What we are for, quite simply, is a total revolution . . . that old system is dying all around us and we joyously come out in the streets to dance on its grave. With our free stores, liberated buildings, communes, people's parks, dope, free bodies and our music, we'll build our society in the vacant lots of the old and we'll do it by any means necessary. Right on!

And according to fellow yippie Jerry Rubin:

People are always asking us "What's your program?" I hand them a Mets scorecard. Or I tell them to check the yellow pages. "Our program's there." FUCK PROGRAMS! The goal of revolution is to abolish programs and turn spectators into actors. It's a do-it-yourself revolution, and we'll work out the future as we go.[12]

The radical Left, defined on one side by the PLP and on the other by the yippies, was self-destructing. Chicago convinced most of the SDS leadership that confrontation in the streets was unavoidable (one person was shot to death by police, over 100 protestors ended up in hospitals, over 600 were treated by medical centers, and at least another 600 nursed their own wounds). Once capable of attracting a mass following, the student movement was now repelling liberal students and nonstudents back to mainstream society. And mainstream society, in the form of the "legitimate" antiwar movement, welcomed them with open arms.

The confrontation between the antiwar movement and the Nixon administration between 1969 and 1972 was often dramatic. The year 1969 is memorable for three things: the inaguration of Nixon in January; the last, self-destructive national meeting of the SDS in June; and the massive, nation-wide Moratorium in October. In 1969 "the longest and most violent student strike in American history" was held at San Francisco State, lasting four and a half months and resulting in 700 arrests. At Cornell, black students armed with rifles took over a campus building. At Santa Barbara a custodian was killed by a bomb planted by protestors at the faculty club. At Berkeley police fired into a crowd of demonstrators, killing one and injuring at least 100 others; another student was killed by police at North Carolina Agricultural and Mechanical School. Two Black Panthers were killed, though possibly by a rival black group. Protests occurred on over 300 campuses (nearly two a day), involving as many as a third of the nation's students. One in five protests involved bombings, fires, or destruction of property; one in four involved strikes or building takeovers; and one in four involved the disruption of classes and college functions. In all there were eighty-four bombings and acts of arson on college campuses in the first six months of 1969, and another twenty-seven bombings or bombing attempts in high schools.

Off-campus confrontation also increased. Protests by veterans and by active military personnel became common, as did those in the churches, ghettos and workplaces of Detroit, Chicago, and New York. In the first half of 1969, ten bombings that were associated with radical activities occurred off college campuses.

With this war between radicals and police raging as a backdrop, mass demonstrations like those in April, which drew 150,000 people in over fifty cities, came close to defining the political center in the United States. Still these marches, while drawing support from Middle America, were not being run by it. More to the point, they were increasingly not being run by anyone. The SDS national council no longer commanded the loyalty of its own members, let alone the unaffiliated protesters. In June, at a poorly attended and contentious meeting, the national council and the PLP broke ranks, each claiming official control of the SDS. By this time, however, the point was moot; the SDS was no longer a national or local force. The radical leadership of the SDS (in particular Bernadette Dohrn and Mark Rudd) formed the Weathermen, an organization committed to the use of violence in the cause of revolution.

In October 1969 the Moratorium, the largest of the antiwar protests, took place. Organized by former members of Eugene McCarthy's campaign staff, it represented the left wing of mainstream politics. More radical groups had no formal role in this demonstration. The Moratorium represented a turning point at which the legitimate Left took the mantle of the antiwar movement. This, of course, made the movement more dangerous to the Nixon administration since it now included a sizable, well-heeled portion of the public. It also, however, made the movement less dangerous to the political system in general. The issue was now clearly and simply the involvement of U.S. troops in Vietnam. To the extent that U.S. troops were withdrawn and the war was fought by the South Vietnamese, the antiwar movement was content.

After 1969, radical politics continued to follow a now familiar pattern: sporadic, often violent confrontations between students and authorities; bombings, arson, and the destruction of property (there were over 170 bombings in the 1969–70 academic year); a growing distinction between legitimate and illegitimate protests. Occasionally even the administration found itself outside the new consensus, as with the illegal bombings of Cambodia in 1969, the invasion of Cambodia in 1970 (and the subsequent confrontations between students, police, and the National Guard which ended in six students being killed at Kent State and Jackson State), and the invasion of Laos in 1971.

However, as long as Vietnamization and troop withdrawal continued, mainstream demonstrations were more nostalgic than politically charged. With the granting of the vote to eighteen-year-olds, the opening of the Democratic party to blacks, young people, and women, and the failed campaign of George McGovern, the New Left was, for all intents and purposes, co-opted by mainstream channels of electoral politics. By the end of U.S. involvement in Vietnam the New Left as an alternative, radical force was consigned to the same minority status as the old Left. The uncovering of Watergate and the eventual resignation of Nixon symbolized both the triumph of liberal democracy and a final trophy for the radical New Left.

What about the Right?   This essay has focused on the New Left for obvious reasons—during the Vietnam years it represented the most visible, organized, and far-reaching challenge to the liberal democratic consensus. It was the political movement most immediately and profoundly affected by Vietnam. The New Left grew from a political philosophy advocated by a handful of students on a few college campuses to a major influence in American politics because of its opposition to the war.

Because the Right (in its various guises) supported the war, and because fighting in Vietnam was U. S. policy for most of the decade, the radical Right could not capture the attention of America the way the New Left did. In addition, because the New Left was most closely identified with young, white, middle-class America, it was easier for it to draw mainstream attention than it was for the older, less educated, more rural or working-class supporters of the populist Right.

As a result, during the sixties the Right remained reactionary rather than instigatory, responding to challenges raised by the New Left rather than articulating a coherent philosphy of its own. Most of the decade was spent trying to hold the line: to prevent the integration of the South and the de facto enfranchisement of blacks; to prevent the national government and the liberal establishment from further imposing its will on local communities; to preserve religious, family, and ethnic traditions they saw being chipped away by the courts, the legislatures, and the New Left. To preserve "our way of life" from the threat of communism by fighting the red menace at home and abroad (remember that the decade of the 1960s opened with the continued hearings of the House Un-American Activities Committee). In the early 1950s these views were all part of the American consensus. A decade later, they were all under fire.

As the New Left grew, so too did conservative reactions to it. With the rise of the civil rights movement came a rise in Klan activity. As opposition to the war grew, a conservative backlash developed. It too had its radical organizations, such as the John Birch Society. It too had its undisciplined supporters, exemplified by the spontaneous actions of Northern hard hats. And it too had its mainstream spokespeople, like Barry Goldwater in 1964, George Wallace in 1968, and Spiro Agnew in the 1970s. In many ways the populist Right was also co-opted, having its least radical reforms accepted by the Republican party in 1964 and 1968, but finding its more radical suggestions about segregation, prayer in schools, and escalating the war effort dismissed. And yet in every instance, for the reasons noted above, the populist Right was less of a force than the New Left. The 1960s was the decade of the Left in part because the 1950s consensus had been dominated by the Right.

The Political Legacies of Vietnam: Contemporary Policies and Ideologies

What, then, has been the lasting impact of the Vietnam era on domestic politics? The liberal democratic consensus, challenged by at least part of the New Left in the 1960s, remains essentially intact; protection of individual rights within the context of a propertied, class society remains the underlying norm, and the periodic election of representatives remains the single most prevalent form of citizen participation. To be sure, as with other periods of political conflict, the 1960s helped engrain discrete beliefs that are inconsistent with liberal democracy into the public psyche, but most of these are the reemergence of tendancies that can be found throughout U.S. history, and are not distinct to the Vietnam era itself.

The Vietnam experience appears to have had a more lasting impact on the ideological coalitions that form within this liberal democratic consensus. While the terms liberal and conservative have always been oversimplifications of the various factions in America, they have usually served to capture something of the basic cleavages that exist during the long periods of "normal politics." Today, over twenty years after the domestic fray discussed in this chapter peaked, one still senses a fragmentation within both the Left and Right in the United States. This fragmentation is found in the ideological rhetoric, as well as in the policies and agendas, of contemporary domestic politics.

The Left in America   Prior to the 1960s, the Left in America was defined by its stand on economic and social welfare issues, and by its coalition of supporters. This old Left advocated national government programs that stimulated the economy, supported unions, and provided jobs when possible and unemployment insurance and welfare for those unable to find work or no longer part of the work force. This emphasis on jobs and social welfare was the heart of the Democratic party from 1932 until the early 1960s, and enabled the Democrats to count on the support of blue-collar workers, union members, urban blacks, and the poor. Socialists and communists, also emphasizing economic and social welfare issues but advocating much more radical programs of government intervention, equalization of wealth, and nationalization of industry, played a very marginal role in this mainstream agenda (though it was in part through their efforts in the early 1930s that the Democratic party developed its moderate variant of the welfare state).

First through the civil rights movement, then through the student movement, and finally through the women's movement, the Left in America was expanded and altered. These movements advocated economic justice for the poor and the working class, and so both were firmly in the old Left tradition. They also found early support within the Democratic party. But all three added new concerns and strategies that went beyond the old Left's version of the liberal consensus.

The Vietnam War opened the way for this New Left to become a more visible force in America; it served as a magnet for attracting those with diverse grievances and goals, and it became a mercurial symbol, representing what was wrong with American politics and society. In the end, however, differences among the various groups opposed to the war were too great for the formation of a stable leftist coalition. Instead, the war became the catalyst for exploding the Left into a myriad of more distinct movements.

The New Left did briefly control the Democratic party. Due to internal reforms begun at the tense, often violent 1968 convention, the party opened up in an unprecedented fashion to blacks, young people, and women. It also decentralized its delegate selection process, giving local voices more say. The result was the primary success of George McGovern, the only New Left candidate ever nominated for the presidency. His platform and early rhetoric reflected the agenda of the New Left as it had evolved by 1972: an end to U.S. involvement in Vietnam; cuts in the defense budget; support for civil rights (which now included women and gays as well as blacks); greater tolerance of behaviors that cut against the grain of traditional morality (premarital sex, homosexuality, marijuana use); greater emphasis on quality of life in the workplace; and protection of the environment. But the only issue that really found majority support in 1972 was getting out of Vietnam, and most people felt Richard Nixon was better able to do this. McGovern was crushed in the 1972 general election, and with him any real hope that a New Left agenda could attract national, majority support.

While the New Left has been unable to recapture the Left's agenda, neither has any other group. The result is a left composed of several distinct philosophies. The old Left is still an active if not dominant force. Within mainstream politics its influence is seen in national unions, and in the continuation of New Deal politics and policies in the Democratic party. The candidacy of Walter Mondale in 1984 reflected a brief return to the fore by the old Left, and his defeat indicated its failure to generate majority support. Outside the mainstream, the Socialist and Communist parties continue to operate, again as peripheral actors.

The New Left remains a force in mainstream politics, with its most obvious legacy still found in the Democartic party. For example, Gary Hart was a former member of McGovern's 1972 campaign, and his own platform reflects many New Left ideas. Tom Hayden, coauthor of the SDS's Port Huron Statement, held state-level office and ran unsuccessfully for a Democratic senate nomination. Jesse Jackson, former CORE member and aid to Martin Luther King, Jr., was active in the Black Power movement. Peter Shapiro, Democratic candidate for governor of New Jersey in 1985 was an antiwar activist. Marion Barry, Jr., former leader of SNCC, was elected Democratic mayor of Washington, D.C., in 1978. Ted Kennedy was a vocal, if belated, opponent to the war in Vietnam. The Democratic party's emphasis on women's rights, gay rights, black rights, the environment, the poor and homeless, their predeliction to limit defense spending, and their suspicion of military adventures such as funding the Contras all have roots in New Left politics. And while this brand of politics has come under increasing attack by members of both parties, it remains a viable part of the Democratic platform.

In addition, many sixties activists, as well as a new generation influenced by them, have shifted their emphasis from national politics back to the grass-roots, populist, local politics from which the New Left emerged. Whether it is called progressive populism, economic democracy, or democratic socialism, the examples abound: the Sanctuary Movement, Committee In Solidarity with the People of El Salvador, SANE, Association of Community Organizations for Reform Now, Citizen Action, Public Interest Research Groups, Campaign for Economic Democracy, National Organization for Women, National People's Action—all have ideological and strategic roots in the New Left, and are populated by former activists or their ideological offspring.[13] Governments of cities, such as Burlington, Vermont and Santa Clara, California have been taken over by sixties activists running on New Left–style programs. Ironically, even the administration of Chicago, under the leadership of the late Harold Washington, was influenced by and populated with the ideas and activists of the New Left.

Despite the proliferation of New Left groups at the local, state, and even national level, they remain at the periphery of mainstream politics. In part this is strategic—many organizations prefer to work at the local level. In part it reflects continued splits within the New Left. And there is concern about compromising the New Left's agenda and tactics while broadening its base of support, an issue currently being grappled with by Jesse Jackson's Rainbow Coalition. But ultimately the peripheral status of most new New Left groups is a reflection of the continued strength of the liberal democratic consensus for which the more extreme proposals of these groups are anathemas.

As evidence of the Left's identity problem since Vietnam, consider one of its most recent incarnations, neoliberalism. Neoliberalism combines the progressive urge for good government, the New Deal emphasis on government control of the economy and social welfare, the cold war disdain for communism, a philosophic defense of individualism and liberalism, and an emphasis on economic growth by aggressively identifying new industries (most often, high technology) and new markets. Most neoliberals are Democrats who want to meld some of the New Left agenda (concern over the environment, a noninterventionist policy in the Third World, social tolerance concerning issues of race, gender, homosexuality) to a philosophy that is tied to a liberal rather than socialist ideology.

The Right in America   The inability of the Left to identify a coalition capable of dominating the American political agenda, coupled with the pervasive sense that the "excesses" of the 1960s are responsible for a national malaise has opened the door for the Right. Much like the Left, however, the experiences of the last few decades have left them in a rather factionalized state.

The populist Right, with roots reaching back to the agrarian movements of the eighteenth century, is still alive in the United States. Known alternately today as the new Right, the religious Right, or the (recently disbanded) Moral Majority, it is the direct descendant of Agnew's silent majority. The new Right is the group most politicized in opposition to the New Left. Socially conservative, tied to the traditional institutions of family and church, fiercely patriotic, individualistic, and anticommunist, this group felt betrayed by the New Left's politics and the Nixon administration's dishonesty. But they learned a great deal from the New Left about the strategy and tactics of grass-roots organizing, direct confrontation, civil disobedience, and the pitfalls of media politics. The result is the success of direct mail wizards such as Richard Viguerie, conservative political organizations such as NCPAC, and preacher politicians such as Jerry Falwell and Pat Robertson. The election of new Right candidates to Congress and the Senate in 1980 (in conjunction with the defeat of a number of New Left incumbents), and the election of the head moral majoritarian, Ronald Reagan, can be attributed in large part to this wing of the Right.

Another variant of conservatism found on the current scene has roots in the classical liberal tenets of individualism and limited government, and in the more fundamental conservative belief in maintaining social and cultural traditions. This conservatism has existed, in various guises, since the founding of the nation. Its current incarnation, and one that results directly from the Vietnam experience, is neoconservatism which emphasizes individual freedoms and laisser faire economic practices. Neoconservatives oppose government attempts to cure social problems and argue strongly against the welfare state, affirmative action, quotas, and the like. The only place where they advocate government activism is in the exporting of free market capitalism, in maintaining a strong defense, and in constant vigilance against the threat of communism to the American way of life.

Neoconservatives represent the intellectual and elitist wing of the Right today, making up for lack of numbers by the influence of their writings. Neoconservatism can be found in the writings of Irving Kristol and Daniel Bell (cofounders of the neoconservative magazine, *Public Interest*), Norman Podhoretz (under whose editorship the intellectual magazine *Commentary* took a decidedly neoconservative twist), Edward Banfield, Nathan Glazer, Seymour Lipset, Daniel Moynihan, Aaron Wildavsky, and James Q. Wilson. While much neoconservative philosophy has roots in the traditional thinking of people like William Buckley and Milton

Friedman, those who use the label most often are ex-liberals, ex–New Leftists, and even ex-socialists who, reacting to the social policies, anti-war protests, and the New Left agenda of the 1960s came to believe that the only solution to America's problems was in a return to order, traditionalism, and the free market. In essence they represent those who in advocating limited social reforms and opposing the war as a policy, were shocked by the more extreme policies and tactics of the radical Left. Fearing both the New Left's anarchistic tendancy and the old Left's communist one, they retreated to a reactionary conservatism. Some political activists of the 1960s have even turned back to such traditional institutions as religion.[14]

Mass Politics in the Age of Neopolitics   Underlying this set of political philosophies is an even broader array of ideological and policy hybrids. For example, conservative can now mean any combination of social conservatism (pro-religion, pro–traditional family values, anti-drugs, anti-sexual liberation), economic conservatism (low taxes, limited spending on social programs, limited regulation of industry, antiunion, pro-business), and foreign policy/defense conservatism (anticommunist, anti-soviet, pro-defense, pro-intervention, pro–covert operations, pro-nuclear). Liberal can mean liberal on social issues (women's rights, gay rights, black rights, drug use, the environment, criminals' rights), on social welfare issues (social security, national health care, welfare), on economic issues (progressive taxes, pro-union, full employment), and/or on foreign policy issues (self-determination, détente, antimilitarism, limited defense spending, antinuclear).

More than ever before, and as a direct result of the experiences of and reflections on the 1960s, various types and subtypes of liberalism and conservatism can be found in unusual combinations, within individuals, within organizations and movements, and across coalitions. Even more confusing, in the complex aftermath of the 1960s, even being conservative or liberal on a particular issue can mean different things. I may be economically conservative, but am I a fiscal or monetary conservative? Is protectionism liberal or conservative? If I'm liberal on the economy, am I pro-union? The cross-cutting nature of issues, in large part due to the opening up of the political agenda in the 1960s, has made politics a much more confusing game of shifting, sometimes invisible alliances.

The strategy and tactics of politics has also been greatly affected by the sixties, and again these strategies and tactics have been adopted by old and New Left, old and new Right, and hybrid movements like the neo-conservatives and neoliberals. Civil disobedience as a means to judicial remedies, a favorite strategy of the civil rights movement, has been used by the antiwar movement, the women's movement, and the new Right.

Boycotts are now popular tools of the Left (against, for example, corporations investing in South Africa) and the Right (the boycott of Seven-Eleven stores for selling *Playboy*). Petitions, protests, and marches are common outlets, whether opposing or supporting nuclear energy, nuclear arms, abortion, or Contra aid. Disruptive tactics, whether by blacks stopping the subways in New York City to protest police brutality or antiabortion activists blockading a Planned Parenthood facility, are part of normal politics today. Finally, violence, whether by the Left or the Right, remains a much more viable option since the 1960s, as testified to by the frequent bombings of abortion clinics, bombings by groups such as the Jewish Defense League and the Puerto Rican Liberation Front, and acts of violence by both white and black separatist groups.

Contemporary National Politics and Policies   The failure of either the Left or the Right to define itself coherently is particularly problematic within the context of the contemporary U.S. system. The nationalization of politics and the institutionalization of first the two party system, and then the Democratic and Republican parties, makes preelection coalition building critical. In addition, with the exception of certain groups in the 1930s and the 1960s, over the last fifty years citizens have increasingly become consumers rather than producers of political meaning. Average citizens react to the rhetoric, policies, and conditions produced by political and economic elites, rather than engaging in that production themselves. In times when such elites are able to produce rhetoric, policy, and conditions that are acceptable, this is a tolerable, if not strongly democratic state of affairs. In times when they can not—and we are in such a time today—it offers few solutions for democratic change.

The political changes instituted in the great realignments of the past (the 1860s, the 1890s, and the 1930s), while operating within the confines of representative, liberal democracy, still required grass-roots involvement, even agitation. They required a general public attuned enough, informed enough, and efficacious enough to react to this growing agitation. They required political leadership able to turn this new agenda into government action. And they required enough commitment to particular solutions to allow policies to have an effect. While this process seldom did full justice to the issues being raised, it is hard to deny that it did them some justice.

Can the same be said in the aftermath of the 1960s? Is there a grass-roots legacy akin to the establishment and growth of unions after 1932? Is there an attitudinal legacy akin to the public's support for the Democratic party, or for that party's economic policies and reforms? Is there a new leadership that has translated grass-roots and public concern into coherent, programatic policies akin to those of the elected officials swept into office in 1932 and 1936 at the national, state, and local levels? Is there evidence of long-term commitment to a particular philosophy, party, or set of policies akin to the New Deal coalition that dominated domestic politics from 1932 to 1980? And, ultimately, is there a set of policies that have resulted from the era of the sixties and that have had a tangible effect on the material well-being of the public akin to the economic reforms of the 1930s?

By some accounts there is more grass-roots organizing today on a greater set of issues than ever before in American history. Most of these groups can trace their lineage from, through, or in reaction to the politics of the 1960s. In several areas there is also evidence of attitudinal change among the public, especially in the areas of civil rights and equal opportunity for blacks and for women. There is also a greater tendency for people to include "sixties-style" issues (for example, concern over the environment, abortion rights, nuclear disarmament, and so forth) on the political agenda. Finally, citizens appear to have a consistent, if not well-informed, negative reaction to any U.S. military involvement that smacks too much of our involvement in Vietnam.

And yet none of this translates into a coherent, identifiable, or stable agenda. Despite evidence of increased liberalism (in the modern sense) like that mentioned above, there is evidence of greater conservatism as well: less willingness to support tax increases, greater suspicion of some government social programs, increased hostility towards criminals' rights, greater concern over drug use, growing hostility over certain racial and sexual affirmative action programs, renewed opposition to abortion rights, a return in popularity of certain traditional lifestyles, and so forth.

While some of this tension between liberal and conservative views reflects differences among groups of people, it also reflects tensions within individuals themselves. Lacking a public rationale for linking particular opinions into a coherent worldview, these opinions remain discrete and often unstable. The result is a popular will that is difficult to read, since it can change depending on which underlying value or belief is tapped by the issue at hand. Again, this is not to say that such inconsistencies are new nor that they are always a sign of pathology—politics is by its nature ambiguous. We do, however, appear to be in a period when such inconsistencies are more prevalent and less likely to be addressed individually or within political coalitions.

Nowhere is this lack of a coherent politic clearer than in the electoral process. With the exception of the Watergate-related victory of Jimmy Carter, the Presidency has remained firmly Republican since 1968. At the same time, Congress, with the exception of the House from 1952 to 1954 and the Senate from 1980 to 1986, has remained Democratic since 1932.

Voters, down to about 50 percent of the eligible electorate in presidential contests and 35 percent or less in off-year elections, are as or more likely to be independent as Democrat or Republican, and less likely to vote according to party affiliation than ever before.

When one examines party leaders and the parties themselves, one can see either a reflection or a cause of the general public's instability. While engaging in more ideological rhetoric over the last few years, it is hard to argue that any wing of either party, let alone either party as a whole, has developed anything approaching a coherent platform that strikes a responsive chord with the public. Ronald Reagan, heralded as the great hope of a populist conservative Republican resurgence, appears to have had little lasting impact in this regard. Ironically, his most important legacy may well be the negotiation of a nuclear arms agreement, the thawing of relations with the Soviet Union, and the bungled, covert sale of weapons to Iran, hardly what was expected by his conservative supporters.

In the absence of any new or old mix of liberal democratic tenets to reinvigorate domestic politics, most of the current battles have been fought over particular policies and programs. National domestic policy emerging from the 1960s and early 1970s clustered into several specific areas.[15] The Voting Rights and Civil Rights Acts of the early 1960s, in conjunction with Supreme Court cases in the area of de jure and de facto segregation in housing, education, and the workplace, have led to tangible improvements in the political, social, and economic status of blacks.

Johnson's War on Poverty instituted numerous programs aimed at easing the lot of the poor and helping to raise them out of poverty. C.E.T.A., the food stamps program, school lunch programs, financial aid for education, legal aid programs, among others, all had measurable, if sometimes small, impacts on the level of poverty in the United States.

The late 1960s and early 1970s saw a wave of legislation and litigation that increased the ability of citizens and government to regulate business. Most of this regulation fell into the areas of occupational health and safety, consumer protection, and environmental protection. Between 1970 and 1980 as many new regulatory laws were passed (the vast majority of them involving social regulation) as had been passed from the New Deal up until 1970.

The late 1960s and early 1970s also saw increased attention in the courts and legislatures to issues of women's rights. The Supreme Court decision in Roe v. Wade gave women the right to decide for themselves whether or not to have an abortion during the first three months of pregnancy. New legislation and litigation extended to women the protections granted to blacks in the early 1960s in the areas of education, housing, and workplace discrimination. More recently some of these protections have been extended to homosexuals as well.

Finally, the 1960s saw an extension, largely through the courts, of civil liberties in the area of criminal rights, rights of the poor, and freedoms of speech and association.

These changes fell far short of those advocated by the civil rights, Black Power, student, women's, and general New Left movements, and their most tangible effects occurred in the late 1960s and early 1970s. There were also many failures, most notably the defeat of the ERA. Nonetheless they all had tangible, measurable effects on the material condition of the groups they were designed to help.[16] They have also, beginning in the late 1970s and escalating in the 1980s, all come under attack by conservatives, with varying degrees of success. The Civil Rights and Voting Rights Acts have remained largely intact, despite a concerted effort on the part of conservative Democrats and Republicans to show that many of the bills' specific protections were no longer needed. The federal courts have slowly but consistently whittled away at many of the protections afforded blacks, women, and those accused of crimes. Much of the economic and social regulatory system put in place in the 1960s and 70s has been dismantled or made ineffective by funding cuts and the hiring of antiregulatory proponents to head various regulatory agencies. Programs aimed at helping the poor have had funds frozen or slashed or have been eliminated. While none of this has resulted in the dismantling of the social, political, and economic reforms of the 1960s, it has made them much less effective, thus helping to make the notion that such programs do not work a self-fulfilling prophecy.

The Vietnam Era and the Battle over Political Meaning   The battle over the legacy of the 1960s continues today, although because of a lack of an overarching philosophy with which to advocate for or against these programs, this battle is fought in piecemeal fashion, among loose, often improbable coalitions, and with erratic shifts in direction. And in this battle, control over the definition of the 1960s, over the symbols of that decade, and, ultimately, over its recreation in contemporary society is key. In the 1988 presidential campaign, George Bush, following in the footsteps of Ronald Reagan, was able to define Michael Dukakis as a liberal, and to define liberal as a combination of the worst (often imagined) excesses of the 1960s and the worst (often imagined) ineffeciencies of government bureaucracy. Such battles over meaning are commonplace. Those on the Right paint the current failures in the educational, economic, criminal justice, and international political systems as resulting from the "social experimentation" of the 1960s: children can't read because of liberal education policies; adolescents buy and sell drugs, carry weapons, mug, shoot, and rape each other because of the breakup of the traditional family, the use of day care, the "problem" of working mothers; poverty is on the rise because government programs encourage dependency on the dole; American business can't compete because concern over equality has come at the expense of merit. And so on.

Nor is there a lack of the use of the symbols of the 1960s by the Left. It is impossible to have a protest, demonstration, or boycott without reference to the sixties. Almost any use of American military force immediately brings comparisons to Vietnam. Defense of programs, policies, and strategies are often as much based on nostalgia and habit as on political logic. Much as the Right was largely reactionary to the Left in the 1960s, however, the Left appears the more defensive ideology today and, hence, is less influential in defining the 1960s. The implications of this are found in the way the Vietnam era is remembered and used politically. The current dominance of the Right in this re-presentation of the 1960s accounts for the conservative shift of the political center over the last decade.

In the long run, however, as long as the battle over political meaning is fought between liberal and conservative elements *within* the liberal democratic consensus, the tangible and symbolic legacy of the 1960s is destined to be a highly domesticated version of the decade. The results will be, as with other periods that challenged the liberal democratic consensus, minor reforms, shifting boundaries, and, occasionally, values and norms that are held despite their inconsistency with the more fundamental tenets of U.S. society. To the extent one remains convinced of the ultimate superiority of liberal, representative democracy, this self-righting tendency is to be applauded. To the extent one believes that many of the current problems faced by our nation result from the limitations and inconsistencies found in this ideology, however, it serves only to limit discourse, to limit what is politically imaginable, and so to limit what is politically possible.

NOTES

1. The work of Jean Jacques Rousseau (1712–1778) argues for universal suffrage and direct participation in decisions about the allocation of goods, services, and values. Rousseau, who advocated a relatively equal distribution of property so that "no citizen shall ever be wealthy enough to buy another, and none too poor to be forced to sell himself," and who believed in participation as a good in itself, influenced the thought of Thomas Jefferson, but was not a liberal democrat and had a minimal impact on the structure of American culture and politics. His thought does reappear in the numerous social movements to be discussed.

2. For a detailed discussion of political movements in the United States and their relation to "normal politics," see Russell Hanson, *The Democratic Imagination in American Politics* (Princeton: Princeton University Press, 1986); Richard

Hofstadter, *The Age of Reform* (New York: Alfred Knopf, 1955); and Seymour Lipset and Earl Raab, *The Politics of Unreason* (New York: Harper and Row, 1970).

3. For a detailed discussion of the culture of the 1960s, see Barbara Tischler's chapter, "Counterculture and Over-the-Counter Culture," in this volume.

4. Landon Y. Jones, *Great Expectations* (New York: Ballantine Books, 1980), pp. 40–41.

5. Judge Clayton Horn, as cited in Edward J. Bacciocco, Jr., *The New Left in America* (Stanford: The Hoover Institute Press, 1974), p. 12. See Barbara Tischler's two chapters in this volume.

6. For a discussion of the role of the civil rights movement in the Vietnam-war era, and of the role of blacks during this period, see Peter Levy's chapter in this volume.

7. Unless otherwise noted, the historical documentation for this section of the chapter is derived from Bacciocco, *The New Left in America,* and Kirkpatrick Sale, *SDS* (New York: Vintage Books, 1974).

8. Bacciocco, *The New Left in America,* pp. 184–85.

9. For a discussion of historical and philosophic issues surrounding the draft, see Michael Shafer, "The Vietnam-Era Draft," in this volume.

10. For a discussion of the role of the media in covering the Vietnam and the protests at home, see Michael X. Delli Carpini, "Vietnam and the Press," in this volume.

11. For a discussion of the relationship between the women's movement and the Vietnam War era, see Ruth Rosen's chapter in this volume.

12. Bacciocco, *The New Left in America,* p. 214.

13. For a more detailed discussion of these new New Left organizations, see Harry Boyte, *Backyard Revolution* (Philadelphia: Temple University Press, 1981).

14. For a more detailed discussion of these new liberal and conservative ideologies, see Kenneth Dolbeare and Linda Medcalf, *American Ideologies Today* (New York: Random House, 1988).

15. For a discussion of the effect of the Vietnam War on U.S. foreign policy, see Lloyd Gardner's chapter in this volume.

16. For a discussion of the material impact of the social programs of the 1960s, see J. Schwartz. *America's Hidden Success* (New York: Norton, 1988).

NOTES ON THE CONTRIBUTORS

Editor MICHAEL SHAFER is associate professor of political science at Rutgers University. Professor Shafer received his Ph.D. in political science from Harvard University. He teaches international relations, American foreign policy, and international political economy. His first book, *Deadly Paradigms: The Failure of U.S. Counterinsurgency Policy*, was published by Princeton University Press in 1988. His articles have appeared in *Comparative Politics, Foreign Policy, International Organization, Political Science Quarterly, Third World Quarterly*, and *Southern Africa*.

BENJAMIN BARBER is Walt Whitman Professor of Political Science at Rutgers University. He is the author of numerous books, including *The Conquest of Politics: Liberal Philosophy in Democratic Times, Strong Democracy: Participatory Politics for a New Age, Liberating Feminism, The Artist and Political Vision, The Death of Communal Liberty*, and *Superman and Common Men*. Professor Barber edited the journal *Political Theory* for ten years (1974–84) and his essays and articles have appeared in collections and in such diverse periodicals as *Deadalus, The Atlantic, Harper's, Dissent, The New Republic, Political Studies, Ethics*, and the *American Political Science Review*. He has collaborated with Patrick Watson on the television series "The Struggle for Democracy", screened in 1989, as well as on the book which accompanied the series.

MICHAEL X. DELLI CARPINI is assistant professor of political science at Barnard College, Columbia University. He received his B.A. and M.A. from the University of Minnesota. He is the author of *Stability and Change in American Politics: The Coming of Age of the Generation of the 1960's*, published by New York University Press in 1986. His articles on the role of the mass media in American politics, on American public opinion, and on the effects of generational change on American politics have appeared in *Public Opinion Quarterly, The Journal of Politics, Western Political Quarterly*, and *American Politics Quarterly*.

LLOYD GARDNER is Charles and Mary Beard Professor of History at Rutgers University and President of the Society of Historians of American Foreign Relations. He is the author of numerous books, including *Approaching Vietnam: From Anticolonialism to Nation-Building, A Covenant with Power: America and World Order from Wilson to Reagan, Safe for Democracy: Anglo-American Responses to Revolution in the Wilson-Lloyd George Era, Imperial America, American Foreign Policy Present to Past, Architects of Illusion: Men and Ideas in American Foreign Affairs, 1941–1949*, and *Economic Aspects of New Deal Diplomacy*. His work has appeared in many collections and virtually every major scholarly journal in the field.

PETER LEVY is assistant professor of history at York College. He is the author of

The New Left and Labor (forthcoming) and editor of *The Modern Civil Rights Movement: A Documentary Collection* (forthcoming).

RICHARD MOSER is a doctoral candidate in history at Rutgers University. He is an American historian whose interests center on the domestic social and political consequences of the Vietnam War. His dissertation explores the nature of GI and veteran antiwar protest. Mr. Moser's work is based on extensive oral history research, and he teaches courses on both the practical and theoretical problems of oral history research.

RUTH ROSEN is professor of history at the University of California at Davis and Research Associate at the Institute for the Study of Social Change at the University of California at Berkeley. She is editor of *The Maimie Papers* and the author of *The Lost Sisterhood: Prostitution in America* and *The Second Wave* (forthcoming).

RICHARD A. SULLIVAN is associate professor of English at University of Wisconsin-La Crosse. He received his B.A. and M.A. degrees in English from Oklahoma State University, and his Ph.D. in modern letters from The University of Tulsa. He specializes in twentieth-century British and American literature, with an emphasis on literary modernism. He has recently completed a book examining the intellectual and cultural backgrounds for the writing, initial reception, and early critical reputation of James Joyce's *Ulysses*. He has published articles on Joyce, T. S. Eliot, Flann O'Brien, and Thomas Davis, and he is currently completing a monograph study of avant-garde and experimental literary movements and styles in France, England and America at the turn of the century. He has lectured on Vietnam literature at Rutgers University and University of Tulsa, and is currently completing an article on John Del Vecchio's *The Thirteenth Valley*.

BRUCE TAYLOR is professor of English at University of Wisconsin-Au Claire. He received his M.A. and M.F.A. from the University of Arkansas. Professor Taylor teaches "The Film and Fiction of the Vietnam War" and has organized an ongoing Vietnam speaker series at University of Wisconsin, bringing major military, political and literary figures to campus to discuss both the war and its legacy. Professor Taylor is also a practicing poet whose poems have appeared in such publications as *The Nation, New York Quarterly, New Orleans Review,* and *Rocky Mountain Review.* He is poetry editor of *Transactions.*

BARBARA TISCHLER is associate professor of history at Barnard College. She received her M.A. and Ph.D. in history from Columbia University. Professor Tischler is the author of *An American Music: The Search for an American Musical Identity, Propaganda and Protest: Studies in Culture from the Spanish-American War Through Vietnam* (forthcoming), and *A Career and Social History of Professional Baseball Players* (with Steven Tischler, forthcoming). Her essays have appeared in many collections, and her reviews and articles in such journals as *American Music, The American Historical Review,* and the *Labor Studies Journal.* Professor Tischler is editor of the Rutgers University Press series on the 1960s.

JAMES W. TOLLEFSON is the author of *Alien Winds: The Reeducation of America's Indochinese Refugees.* Between 1983 and 1986, he spent sixteen months in refugee camps in Southeast Asia. He is currently associate professor and co-director of the M.A. program in teaching English as a second language at the University of Washington.